Legacy of Silence

Legacy of Silence

Encounters with Children of the Third Reich

Dan Bar-On

Harvard University Press
Cambridge, Massachusetts, and London, England

Copyright © 1989 by the President and Fellows
   of Harvard College
All rights reserved
Printed in the United States of America
10 9 8 7 6 5 4 3 2

First Harvard University Press paperback edition, 1991

Library of Congress Cataloging-in-Publication Data

Bar-On, Dan. 1938–
   Legacy of silence / Dan Bar-On.
      p.   cm.
   ISBN 0-674-52185-4 (alk. paper) (cloth)
   ISBN 0-674-52186-2 (paper)
   1. Holocaust, Jewish (1939–1945)—Psychological as-
pects.   2. Children of war criminals—Germany
(West)—Interviews.   3. Germany (West)—Social condi-
tions.   4. Holocaust, Jewish (1939–1945)—Public opin-
ion.   5. Public Opinion—Germany (West)
I. Title.
D804.3B36   1989
940.53'18—dc20   89-7484
                                                  CIP

Designed by Gwen Frankfeldt

Shemà

You who live secure
In your warm houses,
Who return at evening to find
Hot food and friendly faces:

> Consider whether this is a man,
> Who labors in the mud
> Who knows no peace
> Who fights for a crust of bread
> Who dies at a yes or a no.
> Consider whether this is a woman,
> Without hair or name
> With no more strength to remember
> Eyes empty and womb cold
> As a frog in winter.

Consider that this has been:
I commend these words to you.
Engrave them on your hearts
When you are in your house, when you walk on your way,
When you go to bed, when you rise.
Repeat them to your children.
Or may your house crumble,
Disease render you powerless,
Your offspring avert their faces from you.

10 January 1946

Primo Levi, *Collected Poems*
(translated by Ruth Feldman
and Brian Swann)

Contents

Acknowledgments   ix

Introduction   1

1   The Physician from Auschwitz
and His Son   *14*

2   Conjuring the Darkness   *42*

3   Those Blue-Eyed German Songs   *71*

4   The Camp Doll   *96*

5   The Hidden King   *115*

6   The Crown Prince   *135*

7   The Rabbi from Jerusalem   *160*

8   Freedom and Responsibility   *179*

9   Small Hills Covered with Trees   *200*

10   The Divided Self   *218*

11   Gathering Evidence   *245*

12   My Father, My Self   *268*

13   The Narrow Bridge   *291*

14   The Dark Side of the Mind   *321*

Glossary   337

Acknowledgments

Many people were very helpful in the preparation of this book and in the research project on which it is based. I would particularly like to thank an anonymous friend in Germany, whose personal commitment to these issues attracted me to the subject.

Professor Israel W. Charny, director of the Institute of the International Conference on the Holocaust and Genocide in Jerusalem, helped me conceptualize the research proposal and move it through its early stages; the first three chapters were written with his cooperation, and the Institute provided a grant that enabled me to devote six months in 1988 to the project.

I would like to acknowledge the generous financial support of the Sidney and Esther Rabb Center for Holocaust and Redemption Studies of Ben Gurion University, Beer Sheva, and of the Joint Distribution Committee, Jerusalem.

Gonda Scheffel-Baars of Holland gave me valuable insights about the individuals I interviewed in Germany.

Through their assistance and warm friendship, Professor Manfred Brusten and Professor Friedhelm Beiner of the University of Wuppertal, along with their graduate student Bernd Winkelmann, enabled the research to move ahead and made my stay in Germany easier. In addition, the University of Wuppertal was kind enough to invite me to be a guest-professor during several of my interviewing trips.

Gitta Sereny and Don Honeyman warmly supported the research from its earliest beginnings and provided useful information through their humane and critical reaction to my own responses and their comments on early versions of the manuscript.

I am grateful to Dr. Bettina Birn and Dr. Dieter Hartmann of Tübingen and Professor Don Schon of MIT for their enormous helpfulness and friendship. For their support and their interest in this project, I thank Professor Saul Friedlander of Tel Aviv University, Professor Amia Lieblich and Professor Zeev Klein of Hebrew University in Jerusalem, Professor Shimon Redlich of Ben Gurion University, Professor Benno Müller-Hill of the Institute for Genetics at the University of Cologne, Professor Gertrud Hardtmann of the Technical University of Berlin, and Dr. Tamar Bermann and the late Professor David Herbst of the Work Research Institute in Oslo, Norway.

I owe an enormous debt of gratitude to Zeev-Bill Templer. When I returned from my first trip to Germany and began looking for a transcriber and translator, I discovered him just across the street studying Hebrew. He became the sole translator of the interviews presented here, and he devoted considerable time and energy to getting out of the tapes all that was in them. I could not have done what I did without him. Later, Miriam Lavi contributed her excellent and sensitive editing. Tzilla Barneis, Jehudit Brill, Antia Scheaffer, Kerstin Kessler, and Hannah Bahat also devoted many hours to typing, transcription, and translation. I also wish to thank Angela von der Lippe and Linda Howe of Harvard University Press for their help in seeing the project through to book form.

Finally, I want to thank my wife and children. During a difficult time, their love was for me a candle in my own darkness.

Legacy of Silence

Introduction

It was the autumn of 1938. Andre was twelve years old and lived with his parents in a small town in northern Germany. One evening he came home from his youth movement meeting.

"Daddy," he said to his father, "we were told at the meeting that tomorrow we are supposed to throw stones at the Jewish shops in town. Should I take part?"

His father looked at him. "What do you think?"

"I don't know. I have nothing against the Jews—I hardly know them—but everyone is going to throw stones. So what should I do?"

Their conversation proceeded, the son presenting questions to his father, the father turning the questions back to his son.

"I understand," said Andre. "You want me to make up my own mind. I'm going for a walk. I'll let you know what I've decided when I come back."

When Andre returned a short while later, he approached his parents, who were sitting at the table.

"I've made up my mind, but my decision involves you too."

"What is it?"

"I've decided not to throw stones at the Jewish shops. But tomorrow everyone will say, 'Andre, the son of X, did not take part, he refused to throw stones!' They will turn against you. What are you going to do?"

His father's sigh was one of relief tinged with pride. "While you were out, your mother and I discussed this question. We decided that if you made up your mind to throw stones, we would have to live with your decision, since we had let you decide, after all. But if you decided not to throw stones, we would leave Germany immediately."

And that is what they did. The following day, Andre's family left Germany.

* * *

I learned this story from a colleague of mine who had heard it from Andre himself in 1942, in Lisbon, Portugal, where the family was then living. She had stayed with them while she herself was in flight from occupied France, awaiting a visa to go to the United States. "One can try to spoil the story," she told me. "The parents were probably deliberating such a move before this incident, they must have had the financial means to carry it out at once, and so on. Still, the fact remains that they made up their minds in this way. The question is, why did so few others do the same?"

As a psychologist, I was supposed to have an answer, but I could only pose more questions: Why did so few have the courage to speak out about what was happening in Hitler's Germany? How were Andre and his parents different from the majority, who would follow orders to throw stones—and later, to commit other atrocities?

Andre's story embodies a certain naïveté, a positive view of human beings one rarely encounters in dealing with the Holocaust; although unexpected acts of humanity occurred, they were the exception. My generation grew up with the terrible knowledge of the Holocaust, a knowledge that deprived us of Andre's innocence. Our awareness that such an enormity took place in a highly "civilized" society, in this century, and that no one tried to stop it, has constrained our view of the future. Some have given up the quest for hope, convinced of the inevitability of inhumanity. Others have maintained hope by suppressing part of that knowledge—and by avoiding disquieting questions—as if to push it to the dark side of the mind. Only a very few have succeeded in sustaining a belief in the possibility of hope—and this in spite of the disclosures over the past forty years of how the Nazis organized and systematically carried out the extermination process.

My family left Germany in 1933, early enough to have retained a positive view of their fellow human beings, but also late enough to have learned the harsh lesson that, in an instant, your neighbors can turn against you. Like Andre's father, my father made the decision to leave on the spur of the moment. It is still difficult for me to understand how he did so, because so many others did not draw the same conclusion. My parents regarded themselves as well-integrated German Jews. They both came from large families of mostly well-established bankers, physicians, and lawyers who had lived in Germany for more than two centuries.

In the memoirs my father wrote in 1979, the year before he died, he describes his own father as a German patriot: "He had served as a doctor in the German army; he liked his uniform so much that he even wore it at his wedding." If his family encountered anti-Semitism, it was marginal to the mainstream of their lives: "My father studied medicine at Heidelberg and became a doctor in 1897. He intended to start an academic career, but his professor told him that with the name Levy he could never be a lecturer or a professor. So he changed his name and chose his father's first name, Bruno, as his family name."

In January 1933, my father and mother went on one of their favorite cross-country ski tours in the Alps:

> One morning, when we turned on the radio in one of the cabins, we heard the announcement of the Reichstag fire . . . But we were so completely involved in the enchantment of skiing that we did not grasp the importance of this event . . . The next day we arrived in Munich and found the whole town covered with Nazi flags and swastikas. Back in Hamburg, we went to a Furt-wängler concert, showing off our deep tan and still-exalted mood. Our enthusiasm (today I would say euphoria) left us quickly when we met our relatives and Jewish friends; they were gloomy about political developments.

In April 1933, when Josef Goebbels ordered the boycott of Jewish physicians, my father, unlike many others, became alert:

> Many of my patients turned up and said, "Doctor, I am not permitted to come to treatment today; but here I am." Where I was working in Hamburg there were mostly socialists who hated Hitler . . . My mother came to "comfort" me. I still remember our conversation vividly. I said, "You should know, Mother, they start with a boycott and end with a pogrom. I shall definitely leave Germany." She answered, "How can you say this? Everything will blow over in a few months."
>
> The next few months I spent mostly looking into where we would go when we left Germany. I first traveled to Holland, where one of my mother's cousins worked as a doctor. He was willing to take me as his assistant till I could get my license there. I could not make up my mind immediately and promised to return some weeks later after having talked things over with my wife. When I came back to Scheveningen, where the cousin lived, the whole town, from the railway station to his home, was covered with Dutch Nazi flags. This decided the issue finally . . . Most of my cousin's family were later deported to Bergen-Belsen and perished there.

My father considered Denmark, but with the same result. He also received suggestions about working in one of the French colonies, in

Algeria or Morocco. Some of his close friends decided to go to China, others to Brazil. But he finally chose to go to Palestine.

> We had never been Zionists or shown any interest in Palestine before. However, our neighbor, Dr. Wiess, had been a Zionist all his life. For months he had brought us *Die Jüdische Rundschau,* the weekly of the German Zionists, without saying a word. His silence proved to be stronger than any eloquent propaganda . . .
>
> We left Hamburg on October 30, 1933. When we came to the Austrian border, the German customs official checked our passports, saw our immigrant visa to Palestine, and looked at our little boy, sleeping on the bench; then he wished us all the best for our future. He seemed to be one of the "good" Germans. So ended the first period of my life.

As an Israeli, I live in a victims' culture. The Holocaust is still an open wound for many of the people around me. More than a quarter of the population has been affected, directly or indirectly. I meet some of them daily, at the university where I teach and during the course of my private practice: Alona is named after her father's first wife; they both survived Auschwitz, but she died shortly afterward "of sorrow." Zelda is named after her grandmother, who was killed in Auschwitz. Shlomo, whom I interviewed for my Ph.D. thesis, saw his mother murdered by an SS officer; he still screams in his dreams every night. Even people like my parents, who managed to leave in time but lost many friends and relatives, are "survivors"; like those who came out of the camps alive, they suffered from deep guilt feelings, although for years they did not consider it legitimate to have those feelings.

Within this culture, the perpetrators of the Holocaust are still synonymous with evil. Many believe that one should not relate to them as one human being to another because of "what they did to us." Like other children of my generation, I inherited this "black and white" view of the world: the inhumane versus the humane, the victimizer versus the victim. At the same time, the culture exerted constant pressure on us to "learn from the Holocaust": We must be strong so that no one can do it to us again. We must demand justice and punish the perpetrators. We must remind the world of what was done to us and educate our people so they will not forget. We must be alert, unlike those who went to the gas chambers "like sheep to slaughter." We must document what happened and seek restitution for our loss.

Although these demands seem justifiable from a survivor's perspective, they reveal little wisdom—pain and fear, perhaps, even a desire for revenge, but little in the way of understanding. I am afraid that evil is more cunning (the "banality of evil," Hannah Arendt wrote, after watching the Eichmann trial in Jerusalem, and she did not mean stupidity). One cannot defeat it with solutions like these. I have learned not to underestimate the minds that planned and executed the murder of so many of my people, perhaps because I draw on personal experience: the struggle with my own potential for evil.

One day when I spoke about this with my friend Naomi, a survivor of the Lodz ghetto who came to Israel thirty-five years ago, she looked at me and said, "Hitler is dead. Still, he may yet achieve his goal of destroying us if we internalize the hate, mistrust, and pain, all the inhumanity that we were exposed to for so many years." She paused a moment and then added, "I have no mercy for those who did it to us, but I care about ourselves, and I am afraid we might have come out of it lacking the human capacities we had before—to hope, to trust, and to love. Have we acquired the wisdom to prevent such a terrible outcome?" I was much taken with what Naomi said. As the sole survivor of her large family, she was expressing the terms of her own personal struggle to maintain love and hope. Perhaps she spoke for others too.

It will take a long time to acknowledge the complex psychological issues Naomi defines so clearly. After the war, there was a widespread illusion that one could smooth over the actuality of the Holocaust by framing it "rationally" as a problem to be solved—by carrying out de-Nazification, bringing the decisionmakers and the perpetrators to trial, building a democratic welfare society in Germany, and making economic and legal restitution to the victims. But the shadow of the Holocaust became longer the more successful these measures were.

These approaches helped society distance itself from the Holocaust, as though one could be infected by getting too close to such an eruption of evil, but it was like covering a volcano with cement. The basic questions—How could it have happened? How could human beings do such things to each other within a civilized society? Why did no one interfere?—remained unanswered. More recently, Ronald Reagan's visit to the military cemetery at Bitburg and the *Historikerstreit* or "historians' quarrel" in Germany over whether the Holocaust was a unique event have only sharpened the feeling that many would prefer to "sum up" the past in order to forget it. Yet I sense that another process is beginning, a movement toward a deeper understanding of the Holocaust as a human possibility.

When my friend told me Andre's story and asked me, rhetorically, why so few others followed his family's example, I felt ashamed. It seems that we psychologists do not succeed very well in our efforts to answer such questions. Despite all the knowledge we have accumulated in our laboratories, clinical experience, and field experiments, we can say very little about the psychology of those who carried out the Holocaust. How could civilized people commit such atrocities? How could they live with what they had done? In what ways are they different from us—if at all?

The Holocaust divided people according to broad categories: the victims and the survivors, the perpetrators, the rescuers, the bystanders and the noninvolved. One could further refine these categories: survivors would include those who survived the extermination camps, those who succeeded in hiding in gentile homes, those who were transported at night to a neutral country, and those who fought with partisans in the woods. In the same way, one could define bystanders according to their proximity to the extermination process, perpetrators according to the atrocities they committed, and so on. Were these divisions incidental? Clearly not for some: the Nazis selected the Jews, the Gypsies, and the mentally retarded to become victims of the extermination process. For survivors, however, there is a subjective sense of incidence: part of their trauma is the fact that, by mere accident, they lived while others perished. The perpetrators, the rescuers, the bystanders—no one selected them. Was the role they played accidental? Could we find ways to predict who would do what?

In the years since the war, psychologists have tried to identify a clear-cut psychological typology or sociocultural profile for each of these categories: Perpetrators were defined as pathological sadists,[1] a personality type traced to their Germanic heritage.[2] Bystanders or followers were supposed to have an "authoritarian personality,"[3] and rescuers an "altruistic personality."[4] But these labels have proved to be too simplistic. Others have wondered whether the psychology of the perpetrators was based on a dynamic different from that of the rescuers, or the bystanders, or the victims, or whether one particular psychological profile was especially susceptible to manipulation by other, more powerful forces.

1. G. M. Gilbert, *The Psychology of Dictatorship: Based on an Examination of the Leaders of Nazi Germany* (New York: Roland, 1950).

2. Elie Cohen, *Human Behavior in the Concentration Camp* (New York: Norton, 1953; Westport, Conn.: Greenwood, 1984).

3. T. W. Adorno et al., *The Authoritarian Personality* (New York: Harper and Row, 1950).

4. Samuel Oliner and Pearl Oliner, *The Altruistic Personality* (New York: Free Press, 1988).

Newer approaches have suggested a psychology of "ordinary people." In his now-famous research, Stanley Milgram showed that, in obedience to authority, ordinary people could become involved in experiments endangering human life.[5] Nechama Tec found that rescuers could not be sorted according to any particular personal trait, social class, religion, or education.[6] Israel Charny has pointed out in this connection that psychologists have no way of identifying mass-murderers, because many would probably score within the normal range on all existing psychopathological scales.[7] Being able to identify potential perpetrators and rescuers only in exceptional cases means that there is no simple way humanity can defend itself, psychologically, from similar future calamities. Coupled with this is the problem of disbelief. It is clear that the Allies (including the Jewish leadership in Palestine and the United States) did not believe the information they received about the nature and scale of Hitler's extermination system, even during the years when intervention might have saved lives. Disbelief also characterized potential victims who, because they were unwilling to foresee their own devastating end, sometimes reduced their chances for rescue.

Obviously, these disquieting facts require a new definition of "normalcy." If we cannot identify potential genocide victimizers (or rescuers) beforehand, since they are part of the ordinary population, and if we tend to normalize unexpected, extreme events and thus to ignore the danger they pose, how can we respond effectively when catastrophe threatens? What is this willed ignorance that does not allow us to acknowledge the human potential for evil? Does it have to do with the refusal to recognize the evil within ourselves?

One could claim that the Holocaust revealed the "weakness" in human nature: vulnerability to the influence of an evil and powerful person like a Hitler or a Himmler. Some psychologists have identified this tendency as inborn, the beast beneath the veneer of civilization. Still, this also sounds too simple. It is yet another kind of retrospective classification.

Could this "weakness" paradoxically be positive, a sense of trust within individuals that others can co-opt for evil ends? It is easy to observe such human trust among the victims of the Holocaust. It is

5. Stanley Milgram, "Behavioral Study of Obedience," *Journal of Abnormal and Social Psychology* 67 (1963): 371–78.

6. Nechama Tec, *When Light Pierced the Darkness: Christian Rescue of Jews in Nazi-Occupied Poland* (New York: Oxford University Press, 1986).

7. Israel W. Charny, "Genocide and Mass Destruction: Doing Harm to Others as a Missing Dimension in Psychopathology," *Psychiatry* 49 (1986): 144–57.

also understandable that the same psychological explanation applies to those who heard about the extermination process and could not believe the reports were true.

What is much more difficult to accept is that the initiators of the extermination process shared a similar psychology. They knew they were killing human beings. How could they maintain their own sense of themselves as human, as moral people? Did they assume that ordinary people would go along with them and become murderers of men, women, and children? Or that these same people would not break down, even after exceeding their own inner moral or psychological limits? Did they have some unique insight into human nature?

We know of only a small number of Einsatzgruppen members and commanders who suffered a nervous breakdown while involved in the mass killings of 1941–42. Heinrich Himmler devoted part of his famous Posen address in 1943 to the "difficulties of carrying out this most important task." He himself almost fainted while observing a mass-shooting, and he may have suggested that the gas chambers be introduced because they would provide "a more efficient process for overcoming these human limitations." Still, very few of the shooting units asked to be transferred, and the vast majority did their "duty" without showing psychological stress.[8] But how could they carry out the massive killing of women and children and then go home to their own wives and families? Many of them moved back and forth between these two realities for years. What kind of hope did they have, or transmit to their own children?

Historians tell us that Nazi bureaucracy and an indoctrination system describing victims as *Untermenschen,* as less than human, made it possible;[9] sociologists emphasize the strong interpersonal bond between the leader and the group;[10] and psychologists add the concept of "splitting" or "doubling," which enabled perpetrators to go on killing Jews while maintaining their humanity within their own family circle.[11] Yet if these historical, sociological, and psychological explanations help us understand how ordinary people could commit atrocities under the Nazi regime without breaking down, they cannot account for what happened after the collapse of the Third Reich in 1945. Once the indoctrinators were gone and the enormous extent of

8. Raul Hilberg, *The Destruction of the European Jews* (Chicago: Quadrangle, 1961).

9. Ibid.

10. Joel E. Dimsdale, ed., *Survivors, Victims, and Perpetrators: Essays on the Nazi Holocaust* (Washington, D.C.: Hemisphere, 1980).

11. Robert J. Lifton, *The Nazi Doctors: Medical Killing and the Psychology of Genocide* (New York: Basic Books, 1986).

the atrocities became publicly known, what prevented these people from acknowledging what they had done? Certainly they were afraid of retribution (and fear helped maintain the "doubling"). But did the wall between their own moral selves and their atrocious deeds never crack?[12] One could argue that their need to be coherent and consistent in their own minds made them look for justification: "I only followed orders." Although there are many ways to "leak" repressed and denied thoughts,[13] some of these were foreclosed: Many people had left the church when they joined the Nazi Party and found it difficult to return. Few would have sought psychological treatment, since that would seem to admit weakness. Still, have they no moments of regret? No nightmares? No signs of sorrow or guilt after all these years, even now as they face their own deaths?

In the summer of 1984, I began my search for answers. To my surprise, I could find little information. The psychological literature was loaded with research findings and reports about the children, even the grandchildren, of survivors. But I could uncover hardly a word about the perpetrators and their children. Was it that the children remained unaffected by their parents' past, or was it that nobody had tried to find out? At that time, I was not courageous enough to undertake the search myself. I had never traveled extensively in Germany, although once I had gone by train from Zurich to a conference in Stockholm and deliberated about stopping in Hamburg for a night—my mother had always urged me to go and see her "beautiful city" (though she herself went back only twice). I even took the first step during the train's short stop in Hamburg by asking what an overnight stay would mean in terms of a ticket exchange, but the harsh, commanding tone of the ticket clerk's reply put me off. I returned to my seat and traveled on to Stockholm.

An additional problem was the language. I had spoken German in my early childhood because I had stayed with my grandparents, who did not speak Hebrew, for long periods. But as an adult, I had used German only on isolated occasions. I wondered if I could handle the delicate conversation that would be required in interviewing perpetrators' children.

Then one day, a German professor from the University of Wuppertal and his wife came to visit my department. Wuppertal and Beer

12. Gitta Sereny, *Into That Darkness: From Mercy-killing to Mass Murder* (New York: McGraw-Hill, 1974).

13. Donald P. Spence, "The Paradox of Denial," in *The Denial of Stress,* ed. Shlomo Breznitz (New York: International University Press, 1982), 103–23.

Sheva, where I teach, are "twin cities," and the local German university had decided to develop ties with its twin institution in Israel. We sat in my office, and I told the professor about my work. His wife, who did not speak English, listened but did not participate. At some point in the conversation, I asked the question: What do you think happened to the children of Holocaust perpetrators? The room was suddenly silent. The professor's wife looked at me and said in German, "I can tell you from my own experience . . ." We talked for two more hours. When I returned home, I was upset, yet also stimulated. I felt that I could do it, I could go to Germany.

Before I left on my first research trip, I told Tova, one of my students, whose mother had been "there," where I was going and why. She looked at me and said, "Ask them if they still want to kill in their dreams as I still want to die in mine."

In August 1985 I arrived in Germany for the first time. Because I knew very little about how to find subjects for my interviews, I consulted two professors at the University of Wuppertal. We decided to put advertisements in the local newspapers: "A psychologist from Israel, guest-professor at our university, is conducting research about family memories of the Third Reich. Persons born between 1925 and 1940 who had fathers in the war, please contact Professor B." I arrived in Wuppertal to find the professor very excited. He had received twenty-five responses. We immediately decided to run another ad, but this time it read: "Persons whose parents were in the SS, or took an active part in the persecution and extermination of Jews, Gypsies, and other minorities . . ." Twelve more people responded. (A few others called to curse the professor and the university for "continuing to dig up the past with this dirty Jew!") I decided to interview all of the ad respondents, but as I had expected, only a couple of them turned out to be children of perpetrators.

In Frankfurt, I met with a psychologist who, I had been told, was personally interested in the topic because of her own past and had offered to help me find names and addresses. We talked for several hours, and she told me about her parents' role during the Third Reich and how it had affected her life. She was very open and tried to be helpful, yet despite her efforts, she was unable to remember anyone whose parents had taken part in the extermination process. But as I was about to leave, she said, "You know, it has suddenly occurred to me that my sister is married to the son of . . . He was one of the top people in the euthanasia program." This was my first lesson in what repression is like in Germany.

Some of my best leads in locating other subjects came from my first few interviewees. Once we had met and gotten acquainted, they became helpful. They mentioned names and addresses, though many of them had never spoken with each other about their common lot. It reminded me of my situation at home: children of survivors are very quick to identify others with a similar background, but rarely do they talk to each other about this aspect of their lives. "I don't want people to relate to me through this label," a student once told me, almost as though one could be contaminated by the label itself.

In a few cases, the interview experience was frightening. I recall one case especially. I had traveled all the way to a small town in southern Germany where I was to meet a lawyer, the son of an Einsatzgruppe commander who had been given a death sentence at Nuremberg (this was later commuted to a life sentence, and he was eventually released after eight years in prison). On the phone, the son sounded suspicious, but several days later he invited me to his home. As I approached the house, I noticed his face at a window. When I asked his permission to tape-record the interview, he said he had to consult someone and went into another room to make a phone call. I felt sudden fear. Maybe he was affiliated with some organization? When he came back, he let me know that it would be quite impossible to record the conversation. He still admired his father and disputed the nature of his role during the Third Reich. As I drove away, I had the feeling that I was being followed, that the car behind me was tailing me. It took me several hours to calm down, to remember that the Nazi era was over. I was hunting no one and no one was hunting me.

I intentionally avoided children of famous perpetrators, like the sons of Rudolf Hess or Josef Mengele, who had already been the subject of media attention, because I suspected that they had developed an "external self" in talking about their fathers and the Third Reich. I looked for people who had been left alone, for whom the past might have become part of an internal dialogue.

Of the fifty-eight children of perpetrators I made contact with during my four visits to Germany (1985–1987), only nine refused to see me. No one has yet succeeded in interviewing Himmler's daughter, so I summoned up the courage to phone her. I described my research and asked if she would meet with me. There was a pause, during which I could hear only the pounding of my heart. "No, I am sorry, I don't see people on this subject." We talked for a few minutes more, but she did not change her mind, and I am not sure which one of us felt more relieved. Later, I learned about her involvement in neo-Nazi activities.

By 1987, the atmosphere in Germany was changing. The postwar repression of the Nazi period had begun to ease: a few newspaper articles, several letters to the editor, two books,[14] and a television program openly addressed the subject of children of perpetrators. The interviews presented here, however, took place at a time when the matter was totally hushed up in Germany. The interviewees spoke as if in a vacuum. Almost no one had discussed the subject with them before, and no one knew about their own particular relationship to it.

All those who agreed to talk with me were openly informed about my research and its purpose. With one exception (see Chapter 6), I have protected their identities with pseudonyms throughout. The original tapes were transcribed and translated verbatim into English. The interviews included here were edited for length, and additional personal details were omitted to further ensure anonymity.

In the first of the interviews, I am very angry. I have not yet worked through my own need for revenge. But gradually, my anger fades. I train myself to be open and accepting, even when I face manifest or covert aggression, denial, numbness. The interview process demands restraint and empathy, a spirit of inquiry combined with a nonjudgmental approach. I do not always succeed, despite my best efforts, but I know that my interviewees' difficulties with the role their parents played during the Third Reich do not begin here, just as they will not end here.

I soon realize how quickly I can dissociate my emotions from the stories I hear daily. I try to maintain a kind of balance that will allow me to understand Naomi and Thomas, or Tova and Rudolf, at the same time. Sometimes I become so empathetic with my interviewees, I feel the need to remind myself of what happened to my own people in order to justify continuing my research in Germany.

During the course of my research, I traveled by train, although it took me some time to get over the emotional symbolism of trains in Germany. I traveled for hours, almost daily, because I usually met my interview partners at their homes, and they lived all over the country. As I sat in the train compartment, I scrutinized the other passengers, trying to guess where they were during the Nazi period, or where their parents were. I also found myself holding imaginary conversations with people at home. I still felt guilty about meeting the children of their victimizers.

14. Peter Sichrovsky, *Schuldig geboren: Kinder aus Nazifamilien* (Cologne: Kiepenheuer & Witsch, 1987), trans. Jean Steinberg as *Born Guilty: Children of Nazi Families* (New York: Basic Books, 1988); Dörte von Westernhagen, *Die Kinder der Täter* (Munich: Kösel, 1987).

Back in Israel, when I spoke about my experiences with friends and colleagues, many of them couldn't listen. Shlomo said, "We have enough trouble of our own. Why do you have to tell us their side of the picture? *We don't want to know about it!*" When I looked for someone who knew German to transcribe the interview tapes, an elderly woman, who does this professionally for conferences, was willing to try, but after a week she called me. "I can't handle this material. I get too upset."

On my first visit to Germany, my wife, who had helped me overcome my own initial inhibitions about the project, accompanied me, but she returned home after ten days to take care of the children. I myself had planned to remain in Germany for two months that first summer but shortened my stay because Yariv, my wife's fifteen-year-old son, had been diagnosed with lymphoma. This event clouded our lives, and I put off the new research for a while. On my second trip I went alone, but Yariv's illness kept me on call. When I took my third trip, Yariv was no longer alive.

During one of our last conversations, Yariv wanted to hear about the people I had met in Germany. I told him about some of them, and he asked, "Why is it so important to you?" (Yariv had the ability to ask questions one was compelled to answer frankly.) I groped for an answer, but suddenly his face lit up in a wide smile. "I know why, you are looking for hope, for them and for yourself."

"What do you mean by that?" I said, surprised by his directness.

"Because you told me once that, for you, the quest for hope has to do with confronting the truth."

chapter 1

The Physician from Auschwitz and His Son

In the small Bavarian village, a sign shows the way to the doctor's house. I leave my wife sitting on a bench in the village square and drive down the road to keep my appointment. It is a beautiful morning. We have enjoyed a good night's sleep in a little hotel off the main road and wakened to a pleasant rural scene, an atmosphere of serenity. It seems as if I am heading out to a family picnic rather than to a painful interview. I ring the doorbell, and an intelligent-looking, white-haired man greets me with a warm smile. He is the first of the Nazi generation I am to meet in Germany. I immediately picture my own father, who was also a physician. I notice a certain similarity in facial expression and realize that if my father were still alive, he would be the same age. I have decided to get in touch with the doctor first because my informants do not know of any other way to reach his children. "Go see the good old man—you will like him."

From the panoramic window in the living room, there is a magnificent view of the Tyrolean Alps. Ernst sits down in his comfortable armchair and lights his pipe (my father also smoked a pipe). He seems at ease. After the war, he was tried and acquitted for his role as a physician at Auschwitz, because inmates testified about his helpful and humane behavior toward them.

I have just begun the interview when the telephone rings. It is the mother of a sick nine-year-old. Can he come over immediately? He listens, asks a couple of questions, and says he will drop by in an hour or so. I am seeing a physician in action, but I also realize that this hour is all the time we will have.

B: Where do your parents come from?

E: From the Palatinate, the west, near the French border. My mother grew up in Geneva, in Switzerland. Her father was a pathologist there. My father came from a clergyman's family. He was a forester, but he didn't enjoy the practical side of it. He built himself a lab in the basement and taught himself. Pretty soon he made it to the university as a plant physiologist. He came from a milieu that actually had only negative contact with the Nazis. My mother was a fanatic, you might say, she really hated Hitler. My father, politically, was completely uninteresting as far as I was concerned. As the son of a clergyman, he had rebelled, he had something against religion, but otherwise he was quite liberal.

B: When Hitler came to power, you were twenty-two. What do you remember?

E: Well, the discrepancy between my mother's emotions and my own. I was pretty much indifferent to National Socialism, to Hitler. My mother, on the other hand, was exceptionally nationalistic, she had a German nationalism different from National Socialism. I'm sure you know what I mean. Well, she tried to raise me on that. On the other hand, in my age group there were some who really liked the Nazis. It was the "in" thing. I wasn't able to avoid it. I saw some positive things in it too, till I became a student at Tübingen in 1932 and then was confronted with the practical side of it. That looked very different. That caused me to turn away from it completely.

But that was difficult at the time. There were already registration quotas at the university for certain subjects, not comprehensive quotas, but it was still hard to get in as a student. It was not advisable to be conspicuous. You were expected to be active, to go out on demonstrations. And besides, there was no opposition within the student body at that time, although in Tübingen the student body was to a considerable extent made up of theology students. And there was an obligation, you had to be integrated in some way, in '33, '34, '35, '36, either in the SA, the Student Organization, the Pilots' Corps of the SS, riding clubs, something like that. Each student tried to join the organization where he would have to be the least active, you understand?

Anyhow, I was able to avoid all that until I went to Munich. That was in 1935–36. There, it was handled very strictly, and the easiest organization to get involved with was the National Socialist Automobile Corps, which was part of the university Student Organization. But there was also this other tendency: to get away from the nonsense of having students march and to put them instead into National Socialist study groups. They tried to motivate and interest the students in racial-biological theories, that sort of thing.

The sequence of the account and his frankness are convincing.

B: Did you have a particular instructor for that?

E: No, nothing like that. I just had to go there. They tried to funnel this National Socialist propaganda from below up into the academic structures. They set up study groups in this manner. As for me, I didn't like all the marching and definitely didn't like all the rest of it. I was working at the Institute for Hygiene at the time. I came up with the idea of setting up a study group to investigate a poor area in order to find out what might be done there in economic terms. The idea was accepted, and I set up this group for hygiene studies in the Bavarian Forest within the Student Organization. That was my political involvement. I took final exams then—it was 1938—and if you were a graduate student, well, then you had to be in the Party. Couldn't avoid it. So I joined up and became a pro forma member.

B: Was this discussed with your parents at the time?

E: Very little. My mother didn't accept the fact that I had taken such a step. My mother didn't know much about what was happening. She no longer had any contact with the outside world, so to speak. She was already very old. But my father was aware of what was going on at the university. He knew. There wasn't any discussion about it.

B: Was there no other alternative for you at that stage?

E: Well, either you went along to march, once or twice a week, paramilitary training, or there were these other options. It was definitely propagandistic, ideological. The full professors, the senior people, were opposed. The middle level, that of the assistants, the guys trying to make a career, the second stratum at the university, had greater contact with the more political institutions. When I left the university, I was at the Institute for Hygiene, and I didn't do any military service. That was something unusual, because normally every graduate in medicine tried to finish his military service as soon as possible, simply for economic reasons. Then you could do outside work, but you were paid for that. Pay at the university was rotten. So I was sent out as an assistant doctor with the General Sick Fund to practices where the doctor in charge had been drafted. And I got married at this time. I had met my wife at the university—we were both medical students. She comes from a military family. So I had to take care of three different private practices. It was an enormous amount of work, and it wasn't pleasant. I wasn't frustrated, though. On the contrary, there was a lot I could do, I was enthusiastic. Well, I was living in the house of one of the doctors who'd been conscripted into service. His wife was very bitter about the fact that her husband had been drafted and that I, a younger doctor, was not in service. It was quite an uncomfortable situation . . .

So then I got to thinking. There was this change in attitude that took place in me. I can't say that I'd been a pacifist earlier on, nothing like that, but I had no ambition to join the military. Then I became convinced deep down inside that I didn't belong there, I had to get out, in spite of the fact that I was married and already had a child. It was simply some sort of mass psychosis, a mass hysteria, those first two war years. So I tried after one year to get sent to the front, tried in any way possible, with a lot of support from all those who had an interest in seeing me get out of there. But it simply wasn't possible, because I was stuck, caught up bureaucratically in so many institutions that I had become indispensable. There were these three District Offices, all linked up with the Chamber of Physicians. As soon as I had gotten permission from two of them, I was faced with dealing with the other two. So for all practical purposes it was simply impossible.

One day I was in Munich for an appointment, and I met a former colleague in the street, someone I'd been together with at the Institute for Hygiene, a man from Strasbourg. I'd always assumed he was Jewish, didn't know him particularly well. And so I asked him, "Don't you have any problem?" And he said, "None at all, I can arrange things. I've got excellent connections. I'm in the Waffen SS." I guess he wasn't Jewish after all. I don't know for sure even now—he didn't look Jewish. Well, when I first knew him, he hadn't been politically active in the least. So I was astonished, I didn't take the thing seriously. But after a short time I got my papers telling me to report to the Waffen SS, and I didn't think there was anything wrong with that. The Waffen SS at that time, 1942, was considered to be a part of the army, the Wehrmacht, led by regular generals. Even today it is accepted as having been that kind of unit.

I wonder if this was the only thing known about the Waffen SS at that time. Only weeks later do I learn from a source close to his sister that when she had heard about his "eagerness" to be recruited, she succeeded in arranging a job for him in the Luftwaffe—the air force—where she held an important position, but he would only go into the Waffen SS.

E: So I went in and was sent to Pomerania for eight or nine weeks of military training. Since I had had training in pathology and hygiene, I was then assigned to the Institute for Hygiene of the Waffen SS located in Berlin. My job was to take care of the various units pathologically and hygienically. So I reported to the boss, and he said, "Oh good, you've come. You know this man Weber from the Institute for Hygiene, don't you? He's already asked for you to be transferred. He needs someone." "Where is he?" "He's at the Institute for Hygiene, Southeastern Outpost." "Where is that?" "Auschwitz, in Poland. We've got our lab there and our job there is to take care of the concentration camp, particularly the personnel. They're in danger—typhus, yellow fever—because the camps are so filthy. Go on out there and see for yourself."

So I went there, and it turned out that I knew Weber better than the fellow from Strasbourg. He was very pleased, and he said to me, "I asked for you to be sent. We're part of the Waffen SS. We don't have anything to do with the concentration camp. A hundred prisoners work in the labs in these institutes. There's a unit that takes care of the work in the labs. All you have to do is supervise the routine operations. Aside from that, you can do what you want; we're very well-equipped. In the camp itself all you have is an advisory function."

I had no idea what a concentration camp was, but after a short time, I learned, particularly about the way it was arranged as an extermination camp, with crematoria and all that. It took me about ten days before I understood what was going on. Then Weber left for Berlin, so I was alone and experienced it all myself. I was horrified, desperate. But there was nothing I could do, no alternative, you just had to try to keep clear of anything that was inhumane.

B: What was your job there?

E: Actually, all I did was supervise the labs. The routine operations were done by other lower-ranking people who knew them better than I did. They needed someone to give a signature. Weber had already gotten out of all this and left. He was still there as official boss, but he was consulting expert for hygiene in the outlying production units set up in mines and for the V-2 rocket. He had to be away quite often, and then I was in charge. I had the enormous advantage that Weber was not a totally committed, die-hard member of the SS and that he didn't like all this one bit (es hat ihm nicht geschmeckt) so I was able to speak openly with him. Pretty soon this conflict arose between the camp commandant, who was our superior, on the one hand, and the Institute for Hygiene, which had assigned us there. Looked at legally, there was this problem: who had the final word, who was really in charge? That was my problem, but it was also purely theoretical. In practice, the situation was such that I was not actually involved in anything initially except the routine operations of the Institute for Hygiene. Occasionally, I had an advisory function, how to disinfect barracks, things like that. That was the situation until the late autumn of 1943. By then, the gassing capacity in Auschwitz was so large that the doctors working on the ramps couldn't handle the job . . .

He says "gassing capacity" as one might say "production capacity."

B: Selections?

E: Yes, selections. There were five doctors. They had to process incoming shipments around the clock. So someone mentioned that there were two doctors sitting around with nothing to do, and then I was assigned to selection duties. It was absolutely impossible to do anything. How could you keep out of it? To refuse to obey in the normal sense of the act would have been completely senseless. Weber wasn't there, and I thought of the boss in Berlin, Professor B. I'd got the impression he was someone you could talk to. So I said to myself, I'll go to Berlin and tell him what's going on. And he understood the situation completely. The representative from the Institute was also there during this conversation. Professor B. asked me what we should do, and I said I didn't know. He said, "That is simply incredible, unheard of, that this commandant thinks they can deal with *our* people in that way. We won't put up with that. I'll take all our men away. Then he won't have any personnel." Then the two of them started to argue, and I managed to keep out of it . . .

Professor B., his superior, did not want them controlling his people.

E: Now comes a very sad story. The commandant told us that someone from the SS training academy (Ordensburg) was being sent to us, a very young fellow who'd just finished training. "He's being assigned to us as No. 2 man," he said, "and he will take over those duties." He was a very young man who had been brought up on the ideals of the SS as they were taught in these academies, which was apparently quite different from the actual practice of the Death's Head units. So he came on down and he was so shocked, and he was ordered to . . .

It's difficult to picture how it was, this process of selection. There were the various officers, the doctor in charge and the unit commander. He had the task of making sure that everything remained orderly. I only saw it twice myself. The Kapos[1] would carry out a large preselection involving children, very old women, and old men. Then there were additional selections carried out by certain personnel, after which the doctor had to decide. Now a lot depended on the size of the transport. If it was very large, the selection process was very superficial. If it was a normal-size transport, then things were done more thoroughly. The transports came at night, and if you had your normal duties during the day and then had to work extra at night, well . . . In any event, this young man, he was so ill after his very first round of selections that he could no longer be used for that work, even though he had been directly assigned to us for this purpose.

B: This was his duty?

E: Yes, it was. However, they showed special consideration for his

---

1. Camp inmates—criminals, political prisoners, and later, Jews—used by the Nazis to head the labor squads.

condition, and he was put to work elsewhere in the camp without having to take part in selection. During this period, some three weeks, he was assigned to someone who had the job of motivating him to work in selection.

Now I come to something I can't describe, something it is only possible to experience. If you had been in Auschwitz, in this milieu, and had repeatedly heard for two or three weeks (as if it were quite natural) that the inmates who were still alive would die soon anyhow, quite soon . . . And they had a terrible life unless they had some special job and could get better food. The amount was calculated in such a way that if the food had been divided up equally, then many would have been able to survive a few years. But that wasn't possible. The Kapos and functionaries found ways of getting enough food for themselves at the expense of the others. It is incredible, but you can simply get accustomed to such a thing, the horrible condition of the inmates, when you stand there with a full belly. You simply can't imagine how you can get to accept the smoke pouring from the crematoria, the transports and all that, the obvious and seemingly "natural" way in which people were being selected and murdered, something that is beyond any kind of comprehension. You can learn to bear all that and in the end even participate in it. Participate without being really involved, just doing your duty. That's what happened to this fellow.

B: During these two weeks?

E: Not necessarily two weeks, but within a relatively short period of time. Then—he was young and just married—they let him bring his wife, he had a beautiful blond wife, and he was allowed to bring her to live with him in the camp. That may have played a role. They were always preached to, told that "they had the most difficult task in this war, in this era, a time when it was imperative to establish the Germanic race and to solve the Jewish problem once and for all. It is a terrible thing, but those who do it are great heroes, and can expect special thanks from Himmler."

B: And so he did the job you refused to do?

There is a pause of several seconds. He is very upset.

E: Yes, and after a few months he committed suicide.

It is still morning, and the Tyrolean Alps are still visible from the window, but in the room I can hardly see the old man's face. We take a short break; we both need it. He is moving now between two different languages: a formal one, giving an Eichmann-like report of what went on at the ramp in Auschwitz, and an emotional one, painfully describing the critical event that still occupies his mind after all these years.

B: How long did you stay in Auschwitz?

E: Right to the end. Right to the very end.

B: With the other doctors who had to, or wanted to do the selections?

E: Naturally, Weber and I tried to keep our distance as much as possible. The usual duties. The only thing I'm still bothered about, the reason there have been so many journalists swamping me in the last few weeks, is that Mengele was the only one I had any closer contact with. Mengele, as has become clear recently, joined the SS mainly for opportunistic reasons. Well, Mengele didn't go around broadcasting his great enthusiasm for the SS in our presence, but I assumed that he was a very solid Nazi, being a member of the SS. Although he was by no means the sadistic torturer he's made out to be—in fact, he had no sadistic traits whatsoever. That's also the reason the prosecuting authorities for so many years didn't really try to find him. Because it was known through sworn statements that he was nothing but an SS camp doctor. And the experiments that he performed—I have to repeat this again and again—they were nothing out of the ordinary in terms of the usual Auschwitz daily routine. His experiments with twins were performed on human beings who had, in any case, been condemned to death.

Mengele's experiments were "nothing out of the ordinary"?

B: Hard to imagine . . .

E: These things are difficult to understand. And they are written about in the papers by people who are interested in something sensational, in getting a story. It's unusually difficult, an enormous dilemma, one should really listen only to the authentic people, those who have something to say, people who were involved or somehow affected.

B: Did Mengele say it was as difficult for him as you felt it to be yourself?

E: No, not at all. In moral terms, a selection in Auschwitz was nothing special. Besides, Mengele was an enthusiastic Nazi. He did not act the way I did, but he was always concerned with trying to pick out what was going wrong technically over the course of a day's difficulties. "Crazy, that idiot did not do his job. We won't be able to finish this. This is no way to run things!" He was terribly involved in an objective sense, a technical sense. So, I said to myself, well, if a person can be so enthusiastic and want to see to it that things are done in the best way possible, then he must be completely convinced about it all. We had a lot of discussions—he was someone who liked to talk about things. I mean, the "Final Solution," the killing of all the Jews was something wrong, totally wrong. Transportation to Madagascar and many other ideas that had been proposed would have been best, possibly assimilation too. But Mengele was absolutely immune to argument on that point and said, "You don't have to be a historian to see that that's impossible. Others tried it with other possibilities, and it didn't work."

B: As a physician, could you accept his attitude?

E: If you're a doctor in the field and after a battle have to decide who'll be taken care of, and who is treated first—do you take care of the Russian, the Frenchman, the German? Morally speaking, that's a far greater responsibility. If you go into this topic in detail and want to justify Mengele's standpoint, you can do it in many different ways.

I try to make sense of the old man's scale of morality.

B: All this went on for how long?

E: Two-and-a-half years.

B: Your wife was here and the children were small then?

E: They were small. The kids were born in 1940 and 1942.

B: What did your wife and children know about your experiences and activities at Auschwitz?

E: Let me think. I returned from Poland in 1948. Our daughter had been born in 1940, and she had been told about things by my wife, at least during those first years after the war, 1945–46, when I was in Poland. She had been told, sort of indirectly, that I wouldn't be coming back. My wife didn't think it was possible. She didn't believe I could somehow be found innocent.

B: Were you found guilty?

E: No. In this big Auschwitz trial in which almost all the important people were found guilty, I was acquitted. So I returned reinstated, and the children didn't learn anything about the negative side of it, at least not at that age.

B: Their father returned from the war and was acquitted?

E: He'd been in the SS and hadn't been involved at all in criminal acts. On the contrary, the Poles had sent him back home, and former inmates used to come to visit us. So there were no negative connotations then.

B: Is it difficult to explain to the children what Auschwitz really was?

E: [*Playing with his pipe*] That is also something strange. You know, this generation, these children, they just can't relate to this period, they are uninterested. It is strange, these human problems, the fact that millions were killed. Just imagine: turning as many people into ashes in one night as there are inhabitants in this village. In twenty-four hours they are all a pile of ashes! I mean, these are dimensions that young people just push far away from themselves, they don't want to deal with it. And when they hear that those who did it were Germans, they just want to repress it.

B: How did your wife react when you told her about Auschwitz?

E: [*Absorbed in his own thoughts*] Well, there is a very touching and warm human story. For a long time we hadn't been able to write. I don't know if any letter of mine ever arrived normally. First I was in American custody, and then my wife found out somehow that I'd been handed over to the Polish authorities. One day she received a message that she should come to Nuremberg, that there was a Polish prosecutor who wished to speak with her. So she went, and he asked her whether she didn't perhaps have some photographs of her husband and the children with her. She thought they were going to tell her I'd been hanged or something. But they told her that, as far as the government prosecutor was concerned, there was nothing against me, and that they couldn't imagine I would be found guilty. They told her I would probably be in custody another week or so, and that she should go home and get some photos to pass on to the official. I had contended all along that I'd had absolutely nothing to do with the killing. A few letters arrived from former inmates of the camp, who felt obliged to offer their assistance, people whom I'd helped personally, either directly or indirectly. In this way, the situation for my wife was not so bad. What was bad for her was that I'd volunteered for duty against her wishes, that I had tried to leave the warm nest of the family at all.

B: She resented that?

E: Yes, she did. Naturally, my entire life I have felt guilty about this. And it colored our marriage.

B: Did you return to your job in the village after the war?

E: When I returned, my wife was very pessimistic. She said, "Sure, we have good papers, but if you were in Auschwitz, you will never be able to practice medicine again." But I did. I've been very active in my profession, and I like to work at it.

B: Did your experience at Auschwitz affect your work as a doctor?

E: No, I can't imagine being anything else but a doctor. No, I can't.

B: What's it like to live with all this afterward? It's more than forty years now. Have you had any dreams or nightmares?

E: [*Thinking for a few seconds*] There is always a key experience. Mine was rather peculiar, quite strange. One of the first weeks I was at Auschwitz, I was standing at the gate. I wanted to get into the camp, but these columns of prisoners were marching in, so I had to wait. You couldn't enter—they used to count the prisoners—you just had to wait at the gate. I was standing up above to have a good look watching these men filing in, and suddenly, I saw someone. Even today, I would swear that it was Leo Oppenheim. He had been a schoolmate of mine, a very close friend, because our situations were very similar. So all I could think of was how I could get in touch with him.

First I asked this noncom, and he said that if I really wanted to see him, if that was really important to me, then we'd have to ask about him. He wouldn't be known by his given name, but rather by his prisoner number. Naturally, there were indirect ways of finding out, checking the files. But if an SS officer showed a personal interest in a prisoner, that was always bad for the prisoner. He would be carefully scrutinized. For someone who was not an insider it was all but impossible. To get in touch via other inmates was even more difficult, because they wouldn't tell someone's name to anyone they didn't have complete trust in—initially the prisoners always assumed something negative. It didn't take me long to understand that. I waited. Later I established good contacts with inmates who were able to inquire in the records section. In addition, I kept on the lookout for him, trying to spot him. But there were a hundred thousand people in the camp. I never learned anything that would point to his having been there, and according to everything I could find out, he wasn't there anymore. The individual life of this one man I had known, my concern with the fate of this one man, made me experience something very personal. All the rest was just general.

B: Do you believe he saw you there?

E: No, he wasn't able to see me. He had to march past this inspector with his head turned at an angle. But I was able to see him very clearly. You can imagine, they all had shaven heads and had to march past in a military manner, with a military expression on their faces, this last march of the day, for which each person had saved up his last reserves of energy. Objectively speaking, the possibility that it was Leo was not very great. But I was absolutely certain. At that moment Leo became real for me again. This memory has always played some sort of role for me ever since. Naturally, when you saw—how could you miss it?— the large transports rolling in from Poland, Hungary, the crematoria were insufficient, piles of corpses had to be burned, a burning pile of human corpses . . . Terrible, horrible! You understand, that's something quite different. In a purely personal sense I was quite involved. I was on close personal terms with prisoners who also testified at the trial. [*Suddenly very agitated*] Friendships developed there, close contacts that went beyond . . .

B: I can well imagine that you came home rehabilitated after the trial, and your children and wife welcomed you, but your awful memories persisted. How did you sleep at night? What happened later on? After you had time to think about the whole thing, how did you relate to other people? How did you pass your days, your nights?

E: I didn't have any dreams. I had quite different experiences. It's not the actual horror, the terrible fate of the people, that's not it, you understand. It's strange, but you get used to that. No, it's the fact of the selection that I think of, like when I'm in the garden digging, and there are snails. It's like a compulsive idea. Not that I can't kill the snails, that's no problem. But then there's one that I miss, that I see and have to kill, to dig up and kill the last one. That's what's so unpleasant. Take this one snail out especially, and it's such a disturbing, phobic experience. The notion that selection is continuing, going on. Or when I see cattle being transported, I . . .

B: The images return?

E: Yes, the images come back. The others must also have gone through such experiences. I spoke at length with Gitta Sereny, who wrote an excellent book about Franz Stangl, the commandant of Treblinka.[2] I don't recall whether she told me directly or if it's described in the book. She asked him the same question you asked me, and he said that once on a train track, some cows on the way to the slaughterhouse looked at him, and the eyes of these animals . . . In my case, it's not the eyes, but rather, the fact that something is being sacrificed, killed by hand. That's it.

The interview is over. As I leave, the old doctor suddenly appears lonely and defeated. On the way out, I glance at his vegetable garden and try to imagine him working there in a few hours, killing the snails one by one— including the last. This last snail and Leo Oppenheim are all that is left to him of the thousands he watched being gassed and burned to ashes.

When I reach my wife in the village square, these are the first thoughts I share with her, along with his comments on Mengele. She looks at me as if I am contaminated by a terrible disease and urges me to drive away from the village at once. As we drive back to Munich, I think about this man. He tried to keep away from the dehumanization and succeeded in his attempt, only to see a young colleague dragged into the job, and eventually commit suicide. Why didn't he break down? I could have understood crying—any human reaction. Instead, he is looking for a way to sound reasonable. It occurs to me that I could easily have been one of those "snails" had my father not left Germany.

That night I have trouble falling asleep. For weeks afterward I think about the doctor, who has added a new chapter to my understanding of

2. Gitta Sereny, *Into That Darkness: From Mercy-killing to Mass Murder* (New York: McGraw-Hill, 1974).

humankind. On the one hand, he was moral: he did not agree to participate in the selections, unlike many others. On the other hand, he remains fascinated by "workload" and "gassing capacity." Auschwitz must have been the peak experience of his life.

This man is trying to distance others from his own inner turmoil because he can't face it himself. In his own way, he has become for me the gate-keeper of what I am looking for, but he is doing his best not to let me in. I wonder what this village physician told his own children about his experiences at Auschwitz, what thoughts have replayed in his mind over the last forty years.

Peter answers the phone. I introduce myself briefly, adding that I have been referred to him by his father. There is a short pause; he asks for several days to check my story out. When I call again, the matter has been settled. He will see me at his restaurant anytime I wish. I suggest 2:00 P.M. I know he lives in a village very close to the Swiss border, almost a day's journey by train. Since my mother is spending her summer holiday in Switzerland, we have arranged to meet after the interview. She is even willing to cross the border into Germany, although as a rule, she does not wish to see her homeland.

I arrive by train around noon, but no one at the train station can tell me how to reach Peter's village: no regular bus goes there at midday. I call him and ask if he can advise me. After a few minutes he offers, "My wife has to go to town. She will pick you up." I hesitate. I would prefer to get to the restaurant on my own—but I realize that this is impractical, so I accept.

A little while later a short, blond woman approaches me. When we are well on our way, she asks me if it is true that I have come all the way from Wuppertal to see her husband and to talk with him about "that period." "Yes," I answer, "even from as far as Israel." She glances at me with a mixture of surprise and pity. "I am afraid you are going to be very disappointed. He is not the kind of guy who likes to talk, you know what I mean?"

I am seated at a corner table in their simple but well-ordered restaurant and offered coffee and cake. He addresses me bluntly, a tall, blond, somewhat athletic type, with clear blue eyes that look at me for only a moment. No handshake. "My name is Peter. I will be with you in a few minutes. I still have some matters to clear up." I wait patiently, letting my mind wander. How did the son of the educated man I met a month ago become a restaurant chef? Then he is sitting in front of me with a pack of cigarettes in his hand, ready to answer "any question" I wish to pose. There is a quick flash of irritation in his eyes when I ask permission to set up the tape recorder, but his answer is, "No problem."

P: I was born June 21, 1942, the second child. My sister's older, and I have a younger brother.

B: You were born during the war. You probably don't remember much from the earliest period . . .

P: Well, I'd say more or less nothing. Sometimes I think I do remember something, but when I talk to my mother or to other people, they say it's all fantasy. For example, I seem to remember that the Americans came, mainly blacks and Indians, and that I felt very good among them. And if I tell other people this story, they say that there was no real occupation, they just drove on past very quickly. But I have this idea that I slept with them in their tents. It's probably just a fantasy.

B: Are those your earliest memories?

P: Those are about the only memories I have of the war. Otherwise there's nothing. Not that I had any bad experiences. I can still recall when the refugees started coming: I remember that they'd had a rotten time. But we never had any problem with food, for example, maybe because my mother was a doctor, I don't know. Problems that other people probably had, because there were break-ins in bakeries, butcher shops, people were stealing, when these refugees came from East Prussia with lots of kids. I do know that we always had enough to eat. In fact, because my father wasn't around, my mother used to give other people some of our ration stamps. I actually didn't understand then how anybody could go hungry.

B: And did you continue to live in the same town?

P: We lived on a farm for relocated families, and we children were out in a very isolated farm most of the time, even farther away. But when I was six, in 1948, we moved to W.

I sense an openness, a sincerity in his reflections.

B: What are your earliest memories of your father? When was he around?

His color rises for a second. I see that he has been waiting for just such a question.

P: Now, let's see, the first memories of my father . . . Well, I haven't talked about it for a long time, but he came home once and he had these blue pills. And for me they were candies. So I ate them, and then I threw up something awful, all over his boots. That's the earliest memory I have of my father. And he was home only two or three days. Now whether that was during the war or when he was in custody, I don't know. I never talked about it again. But that's the earliest memory, the only one I have of my father from that period, and that my mother was happy that he was home. So we all thought we were happy, and then I threw up all over his boots, and he started to yell at me. Those are the first memories I have of my father.

B: What later memories do you have when your father was at home and around a little more?

P: Later on, my dad—I'm not sure when he came back—but when he was there, well, he would get up at an ungodly hour, at five or six. He had this motorcycle, and a motorcycle makes such a terrible racket. And I remember that he would ride to his office. Now if you mean the time of transition, when he wasn't around yet . . . well, I think we grew up in a very protected environment, so that we didn't even notice when he was gone or when he'd returned. One day he was just back home again, that was it. Life went on in its normal way. He just did his work.

B: What did you do together with your father after he came back home?

P: With my dad? Nothing, I was just with the other kids, and he was always busy. If I look at doctors today, they're also always busy. The only thing that bothered me was that I had to go along on Sundays.

B: To church?

P: No, no, mountain climbing, or on an excursion. I would have preferred to spend the time with my buddies. Well, that was really a must. They couldn't leave me alone at home, because something would always get broken if I was at home alone. So that's why I had to go along with them.

B: Did you quarrel a lot, or was it a quiet family life?

P: Quarrels, well, there weren't any quarrels at all, not at all. I used to get spanked. I mean, I got spanked and deserved it. My sister, for example, she was quite a different sort of child. Everything was always in order. But in my case, that was the only way possible to deal with me. When I think back, I would say that he was very, well, I would use the word "humane." For what I did, I think I was punished very little, though I certainly got my spankings. For example, I'd be holding a stone, and I knew that if I threw it, I'd break the window. And I'd throw it anyway. Naturally, I'd get spanked. All I can say is that it was quite normal.

Why does Peter emphasize that his was such a "normal" family?

B: Do you know why you reacted that way?

P: I don't know. In my son's case, I don't know either. Must be character, temperament. He's a chip off the old block, so to speak. If I look at my son today, I'd say it's almost the same thing. But there was no explanation for it, no reason why. It was just for the fun of it, I guess. I assume it's just a person's character.

B: When and how were you told about what had happened during the war?

P: My parents didn't tell me anything at all as far as I know, nothing at all. The first time I learned what my father had been, I was training as an apprentice cook in S. There happened to be this program on TV in which something was mentioned, and I saw my father there. Anyhow, I think that's the first time I knew or found out anything about what my father had been. It was never talked about, and let me add that I never asked about it either.

B: And when you saw this program on TV, did you ask him anything after that?

P: No, I didn't. As I said, I was away from home at the time. I didn't get back very often.

B: And the first time you heard about it was on TV?

P: Right, on TV, I think. I don't remember anyone talking to me about it before that, neither my mother nor my father.

B: And when you saw him for the first time, how did you react?

P: Right from the start, all I heard were positive things. I never heard a negative word about him. There were also various people who came here from Poland and really, they had only the best things to say about him. Actually, I never had any problems with that.

B: What did these people tell you?

P: Well, they didn't talk about much. They were simply vacationing on Lake Constance and came over to pay my father a visit. All they said was how much they owed my father, things like that.

B: Although you heard only positive comments, when you learned he'd served at Auschwitz, did you know what that was?

P: [*Hesitating for a fraction of a second*] At that point we didn't have any idea at all. We were never told about it in school. It was totally . . . What I do know I learned more or less on my own initiative. I don't know if the picture I have is the correct one, though. Sometimes I think it's really a bit distorted, not in the sense the neo-Nazis distort things, but rather that maybe it's a little exaggerated. That's what I figure. Like this fellow Mengele. Sure, I don't think it was right. But sometimes I have trouble imagining that he was as brutal as they describe him.

B: Did you ever try talking to your father about what happened at Auschwitz?

P: I think I did once. Can't quite recall. I think I spoke to him once about this, and he said—I'm actually not quite sure if it was my father or someone else—but he said he didn't have the heart, the courage.

We didn't talk about the brutality and all that, but we talked about how men were able to do that. And he said he simply didn't have enough strength of character to say no. Now whether *he* was as sadistic as he is described . . . Anyhow, he said, he had his orders and he carried them out. He wasn't able to say no.

B: Who? Your father?

P: No, Mengele. My father tried to avoid those selections of prisoners, he tried to get out of it as far as I know. But *he* didn't try that. He just accepted the order. My father also said that he himself was just lucky, it was just luck that he was able to avoid the selections. He tried to get out of it, consciously. And he said if he hadn't been lucky, well, then he would have had to do it. He said that he was involved in a kind of refusal to obey an order in that sense, you understand? But I don't have any notion of how it really was and how strictly things were enforced, I don't know, I wasn't in the army. And refusal to obey an order, I don't know personally what that is either.

In the eyes of the son, Mengele has become a person who only obeyed orders.

B: Do you think this past history has had some influence on you or on the relationship between you and your father?

P: Not in the least, no way at all, because I was already eighteen when I heard for the first time. Definitely not.

B: Without talking now about your father's activities, how is it possible to understand that things such as Auschwitz were able to happen?

P: Well, now as far as I'm concerned, see, for a long time I didn't worry about matters like that at all. As I mentioned, I grew up out in the country, and it wasn't talked about at all. Now if I'm concerned a bit nowadays, that's simply because today we've almost got to the same point again. I mean, if people see the Turks . . . you have no idea what's going on here. Why, they'll drive them out with stones just like then, that's for sure. The hatred people have for the Turks, what I see here is for me no different from the hatred people felt for the Jews. They'd string people up again in exactly the same way, certain people would. That's what I think anyhow. At least 60 to 70 percent of the Germans, if you let them have their way with the Turks. It would happen again.

B: But something like Auschwitz, that was a one-time event.

P: What are you getting at?

B: I mean, before Auschwitz there was never a camp whose purpose was to murder human beings.

P: That's not true. You've always had camps like that. Auschwitz, you can find that even today, and it existed in the past too. Look at Idi Amin, for example. Maybe he didn't build camps, but he's got prisons. And what's so shocking is that the whole world knows it but nobody says anything. That's what I find so shocking. It's that way in South Africa too. Maybe not as extreme, but, well, just as bad. Or Khomeini. It's all the same. Except that it's not talked about, it's kept quiet. I don't know, but as far as I can find out, in Hitler's case too, the whole world kept its mouth shut. And after we'd lost the war, that's when they started making all the noise.

B: But don't you think Auschwitz was something special?

P: No, I don't. I think places like that existed before and still do. Maybe not in this concentrated form. Whether it's racist genocide or this murdering nowadays, it's exactly the same as it was then.

B: But murder as an industry in a civilized country like Germany?

P: Well, you know, if you read nowadays: so-and-so killed this many, and that one killed that many, and so on, why, that amounts to so many people, it's almost hard to believe. But what's the difference whether I put them up against the wall or in gas chambers?

B: The difference may not be very great. But people who committed these acts, don't you think they were finished, that they couldn't go on living their own lives, loving their own children?

P: Well, that's what I don't believe, as I said, based on my experience here. Since I was twenty I've been going regularly to this bar and talking with people there. You know, if you talk with primitive workers, they don't have any scruples. I can admire a guy at the Munich stockyards who kills hundreds of pigs a day. I can admire him for it, the fact that he's able to do it. That he doesn't say at some point: it's impossible for me to go on. But I believe there are many people who could do the exact same thing to other human beings even today. I think a lot of people are capable of that, just from the way they talk. And if you get to know them a bit better, their character, then I have no doubt that they are capable of it. Probably the people who do things like that, they're the primitive types, the bad ones, so to speak. They simply have no feelings.

B: What do you think would happen to you if you were to go through the same experience as your father?

P: [*Surprised*] Never thought about it. Never imagined.

B: You can't imagine how your father actually worked in such a camp, day after day, for years?

P: No, I can't. [*Taking a cigarette*] I don't even know where he was jailed. And I don't have any idea whether he had anything to do with the gassing and shooting of people. I only know that he was a camp doctor and that he somehow . . . As far as I know, he wasn't . . . But he must have known, otherwise . . . To what extent he was involved, I don't know.

B: But if you know that your father was working on a daily basis in the camp, he had to watch people being killed in one way or another. And he came home and was nice to his wife, his kids, a good father. Then he went back and continued with his work, month after month for years.

P: I never thought about it. I don't know what went on inside my father's head. And, as I said, I don't know how closely he was implicated, whether he just suspected what was happening or really knew. Because every German says, "I didn't know," though he certainly must have known. But I never gave it a thought. As I mentioned, for as long as I can remember, he was just a normal father.

He "never gave it a thought." It is a relief to hear Peter say these words and to make real eye contact with him for the first time. Perhaps he has never allowed himself to question his father's normalcy. Maybe no one has ever asked him to put himself in the victims' place, or his father's. I want him to stay with it a little and suggest we take a short break. Ten minutes later, when I return to our table, he is still sitting in the same position, shoulders hunched. I now feel some warmth toward him. To be the son of an Auschwitz physician, even a "humane" one, involves a life-long struggle.

B: Is it possible to learn anything from the past? Have you learned anything?

P: Nothing at all. Because, well, for example, I have two Turks working for me. I'm on the best of terms with them, and so I get a bit excited about this topic. But what do you mean by "learned"? Actually people haven't learned a damn thing. It's just another period in time.

B: That happened and is past history?

P: It's true that it took place. As I said, that's true all right. Somehow I've pushed it away from myself, repressed it in my subconscious. Whether consciously or unconsciously, I do push it away from me. That's for sure, that's for darn sure! When there was that movie on TV about the Holocaust, well, I thought about whether it was right or not, and I thought a couple of times that it wasn't right that people were showing it. I said to myself that there are two types of people, the ones who are troubled by it, the way I'm troubled, and the ones who take pleasure in it.

B: How did it trouble you?

P: I was troubled about the fact that something like that could happen at all. As I recall, I didn't associate it at all with my father. The fact that he was involved, that's something that I've started to think about now, during our conversation. But you mean Auschwitz in particular. Well, I haven't looked into that much, far too little, never was in a situation where I would have been forced to think of it.

His voice is subdued, his remarks very different from the brisk, almost arrogant answers at the beginning of our interview. I see the same loneliness I noticed in his father's eyes as he talked about the snails in the garden, about Leo . . .

B: It must be very difficult for your father, because he has all these thoughts he doesn't want to tell you about . . .

P: I do believe that if I were to go home today and ask my father about it, he would answer my questions directly and fully. But I've never asked him. I don't know why. Once or twice we've touched on it, although even then it was some odd reason that got us on the topic. But that I asked him or he told me, no, there was never anything like that. Maybe it's possible I repressed it a bit in my subconscious, didn't want to know about it. That's possible.

B: Among your circle of friends, do you know whose father did what during the war?

P: I don't know a single person whose father was a Nazi.

B: There's no discussion about this?

P: I don't know anyone among my schoolmates or my other friends who says that his father was a Nazi or a member of the SS or whatever. There's a lot of talk now about how this one or that one was such a monster, but, as I said, in my circle of friends, it's never discussed. Never. And I don't say that my father was in Auschwitz. OK, quite recently there have been programs on TV, and then they sometimes ask me if that was my father, and I say, "Yes, sure." But nobody expects any further discussion, and nothing more is said. Nothing more is asked either.

B: Such questions are unpleasant.

P: Listen, the whole time I was in school or whatever, well, I can't recall a single one who ever said, "My dad was a Nazi." And nobody said, "He fought against the Nazis." None of that either. It is simply pushed out of the sphere of awareness, repressed. Not a topic worth talking about. Today I think it's a disgrace that in school, after the war, we didn't learn anything at all. Nothing! The word *Hitler* didn't exist. I think it's a damn shame. We just had to scrape it together for ourselves, my generation. That's why you have this situation where one guy believes it and the other one doesn't. We were old enough when we finished high school, but Hitler just didn't exist. We didn't learn anything except that the war started. That was all. As I see it, that was a big mistake, because as a result nobody—well, very few anyhow— became concerned about the matter. You just had to piece it together from newspapers, stuff like that.

B: Is this matter talked about in your own family? With your wife?

P: Yes, we talk quite a bit about it. For example, the film *Holocaust*, which I thought was more harmful than useful, she says it ought to be shown much more often. It's my view that programs like this serve to breed more neo-Nazis, or at least totalitarian types, that you breed such people by showing it. So we talk about it a lot. If we were both of the same opinion, we probably wouldn't talk about it.

B: Did your mother ever talk about your father's role during the war?

P: When I was small? Never.

B: And later on?

P: I can't recall that the topic was ever discussed in our family. As I mentioned, I found out about it via TV. The first discussion was the result of friction between my mom and dad. My mother was worried after that big bombing at the Oktoberfest in Munich, I think it was 1981, that the neo-Nazis would try to kill my father because he had helped free Jews during the war. That's the first time there was any discussion.

B: Do you know the story of how your father came to be at Auschwitz?

P: We discussed it once. He finished the university and a little later on he was assigned to work as a country doctor. But everyone in Germany wanted to go to the front. There was a kind of hysteria, and propaganda to the effect that you're not a good German unless you go to war. And so my father volunteered, but he wasn't taken, because he'd been sent to serve as a rural doctor. But then he got there via some connections or other. And his connections were such that he was sent to Auschwitz. Under normal conditions, he wouldn't have gone there at all.

B: Did your mother ever say what he did there, or voice her opinion about it?

P: No, never.

B: Do you know whether your mother or father had any Jewish schoolmates who died during the war?

P: I don't know. I mean, I can hardly imagine that. I can't imagine that in Bavaria.

B: Well, maybe in Munich.

P: Yes, Munich. But I never heard that they had schoolmates who were Jewish.

B: Would you be willing to talk with someone who knew your father back then and might know about what he did?

P: Yes, I certainly would. As I said, it would definitely interest me, but it would have to be someone who wasn't positive or negative, but rather, who realistically . . .

B: Would you find it interesting to speak with Mengele about these matters?

P: That would be very interesting. I actually defend this man in my subconscious. I don't know why. I mean, I just can't imagine that he was so bad. It's possible that I want to repress it, but it would have been very interesting to have had the opportunity to talk with him. On the other hand, when you hear that all these ex-Nazis were put to work in South America, principally to fight terrorists and that sort of thing, well, then you can imagine that they were the right types for that.

B: So you no longer think he only carried out orders? Anyhow, it is possible to carry out orders in several ways . . .

P: That's what my father said too. You can stretch orders a little. Though I say to myself, well, someone had to, because the order had been given. If I think of that fellow Eichmann . . . I didn't follow that much at the time. He wasn't directly involved in the killing. Maybe it's because those who were directly involved were different, like the one the French captured [Klaus Barbie]. But Eichmann, he just organized the transports. Maybe that's easier, I don't know. He just transported people.

B: Were there many who tried to "stretch" the orders?

P: [*Hesitating*] Well, perhaps not, but they said, "An order is an order." And some were put up against the wall and shot for refusing to obey orders. I can well imagine that Hitler and his staff picked out the right people for the job. They probably said, "Well, if you don't want to, then join the prisoners." I mean, I don't know how it was, it's hard to imagine. And I must say that among my peers, this is almost never discussed, it's given far too little thought. And when I hear those barroom discussions, then I figure that it could also start up again tomorrow, just like before, and take on the same proportions. However, I assume that it depends on a person's character, that it's international. Why, from a purely theoretical point of view, the Germans ought to be so shocked about what took place during the Third Reich that they praise every foreigner, every Jew to the heavens. But that is by no means the case. I figure that it's simply human nature, the human character.

B: Innate?

P: I assume it's innate. You're born that way, so to speak. I see it like this: a lion will attack a gazelle and tear it apart; the gazelle defends itself, but the lion tears it to pieces. I mean, it's in the genes, simply in the genes in certain people.

B: But how can you know who has it and who doesn't?

P: Well, by talking with people. Their appearance won't give them away. I don't even think it's something intellectual, it's just in the blood.

B: Could you imagine an Auschwitz for Turks being built?

P: Legally that's not possible, but, as I said, give the Germans the chance and they'd do it right away. Not *the* Germans, but, I mean, certain types would do it as soon as they got the chance. And I figure *they* were able to find those types, they put them there and they did these things. In my view, it's not difficult. Take a meeting of the Metal Workers Union, for example, with four hundred men attending. If you are looking for some guys to murder Turks, you'll find them, more than you need. They go into the meeting cursing the policies of the union, and they come out thirty minutes later and say that it's the only real solution. Incredible how you can turn people around completely in just thirty minutes. It was probably the same thing back then, the simplest thing in the world.

B: And you can't prepare yourself to deal with this?

P: [*Angrily*] Sure, one or another individual. But not the masses, they won't be able to prepare for it. There'll be some who think for themselves and they'll resist, but the great mass of people, they'll go along.

B: What effect has it had on you that you grew up after the war?

P: I have to exclude myself from this, because I've been on my own since I was twenty, but what I've noticed is that my generation has had an enormous need to experience things they missed out on (Nachholbedürfnis), to make up for lost pleasure and amusement.

B: Your sense of independence, did that have something to do with the war, the postwar period?

P: No, that was pure luck, you might say. Maybe I subconsciously set myself a goal. I was supposed to study at the university, that's what they wanted at home, but I just wasn't the type. So I set this goal for myself. My parents, well, actually they never really supported me in what I did. You can almost say that I left home, though not that I wanted to break with them. Rather, I just didn't want to study, and I wanted to prove to them that you could get along without it. And I did it too.

B: You were successful in that . . .

P: Yes, because they thought you couldn't get anywhere without studying.

B: Was this discussed?

P: Not in the least, not at all.

B: So you went your own way without their support?

P: Well, the thing that was most important to me was to get away from home, get out on my own. I was a pretty rambunctious guy at that time. My classmates used to be out until nine or ten in the evening, but I had to be home by eight at the latest, and that used to upset me somehow. So, as I said, one day I hitched a ride over to S. and looked for an apprenticeship for myself. And then I put my dad in the position of having to sign the apprenticeship contract papers. It shook him up a little, but he did it. Probably in my subconscious it was more because I wanted to prove that I didn't need them at all, that what they thought was wrong. I think that was the main reason.

Is he revealing the roots of his anti-intellectualism? Did he learn from his father's experience that one can be an intellectual and yet still be involved in a place like Auschwitz?

B: You decided very early on, I think, to go your own way. But many in your generation ask themselves even today whether they have a right to live their own lives, whether they're entitled to start afresh, independent of their parents' past.

P: People I know have never talked about that, so I don't know if I'm an exception or if they are. I think probably they are.

B: That's hard to know. But in any case, I think there are relatively few who go out on their own and become independent, as you did, at such an early age, who say, "OK, I'm going my own way," without breaking off completely.

P: But, as I told you, when I broke away from home, I still didn't know anything at all about my father or the war, nothing at all. We knew there'd been a war, and somehow we heard that something had happened. But, as I said, in school we didn't hear anything. Out in the countryside people didn't know anything at all about the crimes that had been committed. It was *totally* suppressed. Totally.

B: Well, the teachers had probably been very affected by it and . . .

P: I figure that the authorities were behind it. Maybe both. Probably even the Americans were involved—they controlled a bit of everything. They probably also had control over the school authorities. On the other hand, I can't imagine that it could have been any different, that I would have reproached myself, felt guilty, because of the generation that did those things. I've never reproached myself for being a German. It was our fathers who did all that. I have never reproached myself.

B: Can you imagine what would have happened if Germany hadn't lost the war?

P: Yes, I can, and I must say, thank God that we *did* lose. Today it would probably be different, but in the first few years what you'd have had was a situation in which Germans—blond, blue-eyed types— would have been sent as district heads. I could well imagine that, though in the meantime, everything would have been destroyed by revolution. There simply aren't enough Germans to be able to control all that. But, as I said, we have to be grateful that we didn't win. Otherwise, we wouldn't have made such progress economically. We'd just be spending our time making sure there were no revolts or rebellions . . . I mean, when you occupy so many countries.

B: I believe this process of repression has an impact on the person, although we still know too little about it.

P: I think this process of repression never took place. It was simply never talked about, that's what I think.

B: [*Surprised*] But that in itself is a kind of repression, isn't it?

P: Look, if you don't know anything, then you can't repress anything. My parents didn't talk to me about it. Older people didn't. It wasn't mentioned at school. Young people didn't know anything about it, so how could they repress anything? How can you, if you don't know anything?

He is somehow party to my own reflections. In his own simple words, he has expressed the complicated idea of the "paradox of denial": you have to know something about the location of the place you do not want to look at.

B: But you can sense that something happened. Don't you sense that with your parents?

P: Look, when you go to school and learn that there is some kind of horrible war somewhere every three months—I mean, persecution of Christians, or the killing of witches, or who knows what—but you hear nothing from your father or your father's friend, who knows he was involved in it too, well, how could I repress anything? I simply didn't hear about it. We knew there was a war, but you had wars every three months. I learned that at school: there was a war every few months somewhere or other. But you didn't know what happened. And what happened in this war, well, we didn't know, at least those of us here, that's for sure.

B: But there are ways of saying things on the surface, and you can go on without really registering what was actually said . . .

P: That came later on. It started with Eichmann. That's when I heard for the first time. It was all over the newspapers. That's when it more or less started for me. Now, maybe there was a kind of subconscious repression, because people simply had not dealt with the matter before that.

B: I often speak with people who say, "Our neighbors were Jewish.

And then suddenly one day they were gone." Or in school, "One day he wasn't there anymore, suddenly he wasn't there." Do you remember anything like that?

P: No, I can't tell you anything in that regard. As I said, out in the country, there just weren't any Jews . . .

He moves in his chair and looks away.

B: But that's an example of how repression can work for some people.

P: I can't imagine how something like that can be kept secret. These camps. If you hear Dachau . . . People were living in Dachau, around the camp, and they must have known about the shooting. And yet they stayed so quiet this information didn't get as far as Munich? And once they knew in Munich . . . well, I just can't imagine . . .

B: I know of a young boy who used to go to school every day through the Auschwitz railroad station. And many years later he told me that he would sit in the train every day talking about Jews being gassed. He said to me, "I didn't know at the time what that meant, but I was compulsively talking about it to my fellow passengers on that train, always talking about the same thing . . ."

P: So people even then repressed *these* matters, so to speak. Hard to imagine. Some certainly knew, that's clear. But, for example, here in the countryside, I've never met anyone from the generation who are between sixty and seventy years old now, who said . . . some knew there were extermination—they don't even say concentration camps, they say "work camps."

B: You see how language is used as an instrument of repression. When you say "work camps" . . .

P: [*His eyes light up*] You know, I suddenly remember something I find very surprising. There are three or four Poles buried here. Several girls in the village were romantically involved with the Poles. They were hanged. The whole village was present. And the girls' heads were shaved and they were taken in a cart through the village. People cursed them, threw things at them. The way people have repressed this memory, that's a riddle to me. The girls are still alive and still speak with those people. They hanged the Poles somewhere, and the people who did it are still alive, respected citizens. It's a riddle to me how that works.

B: Collective repression?

P: Sometimes they even talk about it. They hanged that fellow back then, and today they are the ones who want to fix up the grave. There's even a farmer here: just before the war he denounced his neighbor, and that guy was almost taken to a concentration camp, and he knew it. Well, today the two of them still talk to one another. Hard to imagine. They're still neighbors. It's a mystery to me. The son of one of the men is still alive. He told me that his father was just about to be taken away to be killed. And they still speak to one another. I don't think I could ever forget something like that! And the son was old enough at the time to understand what was happening. I knew both men. One simply wanted to swallow the other, so to speak. He wanted his job. As I said, people are a mystery to me. But I think it's predestined. You can't do anything if that's the way a person is.

There are two kinds of people: meat eaters and plant eaters. The meat eaters are the dangerous ones. Probably has to do with the genes. Born that way. I can't imagine you can educate somebody. He has to be born that way. He can do it or he can't. I don't think you can force someone to do it . . .

B: Well, I can imagine that people were put in the Einsatzgruppen who didn't initially know what they were getting into or what would be expected of them.

P: Right, there were orders, so they had no choice. But afterward they were finished. They'd had it, so to speak. I'm certain of that, that they were wrecks afterward in any case. At least they didn't go on to South America and continue what they were doing. You have to be born to do that, go back to the same type of job.

I need air. I stop the tape and thank him very much for his openness. He is mildly surprised at this abrupt conclusion. When we step outside the restaurant on this sunny day, we meet his wife and a stranger, who are sitting at a table. Her glance seems to ask what we could have talked about for such a long time. We join them for a cup of coffee, and Peter suddenly looks at his wife. "Tell me, do you know anything about these Poles here in the village?" They discuss the subject briefly, and then she looks at me and says, "People are lying. They all knew. You couldn't help hearing the sound of the forced laborers' wooden shoes when they were chased through our place at 5:00 A.M."

Her husband shifts to another train of thought. "Do we know who of our friends' fathers were in the SS, in concentration camps?" The stranger smiles and answers without hesitation, "Sure, I can tell you. My father was in the Waffen SS in Russia. He told me lots of things . . ." Peter speaks hastily, "Please meet Dr. Bar-On from Israel, who is doing research about family memories from the Third Reich." The stranger is immediately silent, and I search for a polite way to take my leave.

As she drives me back to town, Peter's wife describes to me in detail the members of her family who were in the SS, an uncle here, another one there. "Why were so many of her uncles in the SS?" I wonder, as I gaze out at the rolling green countryside. I am searching for the hidden graves of the Poles, which still have no headstones, like so many of the graves of my own people.

Two hours later, my mother and I are sitting near beautiful Lake Constance, chatting over dinner. She tells me how she felt crossing the lake from Switzerland, her summer refuge, into Germany, her lost homeland, and I try to describe to her what it was like to meet an acquitted Auschwitz physician and his son. But I find myself thinking, what does it mean that all these people seem so "normal"?

I wonder if Peter is having as much difficulty eating dinner tonight as I am. I ponder his puzzled resignation to the recurrence of evil. At one point during our interview, he was considering the link between his early need to get away from home and what he did or did not know about Auschwitz. Perhaps that was his solution to his terrible dilemma: not to know and not to feel close. I still wonder if he is truly unable to grasp what went on at Auschwitz or if he is only protecting his own sensibility. How does the realization that educated and intelligent men like his father, like Mengele, could become involved in mass killing affect a man who, wittingly or unwittingly, has fashioned his entire life as an antithesis?

chapter 2

Conjuring the Darkness

"You can't go to see him,*" my friend exclaims, "he'll throw you out." His wife adds, "He is such a conservative professor, and he hates Jews!" My wife gives me a frightened look. I am at a loss. I have come to Germany in order to interview children of Nazis, and now my friends, who keenly wish to help me, are trying to protect me from myself. "Listen," I reply, "I am going to try. If worst comes to worst, he* will *throw me out. So what?" In my mind's eye, however, I see pictures of the horrifying death camp where the father had been stationed. Do I have the courage to meet with the son?*

I phone him and identify myself and what I want. We promptly make an appointment for the next morning; it is almost as if he has been waiting for my call. I get up early and assure my wife, only half-jokingly, that she can call the police if I am not back by 1:00 P.M. I take my small tape recorder and walk over the bridge to the older part of this time-honored university town. It is a bright, crisp Sunday morning. The streets are quiet at this early hour, and I enjoy my walk. In front of his house, however, I am suddenly aware of my fear. A tall, athletic man opens the door. "Manfred." He utters his name abruptly, and I am still afraid, although I detect some warmth in his expression, which reassures me a little. Inside, I look around. The room is well furnished and somewhat familiar. I recognize a print of a Hamburg waterfront on one of the walls. Its twin had hung in my grandparents' home in Haifa.

B: Maybe you could start things off by telling me briefly when and where you were born, and your earliest memories.

M: Well, I was born in May 1947 in a small town in Württemberg with about seventy-five hundred inhabitants, and later on I went to school there too. Elementary school, then a kind of middle school. It wasn't possible to complete high school (Gymnasium) in that town, so after six years there, I went to a school in another town for the final three years. But you have something definite in mind. What would you be interested in hearing about? World War II?

B: Were you an only child?

M: I was an only child. My father died when I was only eight months old, so I was raised by my mother and grandmother, and later on by my great aunt.

B: So you didn't know your father personally?

M: My father, no, not personally. My mother told me—you'd like me to get to talking about World War II, right?—well, naturally my mother told me a great deal. She was from Hamburg and was able to tell me many stories about the nighttime air raids, about feeling threatened, afraid. At that time, in Hamburg—she wasn't as yet together with my father—she was engaged to a fellow from Ulm. Then she left Hamburg and moved down near Ulm.

B: When was that?

M: In 1943. That was after, well, at that time there were these very heavy air raids on Hamburg. She'd gone through one of them, and right after that, she left Hamburg with my grandmother. My grandfather passed away in the 1930s. He had been an executive with the Hamburg-Amerika Line. So my grandmother was mobile, my mother too, and for that reason they were able to get out of Hamburg.

So she came from Hamburg. The familiar picture is not a random phenomenon. I am tempted to say, "I am also from Hamburg in the same way you are: my mother's family comes from there."

B: So your mother met your father only after that?

M: They met in B., but that was after the war.

B: What was your mother able to tell you about your father? Did she talk about him with you?

M: Yes, well, when I was at school, about seven or eight years old. But naturally, since she'd only known my father for a relatively short time, practically speaking, well, she didn't know much of anything about his life before they'd met. So actually she wasn't able to tell me anything. What she was able to relate to me were her own impressions of the war.

B: So you grew up as a child without a father . . .

M: Yes, as a child without a father.

B: What notions did you have about who your father had been? At that time . . .

M: I'd say that, as a child, I didn't think at all about my father. I mean, when you don't have a father . . . naturally I felt that, in contrast to other kids, my friends, I didn't have a father, although I grew up in a generation in which that wasn't so uncommon. There were quite a number of my friends, say two or three years older—in small towns, you know, the classes were not organized by year or age but usually were a bit broader in terms of age grouping—well, so, in point of fact, it was not so uncommon to grow up without a father then. And I have to say that I had relatively few fantasies and all that about my father, though I can't remember back all that far . . .

B: Do you have any photographs of your father?

M: Yes, but basically I was closer to my grandfather, though he didn't live in the same town . . . But I'd say, if I try to remember back now, that I had a very close—well, maybe that's exaggerated—a close relationship with my uncle, the husband of my mother's sister. He's an archaeologist. Now when I was young I was very ill, I suffered terribly from asthma, and we'd always spend two months up north in their house so I could get over the asthma by breathing in the sea air. And in that house, well, for me it was a very strong formative intellectual influence. You see, my father was a scientist.

An interesting choice of terminology.

M: My relatives on my father's side were lawyers, but my uncle was an archaeologist, my aunt a historian and a geographer, and I'm a historian, too. So that house had an important influence. My uncle was an assistant at the Schleswig Museum for Prehistory and later on became the director. Well, there were all these prehistoric exhibits, and that also had its formative influence on me. My uncle would take me along sometimes on digs. He was always very interested, curious, and I always tried to question him about his work. I can still recall that I used to bother him all the time. A scientist has to be able to work without any interruptions, and as a child I just wouldn't let him work. I'd say that the influence he had on me was similar to that of a father. If the distance hadn't been so great—it was over a thousand kilometers—it would have been possible to spend longer periods of time up there every summer. And if those long stays had been possible later on as well, I'd probably be an archaeologist today. Actually, that was what I wanted to be. But then came this more historical direction, something I developed myself.

B: When was it that you started to ask yourself about your father, tried to learn more about him?

M: [*He looks at me, perplexed*] Well, I was maybe ten or twelve. Actually, though, I'd say that the father figure never played much of a role in my case. A very weak role. My mother never let my father have any part in bringing me up. The marriage only lasted a short time.

B: From when to when? When did he die?

M: How long was it? My father committed suicide because of certain political matters from the Third Reich that finally caught up with him. And the way I see it now, things that my mother probably told me . . . I mean, she was never a part of a political opposition movement, wasn't active in a movement, but as a young girl she'd been brought up in a certain atmosphere. She attended the Loewenberg private high school in Hamburg. In the history of Hamburg's schools, this school was special. It was not Zionist-oriented but rather assimilationist, and nationalistic in ideology . . .

I look at him in startled amazement. My mother had studied in the very same Hamburg school. Soon we are going to find out that they were classmates. What an unbelievable coincidence.

M: And naturally my mother was very, what should I say, horrified, she was very upset, but never talked to me in detail about it all. At the end, in her last years of suffering, she expressed her wish not to be buried in the grave next to my father. She even wanted to be buried in another town. That says a great deal . . .

B: Is your mother dead?

M: Yes, she passed away four years ago. My father is buried in my hometown, where I grew up, and my mother is buried in R., as she wanted. Naturally, I followed her wishes in this regard, although she never actually expressed herself to me openly on these matters. She suffered a lot on my father's behalf, then with all the money problems she had later on . . . She hadn't learned a professional skill, had to keep her head above water by taking in sewing. That's how she raised me. And I believe that these other difficulties, along with the disappointment she experienced, led her to eliminate the father figure as much as possible from the way she brought me up. I don't remember her ever saying things like, "Your father would have done it this way."

B: Did she make any critical remarks about him, things like that?

M: Not that I recall. No, never. My mother met my father in the fall of 1945. They married about a year later, and I was born in May 1947. So the marriage, as such, was of relatively short duration. And my mother had been married once before. She was born in 1908 and married a Baltic German in 1932. She got a divorce in 1942 and was engaged to this painter from Ulm, who never came back from the Russian front, and then she met my father in the fall of 1945. The interesting thing is that she got involved with him because he was the spitting image of her fiancé, even down to his handwriting. I was also able to find out that her fiancé was from a family of Viennese sailors who worked on the Danube; my father and his family have some of the same ancestors. They used to go up and down the Danube. Now, whether there is an actual relationship, kinship ties in the last century, I couldn't establish that.

I'd say the formative influences on my mother were her home and then the very strong influence of her years in the Loewenberg school. That shaped her more in her religious and nationalistic sentiments than her parental home. Loewenberg, her schoolmaster, was very nationalistic in his orientation—what can be termed "German-national," faithful to the Kaiser—and he stressed this nationalism very strongly in the educational philosophy of the school. And her first marriage molded her a great deal as well. The Baltic connection, through her first husband, shaped her for some ten years. I'd almost say that my mother was able to tell me more stories about her first husband than about my father. Let's say she passed along more to me from this experience, about how one should live, than what she had learned from my father. You can see that in my case, since I was separated from him myself when I was just eight months old.

B: What did she tell you? What were the first things that influenced her?

M: Well, staying in her first husband's home and contact with his circle of friends, who at that time were part of this rather highly educated Baltic-German milieu. When I was quite young, six or seven, maybe eight, she used to tell me about the trips they'd go on, his school friends—for the most part, they were from the nobility—and she told me about what songs they'd sing, what kind of music was played, Beethoven, Bach. They would have conversations in this house, while back in Hamburg, when my mother was growing up, children of ten or twelve weren't allowed to say anything or show their reactions . . . So that impressed her. She came as a young fiancée to the Baltic, and people were discussing things around the table in Estonian, French, German, Finnish, even Russian. Why, they were speaking five different languages, no problem. All these recollections, which went back twenty or twenty-five years, these were things she passed on to me in a much more vivid way than anything connected with her relationship with my father. Naturally though, her relationship with my father's family only developed after the marriage, later on, when I was already around . . . The type of education, of behavior, was quite different in this circle, and very early on she'd say things to me like, "Look, I don't like what you're doing." Another difference, let's say, was that politically they thought and argued along different lines, not as liberal. She was used to a liberal, open atmosphere, and that was a totally different thing, that Austrian-German circle.

His voice changes slightly when he describes his father's milieu: it is flat-
ter, less involved. He speaks to me about his past as if his father were a
historical figure.

M: Then, when I was fifteen, maybe sixteen . . . when a child, a son,
grows up alone with his mother, grandmother, and great aunt, the
child slips into being the father in the family to some extent. You learn
about matters, such as the financial situation of the family, that you
wouldn't hear about if there were both a father and a mother. I can
still vividly recall my mother saying, "We only have so-and-so much
money, it's impossible, I can't give you that, it's impossible." I mean,
maybe you learn to have a greater sense of responsibility earlier
on . . .

B: Earlier than if your father had been around?

M: Right. On the other hand, I have to say, how should I put it,
part of my youth was stolen from me. Maybe that's putting it too
strongly. It's a criticism of my mother, you understand, and I wouldn't
say that now. But in the families of my friends, where the marriages
were intact, where all the children were still at home, such problems
were kept completely away from the kids. So I noticed at a very early
age that we were different, and that we simply saw many problems in
a different light. Yes, that we were more cautious, that we approached
life with a certain seriousness.

B: Did your mother talk to you about National Socialism? About
the Nazi Party? Not only her experiences, but what she thought about
all that?

M: Actually, a great deal. I mean, she was not one of those who
resisted it, she was a follower (Mitläuferin), but she was opposed, for
example, when her first husband—the marriage was in '32, the divorce in '42—wanted to join the Party, after 1933; she was quite
against it. She said, "For what?" But he thought it would be good for
him from a professional point of view, for his career, since he was a
lawyer. But then she herself was asked to take part in the Women's
Auxiliary (Frauenschaft) and she didn't want to. Then her husband
said she ought to join the League of German Girls (Bund Deutscher
Mädel) but she said she wasn't a young girl anymore. She absolutely
refused. So my mother actually succeeded in keeping out of any and
all Party organizations.

She had received a musical education, as was customary for young
girls from a certain social class at that time. She told me that many of
her schoolmates in the Loewenberg school were Jewish. The school
was attended almost exclusively by Jewish girls, along with four or five
Protestant girls. What upset her very much was that in 1941 she met

one or two of her former classmates and they were wearing a Star of David. Apparently she said to her first husband, it must have been before 1942, she said, "What we're doing to them now, that's just how we will be, with some star or cross, roaming the countryside in a few years. You can't do a thing like this." And that gave her the inner strength to resist.

She once told me about another experience. They had been invited to a wedding of some friends, and the husband must have been in the Party. Anyhow, some important Party official gave a speech, talked about giving the Führer four children, that sort of stuff, the line that was propagated at that time. And my mother must have gotten upset and protested. Now my mother was a very attractive woman and had no involvement as far as Party politics was concerned. So she made some remark, that you couldn't say things like that, and her first husband was terribly angry.

B: When she met your father, what did he tell her about the war?

M: Nothing, my father never told her anything.

His tone is suddenly sharp, almost abrupt.

B: That's what she told you?

M: Yes, that's what she told me. And I believed her too. I don't think it interested her much then. The personal relationship was more important. Of course, I don't know to what extent it would have revolted her if she had known any of the details, if he had taken her into his confidence completely. I mean, naturally there's a difference if a woman thinks about it at the age of sixty or at the age of thirty-seven, and if the person involved has been dead for twenty years or is still living. She wasn't in agreement with the regime, and in a city of a million, well, you could slip through the net, so to speak, you could ignore invitations, not appear, not be interested. On the other hand, her husband was in the Party, and this served as a kind of cover for her. I mean, she didn't have any government position, she was a completely private individual. She was interested in music and wasn't active in any way in public life. So she could behave that way.

B: Your father took his own life. Did she know why?

M: Initially she didn't believe it. Afterward, in the course of time, she learned about things. There were later trials, sentences, facts were presented to her, so that she simply had to believe it.

B: What was her reaction?

M: You mean, psychologically? Naturally she still defended my father. I mean, if I may put it in psychological terms, she was defending herself in this way.

B: And she didn't talk to you about it?

M: Oh, very early on. She told me about my father's death quite openly even before I started school, or maybe it was just as I was starting school. I must have been six or seven. But she taught me, she told me in such a way that I never gave it any thought afterward, never worried about it, you understand? If she had cloaked it in secrecy, and if classmates had then told me that this and that had happened, it's not true, your mother lied to you, then there might have been a break, a rupture in the family, a lack of trust. But I knew about it from her, and for me that was something self-evident.

B: What did she tell you?

M: She told me my father had taken his life because he was a Nazi . . . had held certain positions in the Nazi regime, but she didn't know about anything in detail, she hadn't been interested, because all that had been before she had met him. But she told me quite clearly that he was a Nazi, that he had done bad things during National Socialism, criminal things. Now I don't want to exaggerate, but she presented his death to me as a just punishment. Maybe that is an exaggeration, but, well, she didn't have any pity for him, let's put it that way. Rather, she described it to me quite objectively, unemotionally, and I never associated any emotion with it. For me, right from the beginning, my father was my father. There were certain secrets spun around him, but he was never present in this house as a person or perceived as an intellectually compelling presence. Rather, he was dead and had departed from the house, so to speak. He was a nonperson. So the matter was addressed quite openly, in a very cool and objective manner I'd almost say, like a legal brief. There was never any subjective coloring, although my mother was generally quite an emotional woman. She placed the facts on the table in front of me, and I was then able to confront them myself.

B: Did the kids in your class ever say anything?

M: Well, of course, sometimes swastikas were drawn on my school bag, stuff like that, though I must say that was very rare. And it was surprising. In this village community, children didn't do things like that to each other.

B: In later years, when you were grown up, did you know what your father had done?

M: It was brought up repeatedly in the press. But I never dealt with it any further, because [*he suddenly looks defeated*] . . . I could deal with these things as a scholar, a researcher, but I actually reject such an approach. My reason is that what I might dig up could appear to be an attempt on my part to try to clear my father in some way, and I don't want to do that, I can't do that. He does appear to have been . . .

[*Very excited*] Based on what we know from other sources, well, he had also been married before, to a woman from Ulm who had a rather important role in the Party. And she died in quite mysterious circumstances a few days after the attempt on Hitler's life on July 20, 1944. I heard about it from her relatives. I know that my father was relieved of all his duties at that time and sent to the front, in August of '44. So you could almost assume there may have been some connection with the July 20 business, in some form or other. I don't know for sure, and I'm not interested. It couldn't erase what went on before, it couldn't wash him clean of guilt for what he did.

Now, the fact is that he had to flee from Austria as a penniless doctor in 1936. Under the Schuschnigg regime, as an adherent of National Socialism, he was forced to flee from Austria to Germany in twelve or twenty-four hours. So he came to Berlin, and it was there that he met his first wife and entered Nazi circles. And, if I understand how his career developed, first they got people involved in those euthanasia activities, they got in deeper and deeper, and then they had you in their pocket (im Griff), so to speak: either you go along now, or it's your own neck. That's how I'd see it, in argumentative terms.

B: Did you know any friends of your father's who might have been able to tell you . . .

M: No, none. And my mother never—wait a second, there was someone. My father had a boyhood friend, someone who'd been in school with him till they graduated. Whether they were together at the university later on, I don't know, but I don't think so. My mother and father visited him after the war, in '46 or '47. But after he heard about all those things, about my father's suicide, he broke off all contact. He was a very religious Christian. We were, so to speak, dead as far as he was concerned. Maybe this is also connected with the fact that my uncle and my grandparents were happy to leave my father dead. To a certain extent, his wife, his widow and child, were forgotten. I can recall what my uncle once said. He's still alive, quite old, he lives in my father's hometown. Once we were on a visit to my grandmother, and he said to me, "I'm going to visit the so-and-sos tonight, but I can't take you along, because they don't know anything about your existence." So my father had died after the war, and on my father's side of the family they pulled a kind of veil over the whole thing. But I must say that my mother never tried to pull such a veil over the matter. My mother just sort of stumbled into the situation. And to a certain extent her life was destroyed by all this.

B: Did she feel that way too?

M: Yes, well, emotionally, maybe she did. And I'd also contend that her later wish to be buried in a separate grave expressed this very clearly to me. My father had died and . . . but in rational terms I think she never really wanted to make it a conscious realization. But it's to her credit in my eyes that she never tried to make a secret of it. When we went someplace, or friends asked why he'd killed himself, her attitude was, why should I hide anything? I had nothing to do with it. To a certain extent I'm a victim of all this. And she taught me that too, not to go around concealing anything in this regard. Why should I?

B: Actually very wise of her, psychologically speaking.

M: Yes, but I'd say that it wasn't something conscious. Rather it was unconscious. I mean, if someone is interested in finding out, then he will—so why hide anything? After all, it's a fact. Children of such people very often adopt a totally opposite position, or they adopt their father's position, although I'm not trying to deal with the Nazi period as a scholar in an attempt to work things out. I think it's simply a fact you have to learn to live with.

B: Was it hard to live with that knowledge?

M: Yes, well, that's a difficult question, very difficult. [*Long pause*] It's difficult to live if you constantly think about these things in rational terms. Basically you have to stop—this is my view—at some point you have to stop thinking about them. Because when you think about them, then things are difficult. And you can go on and on in your thoughts, and then it gets very difficult indeed. So I think at some point you just have to tune out, have to say, well, look, I can't change the facts, so what's the use? My father left a farewell letter, and in it he requested that I be told about all this after I'd reached the age of eighteen.

B: Your mother didn't follow his instructions . . .

M: Well, if she had, my personality today would probably be quite different. Psychologically that was a good thing, absolutely. I think my mother had a good natural instinct for what was right in that regard.

We take a short break. He goes to the kitchen to make some coffee, and I remain alone with my thoughts. If earlier I had suspected that Manfred was using his mother as a cover story, I now admit to myself that his sincerity when he discusses his father impresses me. He openly expresses his desire to understand his father's motives, yet his own morality emerges in his decision not to try to clear his father's name. I can see the wisdom of Manfred's mother in the adult son sitting in front of me.

I smile to myself. How afraid I was of him! Now I can even say I like him, and I consider when (not if) I will tell him about my own mother. But then the image of his father and the death camp intrudes. Can I trust my instincts? Can I sustain my role as a detached researcher? Or is my own mind divided, one part unwilling to know about the other? When he returns, I sense that he has used the time in the kitchen for his own reflections. He smiles pleasantly and offers me coffee in a blue porcelain cup. I cannot bring myself to smile back.

B: Did you have any contact with your father's victims? Did you read about them?

M: I read about them. If you mean the death camp, well, that was probably the decisive factor for my mother. Until the 1960s, all they ever talked about was that my father was part of a euthanasia unit. During the trials, it all came out in the newspapers. For my mother, that was the decisive blow, the final shock. Then it all came over her, you understand: all her girlhood friends from the Loewenberg school. If I take out those old photographs, they are practically all of Jewish girls. She grew up in a very Jewish kind of ambience (jüdische geprägte Umgebung).

B: My mother also grew up in Hamburg. She studied in the same school.

M: [*His eyes light up in surprise*] Oh, that's very interesting. My mother wrote down the names of her classmates—she wrote them down later on, after all that became known. It was quite a blow for her. She had never concealed my father's activities, she had always said he was a Nazi and did the things Nazis did, that you could think about euthanasia as you liked. At that time she was still prepared to recognize that. And she would say, "Well, where are the limits?" But she was still ready to excuse him and even defend him when I would say to her, "But that's terrible, such an act." For her, the trials were the beginning of a new period, a rupture.

B: You were about nineteen or twenty then when this came out?

M: I was nineteen or twenty. It was in 1964.

B: Did your mother speak about it?

M: It was discussed, though my mother . . . you understand, it's very difficult. First of all, he'd been dead for twenty years and, after all, they'd had a child together, so it's extremely difficult for such a woman. There's a story she told me again and again, and I believe her too, I don't think she was lying or just making it up, imagining it . . . She met my father once in Ulm. He was visiting friends or maybe relatives of his first wife. She went shopping and then they met in some café. So she came into the café and my father was sitting there at a table. She saw him sitting there, and suddenly she thought, why, that man's a Bluebeard. She went over and sat down and told him what had flashed through her mind. And my father must have been sort of shocked by this. She told me so afterward. And he said, "How can you think that way?" Then, after they had married, she told him on a different occasion—she said this to me too—she told him, "You're hiding something from me. I am not the kind of woman who snoops around, you know, but I can feel that you are hiding something from me. I hope you can for once trust me and tell me about it." She had the feeling something was wrong, that he was hiding something. Naturally she didn't know in connection with what.

B: It wasn't consciously knowing . . .

M: She became conscious of all this only later on. Euthanasia was brought up in the de-Nazification panel proceedings in 1948. She thought that this was certainly incriminating, but she remained proud all the time of the fact that he had presumably had nothing to do with Jews. When this matter came up later about his involvement in the death camp, it was a blow to her.

B: What did she say? Did she cry?

M: There was this trial, and his name was mentioned. Now four or six weeks before the trial, she'd had a dream. And she said to me, "I don't know exactly, but something is not right about this story. It was so strange." Apparently, my father must have appeared several times in her dreams, standing at her bedside. And he said, "You still believe in me, don't you?" And she did believe him. What she actually felt in the dream related to what happened before his part in the death camp came out in the papers. Afterward, my mother broke from him. She expressed her opinion several times, something along the lines of "I'm happy he took his own life." Less for herself, naturally, than for me.

B: Perhaps it was difficult to live with him . . .

M: It's quite clear that that's how my mother felt, absolutely. But not in 1948; rather, later on. Not until the 1950s and then mainly in the 1960s when the death camp was brought up in public discussion. As to my father's behavior, in the light of what was revealed in the trial, he must have been relieved of his duties because of incompetence. And there is the remark he made to his first wife's cousin during a visit to Ulm—she told me this later on—he said, "We Austrians were used by the Third Reich to clean up and dispose of the dirt." Now, to what extent he was taking, even indirectly, a critical position, I really don't know.

I have various photographs—photos, for example, from the year 1944. The way he looked, you have to say that it must have affected him very deeply as a human being. My mother always maintained that he was a very sensitive, feeling, very tender person. And in the POW camp he volunteered to work in the TB tent, where he was infected.

When he committed suicide, a doctor examined him and said he would have died soon anyhow. Whether that is true or whether it was said to protect my mother, I don't know. In any event he had an active case of tuberculosis. Often, this is an indication of psychological troubles. I mean, this matter wasn't easy for him. You can see this just from looking at his photos.

And this matter of his being relieved of his duties after the attempt on Hitler's life in July 1944. That is quite a peculiar story. But it is not my intention to clear my father of guilt and to follow up on all these things. I mean, what use is it? For me, there is always going to be . . . the numbers involved are irrelevant. Whether we're talking about a hundred, a thousand, or just a single person, from a moral point of view it makes no difference. Guilt is present even in the case of a single victim. To deal with it in a scholarly, scientific way—that is obsolete. All that can be done is to draw a theological and moral lesson from it.

B: Looking back today, after thirty or thirty-five years, how do you think all this shaped your life, if at all?

M: It still affects my life today. For example, at one time, when I was eighteen or nineteen, I wanted to become a Protestant minister, though my mother didn't want me to. Probably it would have been better if I had taken such a step then. It shaped and continues to shape me in that I think it places a certain moral guilt upon a person. I think that's quite clear. Of course, what is moral guilt? I mean, I wasn't directly involved. But you think, well, after all, he *was* your father.

B: Have you ever asked yourself what you would have done if you had been alive then?

M: One can't know that. I've thought about it, of course. Probably at times I would have tried to, well, let's say, avoid certain duties, the way my mother did in regard to the Women's Auxiliary and the League of German Girls. I would probably have tried somehow to get out of it. My father was very Prussian as an Austrian, very conscious of his duty, and for that reason, he didn't try to avoid things. And then, he was too much in their hands (im Griff). I myself, if I had noticed what was happening, would have gotten out in time.

In the matter of euthanasia, I think he certainly should have avoided participating in some way. Of course, it's quite surprising for a man of thirty to suddenly find himself in such a powerful position. The National Socialists knew how to place young people in important positions so that they developed a certain kind of overbearing pride. I'd say for my father, if I think about it, the death camp was a kind of watershed. I'd say that for his career, his advancement, the death camp was a critical point. Of course, in a broader sense, there were also career considerations, so that one couldn't openly show active opposition. What would fascinate me as his son would be if he had openly shown opposition at some point. Of course, as a historian coming from a free country and background, I think it's probably impossible to imagine how it really was. I mean, nowadays, this generation can barely comprehend how things really were. And I think sometimes we demand impossible things of my generation in that respect. I mean, a dictatorship exercises such power. And when you haven't experienced it yourself, you just can't understand.

B: Jews put up physical resistance even in the death camps. Don't you think this is hard to imagine? So how could your father not resist, as a human being?

M: Yes.

His gaze wanders. His face has a desperate look, and I wonder if he heard my last question, or if he is finding it too difficult to answer.

M: What fascinates me is that you see in this just how closed the minds of people were. I mean, Polish-Jewish women were very attractive, and yet I know of no case in which an SS man really helped a Jewish woman. Basically this closed-mindedness, this insanity, should be seen as a kind of religious madness. I mean, the way heretics were burned in the sixteenth century. Somehow there's a link between these phenomena. And I believe that when my mother learned about the death camp later on, she wasn't able to comprehend it. It's something you can't deal with properly after forty years. I believe it's actually a warning that people should not be inspired by ideas of any kind— moral, psychological, philosophical—to such extreme acts. Rather, you have to remain an individual, and you yourself must judge what is good and correct. You can't simply follow the crowd, you have to decide whether what is demanded is indeed right. I'd say my mother taught me that very early on. She always said that first, you have to be responsible for what you do in your own eyes, and then you have to ask yourself whether what you're doing is a decent thing: Is it in keeping with the law? Is it honest?

B: A kind of personal accounting . . .

M: Exactly. So you don't slip into a position . . . As for me, I never . . . it is conceivable that I might have developed in another direction as a direct result of my father's influence, say, toward the extreme left. I started studying at the university in 1968, so that would have been understandable. But the education I received from my mother kept me, preserved me from that completely. To keep your two feet on the ground, not to chase illusions, not to go to extremes. These are basic moral principles, ones that shouldn't be abandoned.

B: Do you feel isolated or different from others in your circle of friends?

M: No, actually I don't. I mean, naturally the matter has been broached. I think I have been very much affected by all this, because I believe that one of the most terrible things in National Socialism was guilt by association (Sippenhaftung). After all, I have no personal guilt in the matter. But certainly one does feel different from others—though in certain respects you have an advantage due to your own experience. You can stand up, point to things, say they ought to be different. In that respect I can't throw any stones at my father, and I wouldn't either [*moves uncomfortably in his chair*]. I also can't criticize my father for the fact that he participated in certain things right from the start. But I would criticize him for the fact that he didn't show open opposition at the proper time. That would have been nice, but then, had he done so, I wouldn't exist, you understand. Then he would simply have been executed.

There were such examples, underground movements. He could have quit in a more resolute manner, gotten out sooner. He could have volunteered for service at the front, say, in 1943. This is something I don't understand, how psychologically he was able . . . On the one hand, as my grandmother and mother have depicted him to me, he was very conscious of his obligations. On the other hand, his behavior actually shows me that he wasn't totally convinced, that he had some reservations, that consciously he worked against it in a certain way. What his motives were—it would interest me today to talk to him about it, to ask him, "Why did you . . . ?" [*Almost crying*] But that is no longer possible. It would be more difficult for me as a person, so it turned out better this way, although intellectually speaking, it would be more interesting for me to be able to discuss these things with him.

The notion of talking to his father fascinates him. Perhaps it occurs to him for the first time. He stops, again looking very defeated, then sighs and goes on. He does not really need my questions; he has enough of his own.

M: Something I find positive and praiseworthy: he didn't accuse anyone else or put the blame elsewhere. Rather, he took his own life. In a certain way, he pronounced judgment on himself. I believe he was supposed to be brought someplace for identification, and the night before, he killed himself. The interesting thing, though, is that he never used a false name. He might have tried to hide. That's an interesting point. One shouldn't sit in harsh judgment on one's father.

But sometimes I have the notion that he wanted to have a child, a son, and that that played a certain role. As a son, I don't have the right to pass judgment. It wouldn't be right. After all, to a certain extent he was caught in connection with his marriage to my mother, because his marriage documents were asked for, and that's what got the whole investigation started.

B: After your mother died, did you have a chance to talk about your father with anybody?

M: No. [*Pauses, looks at me*] No one at all. You are the first person with whom I've talked openly about my father. Perhaps I could have, but I never tried, with strangers. I know this colleague of my father's who was involved in those euthanasia operations. He lives in Stuttgart. Now I've never consciously sought any contact with him, but I could pay him a visit and ask him about my father's first wife, about my father. I could say, "You knew my father. What was he like?" Naturally, this would perhaps provide me with a new impression of the situation. But I don't know. What's the point? I mean, I can't change anything by that.

B: It would be interesting to know what this man thinks, wouldn't it?

M: Well, in my case I grew up without my father. He played no role in the family, in my education. It wasn't until the trial that the issue of my father had such an enormous effect. Before that, there had been talk of Nazi crimes, there had been Nazis. That was despicable from a moral point of view. But my relatives were even more critical in this regard than my mother. My mother had a positive approach. She knew that there's a point where you have to stop thinking about things. You can go on and on, and if it's useless, then you simply have to say, "Enough." You can't change anything now.

B: You have to know where to draw the line . . .

M: Yes, absolutely. I mean, it's difficult to know where the limits are. I do feel a certain burden, although it's not something traumatic. If there were only this burden, if I couldn't think of anything else but this, then it would be traumatic as far as I'm concerned. But that's not the case, and I can thank my mother for that. I owe it to her.

B: Your story shows the positive influence of your mother, who was very wise. I know many children of victims who suffered terribly because their parents tried to protect them and told them nothing. And the children had this instinctive feeling that there was something terrible hidden away, but they didn't know what it was. That was much worse for them.

*   *   *

*I leave him this idea as a farewell gift. I glance at my watch: it is after
1:00 P.M. My wife might be calling the police. While I use the phone, he
looks for the names of his mother's Jewish schoolmates. He can't locate them
but promises to send them to me. Do I think my mother could find out if they
are still alive? I promise to ask her, and we decide to meet again. I am not
sure which one of us is having more difficulty with this leavetaking. When
we finally stand in the doorway, he thanks me warmly and . . . clicks his
heels.*

*The narrow, old streets are filled with families taking a Sunday walk, and
I imagine that Manfred and I might have met here, walking with our parents, on some similar Sunday afternoon. When I reach my friends' home,
they find it hard to believe he has spoken to me for such a long time. I try,
but it is impossible to share my experience with them.*

*Several days later, I receive a formal letter from Manfred with the names
of his mother's classmates. I call my mother and tell her the story, but I do
not mention his father's role in the death camp. "Alice, Ruth, Deborah," she
exclaims. They are all a year younger: Alice is in Tel-Aviv, Ruth in New
York . . . I tell her his mother's name and the fact that she is no longer alive.
Would Alice be willing to receive a letter from him? My mother promises to
find out, and when I arrive for the second interview, he has Alice's address.
He receives me like an old friend. The coffee table is set, and on a larger
table there are two stacks of photographs: on the right his mother's family,
on the left his father's. In his father's family album there are photos of
Manfred up to the age of five. The rest of the pages are empty. I am a little
embarrassed by his hospitality.*

M: Last time I did not tell you some details about my mother's will.
She changed her will. My mother's original wish was to be placed in
my father's grave, in an urn. But later she refused. Why, for what reason, well, as I said, all I can do is surmise. She saw this film about that
Jewish doctor and educator of children.

B: Janusz Korczak?

M: Yes, exactly. The one who was killed, along with all the children
from his school, in Treblinka. My mother saw the film and told me
about it afterward. She didn't say much, but I had the impression that
it had really upset her.

Well, naturally I have no personal impressions of my father. And
when you read reports about the trials, I always have the impression
that those on trial, those involved, want to try to get out of accepting
any responsibility. But even if you receive an order, it is you who have
to carry that order out, at least in part. You can also interpret an order
and execute it in a lax manner. You can even get around it to some

extent if you really want to. Now my impression is that this wasn't done by those individuals. Now they would prefer to avoid accepting any of the responsibility.

B: Seeing the Eichmann trial in Israel made a strong impression on me.

M: Did you participate?

B: I was there as a young man, and I was very impressed by all the witnesses who appeared and gave testimony about what had happened. And this man—who sat there like a wall and said only, "I had my orders." No emotion about what had taken place. Like a wall. He said nothing about himself.

M: Yes, but if he did this out of a sense of conviction, I mean, when he says today that he was only someone taking orders, I think that is just a way of protecting himself. He's just saying that. Basically it was a kind of cowardice. He ought to be honest and say, "I did that then because I was committed." And he ought to say he accepts responsibility. It's like the Nuremberg trials, what I have read in the newspaper reports or in other, more extensive coverage; I haven't looked into the original protocols. I think it was Hans Frank [the Governor-General of Poland], for example, who read something in the Bible during the Nuremberg trials and then made a marginal note: "I must speak with deeds." I find that even more despicable. So somewhere along the line you have to see what you're doing and accept responsibility. I can't do something and then try to shirk responsibility for it. They all tried to do just that. I've read newspaper reports about Eichmann's trial too, and Stangl's. They always attempted to put the blame on others. I mean, one single man, Adolf Hitler, can't put sixty million people into motion. That is quite clear. The Allies also bear a certain responsibility. I mean, in 1938 they could have done much more if they'd wanted to. Whatever their reasons were—it wasn't for humane reasons, the way they prefer to see it after the fact—they knew what was happening, people in America and England knew what the score was . . . They knew what was happening and could, for example, have bombarded the access routes. That might have been possible.

B: These feelings of collective guilt are what induced everyone to repress these things after the war.

M: That's right. I have given it some thought as a result of our conversation, and I think there's another element that played a very central role, as my mother said. I mean, if you look at the Bolshevik Revolution, there was this very strong group of leaders. And these leaders were largely of Jewish origin: Trotsky, Zinoviev, Kun, and so on. And the first Nazis came from the circles that were fighting against the Bol-

sheviks. Now I believe that was a factor. As I see it, people had over-
looked the fact that the Communists who were of Jewish background
had basically been pushed into it by the pogroms of the 1880s. So you
can see how hate is passed on and develops. And this antagonism
from the 1920s then linked up with an anti-Semitism that was already
present in the 1930s, which was then made much worse.

B: I'd like to get back to that barrier you mentioned between you
and your father, the one your mother helped to create. Do you recall
times when you felt that this barrier might threaten you?

M: Threaten me?

B: In dreams, for example, or . . . ?

M: No, nothing. I never had a father figure with whom I had to
struggle, to contend. As a young man, for example, I was strictly forbidden to get into fistfights with my friends. Once, when I was twelve,
a teacher said to me, "OK, now start punching back. Don't let them do
that to you. If someone's eye gets hurt, I'll pay for it." I even had to let
myself get beaten up by kids who were much smaller and weaker. I'd
say to my mother . . . well, you know the expression "like father, like
son."

B: We've got that expression in Hebrew too.

M: Yes, exactly, and for her that was to a certain extent probably
the main point. She didn't say so, but I assume that this was a reason,
a rather powerful reason.

B: So it was important for your mother that you shouldn't become
like your father?

M: I can remember that my father's oldest brother said—it was
twelve years after his death, before all that business of the trial—he
said to my mother, "You're playing the martyr," something my mother
never did. My mother never wore a sign saying My Husband Committed Suicide. Sure, she didn't conceal it, but she never . . . I mean, as I
recall, she was a good-natured woman, open-minded. She didn't run
around all the time in a black dress, flaunting her grief or absorbed in
her own thoughts. Basically, she lived in a very normal way. So that
remark really hurt her.

I don't know what my uncle knew. She told me that when they'd
married in 1946, my uncle was in A., and my mother and father paid
him a visit on their honeymoon. That was the first attempt at contact
since the end of the war. And my mother told me that my father and
uncle went upstairs in the hotel where they were staying. They had to
discuss something. And when the two men came back downstairs, she
was sitting in the lobby, they looked so—especially my uncle—looked
so serious, she wondered what they'd talked about. And right up to

the day she died my mother always assumed that my father had told his brother something of what he had done during the war, but my uncle always maintained that he knew nothing.

B: Did you try to approach him, ask him about this conversation?

M: I didn't talk to him about it. He said things were over and done with.

B: In any event, you have the feeling that this boundary, that your mother didn't build it up but rather . . .

M: No, it wasn't threatening for me. As I mentioned, it never became a menace. Vis-à-vis my father, I'd say that he is a historical personage for me, not . . . I don't have . . .

B: An emotional relationship?

M: . . . an emotional relationship with him. For me, yes, he's a figure like Eichmann. Basically he's just as removed from me as someone I would read about, if you really consider it. Of course you tell yourself, "He's my father." But this fact has no direct emotional repercussions. Maybe some indirect ones.

B: Does it influence the way you feel?

M: Well, for example, I don't have kids. But if you were to have kids, you'd ask yourself whether some element of this would surface again in them. It could happen. As I said, that's a problem I wonder about. Acts of murder were involved. When you look at it, is there a possible hereditary element? Actually, I've never come across a case of a murderer among my ancestors, in the family tree as it's been described and as I've investigated it further. It's quite a normal family tree. And when you read the newspapers, the thing you notice about all these individuals is that they were completely average people. And if you compare family trees, people still alive today, normal citizens . . . there's no difference. I mean, is it really possible to incite people to such a point? I saw all that in '68.

"Normal," "average." These words recur in my interviews with Peter and Manfred when they describe their families.

B: Perhaps that's what's so frightening. It's not something genetic, biological. Could it be that each one of us, if faced with a similar situation, would take part in such things in some way?

M: That's what I find so disturbing about this whole thing. That's right. I believe that. I recall a story I heard about my grandfather. I don't know if it's true. I never heard it from him directly, but someone is supposed to have come to my grandfather in 1938, some journalist in their hometown. And he was of a different persuasion. My grandfather had National Socialistic views and he didn't. Anyhow, apparently he asked my grandfather to help him, and my grandfather is said to have refused to do so, quite emphatically. Now that's a manner of going about things my mother never liked. If, for example, someone were to ring my doorbell and say he was of a different opinion but he needed my help, well I think I would always help him in such a case. At least I imagine that's what I'd do. Naturally, you're right. We don't know what's deep down inside us . . . and it's quite clear that what was contained in National Socialism, well, that was something demonic. Much more dangerous is the possibility that something new could arise that might have a demonic effect similar to National Socialism.

B: It's hard to compare, but I believe that some children of victimizers are very much preoccupied with the question: Where is the devil inside me; how can I control it (or do I fail to control it)? For you, such a question is much more limited in scope because of your relationship with your mother. You had no direct personal relationship with your father. So maybe you could say you were free of this feeling?

M: That would be hard to say. I wonder how the son of a normal murderer, a conventional criminal, behaves. That would interest me. I don't know. A mass murderer. But murderers of such a magnitude you don't find. I mean, it would have to be someone who'd committed "normal" murders. How do children react in such a case?

B: I'd say that's different, because there is a much clearer boundary between the murderer and society. Here, there was collective conformity and afterward collective repression. Does that make it more difficult to clarify?

M: Yes. Let me give you an example. I mentioned to you that I had difficulty last December regarding this book I wrote, a study of Ph.D.'s who took their degree in economics at this university from 1830 to 1984. One of the men in the book had also been one of the prominent figures in the Third Reich. He'd received his doctorate in 1928 or 1930. I wrote to his children (his son is an attorney), and they crossed out everything I'd written. They didn't want to have it published. I went ahead and published it anyhow, showed it to my colleague who's coauthor and said, "I'll take responsibility. If someone comes afterward and wants to sue, then I'll say, 'Look, this is the biography I wrote. I don't see why things should be kept secret.'" I have also discovered that these ordinary people, these normal people, don't have any biography for the years between '33 and '45. Yes, suddenly people become very innocent. They become very innocuous, unblemished, although they may have been junior officials in '33 and even high-ranking ones in '45. But they become innocent as lambs. I always had great respect for a teacher who told us quite clearly, "I voted for the

Nazis in '33." I mean, most people, most parents, avoided facing the matter, and this is what led to the student revolt of 1968 in Germany to a great extent. I mean, why can't they say it openly? It was always repressed.

B: Does this repression resolve or enhance the guilt feelings?

M: I had a colleague once, she was ten years my junior, who told me that while she was doing some research, she accidentally came across a file with information that her grandfather had been a Nazi. She hadn't known and was shocked. That was worse for her, comparatively speaking, than what I know about my father. Evidently they had never discussed the matter, and she was from a family that was opposed to Hitler.

He wants to meet the "lady from Tel Aviv" who had been in school with his mother, but he will not go to Israel. Not with his name. He will correspond with her in the meantime. As I get ready to leave, I sense his need to continue the conversation. This time, I am prepared for the heel-clicking, and when it comes, I smile and tell him he is the first person I've known who does it as a habit. He laughs with me.

At home in Israel, when my mother listens to the tape of this interview, she is moved by it but also embarrassed. "A death camp and Loewenberg school," she says thoughtfully, " could one imagine such a combination in one family, in one society?"

A year goes by before I see Manfred again. This time I arrive in Germany alone. My wife has remained at home to tend her sixteen-year-old son, who suffers from lymphoma. The doctors are still hoping for his recovery. Manfred is waiting for me in the doorway, almost impatient to see me. I try to smile. I have learned from my mother that he and Alice met a couple of months before while Alice was on vacation in Germany.

Although I do not know this eighty-year-old woman personally, I feel that I must call her and tell her who Manfred's father was and what he did during the war. There is a long pause. "Strange," she says with a deep sigh, " I could not have dreamed of a worse fate for my poor schoolmate."

B: I understand that in the meantime you were able to talk with Alice?

M: Yes, that's right.

B: What did she tell you about your mother?

M: Actually, she knew very little about her. She was still able to remember, but they were distant memories. She remembered her as a very sweet child, a very friendly child.

B: Did she tell you anything about herself, her life afterward, what she'd experienced in later years?

M: She described her life to me, how she and her husband emigrated. Immediately after the Nazis took over, either in '33 or in early '34, they emigrated to Palestine.

B: Was she able to tell you anything about other classmates?

M: She was still in contact with a classmate who also lives in Israel. That's what she told me.

B: Did she say anything about your father?

M: Yes, she said that in her eyes, my mother's life had been very tragic, because of what happened. She didn't know my father personally, and so she wasn't able to say anything about him as a person. I mean, she could only judge him on the basis of his deeds, so to speak. But she thought it was a great tragedy for my mother. We talked very openly about it [*reddening, sweating*]. Actually, it impressed me very much, the fact that she, well, she had no feeling of resentment against me at all, nothing whatsoever. Of course, against Nazi Germany, that's clear. She did say that today, when she sees a bald-headed German, she has a strange feeling.

B: Did she use the expression "strange feeling"?

M: I can't recall the exact phrase, but that she still thinks, yes, you were there too. Not necessarily involved, but alive at a certain time. There's this element of being torn in two directions among Israelis of German origin: on the one hand, they love Germany; on the other hand, they were oppressed, afflicted. And so they still sense something there. One can certainly imagine what sort of an emotion that is. I assume that your mother will probably tell you the same thing.

B: So this conversation with Alice was interesting for you. Was it difficult?

M: [*Pauses*] No, actually it wasn't. I went to meet her with a, let's say an uneasy feeling (schweres Gefuhl), because I didn't know how she would react, how she would receive me, although on the telephone, she was so completely normal. But all that evaporated after the first five minutes in the hotel lobby. After you, she is the first Israeli I've ever talked to, and the special thing is that she is someone who had close contact with our family.

B: Tell me, how were things this past year for you, since our last conversation together? Have you done any more thinking about it?

M: Well, I read the book, the one you mentioned, *Into That Darkness*.

B: By Gitta Sereny. How did you like it?

M: Well, I thought the book, having been written by an Israeli . . .

B: She isn't Israeli.

M: [*Astonished*] She's not? Somehow I gathered from the context that she was an Israeli, Jewish at least.

B: No, she herself isn't Jewish.

M: [*Looking at me suspiciously*] I was very surprised at how objectively she had written. In many respects, well, she comes to Stangl's defense, let's say. Do you understand what I mean? She doesn't try to excuse him, nothing of the kind. But she does attempt to understand him. And I must say that in that respect I find the book very objective, very deep, with a lot of emotion.

I recall my own reaction when I read the book: the way Gitta Sereny tried to understand Stangl only intensified the horror of his activities in my eyes.

B: Yes, I agree.

M: Well, I don't know how you see it as a psychologist, but I find that her views on Stangl's personality are, well, very accurate. A historian would approach the thing differently, would stay more on the surface of things, not delve as deeply. However, when you form a judgment now—from the historical angle as well—I think you get a more sympathetic picture of Stangl.

B: What was it that impressed you?

M: Well, what he said in that final conversation, that he had outlived his own time. He probably felt then that he'd never actually repented and that basically, you might say, his heart attack was his execution, if you phrase it bluntly. He simply sensed this then himself. She describes his psychological state of mind quite well. Is that really a split personality? I have to say that, in terms of his educational background, he was in fact inferior to my father. Or, not educational background but formal training. My mother remarked once that my father in many respects was, I don't want to say "primitive," please try to understand, but that he acted, let's say, in an ignorant way. I don't know, maybe the word *ignorant* (dummlich) is too strong; perhaps *stupid* (doof). Well, everyone can be a little stupid in some way, not completely stupid, but . . . Now, during those years, what happened is that people were somehow taken in by slogans and then were pushed in a certain direction, more and more, a direction they actually weren't in agreement with and maybe one that in part they didn't even want. Suddenly, however, they were simply . . . In medieval German literature there is this notion of the *tumben toren* [the naive and stupidly innocent fool]. So there is this image then of someone who does things and, in the end, *has* to do things. He's moving initially on his own, because of his own motivation, but ends up being driven from the outside, and he can't stop, can't get off. That's what impressed me in this. My father in fact cut himself off, you might say, in that he took his own life.

B: And in this sense he is different from Stangl?

M: Different from Stangl. I mean, well, Stangl had been captured too but then had gotten away. My father probably simply knew then that he wouldn't be able to escape the thing any longer, and he came to certain conclusions.

Back and forth, from Stangl to his father. He stops, breaks off, can't complete the sentence.

B: Was there anything in Sereny's book that was particularly difficult for you?

M: Yes, I . . . [*Pauses*] I didn't tell you this last year. It's something I only recalled after having read Sereny's book, where she describes the crematoria, the cloud that hung in the air. Well, my mother had a kind of premonition, not very pronounced, but a very strong feeling along those lines sometimes. Now, after I was born, about six to eight weeks after I'd come back from the hospital, just before my father's first arrest, they went out for a walk. I can still show you the place. It was the time of bright summer days, blazing sunshine. And suddenly my mother felt as if they were being approached on the road by a cloud. My father was walking next to me, they were pushing me in the buggy and . . . Well, my mother had the impression that a dark, black cloud was coming toward them on the road, and this cloud . . . now, she told me this story at a time when the two of us still knew nothing as yet about the death camp. I haven't reinterpreted the meaning of the story afterward so that one now could contend that an older woman imagines something and concocts a whole story about it. She told me this story when I was still young—I was twelve or thirteen, maybe fourteen—in connection with her feelings about second sight, that she had premonitions. And in this cloud there were things moving, arms, legs . . . there were creatures inside it that were moving, and they were approaching my mother and father. Then my mother grabbed hold of my father's arm and said, "Now it's all over with. Now something awful is approaching us." And he answered, "OK, well, women sometimes get to imagining things six to eight weeks after having given birth, so don't imagine things."

B: That was his reaction?

M: That was his reaction, yes. And two or three days later, he was arrested for the first time.

B: So somehow she sensed it was coming . . .

M: She sensed that something was going to happen, that's one thing. But the other thing is that the description of this cloud reminded me very strongly of Sereny's description of the smoke in the air—she describes it in two or three words, the soot in the air in Treblinka, the ovens—all this reminded me in an absolute way of this story. I mean, now I'd almost say that my mother was somehow able to . . .

B: To feel it . . .

M: Yes, you understand [*excitedly*]. I'm not able to describe it, that's impossible, I don't have that kind of perception . . .

B: But you now see the connection . . .

M: The description of this cloud, the way my mother described it so vividly to me as a boy. And she described it less, let's say, in respect to my father's situation and more in terms of a situation in which she felt she had experienced second sight, had had a premonition. And she described it so clearly, described this cloud to me as a youngster, that I can see it in front of me. And when I read Sereny's book about Treblinka, suddenly the memory of this cloud flashed through my mind. I actually hadn't thought of the cloud before in this connection.

B: That is really very interesting.

M: And what was so interesting to me, it wasn't just a dark cloud. In the cloud there were somehow—now, I'm intentionally not saying there were human beings, she didn't see people—but rather there were beings of some sort in the cloud. Well, naturally that shows, I mean, as a Christian . . . There is also the tradition about the dead who have no rest but must wander. And my mother . . . every time something appeared in the papers, she would have a premonition beforehand. I think I mentioned that to you already. And I used to tell her, "OK, what of it? Forget it, it's better to forget it." And I can recall that so accurately because at that time she was still writing to my uncle, my father's brother, and he had written back, "What are you getting all excited about? Forget all these things."

[*Excited*] I also found something in *Die Zeit*. A journalist [Dörte von Westernhagen] also lost her father at a very young age, and she interviewed and wrote about victimizers. These were people who did a lot less than my father. And after I read through this material . . . I don't know whether I understand their psychoanalysts, but anyhow, you do ask yourself the question . . . if even today they still suffer, waking up at night soaked in sweat. And these are people who knew their fathers. And their fathers oppressed them a great deal in some cases. They had arguments, confrontations with their fathers, something that didn't happen in my case. Anyhow, sometimes you ask yourself, because after all, I don't have these problems, you wonder, am I *normal?* You understand? Because I don't suffer from this.

B: Because it would be normal to have dreams about it? A more difficult time of it?

M: Yes, I mean, that's something . . . You told me after our first conversation that you thought my mother had been very wise in the way she brought me up, and that she'd made me completely open and didn't build up any barriers. I telephoned the journalist and we met. She told me that her father had also been involved in a certain sense. She herself didn't learn anything about this from her mother, just as it was in the life histories she presented: in some cases the children didn't find out anything at all but woke up, became aware slowly. Though quite candidly and in all honesty, to date I haven't felt any distress, any inner psychological distress. Sometimes I ask myself— and that's what's troubling me now—whether my "working through" of this knowledge (Verarbeitungszustand) is normal.

B: Could you say that a total repression of this material was perhaps functional to a certain point (bis zu einem bestimmten Punkt) and then maybe no longer functional after that point in your own life?

M: I don't see any difference, I really don't. To speak quite frankly, how come I don't have a reaction like that? Waking up in the middle of the night, soaked in sweat . . . Sure, sometimes I wake up perspiring but not because I've had bad dreams or anything. It's simply that I sweat profusely at night. They have anxiety dreams and I don't. And even now, having read Sereny, I don't dream about it, which would be a definite possibility too—to work through these things in dreams. Naturally, I have the advantage that I didn't know my father personally; for me he's a theoretical personality. He is a kind of palpable figure for me on the basis of the stories I've heard, but I've never fleshed him out, as it were, given him substance and form from my own personal experience. I mean, I know him in the same way I know my great-grandparents from stories my mother would tell me. And I figure that you've also heard stories about your own great-grandparents, people you don't know as real persons. That's simply the way my father is for me: standing over me, next to me, in front of me, but not as a person with whom I can really talk.

B: If you were to ask my opinion, I'd say that I can sense two levels or layers in you: an emotional layer that is very tender, very open and approachable, one that feels this confrontation very strongly, and an intellectual layer. It's very strong too, sometimes very strong and rigid. And it's not always clear to me what the degree of contact is between these two layers, whether you don't sometimes have trouble deciding which side or level you're operating on.

M: [*Thoughtfully*] You're quite right about that, that's true, that they run parallel, yes, that's true. In one's early years, maybe one does construct a kind of protective wall against many things, perhaps without even being aware of it. It takes a long time for me to open up. I can be very open, you understand, if I like a person. On the other hand, I'm very suspicious. I don't warm up very quickly to people. It's exactly as you describe: being sensitive on the one hand and having a kind of intellectuality on the other. Though, if I look at my mother in this same light, well, I also felt this in her.

B: These two layers?

M: Yes, in a similar way. My mother was very emotional, extremely so. I can still recall how, as a small child of four or five, I would push my mother away. She was much too emotional. I didn't like that when I was small, I can still remember that quite vividly. Aside from that, my mother was very impulsive in everyday life, very high-spirited, not at all what you'd imagine of a serious, older woman. Students would come home with me and talk with her, and they'd find they had more in common with her, more of a common wavelength, than with me. I was older than she was in many ways, older somehow. I don't know if I'm putting it right. She was still able to be youthful . . . And that's why it's remarkable that after this terrible knowledge was revealed in the trial, even then she didn't react in any way. Externally, I mean. I don't know what was going on inside, in the depths of her soul.

B: Well, I don't know. And I don't know if, when it comes to such things, a woman can open up completely to her son, especially since a child is not familiar with his mother's intimate relationships.

We continue our conversation in a spirit of camaraderie. I find it paradoxical that Manfred wonders if he is normal because he does not have nightmares like the children of other perpetrators. He impresses me with what he has achieved during the past year: meeting Alice, reading Sereny's book, talking with the journalist. Yet he has a much more difficult problem still to solve: how to conjure a father out of the emptiness and to bring him to life for the sole purpose of killing him again. We laugh as we approach his front door: should he click his heels? My friends see him as square, conservative, unapproachable, but I cannot. He has shown me his inner vulnerability and pain. The biological son of a father who did appalling things has become for me a person in his own right. Will he be able to do the same for himself?

It is a beautiful autumn Sunday, just like the one a year before when I first came to interview Manfred. My friends offer to spend the afternoon showing me around. They decide to take me on a tour of some old Jewish cemeteries they have discovered in villages not far from their hometown. In the car, I share with them my feelings about Manfred and how they misinter-

pret him. But they look at me with mistrust: I was with him for such a short time, while they have seen him every day for years.

In a lovely village, with quite a few medieval buildings, we park the car and approach several townspeople to find out what is left of the old synagogue. No one can tell us. Finally, an old woman points out the location, watching us warily. The building that once served as a synagogue is no longer recognizable as such, and we enter the graveyard, which is well kept and green. The old tombstones indicate the size of the Jewish community that lived in this place for almost two centuries. I read the Hebrew script as I walk along: Yaacov Levi, very generous and beloved; his wife, Esther, beautiful and beloved; a four-year-old son who died suddenly; another son who fought in the Crimea, where he was wounded and cared for by a Russian nurse. Most of the newer tombstones date from 1943, and a memorial stone tells the story of the community's end: the Jews were rounded up in the local plaza on August 15, 1943, and taken to . . . 265 of them were gassed in . . . on . . . Several gravestones from the 1960s and 1970s indicate that people have asked to be buried near their family members in more recent years. That is all. A silent testimony to what was once a living entity.

An older couple starts a conversation with my friends. They are local people who thought we were part of a gathering of Jews in a neighboring town. The man and his father used to work for the Jewish goldsmith. They think he and his family made it, that they escaped before the August evacuation. They would so very much like to see these people again, such nice people, would so much like to talk to them once again. I join in and note how carefully they sidestep the more difficult issue: what they did or did not do to help those people during that awful time.

Suddenly, I feel an engulfing sense of sorrow. As long as I am interviewing Manfred or Peter, I am at work. Maybe dealing with individual psyches "protects" me from the vastness of the loss. But here in the cemetery, the tombstones tell the story: whole families vanished in the cataclysm. And I know that tomorrow Helmuth will be waiting for me.

chapter 3

Those Blue-Eyed German Songs

*Look for the Literature sign on his door. That's what they tell me at the
entrance to the local television station. I almost get lost in the maze of corridors and staircases but finally reach the half-open door. When I look in, I
see the back of a man who is leaning over a table covered with papers, books,
and leaflets, all jumbled together in a huge pile. I have never seen so many
papers on a single table. I cough and mention my name, and the man turns
around. From that first moment of our encounter, I remember a sad smile
and kindly eyes peering at me through glasses. When we sit down, it is as if
he is interviewing me for his next TV program. I set up my small tape recorder, and he asks candidly whether it is really necessary. At this stage, I
already know something about his father: he wrote a professional opinion
addressed to the Racial Hygiene Committee proposing that any person
whose ancestry nine generations back was Jewish should be identified as a
Jew.*

H: I was born in Munich in that year of ill fortune, 1933, but we
only stayed there for a short time. I grew up in the town of T. That's
where I spent my so-called childhood. I was the third of four children,
the first son. I have two older sisters and a younger sister.

B: So you're the only son?

H: Yes, that's right. My father wished for a son. There were two
girls, and then I came along, although that was also a kind of disappointment as far as "masculinity" was concerned. My two older sisters
were more "masculine" than I was . . . Now, my earliest memories of
the family . . . well, let's see. That's hard to say. My earliest memories
are probably indirect, based on stories I've heard, photographs. Well,
a memory I cherish very much is of being at the beach on the North
Sea. I'm probably in some sort of sandcastle in the sun, lying in my
father's arms. It's a very pleasant memory. But I'm not sure whether

it's direct or based on the photograph—I've seen the photo. At that time they say I was a trusting, loving child. My father was pretty strict. It was probably connected with his expectations about masculinity, which I didn't quite live up to. I was dreamy as a child, still am. And I was afraid of dogs. He didn't like that. He wanted me to be "a man."

B: And you remember that directly, or did people tell you about that too?

H: I do have direct recollections of this, I certainly do. Unpleasant memories actually, though in connection with rather harmless matters such as help in doing my homework, math homework and Latin. I felt a little—not a little, I felt very strongly—that it was humiliating. He was a bad teacher, had the wrong approach. He thought that he could achieve something by means of intimidation. Now we know better. Even then, one could have known better if there hadn't been an effort to suppress the insights of educational theory and psychology. Suppress—or burn in the flames. This wasn't just suppressed.

B: And that's where he tried to be strict.

H: Yes, that's right. In the form of humiliation as well. Actually, it always ended up with me in tears. And his own life ended in tears. He shot himself. [*Looks at me*] I don't know if you were aware of that, so let me say it right at the outset. Yes, my tears, I . . . I even turned dense, a dull student. And I became what I am today very much in spite of his education, I'd have to say that.

B: Did your mother take part in this?

H: Not very much. Sometimes he'd send me to my mother bathed in tears, and I was supposed to tell her that I'd been a good student again, learned what I had to. But it was also terribly inappropriate, unsuitable.

B: What was her reaction?

H: Actually, I really can't recall. Because my mother is still alive. You probably recall these old memories with such clarity only after there's been a break, an interruption.

B: Do you have any memories of your mother from those early years?

H: Yes, both good ones and bad ones, probably just like you [*laughs*]. I don't really know what I should talk about in that regard. My mother kept a certain distance from us children. I personally, well . . . They say that a mother is the one who shapes men's image of women. I believe, however, that my own image of women was shaped and influenced by our maid and not by my mother . . . though I don't like to say things like that, because I try to live in peace with my parents. And somehow, actually, what I feel toward them is mainly love (überwiegt bei mir eigentlich die Liebe), toward my father as well. Although it was only later on, after his death—and through his tragic, his terrible, fateful entanglement (Lebensverstrickung), so to speak— that I learned to love and respect him. I mean, I don't have any need to settle accounts with my father.

B: But in those early years, it was different then . . .

H: Yes, that's true. I reached the age of eleven-and-a-half while he was still alive. Then, at the end of the war, he shot himself. He said good-bye and took his leave of the family. The way my mother describes it, it was terrible. Yes, he knew he was going to do it.

B: Why did he shoot himself?

H: Because he believed that he himself would be brought to trial, that the Allies wanted to have their revenge on the Nazis.

B: What sort of activities had he been involved in? Why should he have been put on trial?

H: I don't know, I didn't speak with him about it. But I assume that this was so. After all, he was a formidable professor, and he had been teaching the theory of genetics. He was quite a strong ideologist—of anti-Semitism too. He was the local director of the so-called Race-policy Bureau of the Nazi Party (Rassenpolitisches Amt der NSDAP), a terrible name. I can't say, though, to what extent he might have been found guilty of actual crimes.

B: Because you don't know or because you don't believe he committed any?

H: I simply don't know exactly. I assume that my father had concrete guilt in respect to euthanasia, the so-called euthanasia. That is to say, that he was somehow implicated in the way so-called mentally ill patients were killed in the psychiatric institutions.

B: What sort of duties did he perform in those institutions?

H: He was the local director of Health Services in T., though these are all things that haven't been completely clarified. I don't know exactly, I just assume that that's the actual substantive basis to any guilt my father incurred. I also came across a document in a research report on euthanasia. Actually that's the only thing I know. The topic wasn't brought up in my family. I did try to talk with my mother about it, but I didn't find out anything clear or specific. I figure that maybe she doesn't have a clear idea herself, and that perhaps she doesn't have much interest in getting a clear picture of what transpired.

B: Didn't he talk with her about what sort of role he played in the euthanasia program?

H: With my mother? I don't know exactly. During the last year of his life, or during those last years, he did talk a great deal with my mother, but that was in connection with a tragic incident . . . I myself was very much affected and harmed by it too. You see, there was a family in Berlin we were friendly with, my parents, my father. And the father in that family not only committed suicide, he killed the entire family. For years after my father killed himself, I lived in fear that my mother would kill us all. This was a delusion, a crazy idea, because by that time it was quite a different situation and had been for a long time.

I had been awakened by a phone call at about midnight. I barely understood the excited caller, who told me she had found someone for me to interview. "What I know about him is this: at night, while he was supposed to be asleep, he overheard his parents discussing whether the father should commit suicide or kill the whole family as well. He lived in terror for days and was somewhat relieved only when he found out that his father had finally committed suicide." Completely awake by then, I wrote down the address and phone number. I could not sleep any more that night. If I could scarcely grasp what the Nazis had done to us, how would I be able to understand what they had done to their own children?

B: But for you that was a realistic fear, was it not?

H: Yes, it was based on a justified fear. You see, my mother says she talked my father out of this idea.

B: She talked him out of it?

H: Right, that's what she says.

B: He wanted to do the same thing?

H: They spoke about it, discussed it. The father of the family in question, the one we were friendly with, was some sort of important official in one of Hitler's ministries.

B: Did you know why your father wanted to kill the entire family?

H: I think they thought the Allies would take revenge on the whole family. It was perhaps a false assessment of the situation. They were probably projecting their own thoughts and deeds: they were afraid that what they had done to others would now be done to them. Though I think one should trace all this back to its origin. In contemporary terms, my father would have been one of the Green Party. His views were based in biology. He had studied medicine as a young man—the first in his family to go to the university—then athletics, and he had a strong interest in things biological, the forms of plants and animals, that sort of thing. And he had this notion about healthful living that was very formative in his life. He lived very strictly according to his own views of life and in a manner that was in tune with nature.

B: Was he a very strong man?

H: He described himself—I believe he was a physician for sports at that time—he described himself as an individual with a trained, athletic constitution. We have photos in which he looks very powerful.

B: So he believed in it and tried to put it into practice in your case as well?

H: Put what into practice?

B: This philosophy of sports and . . .

H: Yes. For example, there was a certain sun cult in the family, which is understandable in this northern climate. In Israel, there's probably no sun cult in that sense. It's too hot there. And then the notion of the free life . . . he had been in the Wandervögel youth movement. As a student he'd helped set up the so-called Guild, a student organization that had developed out of the Wandervögel. It was a youth movement, populist (völkisch) in orientation. They wore large, open-collared shirts without ties.

B: What did your mother say about these ideas? What sort of ideology did she have?

H: My mother actually didn't wish to have anything to do with all this. She thought that this nationalism was somehow too primitive. In T., my mother was the only wife of a so-called highly placed political functionary who was not a member of a National Socialist organization. She was neither in the Women's Association nor in anything else, though this was not necessarily because of any political insight on her part. It was due more to an instinct. It somehow disgusted her. It was too primitive in her eyes, too "unpleasant," as she puts it.

B: What sort of a family does she come from?

H: My mother's father was a postal official, an educated man. I loved him very much. He came from a family of teachers—there was a tradition of going into teaching in his family. And he was also a poet, so to speak, a club poet, for social occasions. A grandfather who was very close to me, and someone whom I knew for many years. A person who actually became a father to me later on.

B: What sort of memories do you have of this grandfather?

H: Oh, very pleasant ones indeed.

B: For example . . .

H: For example, I named one of my books of poetry after him. Something special I learned from him is that you can isolate a certain motif from its surroundings by looking at it through your clenched and empty fist. He was a very warm-hearted, loving, and witty person.

B: What did he have to say about the question of National Socialism, race crimes, and those notions of biology?

H: It didn't interest him. You never know exactly whether people didn't bother about all this because of a lack of political interest or because they had better insight. I think it was mainly due to a lack of political interest. I think that probably you'll only begin to comprehend the entire calamitous movement of National Socialism if you also bear in mind that for many people, it did indeed have a great fascination, it sucked them in (mitreissenden Charakter hatte). And that people who wanted to be politicized were pulled in by its power, drawn into the vortex.

B: Like your father?

H: Yes, I think so.

B: And so your mother simply withdrew from contact with any such matters.

H: That's right. And in terms of a formal professional connection, she also had no involvement because she was not a member of any of those organizations. And my father's image of himself as a man was predicated on the notion that these matters were not for women.

B: So it was his idea that this was no business for women, that they shouldn't be involved. Did this extend to your sisters too, his daughters?

H: Yes, my older sister was five years older. Let's see, if I was eleven, she must have been sixteen at the time, not an age when you are very political.

B: Were you in the Hitler Youth (Hitlerjugend) movement?

H: I myself was in the Hitler Youth. I wanted to join, I really did, a special group of "cub cadets" (Fähnlein). These cubs built model planes. They weren't a paramilitary group like the other Hitler Youth cubs. This was a group that built model airplanes: small, hand-launched gliders. We were a bit sloppy, didn't have such neat uniforms. At times we had no uniforms at all. And we'd always have glue stains or spots on our clothes. I wanted to join this cub group even before I was supposed to, when I was about nine or so, as early as that. I pestered my parents a lot to let me join.

B: Was your father happy?

H: I can't recall. I assume he was. I only know that it was my idea to join. It's important for me to say it, because I think it's important that people understand all the things that are done in such a mass movement. You can't operate on the assumption that a population consists, in large measure, of criminals. I assume they were just people like any other, basically just human beings. And I think we can only understand the crimes that were committed then if we understand our crimes today—crimes that are committed with a more benign face. I believe that all of us bear a structural guilt, or let me put it more modestly: for me as a child of our times, our guilt is not less than that of my father. I haven't, thank God, become a perpetrator, a victimizer. I'm not guilty of the death of others, though I must utter these words with caution: my son committed suicide.

B: That's a frightening connection you made just now . . . How old was he?

H: He was twenty-six.

B: Were there any specific reasons?

H: He was a very political person. He was living among so-called squatters in Berlin. He was an anarchist. It's difficult to talk about, hard to explain such a thing exactly, I just don't know. Probably politically he'd overextended himself, too much pressure. That's what I assume. We were corresponding, and when I asked him why he was doing this, why he was involved—well, my feelings were a mixture of pride and worry when it came to my son Thomas. Once I said to him, "What you're doing is of great merit, but it isn't really in keeping with your own class affiliation. You don't have to be a squatter. You have a father who gives you money . . ." I said that he didn't have to commit an illegal, albeit socially motivated act in order to live somewhere. And his reply was, "A person can also participate out of a sense of solidarity with others. Besides, I'm *doing* what you write." I felt proud when he said that. He was very close to me.

B: Was he your oldest son?

H: Yes.

B: When did it happen?

H: Just two years ago, it's not quite two years.

B: Did you speak with him about your father?

H: Sometimes. He asked about him once, and he was very surprised that my father had committed suicide. That thought preoccupied him, bothered him. But my son was very witty. No one would have imagined that . . . You would have thought that he would have dissuaded five people from killing themselves rather than take his own life.

B: How did he do it?

H: By hanging.

B: It must be very difficult to have to live between a father and a son who . . .

H: Yes, I feel hemmed in, weighed down . . . by both of them . . .

I listen to this man, and as a therapist and an interviewer I feel pulled in opposite directions. I focus, with effort, on the interview.

B: You were about six when the war broke out. Do you have any memories? Did you talk about that period within the family?

H: Did we speak about the war? Well, I experienced the war very directly: bombing raids and such things. At the end of the war, we were living in a village in the Thuringian Forest. This village was attacked, under artillery fire for a number of days, reconquered by the Germans. Then it was taken again. I can recall such nights, when there were bombing raids, very well. And I saw the dead who'd been killed in the raids. In Weimar I also saw concentration camp prisoners, external detachments from Buchenwald that were working in the town of Weimar.

B: What were they doing?

H: Working in construction on water reservoirs in the neighborhood where we lived.

B: How did they look?

H: Very gaunt, emaciated, and I can recall they were wearing black caps and striped uniforms.

B: Did you ask questions about them?

H: We looked at them. Sometimes the Kapos would send us to get cigarettes—Eckstein was the brand.

He looks at me but does not answer my question.

H: I myself had another encounter with the concentration camp during a school excursion to the Ettersberg near Weimar. Somehow I had wandered off from the main group, gone my own way. I lost contact with my class and walked right into a machine-gun nest. Suddenly, I found myself standing there facing soldiers with machine guns. You might say that I went out hunting mushrooms and stumbled onto the concentration camp. I was terrified.

B: Did you see anything of the camp itself or only this machine-gun emplacement?

H: Only the machine guns, not the camp itself. This must have been just in front of the outer tower. I didn't cross any fence. I don't quite know how it happened. I have another memory. There was a bombing raid on Buchenwald, because the camp contained munitions factories. And there were long convoys carrying the injured, open trucks with trailers covered with straw. They drove them out of the camp, and among the injured there were probably prisoners too. We saw that once, as children, on the way to school. It was right after a heavy bombing raid.

B: You saw these trucks driving through town?

H: Yes, right.

B: And did you ask at home about what you'd seen? Who are they? What's a concentration camp? Why, how come?

H: I assume so, but I can't recall asking any questions . . .

A kind of numbness comes over Helmuth's face, like a mask.

B: Did your parents say anything?

H: I have some recollection of my father speaking about the camp and being filled with disgust. He knew the earlier camp commander, the one whose wife was Ilse Koch. Ilse Koch was infamous, and my father knew this man. Later on, Koch apparently was punished by the Nazis for some transgression or other and was removed. During his last year—or the final two years—I believe my father feared that we would be liquidated. That's what my mother says.

B: That you would be killed . . .

H: Yes. My father had a close relationship with the Party District Chief and must have expressed his opinion in unmistakable terms. By the way, my mother says that this person also expressed a very clear opinion about the concentration camp—I'm only telling you what I've heard, I can't check on whether it's true—that the District Chief said the concentration camp was the only blemish in his district, the only stain. He called Buchenwald an infamous stain (Schandfleck).

B: Why?

H: I believe the two men knew people were being liquidated[1] there. They probably knew that.

B: At what point did your father draw the line between his commitment to the cause, his desire to continue, and what he regarded as a disgrace, something that wasn't good?

H: I assume that in terms of ideology, it's all still relatively simple. My father was of the opinion that there should be planned biological improvement of the human race by eugenics. Those who were pure and noble (echte Arier) should reproduce and multiply, those who weren't (die Unedelen) should not. It all sounds very good, but as my mother, who always talks about this, says, it isn't practicable. That's true. The ideas are in themselves false. Because somehow, well, it's always turned out differently in practice. The human race certainly did not come about by breeding, but rather negatively, though who knows?

His eyes look pained now, as if he cannot simultaneously hold in his mind these ideological thoughts and the sights he still recalls from Buchenwald.

H: But my father also said it was impracticable, couldn't be done. It could only be misused. The so-called "noble" person will not decide whether someone lives or dies; rather, those who are not pure and noble—though this terminology is disgusting—they're the ones who

1. Although Buchenwald was a concentration camp, not an extermination camp like Auschwitz, Chelmno, Belzec, Sobibor, Treblinka, and Maidanek, thousands of people died there between 1943 and 1945.

will decide in the end. These ideas have been around since classical antiquity. They were less squeamish then: weak children were abandoned and left out to die. And my father was a proponent of such notions. The idea that a better human being, both physically and mentally, could be produced by breeding, though we've seen the upshot of all that.

B: When he saw the concentration camp, he thought that was not a way to reach this goal?

H: It was murderous.

It is not clear to me whether Helmuth is expressing his own feelings or those of his father.

H: And then the way they killed the mentally ill in the psychiatric institutions. Decisions had to be made, and the way it was done was a bit hypocritical. I read in one document contained in the book by Klee[2] that they let the directors of these institutions carry out the orders given by the political leadership. Such orders were given very indirectly, verbally rather than in writing, with all sorts of provisos. There was one that let them go hungry. They were killed mainly by being left underfed, undernourished.

B: I don't know if that was the *main* way, but that was also practiced.

H: They were killed by injection.

B: And by gassing.

H: By gassing, where?

B: In a number of different institutions.

H: So there was also gassing. I read about the use of special vans. They made use of that experience, so to speak, in Auschwitz. It was an insecticide, a disinfecting agent—this mania about cleanliness. So they used a disinfecting agent to murder people.

A mania for Aryan cleanliness. I had never thought about it before in those terms.

B: Did your father say anything against this? Against the killing of the mentally ill? Did he express any opinion about it?

H: My mother says that he said it was irresponsible, that it couldn't be carried out, though probably always with various explanations, for example, that it was always the wrong people who would carry out the measure. So I do believe ideologically he was of the opinion, in any event, that . . . You know, they coined these special terms such as [*looks away from me*] "burdensome individual" (Ballastexistenzen), expressions like that. They carried out incredibly petty calculations about

2. Ernst Klee, *"Euthanasie" im NS-Staat: Die "Vernichtung lebensunwerten Lebens"* (Frankfurt: Fischer, 1983).

how much it was costing the public to provide food for the crippled, things like that. There are these wretched computations.

B: And your father basically accepted the fact that one could make such calculations, or that they had some sort of meaning and use?

H: I think my father held the view—allow me to make use of the Nazi terminology—that "life not worthy of living"(lebensunwertes Leben) ought to be . . .

Helmuth cannot utter the word exterminated.

H: Initially he saw this, understood this in a biological sense, that those who were deficient physically and mentally—the crippled, the mentally ill, handicapped people, those who . . .

B: And Jews as well?

H: Probably.

B: Were there any Jews living in your neighborhood before the war?

H: In every family they tell some story about how a Jew was saved. Something about a professor at the university—I've forgotten his name—who gave a party and then his students danced around the bust of Hitler. My father helped to shield and protect him, although I don't know whether this is just a story or whether it's true.

B: Were there any discussions at home you might have heard in which your father spoke about Jews?

H: Something I overheard maybe once or twice. But that was not the decisive, formative factor. What was decisive for me then was my fear of my father, a father I was afraid of. And a man who probably became more strict himself, the more frightened he became.

B: And more strict in his behavior toward you as well?

H: Yes, right, that's what I assume.

B: And less so in his relationship with your sisters? Or was he strict with them too?

H: Mainly with me, mainly with me. I guess I was the problem child, and somehow the naughty boy, though I wasn't particularly naughty. I probably did basically what all boys do: I lied, stole things, went my own independent way. Not for any malevolent reason, not out of malice, but somehow just because I probably wanted to live my own life, for myself.

B: Did you try to get away from your father?

H: That wasn't really possible. I tried to avoid him, and we didn't have all that much contact. He was at the office all day over at the university. We'd see each other evenings, on weekends, and during vacation periods.

B: Did you sense that he was getting more and more severe?

H: I don't know how long it lasted, this severe, strict behavior on his part, the torments I saw myself exposed to. Though this was certainly connected with my own sense of guilt. Because there were always reasons. He would go off on an official trip somewhere, for example, and then he'd say good-bye to me and would warn me not to make any trouble for my mother. He would say something like, "If your mother complains about you when I get back, then I'll kill you!" That's what he said. He certainly didn't mean it, but I thought to myself: he means it. I was genuinely afraid. I was frightened that he would kill me. There's that stupid quote from the Christian tradition, or from the Bible, I think the Old Testament: "The Lord chastises the one he loves."

B: And your mother stood by and watched? Did she take your side or that of your father?

H: I think that emotionally . . . she was on my side. I can't really say. Mainly, she just kept out of it. My mother was a bit cold. You know, I recall the bad things from my childhood, the bad things about my parents, my mother too. For instance, I recall a warning of my mother's that I shouldn't play too near the fireplace, that I might set fire to my new suit. *I* wasn't important.

B: Not you, but the suit . . .

H: Yes, it would be too bad about the suit. You know, those are the stupid things that parents say, and you hope they don't mean it. But I thought they did mean it. I would never say anything like that to my children. And I really did hear such things being said. A person wouldn't remember them if they hadn't had such an impact emotionally. This isn't something I dreamed up or invented. My mother has never mentioned that incident to me since. I was the one who reminded her about it.

B: And what was her reply?

H: "You mustn't take such things seriously, it's just talk." Also my older sister used to tease me for being so timid. They used to tease me in the family because I was so timid, so easily frightened. On family walks . . . I was scared of sheep, I was afraid of almost everything. Even today, they still tell the story that once, I didn't want to walk past a herd of sheep, I wanted to make a big detour. Then, after we'd long since passed the herd, they shouted, "Oh look, another sheep!" And I didn't turn around, I just started running. I ran and ran. I assume that all of this is less connected in specific terms with National Socialism than you might perhaps think. I assume it's pretty common practice all over the world to tease the weak, the timid, to have fun at their expense. I guess it's a common abuse.

B: Do you have a different relationship with your younger sister?

H: Yes, with my younger sister. I was the one who protected her a bit, because I noticed that she was being made the object of certain educational experiments. For example, they were trying to toilet train her, and I saw some very rough, unpleasant things being done in that connection. Now, my parents were very proud that my sisters—the older ones—had been toilet trained at a very early age. Now in the case of my younger sister—she's five years younger than I am—she had also been toilet trained, had started using her potty and going to the regular toilet. And once she was supposed to "go out in the open" (im Freien abgehalten werden). I don't know whether you're familiar with the expression. Anyhow, you take a child, pull down her panties, and then she's supposed to urinate outside, in the open. So once while we were out on one of those many, awful family walks, she was supposed to go, but she wouldn't because she'd been trained to use her potty or the toilet. They gave her a spanking for that. Nothing special, but I thought to myself that she must be wondering, "What does he want? He's interested in having me urinate only when there's a toilet, and now I'm supposed to go when there's no toilet around! So what's a girl to do?" I'm telling funny little stories, but . . .

B: And how did your sisters react to his sudden suicide?

H: I believe it was a hard blow for them. In the beginning, it wasn't for me. I was the only one who was able to sit down and eat anything after we got the news. My mother was desperate, completely beside herself. It was a terrible sight.

B: Did it happen at home?

H: No. My father shot himself in a clinic at the university. I believe that, initially, they were all more traumatized by this than I was. Though I think that over the long term I was the one who was more traumatized. Back then . . . my father said good-bye to me in a very warm way. It was not at all in keeping with the way he usually behaved toward me. I can hardly talk about it. He came to visit us to say good-bye, though we didn't exactly know that this was what was happening. I overheard a conversation between my mother and father. My mother wanted to dissuade him from killing himself. She said, "They [the Americans] need doctors. You have a chance to survive as a doctor." Things like that. But my father didn't believe it. And he took special leave of me, probably because I was the son. He went out of his way to take a walk with me, and though I was a fairly heavy child of eleven, he carried me on his shoulders during the long walk in the forest.

Helmuth is now crying quietly.

H: And he sang folksongs. Somehow my father was a pretty sentimental person. He sang German folksongs, ones that he used to play for me on his harmonica when I was in bed. You know, when you put a child to sleep. Now that's something that doesn't fit in at all with the other image I have of him. That must have been the earlier period, before our relationship hardened. Then he used to play songs for us in the evening on his harmonica. Folksongs, like "Am Brunnen vor dem Tore," "Kein schöner Land," all those songs I can't stand to listen to today, because they are associated with the crime, those blue-eyed German songs.

I am overwhelmed by his suffering. I can see in Helmuth the magnitude of the inner break: he cries for his father, singing in the forest, and he finds it impossible to tolerate these songs today because they symbolize the event that took his father away from him.

B: What was it like when your father suddenly became so soft and gentle, so warm and loving again?

H: I felt that it was something positive, but I also noticed that he was crying.

B: He was crying?

H: Yes, he was.

B: And did you say anything?

H: No, no, nothing.

B: And did you already know then that the end was near?

H: I really didn't know exactly, though I had overheard those conversations with my mother.

B: [*Pauses*] And you realized from this that he loved you very much?

H: Yes, I think so. There's that saying, "God chastises the one he loves." And God is the father . . . There was also this patriarchal concept of father to son, something that was also in National Socialism. And there was this abysmal desperation on my mother's part. And my own feeling of desperation, which was much less intense. Then a period began in which I was afraid that my mother would kill us. I only understood all this rather slowly, and that bothered my mother deeply. My mother was terribly offended by this.

B: By what?

H: The idea I had that she wanted to poison us . . .

B: Did you say anything about it?

H: Yes. I wouldn't take anything to eat at home, wouldn't eat the soup.

B: Because you were afraid she was going to put poison in the food?

H: Yes, right.

B: And what was your mother's reaction?

H: It was a mixture of rage, feelings of hurt, and a sense of desperation. She was angry because it wasn't her intention. On the contrary.

B: Did she try to discuss the matter with you quietly?

H: Yes, but then my older sister started up again with her teasing. And she cured me in a radical way: she always used to pretend that she was sprinkling poison in my plate. That's when I realized it was all a lot of foolish nonsense.

B: But you were afraid nonetheless?

H: Yes, I was, and afterward this fear took on a life of its own (hat sich verselbständigt). It became a kind of crazed delusion (Wahn). At boarding school, for example, we had to bring along silverware from home to use. And I didn't use what I'd brought, because I thought it was poisoned. It even extended to include the personnel working at the boarding school, though they were deaconesses. When I was ill, for example, I wouldn't take medicine from the nurse, because I still thought she was the tool, so to speak, of my parents.

B: How long were you at boarding school?

H: Until my final college-prep exams. From the age of twelve until I was twenty—some eight years.

B: How long was it after your father's suicide that you started at boarding school?

H: Well, maybe about a year after that.

B: So you were at home for about a year and had these fears during that time?

H: The initial period was one of a struggle to survive. This fear hadn't really developed yet. We were in Weimar. Then Weimar was handed over to the Red Army. First Thuringia was taken by the Americans, and then the Red Army came. And we left. We had a hard time getting across over the border to the west. Everything in backpacks. And we had a very hard time surviving initially. Then we went to B., and that's when this whole story appeared and started to develop. After that I was sent to boarding school. I think that, altogether, that was about a year after my father's death.

B: And how long did you have these fears after you went to boarding school?

H: I'd say the first few years, two or three years. And somehow it continued on in the form of a negative religiosity. A very strong fear. After all, I hadn't been brought up in a religious manner. Like all Nazis, my parents had left the church—what they used to call "being a believer in God" (gottgläubig). So it wasn't until I was twelve years old and in boarding school that I had any instruction in religion. That was quite unusual for a child, and so I took to it in a very passionate way and developed a rather negative form of religiosity. In actual fact, it was a continuation of the image of my father that I had. In evening prayers, I always used to have a kind of bargaining session with God. I would say, "OK, I *know* you secretly want to kill me tonight. But since you only do things I'm not supposed to know about—because you're omniscient—you can't do it." Crazy childish notions. I used to pray every evening, "I know you want to kill me tonight" . . . so that he wouldn't do it!

B: How many years did this go on?

H: A couple. I can't tell you exactly. But it went on for a couple of years.

B: Did you talk with your sisters about this period later on?

H: Yes, I did.

B: And what did they say?

H: Well, they were very worried. They knew I was having a rough time of it and . . . We are generally pretty close. Later on, my oldest sister married an American. She says it was on the advice of my father. He had told her, "You can only survive if you go with the victor." She had learned some English and went to live in the States. She married twice. And she's been living for a long time now back in Germany, though she remained a U.S. citizen. We are pretty much in agreement about these matters.

B: What's your sister's image of your father, her relationship with him today?

H: I think hers is similar to mine, although she didn't pass through this traumatic period. But there were traumatic experiences. She is my oldest sister, and was the only one at home the day my father shot himself at the clinic, which is some twenty kilometers from our house. People are pretty nutty, pedantic. When a person shoots himself, they send his blood-stained clothes home. Apparently it's some kind of crazy notion people have that clothes are a person's property and . . . I saw them too. His clothes were in the stove in the bathroom. When we made the fire to heat the water for the Saturday night bath, my sister shoved the bloody clothes underneath the boiler into the fire. I was watching.

He is on the verge of tears again.

B: How do you believe it affected her, this traumatization?

H: I don't know. My sister is actually a rather unconventional and anarchistically inclined woman, someone who is never afraid to tell you her views.

B: Was she that way even then?

H: Maybe even back then. But that's how she is today.

B: So why did she tease you with this poisoning episode back then, because you were more open in expressing your fears and she less so?

H: That was a therapeutic experiment on her part. She wanted to take the thing ad absurdum. At least that's my assumption.

B: She wanted to teach you something . . .

H: Yes, she wanted to teach me something. Everyone wanted to teach me something . . .

B: And your second sister, what did she experience?

H: She was probably my father's favorite. I guess I envied her. She used to get presents from him, a fountain pen, stuff like that. And she was the closest of all to him. It was a very close and harmonious relationship. There were no problems between them. Somehow she was a kind of favorite daughter. She's married to a doctor, lives in K. And she's the only one who still writes in German—in Gothic—script. We all learned how to write that script. Let's see, no, I guess my youngest sister didn't. Anyhow, I can read it, and, if necessary, can write it as well. But my second sister, she writes in that script easily. And it's an expression of a certain bond between her and my father.

B: And this sister, how did your father's suicide affect her?

H: Well, it was a great tragedy, but she's managed to have a family with three children. Her husband is an important doctor. And they have the same sort of family life that came to an abrupt end in our case. My youngest sister also has that kind of life, with a family. But my oldest sister doesn't. She proved to be a very basic failure in respect to those things having to do with a family. Like me.

He loses his concentration.

B: What do you mean a "failure"? In what way?

H: Well, no family, for example, divorced. Myself and my oldest sister, we both have been twice married and divorced.

B: And what about you, do you have any other children?

H: Yes, two. But they're from different mothers. I have a child from my second marriage. Thomas, the one who committed suicide, was from my first marriage. And my son from my second marriage, his name is Isaak. Then I have a young illegitimate son—what am I saying, young, he's already fourteen—an illegitimate son named Eliyahu.

I am moved by the Jewish names. Is this his (conscious or unconscious) way of identifying with his father's victims?

B: Do you think that was connected with your youth?

H: I don't know. I really can't say. I was very inexperienced, a very confused and difficult person. I believe it was basically my fault—I was still pretty much what they call "ignorant of the world" at that time, and I got involved with a woman who was anything but "ignorant" in the ways of the world. So it didn't work out, it broke up pretty quickly. I was an individualist, I actually never wanted to . . . never wanted to be bothered.

You know, I talk a lot to myself. I hope you won't misuse that bit of information. Say, you're not a cop, are you? [*Laughs*] Well, you asked me what my difficulties were. Basically, even today, it's the same . . . I don't know what you know about me.

B: Nothing.

H: I'm a poet, that's the most important thing I do. I've published a few volumes of lyric poetry, so I am, so to speak, a writer. And I work here as a literature editor for the radio. I'm more interested in knowledge, in insight into the nature of existence (Welterkenntnis). Now there's a strange story connected with my father in this—basically that's what you're interested in—a kind of posthumous obedience that has developed in me in association with one of my main loves and passions. I studied biology but didn't finish and take a degree. I switched to literature. Now, when I was a child, my father also used to torment me with nature. I would hope it wasn't his intention to make me suffer, but he did.

B: He wanted you to love nature.

H: Yes, that's what his interest was, and on those family walks that I hated so much, well, he would always ask me questions, quiz me: what sort of a finch is that singing, what kind of bird is that, what type of tree is that? And today I could obediently answer him. I know it all, maybe better than he did then. But then it was a torment for me, it didn't interest me as a child, not in the least. A child isn't interested in knowing about nature in this way. This interest developed in me later on in a very pronounced way. Even now, I still don't know why. I assume that if you probe the deeper paths of the soul, well, that it's a later form of obedience toward my father. Although it has been so internalized, has become so much a part of my own nature, that I don't suffer now from this obedience because it's become my natural life element: knowledge of the natural world . . . And then there's this surrendering up of one's own experience, one's own perceptions. Somehow, even as an adult, you really continue on like a child down odd, eccentric paths, busy with your thoughts, lost in your dreams.

B: And do you try to teach these things to your own children?

H: Yes, yes, I do.

B: As a strict disciplinarian?

H: No, I hold myself back, as the shrewd son of my father. Sometimes I've thought about that, but . . . Are you familiar with Whitman, the great American poet? Well, he developed a kind of cult in his *Leaves of Grass,* a cult with calamus. That is the aromatic, strong-smelling root of a reedlike plant. There was this big cult around it. So I showed it to my son, asked him to smell the root. He asked about it too. And on one of his last walks in the woods, with his girlfriend, he showed it to her. You know, I carry with me a piece of a root that was on his desk. It's almost a cultic emblem of recognition in this cult of male friendship in Whitman's work. A token among friends and comrades. They give it to one another as a kind of emblem, although I always viewed that with a grain of salt. I'm not one to make a church out of something like that. I don't build churches, and I'm not interested in sects. But these elementary and basic forms of behavior, I am interested in them.

B: Was your son Thomas of a timid nature when he was a young child, easily frightened?

H: No, not at all. My father would have liked him a lot. I wish Thomas had been more afraid. He was without fear. Once my younger son Isaak was with us. He was about five at the time and Thomas was perhaps eleven. Thomas had a number of guinea pigs in the front yard. Now a dog, a street dog, had worked its way under the fence and had gotten hold of a guinea pig, almost killed it, you couldn't tell. And the dog was barking, running around, and we were there too. I didn't understand what was happening, but I saw Thomas. He ran angrily up to this dog, a dog one should have been a bit afraid of, anyhow I was, and he took this dog and threw it over the fence! He tossed it right over the fence. What frightened me was that Thomas was so angry, like the good shepherd when the wolf attacks his herd. And I was so surprised at what Thomas had done. He goes and tosses a dog right back over the fence! It was absolutely astonishing. And my little son Isaak, he just said, "Wow!" He was so surprised about what was happening. Oh, well . . . My son was a very independent and fearless child.

B: You said before you would have preferred it if he'd had a bit more fear of things. What did you mean by that?

H: Fear of death too, for example. And fear of the police. There were all kinds of street battles with the police in Berlin, clashes in the street.

B: And he wasn't afraid of that?

H: But he wasn't a militant stone-thrower, except in an emergency. Then he did.

B: Were you afraid then?

H: Yes, I was. I was afraid for him. Not so much in connection with the street battles. He was very amusing in that regard. That wasn't his main interest. My fear was that in this milieu he was the smartest person around, so to speak. The fact that he wasn't together with people who were smarter than he was worried me. I think it's important for people to be together with others who are smarter than themselves. I think it's important that you don't gain social acceptance by being the smartest. And I had the impression that my son had won the love of others because of the fact that he was the smartest one among all those squatters. And that wasn't hard to do, no big deal, because a lot of the people there were almost illiterate.

B: How did you present your father to Thomas?

H: The same way I have described him to you, no differently.

B: Did he ask any questions? Did he try to clarify things?

H: As you are. In a similar way. But I . . . [*with tears in his eyes*] I didn't answer him. [*Long pause*] It's possible that we . . . we tend to want to find explanations for our lives or to develop such explanations. If unusual things have occurred in one's life, then there's a tendency to go and turn what has happened, this exceptional occurrence, into a kind of focus. I'm not sure that's right, I'm not sure. [*Crying*] I myself . . . as a small child I didn't just have a fear of dogs, I had something that is probably rather unusual for children: namely, a general fear of death, although not principally in the sense of the dangers that lurk. Rather, it was a fear of death as a fact, a given. I know it is generally said that children can't imagine that. But that was a fear that predated the fears I had in the last years with my father.

B: But you'd had direct experience of death, you'd seen dead bodies.

H: That's true. I just wanted to broach this question. It's not certain that things are connected the way one understands them oneself. It is possible that one can explain one's own life by the fact that a terrible, fateful event was in progress, that this enormous fate (Schicksal) can explain one's own life story. But it is not certain that one's own story derives only from this fate. It is also quite possible that there are individual paths of searching, which would have developed along similar lines even if there had been no catastrophe. That's quite possible. I'm not certain. People try to explain things. We know, however, just how skeptical you have to be toward all explanations.

B: What intrigues me in particular is your remark that, despite all the fear and anxiety you felt because of your father's severity, there was still a great deal of love between you and your father, that the relationship was actually quite close.

H: That may be. But that might also be the posthumous love I feel for him—a love that links up with earlier periods, with certain wishes, desires, and so on. The strange thing is the political convictions people have that then lead them to political action. In relation to the deeper layers in human beings, this view is relatively superficial. In reality there may be shared emotional structures—that shape movement, language, action—in human beings who, ideologically, are at completely opposite ends of the spectrum. It comes from the structure. You can be a Communist or a neo-Nazi, but the emotions are the same . . .

B: Did you have any inner struggle over your father's possible involvement in the euthanasia program? How the various facets of his personality were able to mesh: his strictness, his warmth, his perhaps murderous ideas, his humanistic side?

H: Yes, naturally I think about that constantly and try to explain it to myself. I have a strong anticapitalist penchant and sympathize with anarchist groups here. So I could well imagine that under other circumstances, if I were a bit less of a coward than I am, I might have become a fighter for some cause. A cause that would have been right somehow and wrong somehow. And I think that capitalism is a crime. Yes, and that much of anti-Semitism developed as a scapegoat function within capitalism. That's why I think that, in a certain respect, my father was no dilettante. Unfortunately he wasn't a Taoist either, wasn't inactive. [*Angrily*] Unfortunately he was a man, and not some person hovering exalted above all these affairs. Quite in contrast to my beloved grandfather on my mother's side, the one I spoke about earlier.

My father's father was a policeman, a Bavarian municipal policeman. He provided law and order, and on payday he'd go down and bring the married men home from the bars so that they could give their earnings to their wives. He would also check the cars and coaches. He was a gauging expert. He wore a spiked helmet and had a long Wilhelminian sword. My father was made fun of at school: "you're going to get a beating at home with the sword" . . . My father stood in some way within a tradition of duty, a Bavarian-Prussian, God-only-knows-what tradition of duty. And these were people who had a rough life, a hard time surviving. There was a certain amount of poverty. For example, my grandfather didn't earn enough to support his family as a policeman. My grandmother had to open up a business, a shop for cleaning mattress and pillow feathers. My father was the only one in the family to go to the university. And this political option was simply there as part of the times. He was a person with a strong interest in ideology. And then he was influenced by those people who were developing an ideology of breeding in eugenics, like Ploetz and whatever their names were. He fell into the trap, so to speak. But somehow that was the best trap available at the time, so that it was somehow almost a noble act to fall into that trap. He was an extremely altruistic person, a man who . . .

B: But there were also human beings he didn't care for, people he didn't even recognize as human beings . . .

H: [*As if waking from a dream*] Yes . . . who didn't he like? What do you mean?

B: Those who were weak, or the Jews . . .

H: Yes, well, the Jews, they were regarded as being very powerful— they were seen as the incarnation of all the negative characteristics of the human race.

B: But also as weak in the eyes of Nazi ideology.

H: Maybe.

B: Maybe weakness such as you had too.

H: That's possible. Younger Jews criticize the ghetto Jews, saying that they didn't put up any resistance except, say, for Warsaw and certain other isolated instances.

I shut off the tape. He invites me to have lunch with him at the TV station's cafeteria. We walk out into a beautiful garden, part of an old medieval-style castle. Helmuth is still absorbed in his own thoughts. He stops at each plant and describes its characteristics to me in detail. I sense something very fragmented in him. I can't put my finger on it, but I feel it behind his love for his father and his anger: the poetic dreamer and the analytic "plant breeder." At the self-service counter I choose prepackaged food (I think of Helmuth's fear of poisoning) and can hardly eat anything. He looks at ease; he eats a lot and becomes very expansive.

Am I a therapist? he asks. He had an experience with a woman therapist, but she only complimented him on his tenderness and understanding. She was probably overwhelmed by his fame as a poet at that time. Yes, he went to therapy with his wife, his first wife, because Thomas broke away from home: he was twelve, got bad marks at school, did not go back to school, did not tell them. When they finally found out, he ran away from home. The woman therapist said it was all due to his wife's harshness with the child. They went to her only a couple of times altogether. I try to listen politely, but I am thinking: the son gave them all these warning signals, but he, or both of them, did not want to listen. Helmuth is such a tender person; does he not know where his aggression reveals itself?

"Wait here, I want to give you something." He returns a few minutes later

with a local newspaper, which contains some of his poems. Here is his first poem about his father. He has written more than a thousand poems, he says, but this is his first poem about his father. Yes, he has been using a pseudonym since his son's death . . . memorializing Thomas by using his name. On the long train ride to Heidelberg I read the short poem over and over:

> Die Sonne
> hat meinen Vater
> Um die Ecke gebracht
> Jetzt muss ich ihm
> heimleuchten
> Tag und Nacht.

In the first three lines, the meaning is clear:

> The sun
> did my father
> in.

In the last three lines, however, the German words have a double meaning:

Now, I have to	Now, I have to
say him back	illuminate the way for him
day and night.	day and night.

An intermezzo: I pay a visit to my grandfather's house in Heidelberg. My grandfather had been a physician and a professor at the University of Heidelberg. He is buried outside the Jewish graveyard in Heidelberg because he committed suicide when my own father was fourteen years old. My father, the oldest of four children, helped his mother raise the younger ones. Still, he managed to make his way and became a physician, probably about the same time Helmuth's father finished his studies. I found myself wishing I had had the opportunity to talk with my father about those strange biological theories: how was it that he did not believe in them himself?

I cannot say that I did not suffer from my father's own biological theories. He believed, for example, that suicidal tendencies are hereditary and feared this would prove so in our family as well, a "suicide gene," as it were. He first told me about his own father's fate only when I was approaching forty. I remember being very angry that he had not mentioned it to me before. As a child I had sensed my parents' fear but could never understand it as anything but the result of my own naughtiness. "You and your theories about suicide!" I thought. "Why didn't you learn some psychological theories as well: that parents can make children feel guilty for nothing." But the incident released the tension that had always been between us. I had felt much more warmly toward him during the last years of his life and think of him now, as I travel toward his hometown.

I have a sudden urge to take a break from my intensive interviewing and stay the night in Heidelberg. I want to revisit the place where my father lived and grew up. A year ago, following my cousin's directions, I found the house on one of the most beautiful of the town's main roads. In pouring rain I stood and stared at the medical sign and the year 1908—the year my grandfather moved into this house—carved into the front wall. I was overcome by intense emotion and drove away at once. This time, I feel like walking over and trying to look in a window to see if I can recognize the wood-carved staircase my father described in his memoirs. It was a piece of true craftsmanship. His father had ordered it brought here from their old home in Mannheim.

I make a phone call at the train station announcing my delayed return to Wuppertal. Then a pleasant young woman at the tourist office directs me to a hotel ("Only one night? We have such good concerts during the season"), where I leave my things. The dark-eyed desk clerk looks at my passport and says with a grin, "From Israel. I am from Iran. But don't be afraid, I'm not one of Khomeini's people."

I walk all the way to the house, enjoying the quiet streets, the bridge over the river, the bookshops, as if coming back to an old acquaintance. When I reach it, I recognize it immediately. A single window on the second floor is lit up. I ring the doorbell, not even thinking about what I will say. I have to push the button two or three times before an elderly man opens the door. "I am from Israel," I say promptly, "and my grandfather once owned this house. Could I come in for a minute?" I am astonished at my own courage. The man in front of me seems in shock. "Please come in," he mumbles. "Lilly, we have a guest from Israel," he calls into the house, almost as if trying to exorcize the ghosts. And there I am, standing in front of the beautifully carved mahogany staircase. I am fascinated by it. I tell the man, who is still staring at me in fright, how I know about it. He calms down a bit and invites me to see the rest of the house. I walk through the corridors of my father's childhood, as if in a dream. The man and his wife, who joins him, chatter easily. How they got the house and when . . . Yes, they know about the doctor who had lived here. This was the room where he received his patients, and here, where their daughter stays when she comes to visit, was his lab . . . and this was his living room, and here the maid used to live, and these were the children's rooms . . .

I barely follow when the man tells me, as he serves me a glass of wine, that he, a Hungarian by birth, ran away from Hungary in 1944 and de-

cided to hide in Germany—from the Russians, of course. At this point it doesn't even stimulate my usual suspicions (Why did you run away? Were you serving in the Army or the SS?). I am off duty, not interested in someone else's past for a change. The elderly couple gather up the courage to ask me if I know whether my grandfather had sold the house or only transferred it to the woman from whom they bought it. Since my grandfather was dead by then, I tell them my grandmother probably gave it away for nothing.

Walking back to my hotel, I feel drained. Helmuth's poem comes back to me: "The sun did my father in. Now I have to illuminate the way for him day and night." Later, lying in bed slowly falling asleep, I have a dream: Peter, Manfred, and Helmuth are sitting with their parents in my grandfather's reception room in Heidelberg. My father and I come into the room to discuss their diagnosis with them. "You see," my father says, "I can accept that some ignorant people will commit criminal acts, carried away by mass hysteria. But tell me, you are educated people. All three of you [looking at the three fathers] swore the Hippocratic Oath, like myself. How could you have taken part in these acts?" I start to say something about their children's struggle to remain normal, that you can pretend to be normal for forty years and then one day . . . but they all start to talk at once among themselves, ignoring my remarks. I wake up sweating and shaking in the darkness of my hotel room.

chapter 4

The Camp Doll

The professor with whom I stay during my first visit to this northern university tries to be helpful, but I can see it is not easy for him. Although he has known for some time that I am interested in interviewing children of perpetrators, it is quite a while before he tells me that such a person lives just across the street. At a social gathering a few years before, this woman had mentioned that her father used to take her to work with him in "those camps" during the war and that it ended in a "very bad way." He did not request further details. "Can you introduce me to her?" I ask. "I'll have to consult my wife. I feel uneasy about it: how should I approach her on this subject? We never talked about it again."

During the next month, as I walk along this street countless times, I find myself looking at women's faces and wondering which might be hers. Behind which door does she live? In which camps had she been and what had she seen there? Why did it end "so badly"? I become more and more curious, but we do not meet. I do not even succeed in finding out if my host has tried to arrange a meeting and was refused, or if he tried at all.

When I return to the town a year later I renew my request. This time, the professor's wife says, "I will ask her." She calls me at the university later that day. "You can come and see her tonight. Please find the time, because she is very nervous about it, and if you postpone it, she might change her mind." After supper, we cross the street and stop in front of the heavy wooden door of a beautifully renovated old house. I have passed this door many times—as I suppose I have passed almost daily doors that conceal similar stories I will never hear.

Hilda opens the door and greets me with a big handshake and a smile. "Please come in. Do you want to join us for tea?" she asks the professor's wife, who declines. After some time we sit down—her husband, who has joined us, Hilda, and myself—and drink our tea. I feel a sense of uneasi-

ness in the air. I ask for permission to tape-record our meeting, and she says, "Of course!" smiling and laughing, gesticulating while she talks.

H: Seven years ago I was lucky enough to get a job writing a recreation-tips column for a widely circulated newspaper. A recreation tip might be something about museums, or painting on silk as a hobby, or . . . I can choose for myself what I want to write about, say, about games—usually I select old games, ones that have been almost forgotten. It's very popular with readers. Two years ago I wanted to stop writing because it was getting to be too much for me. *Every week* I had to write something for the paper. I was under all this pressure. Then they made me an offer where I could write twice a month, every other week. And that's worked out quite well, especially since now and then I get a commission, perhaps to do a children's book for Christmas or something. Right now I have a new project: I've been asked to do a children's book about stars. And then other things come up, so I have to do this or that. We've got this *enormous* family, and not just with the children. Anyhow, I'm the "oldest" of the five kids, then there's my husband, and we have lots and lots of friends. So somehow I've always got this feeling that I don't have enough time. Besides that, I've been working the past nine years on a voluntary basis for the social services department. I'm active in social welfare work.

What we have here in H. is a very special approach. I love to talk about it. The system was established such a long time ago. We've taken an oath. We're official volunteer workers. That's very important, because, for example, the doctor can give us information—what we deal with mainly are the elderly—and the doctor will say something like, "Keep the apartment" or "The apartment won't be needed anymore." I've been working there taking care of people on a volunteer basis for nine years.

B: Let me say something briefly about the project. I'm a visiting professor at the university and I'm directing a research project on family memories from the Third Reich. It's a topic that interests me because I have experience working with the children of victims. But I've found very little in the literature about children of victimizers, how they've come to terms with this fact, dealt with it over the years. So if you'd like to start, could you tell me something about your childhood, when and where you were born . . .

M: [*Husband*] Is this a German project?

H: [*Ignoring his question*] OK, first, I was born in July 1936 in Silesia, though I must say that neither one of my parents comes from Silesia, so I was always a stranger there. My father's family on his father's side is from the Rhineland, and my mother's whole family lives in N., in East Germany. They went to Silesia because my grandfather was a painter, and there was a porcelain factory there; he used to do drawings and designs. So in that village I was always an outsider, I didn't belong even as a child. For two years I lived on farms, and I thought that was very nice. I liked it. But, well, I dressed differently, and there were only two cars in the village—one belonged to the doctor and the other one to my father. And then we became refugees, fled, with just my mother though, and we made it to N. I was there until the Russians came in February 1945. We were on the road for three or four weeks because my mother was pregnant with my youngest brother. It was awful, when we fled. I still have dreams about that. I still see the hands of the dead lying there in the snow. So we arrived in N., and at first there wasn't any school. We stayed there until 1950. My father arranged for us to be sent to Bonn when he was released from Russian captivity as a POW. We were reunited in a legal way, though, by a nun from that resistance group, the White Rose. They helped him out. Out of defiance, I joined a youth group and was so proud. I was chosen by the whole district to participate in the May 1 march on Berlin by the Free German Youth. But we were supposed to cross over the border on April 30, so I wasn't allowed to go to Berlin and felt terribly insulted. For a long time I didn't forgive my parents for the fact that they hadn't let me go.[1]

Then I lived in Bonn, and I wasn't able to continue in school, because you had to pay school tuition fees at that time and things were rough. After that I went to a doctor, a woman doctor, and started training. I liked that a lot. And I was placed in the university clinic because I'd done so well in my exams, although I wasn't able to attend night school at that time. The only school was located in Cologne, so that wasn't possible for me. Then I got married. I went to Hamburg, from there to Bochum and in Bochum—I already had two children— I started up at night school again. Afterward, before I could start anything new, we went to Brazil. And from Brazil we came back again to this town. So the circle kind of closes itself here.

B: What do you remember from the war years?

H: Well, I should add that my father married for the second time very late in life. He was already thirty-five, and he married a very young girl; she was fourteen years younger than he was. My mother had come by bike from Thuringia to Silesia, and they wanted to set

1. Many ex-Nazis did not allow their children to go into East Germany because they suspected that the authorities had open files on them and would use the children as hostages.

up a commune, you know, with long braids and all. They were on a back-to-nature thing even back then. She had contact with the youth movement and had been quite influenced by anthroposophical ideas. So he was a man of the world from Berlin and . . .

B: You're a child from his second marriage?

H: Yes, from his second marriage. He didn't have any children from his first marriage. Anyhow, he had lived a very wild life in those years in Berlin. He wasted money as if it grew on trees, and basically he . . . he was a kind of good-for-nothing. Financially they were very well off. He had studied in Heidelberg for a time, music. Then he went into business, ran out of money, and after that he opened up a store in this village in Silesia. My mother was always busy with the children, so right after the war, I was the one who would steal potatoes, or climb up on the trains and toss down coal. My mother always had books, and she used to read things to us or light candles for an evening of music, though there was almost nothing practical that she was able to do. That was what led to my break with my father. I was in Bonn, and suddenly I was supposed to be a child again. I mean, up until then I had been the one who was trying to raise my brothers and sisters. Then, all of a sudden, when he came back from the POW camp I was supposed to behave properly and become a child again. Yes, and this is a very important point, my father had always wanted— he was thirty-six when I was born—well, he had always wanted to have a girl. So after I was born and had grown up a bit . . . I was exactly in keeping with the ideal of child beauty that was popular at the time, Shirley Temple, or whatever her name was, with curly blond hair and blue eyes. I was terribly spoiled, terribly insolent. So, for all practical purposes, I was *his* child. When it came to my brothers, for example, he didn't bother much about them. Just about me. That's why he used to take me along. I don't know how he got started on that job. Probably he was broke, or maybe it was a chance to have a real job. In any event, I was in a number of camps where he . . . I can only recall that he always said they were building the autobahn and he was the camp head. I don't know if that means anything to you. So I was in a few of these . . .

M: He wasn't the head of the camp. His job was to take care of supplies for the camps.

I can hardly keep up with her free association. She moves from her mother to her father, from her experiences in postwar Bonn to her father's love for his favorite daughter, and then to his work in the concentration camps. Her husband's correction seems to be his way of calming her down, but it puzzles her instead, and she loses her train of thought.

H: Well, I can't say for sure, I . . .

M: He was involved with the *supplies* for a number of camps. At least, that's what I know . . .

B: Can you recall the names?

H: I don't remember any of the names at all. I only know that this one camp was near Brunslau. I remember that because there's this Brunslau porcelain, from Brunslau, that's why. But where the others were . . . Though I could almost make a drawing of them. They were situated in the forest, usually closed off, and there were always these planks on the ground, wooden planks, because the ground was very boggy, and these functioned as a kind of artificial path. And in the camp that I'm thinking of right now, there were barracks up above, and a kitchen barracks, a barracks with an office, and one where I would sleep. And then there were stairs leading down, also an artificial path of some kind. Then you had, it was like a lawn, lots of grass. But out in back there was this section where I wasn't allowed to go . . .

And the one thing I remember particularly well—probably because I always had a feeling of guilt—took place when my father had to go somewhere once and wasn't able to take me along. I was pretty furious. I had a terrible temper then and was a very defiant little kid [*demonstrates with her fists*]. So I was really angry. I threw myself down on the ground and started screaming, "You won't take me, you won't take me . . ." But he wasn't able to, so I had to stay there alone.

I had tame sheep and a fox that was in a kind of pen, and I was supposed to play with them. The people in the kitchen were supposed to look after me, I guess. I started to wander around the place, because I was feeling kind of bored. I can't remember if I heard something then, or why, but I walked on down where I was absolutely forbidden to go. I went on down, and there were a lot of men standing there. I don't know whether they were in rags or . . . but I thought that these people, these men, well they looked just awful. I don't know, I just thought it was awful. The worst thing, though, was that one man was being beaten. He wasn't wearing any shirt, and the blood, you could see he was bleeding. I believe I knew him, I'd seen him at work somewhere in the camp beforehand. Then I started shouting, "Stop it, you pigs, stop it!" And I really worked them over, I was *so* angry. [*Crying, almost shouting*] Because I never got hit. We were never beaten as children. And beating someone, that was such a horrible thing to me, I mean, that you could beat another person . . . So I went over and started to hit them with my fists, striking their boots and shouting, "Stop hitting him, stop it!" Then they tried to pull me away from him. I ran away and hid. And they went out, I still remember, they went out with torches searching for me and calling. I was able to see the torches there in the darkness. I don't remember, it was one night, maybe two or three. Then my father returned. Well, from that time on . . . Before that I'd loved my father so very much, but then there was a kind of break . . .

In any case, my father was sent to the front soon after that. And these old women who were always peeling potatoes in our house, that sort of work, they used to tell me, "You're to blame for your father's being sent to the front . . ." They said things like that. And I recall that there was some kind of break then, a rupture, in our family too. My mom, for example, and I can remember this very well, because the women would say, "She ought to take it easy in that department, not carry on so much . . ." There was this special distinction under the Nazis, something called a "Motherhood Cross." I don't know if you're familiar with that. It was an award you got when you had so many children. Well, my mother said she didn't want the cross, that she wasn't having children for the sake of the Führer but rather because *she* wanted them. And when my father came back on furlough—it wasn't the last furlough but the one before his last—then they said he shouldn't say the sort of things he used to like to say. He'd say, "I'm Jewish too, I'm Ellberg the Jew, look at me and my long nose." So these old women told me, "If he goes on like that, he'll talk himself to the gallows." I remember that. But why, how, I don't know.

She is crying and talking, talking and crying, jumping from one subject to the next. She can control neither her words nor her tears, which run down her cheeks. I understand now why it was so difficult to set up this interview.

B: It was a very hard experience you had in the camp . . .

H: [*Trying to smile*] That was shortly before I started school. I was very young when I started school. I had my birthday in July and then, sometime in September, I started school. The year was . . . '41, '42? That's all I remember, though.

B: Did your father say anything to you when he returned?

H: I didn't speak to him again about this subject.

B: The people who were there, or your mother, did anyone try to talk with you afterward?

H: I think . . . the terrible thing was that I didn't get any explanation. My situation was a very special one when I was a child. I was allowed to go *everywhere*, I had this feeling that it was OK for me to go everywhere. When my father would go away during the evening, I could stay up as late as I wanted. And when they would have a party . . . It was awful, they'd have parties in this barracks, and these horrible women would come. They used to bring me dolls too, and I would throw the dolls right back at them. They used to drink, and then they'd always say, "Put her to bed!," things like that. But I didn't go to bed. So I always thought I had a right to hear something from him . . . but he didn't say anything. He didn't explain it to me. I don't know.

He could tell such wonderful fairy tales. There was always one he'd tell in installments. It would go on and on. It was the story of Gold-food, the first dragon. He was a good dragon, he loved children, and that's why I liked this story. I think we were up to the hundred and fiftieth installment. And I can remember that he wanted to tell me this story again after that incident in the camp, but I didn't want him to anymore. I was so disappointed, though maybe it was just that my childish vanity had been insulted. I don't know.

B: Did you tell this to your mother when you got back home?

H: I had very little contact with my mom at that time. My mother suffered from the fact—she told me so later on too—that I was always so cold toward her. She said that I hardly showed any emotion, any feeling. My sister, on the other hand—she's just a year and a half younger than I am—well, she was very quiet as a child, never got dirty or anything, was always my mother's baby. In contrast, I was always very wild, and actually, I only paid attention to my dad . . . But I definitely didn't tell my mother anything like that. Because I didn't tell her, for example, that I once saw my father kissing another woman when they had a party, after they'd had a few drinks. I didn't tell my mother about what went on in the camp. Later on, though, I had a closer relationship with my mother. When I had children of my own, that's when we became very close.

B: Did you talk with your father later on about any of this?

H: Let's see, I think it was the end of the 1950s or was it in the early 1960s? Anyhow, there was this program on TV, we'd just gotten a television set and for the first time there was a documentary about the Third Reich, in five or six parts, a series.

M: [*Taking charge of dates and technical details*] That must have been sometime between '57 and '59.

H: For the first time. Anyhow, we all watched this program, my brothers and sisters, with my parents. At that time I didn't watch much TV. I was always out in the evening. I wasn't at all interested in TV. But for that program I stayed home to watch. And I remember that *every* time they showed this series, well, afterward there was always a terrible argument, all of us children would leave the living room slamming the door and then go to our rooms and . . . I guess my parents used to try to explain something to us or . . . But we never accepted their explanations, though I can't remember now what was said in those discussions.

M: Criticism of the parents, nothing but criticism. To the effect that they should have known, that in any case, the program indicated that people *must* have known . . . So how could you have gone along with it? You and so many others . . .

H: Yes, and I recall that I said to them, "Well, if all of you supposedly didn't know that there were concentration camps, *I* knew it when I was just six or seven!" And then my mother said, "What do you mean, you already knew at the age of seven that there were concentration camps?" And I told her that I wasn't permitted to talk about it then because I'd sworn an oath, a solemn oath never to . . . I remember, there was this church fair. We used to call it "getting a dispensation." It was connected with sins, with the church and all. Anyhow, there was this fair, a carnival. They had a merry-go-round, different stands and booths and such. And then this girl came in a kind of Gypsy caravan. She had made some caramels. I had this beautiful pink paper, and I gave it to her as a present. I can still see us sitting there. This caravan had wooden boards like stairs going down in back. So we were sitting there. She had a rag doll—she was older than I was, I guess she was already nine or ten—and she said that nobody should touch that doll. Then she told me—and I had to swear I wouldn't tell a soul—she told me that there were others who went from town to town with the fair, they were also Gypsies, and that they'd been put in a camp and gassed. So I whispered, "But that can't be, I mean, just because they're Gypsies . . . what crime did they commit?" "No," she said, "it's *because* they're Gypsies!" And this doll she had was from some girl. The girl had given it to her as a present. Then she said, "They put the children to death there by gassing." But since I had to swear that I . . .

Hilda mimics the voice of a seven-year-old child, almost whispering the oath and the secret of the Gypsy with the doll. The story streams forth, and I wonder for a moment how much of it is real and how much is the product of her imagination. I am fascinated, however, by the events she recalls. I also wonder why, during that confrontation with her mother, she did not talk about her experiences with her father in the camps.

B: When was that?

H: Let's see, I was about seven years old, so it was 1943. So that's why I reproached my mother, "If I knew about that as a seven-year-old, then you certainly must have known." Right?

M: I'd be interested in hearing from you what your research is all about . . .

B: Later on I can go into that. So what did your mother say in reply?

H: Well, my mother said that there'd been some whispering about something like that, but that people didn't really know for sure, and that those people were mainly criminals, the camps were for criminal elements. Then I told her, "No, you know that isn't true!" And she said she did not know. She tried to put me off.

B: Did your father take part in this conversation?

H: No.

B: Did he ever talk about it later on?

H: I always had the feeling that he had a very bad conscience, that he was repressing quite a few things (verdrängte da also ganz viel). And he always said that he too could have been a Jew . . . but I thought that was all so theatrical. I didn't think what he was saying was serious. After I moved to Bonn, well, I didn't like my father so much anymore. On the contrary, I thought it was a burden, the fact that he smothered me with so much love. For instance, he didn't want me to marry. He thought we could travel together to some spa and have a nice time. I thought that was a real burden. And I had the feeling that the time he spent in the camps bothered him. I think that afterward . . . later on he suffered from asthma, and when he felt this terrible fear of dying, well, there must have been something, I always had the feeling that there was something that was troubling him a great deal. I can't say when, but I had this feeling when I was sixteen, seventeen, eighteen. I said then, "He's afraid to die because of something that's troubling him" (den belastet was, in den Tod zu gehen). I don't know whether you understand. [*Painfully*] I couldn't say concretely what it was, but at the time I despised him for that reason. Oh, and there was something else connected with this. Suddenly . . . my mother was Protestant and my father Catholic, so they were living together but not really married, I mean, in the eyes of the Catholic church. For that reason, we all had to become Catholic. They had to sign some document. But he never had anything to do with the church during that whole time. Never. Then, right toward the end, he became religious. It was a kind of insurance on his part. That's why I despised him.

B: And you never spoke with him again about this?

H: I can't recall. These memories are coming back now. Fragments. I think I repressed all of this. Just now, while we've been talking, I recalled something. They used to call me "camp doll" all the time, the people in the kitchen and the women at the parties. This expression, it's been buried [in my mind] for forty-five years. I think I repressed all of this very strongly (ganz stark verdrängt).

B: Camp doll . . .

H: Right, camp doll. Strange that it occurred to me again today. And I don't think I wanted to be that, though at the time, the expression certainly was not something negative. But when I repeat it today, well, it's like a swear word to me . . .

Hilda and I look each other in the eye for the first time, and I understand her tortured expression. Camp doll . . . she still looks a little childlike, even now. Did she ever get away from being her father's beautiful little daughter?

H: And then, when I returned from that life in the camps—I lived in those camps for a few years—then I got a governess, Aunt Wally, and she was very strict with me, because I was so wild. She was supposed to give me some polish, some manners. So I was mainly with her. I can recall that it wasn't this Aunt Wally, no, it was the old women who worked in the kitchen, they were the ones who said all the time that I was to blame for my father's having been sent to the front, or that if my father were to be killed in action, then I would be to blame—things like that. But why, I don't know . . . I didn't ask either. Because I already felt *so* guilty [*crying*] that I didn't want to show it. I always wanted to be insolent. I didn't want to show how guilty I felt. That's the reason I never asked.

M: I think topics like that were completely taboo in your family.

H: [*Looking at him angrily*] No, maybe in *your* family, but . . .

M: In our family, at home, such topics were taboo, with relatives too.

H: But it's different in my case. I was brought up differently than you were. Actually, I didn't have any "upbringing" at all. For example, I askèd my dad, "How did you make me?" My mother was embarrassed when she heard me, but he replied, "In the woods!" He told me exactly. But you would never have been able to talk to your father like that.

M: Exactly, because it was a taboo subject.

H: I don't know, I think it was more because of the feeling of guilt they inculcated in me. Even today, I still haven't gotten over this feeling of guilt.

B: After that incident in the camp, were you in any other camps or was that the last?

H: Well, I was in another camp before then, but that's what I remember. That's the end point of my life in the camps as far as I can remember.

B: Did he serve in other camps too?

H: I don't know. Probably. There's not much I remember.

B: Yet you remember much more than many others do.

H: [*Surprised*] Really, more? Oh, I do remember something else, but it's something quite different. I don't know whether it might interest you. [*Joyfully*] My grandfather, my mother's father, was director of the telegraph construction office in B. I remember that we went there once during the summer. I think I'd already been at school one year and had summer vacation. We took a trip there. My grandfather was living in a villa, the villa of the biggest Nazi in the whole district, the district commander. You just can't imagine what a disgusting person he was, and he also had a terribly disgusting daughter. I used to tease and bother her. It was the last house on the street. Then came the railroad, and behind that there was a munitions factory, something like that. In any event, my grandmother was with us. We used to sit outside all the time. There was a wall, a kind of fence and a wall, and we had these dresses with big pockets and wide sleeves. So she put a lot of sandwiches in my pockets, stuffed my pockets, and she said that when the *girls* came by—I can't remember whether she said Jewish girls or Polish girls—then I was supposed to walk along with them, as if I were marching with them, and give them the sandwiches. So I walked along with them and gave them the sandwiches.

Once, I remember, I had this pan full of cherry pie, and I divided it into pieces. Because my grandmother wasn't around, I took this cherry dessert that was meant for all of us and marched along with them and gave them pieces. Their guard wasn't able to say anything to me either, because I always used to come out of the house where the district commander lived. My grandparents lived upstairs. And I can remember that one evening my grandmother told my mother that Erich—he was my mother's oldest brother and was a Nazi—well, she said he mustn't find out about what my grandfather was doing. It was all so mysterious. I used to sit there and just listen all the time, though it was something I wasn't actually able to understand, and my imagination really caught fire hearing these things.

Hilda is full of excitement again. I can visualize her marching along with the girl prisoners. Even now her hands gesture as she relives the event.

B: What did the women who were marching past look like?

H: They were very young women, in some cases still young girls. Their clothes were torn and ragged, and they had beautiful eyes. Some of them were wearing kerchiefs on their heads, and their hair was very oily. I thought they ought to have a shampoo. Yes, and they always had a very unpleasant odor.

B: Were they always the same group of women, or did you see different groups?

H: Well, my pockets were so full I only saw them when I looked up, so I wasn't able to look at all their faces. I had to hurry too. I used to sit on the wall and wait until they were led along the path. I'd see the women guards; sometimes there were two of them. You should keep in mind that I was on the side where there was no guard. And I had to sing very loudly and pretend that I was one of the group. It was a kind of game. I had to give them the sandwiches, and if the guard looked in my direction, I would bite into a sandwich myself. I knew I had to pretend, to fake. I thought my sister was a stupid idiot, the way she always said, "No, I'm afraid to . . ." "Poor Renate," I always used to say to her, "how can you be such an idiot?" I was always a bit rambunctious.

Another thing I recall is that my grandfather played in a quartet, and he had a very big violin case. Once, shortly before we left, he took me by the hand and we went off. He was carrying his violin case. So we walked along for a while, and I can remember we went through a gate, or maybe it was an archway. Anyhow, we walked through there or walked past it. Oh, now I know, I remember, because I would always look to see if there was a horseshoe hanging there. That's why I remember it so well: there wasn't any horseshoe. Then my grandfather told me that I mustn't breathe a word of what I was going to see to a soul. He said I was his big granddaughter, I was a big girl, and I shouldn't forget what he was saying. So I swore I would. I said to him, "Cross my heart!" Then we went into an area where there were lots of small summer cabins, lots of gardens and cabins. And I can recall that a woman opened the door. I thought she looked so strange. She had a long nightgown on, with a heavy lining, and she was wearing a black skirt on top of it, with black straps. She had black hair parted down the middle, with lots of gray. And she had beautiful dark eyes. She looked at me full of love, and took me in her arms and hugged me. And I thought this was very strange, the fact that this woman who was a stranger was hugging me and crying. There was a man there too. Now the thing that struck me as being especially strange—and this is why I recall the incident—when my grandfather opened his violin case there wasn't any violin. It was full of food. I thought that was very strange.

And to show I didn't imagine all this, well, when we fled to N., my grandparents came over from B. We were all sitting around a big table, and my grandfather said that Mr.—I can't recall now, Mr. Nesselberg or Lesselberg—had saved their lives and that they had testified on his behalf. Otherwise he would have been shot by the Russians or the Poles, I'm not sure which. After that my grandfather had to go for de-Nazification. I remember that, because I always wondered what they were doing to him when he was "de-Nazified." So those are the most important memories I have.

I laugh. "What were they doing to him when he was 'de-Nazified'?" A wonderful idea for a young girl, which the grown woman succeeds in echoing.

B: This married couple, the ones he brought the food to, do you know who they were?

H: That was a Jewish couple. They had been hidden upstairs in the villa of that district commander in a dressing room. My grandparents had hidden them. And Erich, their eldest son, wasn't supposed to find out, because he was a very enthusiastic Nazi. Actually, my grandfather was also in the Party. So the best place to hide them was upstairs in the house of the district commander. Then I guess my grandfather brought them out to this cabin, this garden house. I never talked to my grandfather about it afterward, never. He only said that these people had saved his life.

B: After the war, did you ever try to find out whether they were still alive?

H: No. And I really felt a certain timidity about it afterward. I never asked my grandfather, and we never, ever spoke about it again. Only that they'd saved his life, because they had testified to the Poles—I think it was the Poles, not the Russians. And because he was the head of the telegraph construction office, he had to stay there right until the end. So they testified on his behalf. Oh, I remember, when grandfather first came there, he and Mr. Nesselberg used to play music together in a quartet, but I can't recall much else. These are the key experiences.

B: [*Warmly*] You remember a lot . . .

H: Yes, and to some extent I was really horrified when they showed *Holocaust* on TV. Our children had a very strange reaction, quite different from what I'd expected. That was because of what had happened in Brazil. Our children were only six and nine then. When they would play out in the street, the kids would always call them "Nazi pig" or "Nazi." And they came to me and asked, "What is a Nazi pig, what is it?"

B: These were children playing outside in the street?

H: Yes, Brazilians . . .

M: There are a lot of Brazilians who speak German.

H: So I told my children, "They called you a Nazi pig because they do not understand what happened here. We can't help that, it's not our fault. I was still a child, and if you didn't do anything, how could you be responsible?" And then, years later, after we watched *Holocaust* together back here, our children wrote a letter to the broadcasting authority. They wrote it together. I didn't want to interfere. The tenor of the letter was, "The time has to come when all this is over and done with." They distanced themselves from the whole matter.

M: They refuse to be affected, they refuse to get involved.

H: Yes, they are very resistant.

M: I even think they don't want to hear our stories, what the two of us know, they don't wish to remember all this. They don't even want to hear about it.

H: [*Shaking her head*] Not that, because when I talk about the war years they don't refuse to listen. No, not at all. They listen when I tell them stories about how, after the war, I used to go out stealing things, all my experiences. They enjoy listening to such stories.

B: Did you tell them about the camps?

H: Yes, I told them about that too, yes.

M: [*Persisting*] But they refuse to listen, they don't want to hear about things like that.

H: Well, I believe that's because they don't want to be the "bad" Germans. In Brazil, that aspect came up in a very pronounced way.

M: It's possible that they were also somewhat influenced by their experience in Brazil.

H: And they told me that every afternoon—I wasn't really aware of this—every afternoon when we lived in Brazil there were films about the Nazis on TV. The Germans were always portrayed so negatively in these films, always as Nazis. I don't know just how many of these films they saw. We had a maid who took care of the children. I had a lot of other things to do, so the children were often alone with this girl. And only recently I learned that they'd seen a lot of these films. They had a German teacher there—no, she was a teacher of Portuguese but she was of German background; I don't know how many generations her family had been in Brazil—anyhow, she told the children, and I only found out about this afterward, when we were back in Germany, that the Jews sit up there in New York in the press center, and all they make are films like that so the world will repeatedly see Germans being portrayed as bad.

We were viewed in Brazil as Germans from the Reich. Those whose families had been there four or five generations, why, they glorified us, you understand. Now I thought that was terrible. Once I went to the dentist, and this dentist was of German background. The family had been there for four generations. He said to me that German kids are brought up in a completely different way, that they're good children. He imagined they had qualities his children didn't have at all. Then he told me that he had been ready with his rifle to fight, but Brazil had come out against Germany in the war, and so they wouldn't let him go. I said, "Thank God, otherwise maybe the war would have lasted even longer!" Let me tell you, he was *so* insulted. Yes, well, there were various undercurrents down there. You know, I never thought so much about the Third Reich, dealt with it as much as I did in Brazil.

M: There are some very extreme Germans, ultraconservatives, who still refuse to . . . so nationalistic in orientation. I never met people here who were as nationalistic as Germans are in Brazil. That was also a very special experience for us, suddenly to see that down there.

H: They were so far removed from Germany. Distance helped them keep these notions alive.

M: Yes, right.

You learn more about a German when you live in Brazil than when you live in Germany, is it not so? Hilda goes out for more tea, and I turn to her husband, who moves between supporting his wife and looking for some "objective truth." He is involved in every detail, even when Hilda is doing most of the talking.

B: What were your experiences as a child?

M: I'd really like to hear more about the purpose of this research. If we could turn off the tape recorder a second and talk . . .

I turn off the tape and try to explain my objectives to him. He cannot understand why I, as a Jew and an Israeli, have come to Germany to carry out this research. He persists in his search for some German involvement in it. Hilda returns with the teapot. It seems that she also is full again, full of the need to talk—as if she is saying, "It is my evening, isn't it?"

H: The fact that I have such an ambivalent relationship with the Jewish people, that must be something very deep down inside me. I can remember people talking in the evening and we children listening. Well, there is one scene I recall. We had relatives who had a farm nearby, and they were apparently quite wealthy because they had these big sleds pulled by horses. I have these beautiful memories of riding outside in the winter, wrapped in fur, the moon shining. Once my aunt came to my mother, and there was all this excitement, because one of her sons, they said he was married to a Jewish girl in Berlin, and she had to go into hiding. I was listening and heard it. I always thought this woman was very beautiful. I met her once—a young and beautiful woman. But I always had this feeling that there must be something wrong with the Jews somehow, that there must really be something. Otherwise, why would they be so persecuted? And that idea simply wouldn't leave me.

Now when we arrived in Brazil, we were sitting at the airport in São Paulo, and there was a young woman sitting across from me, a woman my age. We had all these stuffed animals and dolls in our hand luggage and a four-hour stopover before the connecting flight. So this woman was sitting there across from me. Suddenly she said something, and she had such beautiful, interesting eyes. Such dark eyes. They were filled with curiosity. She started to talk to me and asked me whether we were going to stay a long time in Brazil. I told her maybe two years. Then—she had one of her daughters along—she started to talk with my children. And she said to us, "I'm Jewish, and you're the first young Germans from Germany I've ever met." To which I replied that I had never met a Jewish woman before either. After that, she told us she lived in Pôrto Alegre—that's where we were going to live too—and she sat near us on the plane. Then we just talked and talked and talked, Vera and I. She told me that her husband—he was older—was from Offenbach, and that his father had been one of the founders of the soccer team there. He had to leave Germany when he was eleven or twelve, and they went through some terrible experiences. Vera had been born in Brazil. Her family was there. We were both young women, and we got along beautifully. Then Vera gave me her telephone number and said that if I needed anything I should just ring her up. Brazilians will often tell you that. Our German-speaking neighbors had said that too, but they didn't mean it . . . Anyhow, when I really needed something, I thought, OK, give Vera a call. So I called her up, and she said, "Hey, I'll be right over!" This, although we lived very far from each other. So we became very good friends; she would sit there fixing her hair in the bedroom and we would talk and talk.

And then, one evening, her parents were supposed to come by. I was supposed to meet them. And I started to feel terribly nervous, jumpy. I had a terribly bad conscience. Her parents had fled from Germany as refugees. Now as far as Vera was concerned, there was no problem in that respect. But when it came to her parents, well, that was pretty bad. The worst thing was—and this I'll never forget—we met in front of a movie house. We used to go to the movies a lot then, in Pôrto Alegre too, and we would go out afterward for a bite to eat. So we met out in front of this movie house and decided to go in and see the film *Cabaret*. Now I had no idea what sort of a film it was. And there was this dear old grandmother, a very small and delicate person. She'd never learned how to speak Portuguese, she only knew German, she spoke such sweet German. Well, we went in to the show, and after it was over, I didn't want to see them. I felt so terribly guilty. So I ran up to the ladies' room. They were waiting. My husband was outside. They waited and waited, didn't leave, and then someone locked the toilet while I was still in there. It was getting dark. Then I started to knock, and someone finally opened the door and let me out . . . I came down and didn't want to face her grandmother. It was so terrible for me to have to face her grandmother after that movie. [*Cries for several minutes*] Yes, well, they were all still standing there when I came out. And her grandmother was so sweet. She said to me, "Oh, you little dear . . ." There was no animosity, no bad feeling against me. But when I think of it now, I still tremble, because I still have this complex all the time. No problem when it comes to young people, that's OK. But with older people, it's always a problem.

I have a similar problem in Germany. Whenever I see someone with white hair, I ask myself, "Where was he? What did he do 'then,' 'there'?"

H: Oh, and there's something else. I have a girlfriend in Hamburg. I was talking to her on the phone just before you came. That's a very strange story too. She's sixty-five now, or anyhow, over sixty. And I know definitely that she was away . . . she had to leave Hamburg for the entire period of the war. I know that she lived in London, or in England somewhere, and that she no longer has any brothers or sisters. I used to live next door to her parents, and the thing I noticed back in '62 was that her father always wore a little cap in the house. And there was a cousin, Uncle Stein. We loved him very much, and her cousin loved us.

So this isn't just a superficial friendship. Down through the years they kept coming to visit us. And, as I said, she phoned me up just yesterday and told me that she definitely had to see me again soon. She's living with a man, and we talk together, gossip a lot. Now, I know she is Jewish, but we have never spoken about it, never in all these twenty-three years. Whenever I try to probe the subject, she blocks it off. Who knows whether our friendship would end up on the rocks if . . . We never talk about it. Our children go up to visit her. She saw them when they were almost babies, watched them grow up. But there's this one taboo. We're friends, but where we come from, our background, well, she never asks me about the past, never. We've loved each other for some twenty-three years now. Actually, this is something unnatural, isn't it? It's something abnormal . . .

B: Did you ever try to break through this wall?

M: Yes, repeatedly, in a careful, cautious way . . .

H: Very carefully . . . And she knows that Vera and her husband came on a visit from Brazil, that Vera has been here many times. I told her about our Jewish friends, but she didn't say anything.

M: She can't be tempted out of her . . .

H: She can't be tempted. Our daughter lived at her place in Hamburg, and she told us that she has this seven-branched candelabrum, and books and pamphlets from the Jewish-Christian Association. She never wants to speak with me about this, never. We can talk about everything, everything, even intimate matters, and we don't need to . . . When we don't see each other, well, then she phones. She rings me up once a week, especially when she's all alone, in order to talk, you know. But there's this thing . . . though I don't think I want to upset her either.

I wonder how these people maintain such a delicate equilibrium. They need each other to keep this equilibrium stable, and wonderful friendships grow out of such a need. But Hilda is still absorbed in her Jewish experiences. I am surprised to learn that they made a visit to Israel the year before.

H: The greatest experience I had was in a kibbutz, in Israel. There was a man there who was seventy-five. He'd been born in Berlin and was a lawyer then, I think. Anyhow, he had to help out. There were a lot of groups, and because he knew German, he was asked to talk to us in German. So he spoke to the group, and then after a while we sat down and had something to drink. The group gradually got smaller; this young couple from Switzerland was still sitting with us. But at that time we weren't aware that he was Jewish and that his father had fled Germany as a refugee. And then suddenly this man started telling us . . .

M: I think he was one of the founders of the kibbutz . . .

H: Yes, he'd come there very early on with his wife . . .

M: So we sat talking until five in the morning, six or eight of us together . . . It was very, very interesting.

H: And so beautiful! We hugged each other, it was so beautiful! And the man understood me, and I understood him, although he'd been in Israel for forty years. Exactly what I said, what I'd noticed in Israel, the criticisms I had, well, he could understand.

She looks so peaceful now. She still feels this beauty *she talks about. She did not speak about her father with such warmth.*

H: Otherwise, I wouldn't have been able to talk to our young guide. He had come to Israel from Germany when he was eleven, I think. Yet he was so radical in his thinking. And I have always thought that when a people has suffered so much, it ought to become very tolerant. Suffering must soften [the heart]. And I just couldn't understand it when he said things like, "Naturally that man [an Arab] has to be arrested." Sure, I could also appreciate that there is this complicated situation in the Old City in Jerusalem, that bombs are thrown and . . . So my feelings were running hot and cold, up and down, back and forth. It was terrible.

As soon as I met older people and talked to them—those who actually experienced all that suffering, people from Germany who had emigrated—well, these older people were so kind, so forgiving, but what disturbed me was the younger generation. For example, we flew from Jerusalem to Eilat; in this case too, it was a man originally from Germany who helped us arrange things. His son let us have his apartment. And this man was so warm and kind, so full of human feeling. I was very touched by all the effort he took to help us fly down to Eilat.

And in Eilat, we were living alone in this apartment. It was in a block of flats, a residential area . . . Anyhow, what I thought was so terrible was that these young people found such pleasure in handling weapons. They used to shoot, and some pigeons would come tumbling down. I always had such a fright! Or when we were at the beach there'd be a soldier on guard, and somehow they were always shooting. There were always these weapons around, and that frightened me, frightened me a lot. Then there were these roadblocks, and young boys—they weren't more than fifteen!—and they all had guns, and they searched the car, and I felt terribly . . .

M: That made a negative impression on us. It brought us back to these memories of Germany . . .

H: Yes, and we weren't allowed to say that here either. Because when you come back from Israel, then everything has to be nice. You have to tell everyone it was beautiful. That's the bad thing. But we can tell you, even if you get a little upset with us [*laughs*]. That was the experience we had. Which is why this trip haunts me so. I always wanted to analyze this. I wanted to think everything there was fine and beautiful . . .

I welcome their confidence in me yet feel exhausted. After I shut off the tape, they continue talking until two in the morning. Hilda's husband tells me about his family, and she comes in with more tea and more stories of her own. But I cannot absorb any more. For me, the image of the little girl running and hiding in the woods is all I can take in one evening.

It was true for them too. I write Hilda from Israel and thank her for the interview, but I get no answer. When I come back a year later, they do not want to see me again. We meet from time to time in the street, and they are always very polite, but I feel that the subject is closed. Hilda tells my host's wife that I was a very kind listener, but that she got too excited. She can't handle it again. Whenever I pass their door, the image of her face—her sweetness—comes to me, as she said, "They used to call me camp doll."

chapter 5

The Hidden King

It is my first research trip to Germany. I am a guest of the local university, and my host, Professor O, has arranged everything: I have an office, a friendly assistant, and taping equipment. Everyone is trying to make my stay as comfortable as possible, yet I also sense curiosity, even suspicion: What am I really after? What will I uncover?

My host tells me about a member of the faculty whom he thinks I might want to interview, but he is not able to give me any details. He does not know who her father was, only that she lives under a pseudonym.

Several days later he stops by my office. Gerda is willing to see me, but only if he is present. And she has another condition: that I do not try to find out who her father was. She will not answer any questions in connection with his identity. I consent to her conditions, but I also wonder what she is afraid of: The fact that I am a Jew? A psychologist? That I am interested in uncovering the aftereffects of Germany's recent past?

As Professor O and I climb the narrow staircase to Gerda's top-floor apartment, he tells me that she is single and has lived here since she received tenure at the university many years before. When we enter, I am amazed at the smallness of the apartment and its monastic simplicity. An elderly woman with very blue eyes, wearing thick glasses, introduces herself, and I feel her cold hand. She is reluctant about the tape-recording procedure, but "as a scientist," she says, "I can't refuse." She is clearly as uncomfortable with me as she is at ease with Professor O.

G: I was in Berlin last June. I had to visit a federal training institute and took the night train, so I was left with some time in the morning and went over to see again where we had lived. The official apartment has been divided up since then; that took a long time because it wasn't clear who the owners were. I found the same ambience, yes, but, well, very little that was concrete. Anyhow, I didn't ask about it then, I just went back to make sure it was really the way I remembered it.

B: In West Berlin?

G: Yes. I lived there for a time during the war, '41 or '42 until '44.

B: Did you move to Berlin at that time or had you been there before?

G: I was sixteen when my parents divorced. And I lived with my mother, mainly with her from then on. But I also lived for about two years—yes, I believe two—with my father because I was apprenticed as a trainee at the newspaper. We lived in the country, then in Cologne, in Munich, and later on I lived with my mother in Bonn.

B: And then you went to stay with your father in Berlin?

G: Yes. In between I was also a student.

B: Do you have any brothers and sisters?

G: They are all much younger, much younger.

B: You are the oldest?

G: I'm the oldest and the only child from that marriage.

B: And your mother remarried?

G: No.

B: Your father?

G: My father, yes.

B: Maybe you could begin with your memories of your early years, your parents . . .

G: Well, I already told Mr. O that basically, I have a kind of "black-out," a blank between the ages of eight and eighteen.

B: Why those specific years?

G: Well . . . give or take a bit. I remember the primary school in the country, but I can recall much, much less about the following two years at elementary school in Cologne, and even less about school in Munich and then in Bonn. But I think that has less to do with political things and more with the fact that my mother was a very religious woman. There was a lot of tension, although my mother always stuck by my father, even after the war. One thing was certainly very important to me: I couldn't stand it when people spoke badly about my father. I guess I was affected by the tension that existed—not consciously, but half-consciously—and I think the black-out is connected with that.

In addition, my mother was a very level-headed person, not easily excitable. It was much easier for my father to become enthusiastic about something. I like to tell this story [*smiling to herself*] . . . it certainly didn't happen exactly this way but I think it's quite typical of my parents. My mother was an excellent housewife, yet she was actually the one who made it possible for me to go to high school, all the way through to matriculation tests and graduation (Abitur), while my dad, well, at that time he would have been quite satisfied if I had left with a tenth-grade certificate (Mittlere Reife). When I finally did graduate, my father was really enthusiastic, and I like to tell the story that he said, "How about that? Would you have believed it? Would you have expected it?" To which my mother replied, "Of course, certainly!" [*Laughs*] I think that in the whole spiritual sphere, and also when it comes to temperament, their whole view of life, well, there were big differences between them. And I figure that affected me, influenced me. And I remember that. I must have been seven or eight. I was born in 1922, so that must have been before '33.

She appears surprisingly open. Not everyone would tell a stranger about the differences between parents or about their divorce with such simplicity and apparent sincerity. I notice that she still thinks a lot of her father, but I do not yet know his identity, and if, or why, people "spoke badly" about him.

B: Could you say something about what you did as a small child?

G: I can't really remember things from that period very well. I'd have to go to a psychoanalyst first [*laughs*]. As a child and young person, I was very attached to my father, very much so. For me he was the most important person. For instance, he'd take me along to meetings, and then I'd play outside somewhere if it was out in the country. I'd play and wait for him, and I can remember driving home at night in the dark and the headlights on the road. With my mother, there was just normal, everyday life, but with my father, well, it was something special.

B: Those were Nazi meetings?

G: Right, yes, certainly.

B: Did he tell his daughter anything?

G: I don't remember much. He certainly did . . . he certainly . . . Actually, what I can recall better are his own World War I experiences, the stories that would be told and repeated. He was an aerial observer during the First World War. He was shot down and captured. And it's also part of our family history: his leg was supposed to be amputated. He struggled [against it], then they operated and did not take it off, but he was so far gone, well, he had this experience of being almost dead. And that was a very important experience for him. He didn't come back from World War I until quite late. All that played a decisive role in shaping the political path he took later on. But I remember very little about anything political. Later on, I read the introduction to *Mein Kampf,* you know? [*Laughs*] It was a compulsory thing, for school. And I didn't retain much of it. I myself only made it to representative of the head of the girl's organization (Mädchenschaft).

B: Well, sometimes when you travel with your father—I've had this experience—he gets to talking and tells about things that are on his mind . . .

G: Yes, of course. Well, we weren't alone on these trips. There were subordinates too—well, before '33 certainly not—but there were others along in the car, and they definitely talked among themselves about what interested them, and then there was this child sitting there between them all. When I look back, I'd rather say that—Mr. O can say whether or not I'm right about this—but I think that I grew up to an unusual degree surrounded by men, and maybe for that reason, psychologically, I don't have the . . . I mean, I didn't live so much in a woman's world, but also . . . You know me today. I think I don't have many problems at work when it comes to men. What would you say, Mr. O?

O: [*Laughs*] That's how I'd see it too. I agree.

B: So you have that as a result of being with your father? You got it from him?

G: Yes, the trips . . . During my childhood, one of his subordinates lived with us in Munich, and the others used to come and go quite a lot. So I guess I had more contact with men, and there were drivers, people like that . . . on the job. It was known at home that when my father wanted to relax and his subordinates were around, then, well, Gerda would put on a little show, and . . .

B: At home?

G: Yes, certainly. And my father had this warmth, he was so emotional. Didn't I tell you [*turns to Professor O, laughing to herself*] how he punished me once?

O: No, I don't remember.

G: Well, I was four or five. We lived in a row house, and my parents were somewhere in the neighborhood taking a look at a new room at a friend's place. I can only retell the story now based on what I've heard from others, but it was a very profound experience, which I've retained. Well, I was all alone, so I got up and put on the lights and went down to stand at the front door. At that time there used to be these private nightwatchmen. I was wearing my hair the way I do now, a similar style. Anyhow, this nightwatchman went on over and he said to my parents, "You've got to come home. Your little boy is downstairs in the doorway." And now I have this memory: I'm standing there at the top of the stairs, and someone is coming up the stairs in a threatening manner, you know what I mean? Well, that's the only time he spanked me, but then afterward he said he'd never do it again, that he was very sorry.

B: That's what you remember?

G: Yes. While my mother often had a big spoon handy, at the dinner table at noon, because when my father came home then—he had a completely different profession at the time—the meal had to be on the table. Afterward he'd lie down for a while on the couch and I'd lie down beside him. It was the only way to keep me quiet. And he'd fall asleep, because in the evening he'd go to Party meetings and wouldn't come back until very late or very early the next morning.

B: Quite a picture, the two of you . . .

G: Well, I don't know whether I've answered your question. That's also the way he behaved politically too. Verbally, emotionally . . .

B: Can you give me an example?

G: No . . . Party doctrines . . . clichés, really. There were these maxims in the family too. One was that he had always encouraged me, I can't give you a direct example, but that he'd encouraged me to argue with him about things, not topics from the Party, matters like that, but rather things we'd be having in classes at school, literature. That he'd tried to get me to argue and to stand on my own. On the one hand, he would say, "My daughter can do what she wants." But on the other hand, if there was just a letter from some soldier, not even a real relationship, just a few letters—like when I was twenty, later on during the war—well, then he'd have someone look into it to find out who'd written, who he was. Then there'd be a call, "Her father says such and such." Now that wasn't particularly positive or encouraging, if you get what I mean . . .

B: What was your father's job?

G: Well, he was . . . he . . . he had a lot to do with organizational things.

B: Special tasks?

G: [*Laughs*] Well, in the area where he . . . you could say that more generally it had to do with labor, and there was a lot to do with labor at that time, you know what I mean?

Indeed, "there was a lot to do with labor."

B: Was he an organizer in the extermination camp system?

G: [*Agitated*] No, no, no, no. Nothing in any area like that. It was in the civilian sphere. That is probably why my own professional interest grew in that direction as well. And I certainly picked up . . . you asked how my parents influenced me. I'm very sure that from both of them, from very different sources, I got an interest in social questions. Both of them were very open . . . and I think with my mother it was the religious element. My father came from a background of small farmers, and only with his family's help was he able to study, the only one at that time, and then there were his war experiences . . . and there was very little motivation for my father to join the Party. So if you ask what I have from my father, I'd say definitely, without a doubt, it's that interest in social questions.

B: Are they still alive?

G: No, neither of them is alive.

B: Where did they come from? On your mother's side? And your father's?

G: I mentioned that on my father's side, it was a family of small farmers. He was the second youngest of eight children. My mother came from a farming family that was somewhat better off financially. They had a farm and a tannery as well. My mother's family was considered "landed gentry."

B: Can you still remember your uncles and aunts?

G: Yes, very well, on both sides.

B: Did you have much contact with them?

G: Well, in these farming families there was always a lot of contact, keeping together. That continued right on into the war and after. We got something from the family of one of my father's brothers—we'd always get a little something in those difficult years right after the war—and I stayed at a cousin's farm back in 1945. And when I was a student in the early 1950s and was working during vacations, I'd live with other members of the family. That was . . . it wasn't like it is today, you know? [*Laughs*]

B: Do you recall how your family reacted to political issues at that time?

G: Yes, I think basically . . . they accepted my father's opinions.

B: And what sort of conversations did you have with your father during that period?

G: Well, generally what was talked about were private matters, family affairs. I certainly was no simple and easy daughter for my father, and I think that's probably connected with the fact that I used to go along with him way back in early childhood. So we took each other very seriously, as individuals, you know what I mean?

B: You say you weren't an easy daughter to have around. What did you do?

G: [*Laughs*] I wasn't an easy daughter because—Mr. O can probably confirm what I'm saying. [*Laughs*] Well, how should I put it? I was critical in the sense that at the time I tried very hard, quite unconsciously, to be independent. And sometimes I think that if my father had lived longer, it might possibly have led to conflicts, if you know what I mean. And later on, this sense of independence led to my being quite critical. And it's possibly also connected with my mother too: she never deviated, as the expression goes, from her "traditional role" as a woman, yet she was also very independent. So that at a very early age I knew I wasn't going to travel the typical—and what is typical?—well, the route of being a wife and all that. I knew exactly what I didn't want. I didn't know what I did want. And then my father remarried, in 1938.

B: And during the war, your father was . . .

G: A lot of work and worry, a lot of work and worry, and a great deal of not knowing. Not knowing, ignorance to an extent that an outsider would find hard to imagine.

B: Can you give me an example?

She pauses for several minutes, and I can see that she is groping for words. Is she trying to find a way to tell me that, although he was at the top, her father did not know about the extermination process?

G: It's hard for me to pin that down to a specific, single point. But it was connected with the fact that communication between *them* was very limited, very limited. For example, I think he assumed for a long time that this secret miracle weapon, what they called the "miracle bomb," actually did exist. He thought so for a long time, and when he learned that it didn't, it was terrible for him. He almost collapsed.

B: And he told you about it, when he suddenly found out it did not exist?

G: Yes . . . he told me . . .

B: When did he hear about it?

G: I can't tell you exactly. But it was very late, I think it was during the winter of 1944–45. And I think—let me say it once again—you just can't imagine how isolated individual people were, the sections, departments, or whatever you want to call them.

B: Did you hear anything from your father about the persecution of Jews?

G: No, I didn't. Because I didn't see any of that.

She is not answering the question.

B: How were you affected by your father's status?

G: I think that's the problem every generation has: it can't pass on its sum of experience, or can do so only to a very limited extent, because young people have very different sorts of problems. For example, my problem, let me put it this way, was that my father's second wife and her family were from a totally different background. They were theater people, singers, actors, and they tried hard, and it was well-meaning on their part, to make a little lady out of me—a hopeless task! [*Laughs*] And those are the problems you had at that age . . . So I don't think I heard much about other things. In any event, there were these tensions between my parents. Much later on, for instance, I came across a letter from a family I spent a lot of time with as a small child, and in the letter the woman wrote that she was so terribly unhappy. Well, I suppose private life does go on . . .

B: The persecution of the Jews. It would interest me . . . were you aware of it?

G: No.

B: Let's start with the question: Did you know any Jews?

G: [*Reluctantly*] I've already told Mr. O that I certainly had some Jewish classmates, girls at school.

B: You say "certainly." Why?

G: Well, because in the 1930s, in the school in Munich where I was, later one or two [students] weren't around anymore. But I don't think they were sent to a camp. I believe they were able to leave the country.

B: You think so?

G: All I can say is that I believe that was what happened. I think I mentioned before that this thing wasn't talked about at home. The first time I heard about the persecution of the Jews was in February or March 1945, and then not within the family but while we were on the road going west from Berlin, from soldiers who took us along for part of the way.

B: Can you tell me something about that?

G: It must have been near the Oranienburg camp, and that started one of them talking about what had happened in the east.

B: Can you recall what they said?

G: They talked to get things off their chest. I mean, as a third party, I'm not sure I should say anything . . . They talked to relieve their consciences. That's how I knew about this. I heard about it from them before the end of the war.

B: Did they talk about how some were shot?

G: Yes, shootings. How they were . . . that's how I knew, before the war was over, what had happened . . .

B: Any more details?

G: Yes, that was in such a general . . . terrible . . . The image I have before me is a village the Russians had occupied, and when it was liberated by the Germans, the Russians showed them where the women were hiding and . . . people hanging from a tree . . .

B: And didn't you go to your father and ask him?

G: No. My father was no longer around then.

B: How come?

G: He killed himself in 1945 . . . under terrible circumstances.

It is a difficult moment. I can see the sorrow in her eyes as she utters these words.

B: [*Pauses*] Do you think he knew and didn't tell you? Or do you believe he knew nothing?

G: I just can't say. I don't think—and I was never told—that he was personally involved in the killing of Jews.

B: He didn't know about it?

G: Well, that he had anyone sent to a camp.

B: I asked if he knew about the persecution and extermination of the Jews.

G: I don't believe he had that done.

B: And he didn't know about it?

O: That he was actively involved in having someone sent to a camp.

G: Yes, right.

O: Perhaps he knew about it, but . . .

B: . . . didn't have anything to do with it?

G: Yes.

Her father knew about the extermination of Jews, but he had nothing to do with it. I would like to hear how she feels about it, but she does not say anything. Perhaps she understands that once these thoughts penetrate into her consciousness, she will find it impossible to sustain her favorable childhood image of her father.

G: Well, after the war I had to confront the problem, the political thing. And actually, I only consciously registered the presence of Jews for the first time then, you understand. With considerable inhibition . . . Even today I can't have a natural, relaxed response in that connection. That's very clear. But there were Jews who were helpful, and I had other experiences too . . . for example—did I mention this to you? [*turns to Mr. O*]—there was that Jewish bank director who came back. He helped us. My mother and I had received a house after the divorce. Naturally, this house initially . . . well, it wasn't given back to us after the war. So he helped us in this matter.

But I also had an experience in an office once where somebody said, "Actually you shouldn't even be alive today. They should have killed you too!" So I'm surprised myself. Whenever there is anything, anything at all that has any connection, however remote or however irrational, with all this, I react immediately. I can deal, let's say, with people I meet on a private or job-related level. I can do that, handle that . . . But even today, if a Jew approaches me as a Jew, I can't handle that, can't deal with it. It's impossible.

B: What happened then?

G: Well, then there's . . . I . . . it's hard for me . . .

O: Was it hard for you, the idea of Dr. Bar-On coming here? That's very interesting to me. Now we know each other a little better. I'm not so familiar with the problem. I'm younger than you are.

Surprised at the professor's intervention, she ignores his question.

G: Once I was in Romania, in the Carpathian Mountains, on vacation, and quite a number of Jewish guests were staying at this hotel too, people who had gone to Israel. They like to come back on vacation, like to go to a spa and all that. And I had no problem whatsoever [*looks very uncomfortable*]. They spoke German mainly, and it was on another level, you understand? But once, toward the end of the 1950s, I had to deliver a paper at a professional conference. So there was one of them and myself. I think he had grown up in Israel. In any case, he presented this in a very provocative manner. "As a Jew . . . when I come back to Germany . . ." I couldn't deal with it at all, you understand? I didn't know what to say, I lost my entire train of thought, I was unable to discuss anything with him, to explore the matter . . . nothing.

Gerda's body language expresses what she cannot say: how terrible she feels, torn between her love for her father and her reaction to the Nazis' policy toward the Jews. She sits twisted up in her chair.

B: Were you able to tell him about your own past?

G: No. At the time that would have been completely impossible. I told Mr. O a while ago that I experienced certain feelings until 1950, and it was very clear and distinct again at the time of the Eichmann trial.

B: It is hard to talk about such emotions. The Third Reich no longer exists and . . .

G: [*Sighs*] Well, I told you that my mother was very cool, very level-headed. She was someone who always had her two feet firmly planted, you know what I mean? Who continued to live her normal middle-class life just as before, so in that respect it was not a problem. Well, I mean, nobody had anything, you understand? So, I had problems for the first time then, but I'm not the only one who had them. I think men who came back from the war had more problems than I did. Suddenly life was without all that tension . . .

B: Without all that tension or without all that meaning?

G: [*Surprised*] No, not meaningless. Rather, in those last few months, it was . . . well, basically they were living beyond the limit of what was normal . . . and then to return to this normality. I would guess that many men just couldn't handle it. In the beginning, that wasn't . . . that was . . . well, it wasn't meaningless. Politically, then, I had to confront matters, things like the persecution of the Jews, things I can't confront and deal with on a rational level. So for that reason . . . well, what can you do? For example, for a long time I didn't vote for any party.

O: You mean a world falls apart and . . .?

G: No.

O: To compare that with my parents . . .

G: No!

I am surprised at her aggressive tone.

B: Why not?

G: I think I'd put it this way. [*Laughs*] The education I received was in terms of a very fixed and definite set of norms and values. It was Protestant, pietistic. No one ever asked me, but naturally, from the age of fourteen until I was in my midtwenties I thought the norms and values of my parents were terrible, and I rebelled against that a lot. Who doesn't? [*Laughs*] But in the last twenty years, during my professional career, I've actually come to appreciate more and more what that really means for a person. I mean, when I hear young people talking about self-realization and all that, then . . . Well, not only my mother came from this background, my father did as well. Maybe the influence in his case was not as strong as in my mother's case, but it was there. My father went to Sunday services through the influence of my grandmother on my mother's side. But he knew, in any case, starting from the winter of 1944–45.

I try to make sense of the bits and pieces of her monologue. Is she now trying to examine, in her own mind, her family beliefs, her deep admiration for her father (and his belief in God), and what she calls the "political issue"?

B: Can you tell me about it?

G: Maybe at that time he couldn't go on. And he thought, "If I have a small daughter, and maybe I can't go on . . ." [*Long pause*] He certainly did hope that we'd stick together as a family. And he said goodbye. The father I remember was very human, very much so (er war so ein Mensch).

B: It's hard to imagine how your father took his leave, how he said farewell.

G: When Mr. O asked me that question, I told him that it was certainly very important to me that my mother stayed the same, that she had the same opinion before and after. She was, well, let's say, vis-à-vis my father, she was very cool, level-headed, something like a family legend. Once my dad was promoted—I was still a child, before 1933—and someone at home, who is still around, likes to tell the story. My mother just stood there and said, "Well, sew him a fancy little braided ribbon."

O: She was a little disrespectful about the whole thing?

G: Well, that was one side of my mother's character. But after the war she would also say things like, "I can't stand it when people speak badly about him." That was certainly very important to me. On the other hand, it was not until the early 1950s that I was given permission to study . . .

B: Because of your father?

G: Well, naturally it wasn't presented that way, you understand, but doors were simply closed, if you know what I mean. At the beginning of the 1950s I was in such a state that I stood in front of a psychiatrist's door, but I turned around and didn't go in. Because that's all just part of my life, a chapter that's closed. Maybe it was closed too tight. Perhaps now, after so many years, I'm in a position to deal with it more. It took me a long time to break free emotionally from this, and you can see that I'm an individual, how should I put it? And to try to . . .

B: I hear you asking yourself, "Do I have the right to be an individual in my own right, an independent person?"

She seems moved by my formulation.

G: I don't follow you. Finish what you were saying.

B: Whether at the back of your mind there isn't the question: Can I allow myself to be an independent person, an individual in my own right? Do I have the right to start to live my own life at last?

G: [*Sighs*] Yes, that's . . . that's very true.

O: A complicated question.

G: And I think I've tried to express my problem several times now: I just can't deal with it rationally.

B: Has it become any different in recent years?

G: Yes, today younger people don't associate me much with it. And I had the impression recently, in connection with the fortieth anniversary [of the end of the war] that there was actually more of a feeling that things were not so black and white, that maybe now, slowly, things are starting to be looked at with more discrimination, with more differentiation.

B: What do you mean?

G: Well, how should I put it? That people are capable of doing all kinds of extreme things, acts they can't predict and which they don't consciously want to do. So that it's seen in a more differentiated way.

B: Could you be a bit more specific?

G: Well, after the war I tried to inform myself by turning to historians who, as far as I could judge, presented things . . . objectively isn't the right word . . . let's say, in a balanced fashion. And I found that on the occasion of the fortieth anniversary, there were some programs on TV . . . this mixture of weekly newsreels, eyewitness statements of the time, things like that, and I could understand it. But many other things were very abstruse . . .

O: Which have to do with National Socialism?

G: Yes.

The daylight has faded, but Gerda does not turn on the lights, and we sit in half-darkness. I realize that the interview is effectively over, although I feel we are only at the beginning of something. I wish I could persuade her to come to my office at the university to continue the conversation without Professor O.

B: I just want to thank you for this interview. Some of the things I've learned about here, the personal fate of children of the Nazis, what has been repressed . . . it's a terrible fate in my eyes.

O: I have a question, though I think you answered it once when we first met: Why did you change your name? Was that to avoid being approached with questions about your father?

G: I think that otherwise, well, I wouldn't have been able to study. What has helped me these past fifteen years in respect to myself as a person, is that my colleagues on the job, they know about it more or less. It was never broached as a topic, and my colleagues have really been very friendly. I think that was an element, a factor that acted as a stabilizer and gave me confidence. And I think the fact that I did not marry . . . it's all connected. I think that if I weren't busy with my job, I could deal with that again. But at the moment there are still obstacles, barriers. I'm still working, so I just couldn't, I . . . I can only do one thing at a time. And I'll just say that quite openly to my therapist [*looks at me with humor in her eyes*]: I'm afraid and have misgivings about going on and opening all that up again after it's been closed off. And I don't know to what extent I can deal with it.

B: We all have such fears. Two different forces. On the one hand, we'd like to be free of the burden, but on the other hand, we're afraid that maybe our life won't be quite as worthwhile and perhaps even as meaningful.

G: As far as being less meaningful, I'm not worried about that. But there is the fear of having to try to do things, of confronting matters once again, with a feeling of guilt.

We walk out into the darkness. That night I phone a historian who has helped me before in identifying parents who were perpetrators. Within two hours, we believe we know who Gerda's father was. I have unwittingly interviewed the child of one of Hitler's closest associates. Did Gerda try to fool me, or does she really believe that her father did not know about the extermination of Jews before the winter of 1944–45? How could that be true of such a close friend of the Führer? The next day I look through several history books, where her father's hatred for Jews is graphically recorded. Has she never read or heard about his public speeches?

I sense in this woman the high moral standard so appreciated by her colleagues, yet she has not uttered a single word of criticism about her father's part in the Third Reich. Am I encountering a new form of blocking?

She agrees to talk with me again, and the two of us meet in my office a week later. We now play a chess game with a hidden king: I know who her father was. Still, the second interview is very similar to the first. She talks quite frankly and openly about her own life: her relationships with her father and mother; the hard times she had after the war in trying to pursue her career while her family, and society as a whole, were somehow against her. Once again not one word of criticism about her father or his activities under the Nazi regime, only some general comments about how difficult it is for her to confront "certain issues," especially those connected with the Jews. When I try to press her about these matters, she closes up immediately and says, "I have told you, Professor Bar-On, that I am willing to go with you only part of the way. If you do not like it, we can stop now." She feels that her father was presented in a distorted manner by historians after the war and that it is her duty to reveal his true, humane nature. I can sense that she likes talking with me here more than she did during our first interview in her tiny apartment; she does not hurry to conclude our conversation. It is I who become more and more impatient.

We meet again a year later. She says she has something for me and tells me she has been wanting to thank me. She feels that because of our conversations the year before, she has been able to return to some of the unresolved issues in her past and work them through. She is also willing to disclose her father's identity to me. "Did you know already?" She looks at me without surprise when I tell her that I knew even before our last meeting. She says she wants to send me something her father wrote before he committed suicide. She then tells me in detail about a party she has recalled lately, which took

place close to the end of the war. When someone spoke about the extermina-
tion of the Jews, her father interrupted the conversation and said, "We will
never be forgiven for what we have done to them." She repeats her earlier
comment that he was such a Mensch, *even if too emotional sometimes, and*
states again that most people have a wrong perception of him. She is now in
touch with a German historian who has been working on a biography of her
father for the last ten years. He will present her father's different sides accu-
rately, she thinks, closer to the way she herself remembers him.

The next day I find the document Gerda mentioned in my mailbox. It is
her father's "Political Will and Testament."

Do I have any right, after this singular catastrophe, the subject of which is the unfortunate German people, to address that
heroic people? Because many—and I have no illusions in this
regard—many will also accuse me of being among those responsible. I also wish to accept and bear that responsibility. I don't
want to shirk it as a coward might . . .

I have learned to see in all things a fateful design of Provi-
dence. My own obstinacy, my inner strength of will have been
totally crushed and broken. And so I surrender myself uncon-
ditionally into the hands of my Creator, awaiting what he has in
store for me. What he ordains, may that come to pass. He will
also give me the strength to bear it.

God led me to Hitler. God gave me the power of persuasion,
in speech and thought, to win over other human beings . . . It
was God who caused me to write those stirring articles during
the war. It was God who let me fall, it was he who brought me
into this lonely, cold, and bare cell. It was he who caused me to
become nothing, he humbled me as another human being sel-
dom can. He will lead me onward.

That is why I believe, my German people, that God, our Lord,
is now moving me to write these lines, which I address to you.
They are the product of a long period of brooding, which led
me to the brink of madness and despair. Again and again, the
same question: why, what for, because of what? I tried to discover mistakes that were made, omissions, false and pernicious
things. I tested myself, tested the others. My self-criticism did
not shy away from anything, not even from the most exalted
thing I possess on this earth—my memory of the dead Führer. I
have literally tormented and tortured myself. And, aside from
those human weaknesses that are present everywhere, I repeatedly come again and again to the following conclusion: *We aban-*
doned God, and that is why he abandoned us. In place of his divine
grace, we set our human will. And in anti-Semitism we trans-
gressed against a fundamental principle of his creation. Our will

had become defiance. Our anti-Semitic defense turned into a dominating complex.

Today, as I look back on it all, I realize this and could give dozens of examples of just how debilitating, and indeed how fateful, these two factors have become for us. Because of them, we saw many things wrongly. Because of them, we evaluated the situation erroneously. And missed opportunities that could have altered our fate. *The anti-Semitic spectacles on the nose of obstinate, foolhardy men were a disaster.* That must be stated clearly once and for all, courageously. There is no use whatsoever in beating around the bush. Or burying oneself even deeper in defiance, or even apathy. There is a reason for everything, and our catastrophe has its reasons too. If it is true that success is the only proof of the correctness of an idea, then failure is proof that mistakes were made somewhere. In all positive matters, National Socialism was important, great, and powerful. It will prevail, despite everything. In the negative things, in anti-Semitism, it was important only as long as what was involved was a necessary defense against being inundated by Jews, especially from the East. And as long as what was involved was the need to combat excesses. [Illegible addition.] Everything else was an evil that finally led to those blinders that stole our sight from us . . .

It is certainly bitter and difficult to admit mistakes. There are some who will accuse me of treason. Yet it is better to accept that charge and tell the truth than to stick obstinately and stubbornly to certain fundamental positions. *What is at stake here is the very substance of our people.* Political unity has been smashed, a Reich of a thousand years has been lost. Should the substance of Germany now also be lost because we lack the courage to shake off that anti-Semitism that we so stubbornly pursued? We National Socialists must have that courage. Our youth do not believe our adversaries. Should this magnificent German youth now go down to its ruin, as did ancient Carthage? *Never.* Fate can demand my life, yet if I can but be granted a chance to prevent the terrible decline of the substance of the German people by a courageous statement of belief, then I will gladly bear this suffering. Structures may snap and break, many men may fall, parties and systems pass away—*yet the people must remain and live on.* In order to be successful, we must take this step totally. It is not enough to say that we no longer wish to talk about anti-Semitism, that we will put up with Jews, that we are forced by necessity to do so. No, we must take this step completely and totally. Half-hearted measures are useless. *We must remove distrust* by encountering Jews with an open heart, on a new basis. We must *clear up* our mutual relationship. Without reservations, without inner inhibitions, Germans and Jews must find the way back to each other once again. To mutual reconciliation. They must found a new life together on the basis of their advanced knowledge. And agree to this for all time to come.

This clarification in worldview has priority above any efforts toward economic and cultural reconstruction. And the sooner one finds the courage for this, and the more courageously these matters are recognized, the better it will be for our people. Either they eradicate us, or we are prepared to take this step. A defiant hesitation is useless in this instance. And even less a belief in miracles. The only thing that can be of value here is to push on boldly down the path that has been embarked upon.

The Jew should also learn from this. At the moment he holds the trump card. He can eradicate and destroy the National Socialist leadership. He can bring me and others to the gallows. But he cannot destroy eighty million Germans. Nor can he suddenly conjure up paradise in order to buy the Germans with it. The more the Jew rages with revenge, the more martyrs he creates. The more embittered enemies he makes for himself. Because each new suffering engenders new feelings of revenge in almost every German family. Today almost all of Germany has been affected. Does anyone believe that in this way anti-Semitism can be stamped out? *It will only be strengthened and stirred up.* Added to this is the national pride of the Germans. People will point to the great accomplishments of National Socialism. Youth, lacking any other ideal, will cling all the more strongly to the old ideals. The Jews who were expelled will not be able to return without any worries, but rather will find themselves confronted with a secret phalanx of defense and hatred. The occupiers will leave someday, and new political constellations can also bring new opportunities for Germany too. Nothing is eternal—least of all, peace alliances on this earth. But then anti-Semitism would flare up anew once again, openly, and rage in a much more terrible fashion than ever before . . .

In addition to this, there is the fact that now millions of American, English, Russian, and French occupation troops are constantly running up against the Jewish question in Germany. They have to take a stand, one way or another—for or against. Yet this fact alone sets them to thinking. They start making comparisons. Here and there they find certain confirmations of what anti-Semitism says. They begin to reflect. Then they turn into anti-Semites and bring anti-Semitism back to their homeland, their country.

People think they can eradicate anti-Semitism with show trials, if they are cleverly staged. On the contrary, this will achieve just the opposite. The attention of world public opinion is directed to a question that can only continue if it remains hidden—or, if the courage is found *to solve the Jewish question by open discussion and enlightenment, as a conclusion drawn from that singular catastrophe.* You have to continue on at that point where the wave of anti-Semitism took its beginning. You cannot impede and stop the wave suddenly by means of force and terror. Then you'll be inundated by it. Rather, you have to contain the wave, direct it onward and let it run its course out to sea. Then the stormy sea will grow calm once again. And it will not have the disastrous consequences that I predicted above as certain. *German anti-Semites* took the first step—they must also take the next.

Jewry must be reconciled with Germany, and Germany with Jewry— in the interest of world peace and world prosperity. They must not agree on a ceasefire, but rather on a solid peace founded on reason, clear knowledge, and clear rights and duties. The Jew should make Germany his friend, and Germany the Jew. This will then be a blessing for the rest of the world. People should finally understand that what we are dealing with here is a natural event. If mankind is unable to get enraged passions under control once again, it will be destroyed by them.

But it can only gain control over them again if it attempts this calming of spirits and passions proceeding from the point of origin, from Germany. *And in this, the most die-hard anti-Semites must be the pioneering champions of this new—and yet so obvious— idea.* They must find the courage to overcome themselves and to push boldly ahead. The torch of knowledge must shine brightly in their hands so that the people will tread the path with them. God taught me this in my dungeon cell in Nuremberg . . .

My German people! Many will think me crazy for what I have written. They will say that I am bereft of all sense of reason as a result of misfortune. Others will curse me as a traitor who wants to deliver Germany to the Jews. They would rather stand by the wayside defiantly and go to their destruction than admit a mistake. They do not see that I am not admitting any mistake— rather, I am drawing the logical conclusions from events. And then continuing on, just as consistently, toward the goal down the path embarked on.

They fail to comprehend *that one has to have been an anti-Semite first in order to take this next step in knowledge.* That is why no one as yet has ever dared to think and act this way, because he was lacking the basic foundation . . .

Who will give you, the German people, economic assistance, as long as this problem remains unresolved? Reconstruction is a question of trust. But trust can be earned only by being honest, open, and reasonable. *The precondition is—and will remain: a solution to the Jewish question in Germany.* I implore you, my German people, be like the wise father of a family. Make a soberly clear assessment of the situation:

You have been *totally defeated.* But you have a grand and reasonable idea and are a splendid people. God will show you a way. Learn from the catastrophe.

Make peace with the Jew, invite him to find his homeland in your midst. There will be the devil to pay if this project does not succeed and a reasonable modus vivendi is not found. I know the way and am saying this openly.

Yet will Jews tread this path with you? If the Jew is wise, he will. And if a desire for revenge clouds the power of reason—I cannot change that. At least I have done my duty to convey to mankind an insight given me by God. If the Jew closes his heart to this insight, then the world catastrophe, as I have described it in the Jewish question, will take its inexorable course. Yet if Germany should solve this question and recover as a result, the entire world will recuperate. And this most burning of all questions would then be solved everywhere in the world. Zionism, in its present form, will never reach its goal. The Jews must obtain a *Heimat,* a land that is home. Germany is ripe and ready to give them that home in its midst.

And what does America say about this plan? The age of nationalities has passed, the age of races is now dawning. Countries are no longer a factor; it is continents that will contend one with the other. That is the certain—perhaps the only certain—result of this war. America on one side, Asia on the other. And Europe in between. It is for this reason that America has a basic interest in Europe's recovery. Yet Europe can only recover if Germany, its heart, grows healthy once again. For this reason alone, America has an interest in seeing Germany restored to health.

But America, like all nations, is interested in resolving the Jewish question. America knows that if it remains unresolved, then problems the same as in Germany will crop up there someday too. On the basis of all this, it is my conclusion that my plan does not run counter to American interests. Rather, it is quite definitely, and in the best and loftiest sense, in the interest of the Americans. And not only in the American interest, but in that of all mankind.

I realize that my proposals are bold, daring, and audacious. Yet I also know that in these [illegible] times, faint-heartedness and despondency will not lead one to the goal. And if I should be asked what Hitler, your Führer, would say to all this then I would reply: *that [illegible] genius, who was equal to Hannibal as a field commander, certainly does not wish that Germany should go down to ruin as did Carthage.*

All I can say is that I tried, I dared. May people now do what they wish! I place the matter in God's hands, from whom I believe I have received inspiration and revelation.

Some weeks ago I would have been horrified at the thought, I would not have dared to even touch the issue of anti-Semitism at all. Today it is crystal-clear to me. I could speak about it for hours. New and ever more perfect plans rise up in my mind. I am indeed obsessed by these ideas. God must now help me to convey my thoughts to the right destination. I place my trust in him. He will find the right way.

I am intrigued by Gerda's behavior: she holds on to admiration for her father while handing over to me a document that reveals his final thinking about the Jewish question. Is she asking for forgiveness—for her father's arrogance and for being unable to confront this testimony because of her love for him?

I no longer think Gerda has tried to deceive me, but rather, that she has tried to be honest with me. The protective boundary she has set up around her feelings for her father has allowed her to go on loving him and, perhaps, loving other people.

I am left with questions, yet I feel that Gerda has accomplished a lot—by consenting to talk with me in the first place, by meeting with me again, and by initiating the delivery of her father's last communication. In her own way she is trying to confront what she could not confront before: that her much-loved father was a key player in one of the most murderous regimes ever constructed. I am grateful to her for allowing me to witness what such a struggle can mean.

chapter 6

The Crown Prince

I climb the stairs to the apartment with my German assistant. Although it is 1985, the surname on the door still makes me shudder. Reinhard Heydrich remains for me a prototype of Nazi evil. As the head of the Gestapo, he signed the orders that obliterated the lives of hundreds of thousands of Jews. No one knows what went on in his mind in those days: he was assassinated in Czechoslovakia in 1942. His son has refused to see me, as he has refused many others, but his nephew is willing to be interviewed. He is the only one whose real name I have asked permission to use.

Thomas meets us at the door. He is tall and stout, with a heavy beard. Behind glasses his brown eyes radiate warmth. He smiles and greets me with a deep, strong voice and firm handshake. The decor of the apartment reflects his artistic tendencies: he is a stage actor who presents cabaret songs of the 1920s and 1930s in the local theaters.

T: You know, it's a bit odd for a person whose name is Heydrich to talk to someone like you. It's not a new problem for me, because I have so many Jewish friends. But for the first twenty years it was very difficult for me and for those who talked to me. Even today I still find that whenever I deal intensively with this period again—not that of Germany, but rather of my family—I find it a pretty rough experience, unpleasant enough, though I've managed to get over that. And I want to tell you about it.

B: If you're ready, perhaps we could begin at the beginning: when and where you were born, what you remember about your family.

T: I was born on March 2, 1931. I was the oldest of five. My earliest memories are of my father running around in a black uniform. I remember that a lot of people in uniform would come and go at our place in Berlin. As a child I probably thought—I can't really recall—that these men were soldiers, though actually they weren't soldiers.

Initially, it was the black uniforms of the SS, and later the gray uniforms. I'm not sure when, but yes, gray uniforms. Then there's the memory of my uncle. He was quite unimportant to me as a child, but I can remember him very well. He was my godfather, and the sole but quite decisive relationship we had was that I would always get the biggest present from him for my birthday. One of his adjutants would drive up in a car and ask my mother what her child wanted for his birthday. Then, one or two days later, some bombastic birthday gift would arrive, like a model electric train, that sort of thing. My second memory of my uncle is as a fencer. I think maybe he was on the Olympic team, something like that. Though, as I said, my memories of this are mixed with later stories—though stories, in my eyes, are memories as well, at least for me. Our family—which is to say *my* family, not the Reinhard Heydrich family—always liked to tell lots of stories. My mother, for example. As long as I can remember she used to tell us stories about the past. Not in the style of "now pay attention children, I have a story!" Rather, it was always very present and real. My mother was a very vivacious and lively woman. We had grandparents who were Italian, our ancestors . . . not the Heydrichs, but rather the Werthers, my mother's family. And for that reason, I can't separate story from actual memory. But things I've learned from books, well, I'll try to leave all that aside. This athlete—my uncle was a great athlete—I can still see him dressed in his white fencer's outfit. These basically are my personal memories of my uncle. The real memories don't begin until much later—not of my uncle, but rather of what Heydrich is and represents.

Actually, my own family—except for the fact that I see my father standing there in uniform—was completely free of the taint of National Socialism. In our own family, it didn't play any role at all. This was due to the fact that my mother—I must mention this—hated my uncle. Not because he was a Nazi—I don't think my mother gave that much thought at the time—but rather because she simply didn't like him personally. At home he was always called an arrogant fop. And then there was my father, who, according to everything I know from letters, from stories my mother told me, really loved his brother. But for his part, my father never injected anything Nazi into our home or family.

B: Was your father younger or older?

T: My father was a year younger. They were very, very close. In appearance, though, they were quite different. My uncle was very tall and thin, and my father was a real ox of a man, thickset. My uncle had his hair slicked down and always neatly parted; my father always had trouble keeping his curly hair under control. He was a journalist by profession, worked on newspapers, illustrated weeklies. He was the Berlin editor of the *Münchener Illustrierte*. My mother probably also rejected all that Nazi stuff in a rigorous manner. I don't know to what extent she was aware of my father's involvement.

You can read a lot about Heydrich in the book by Shlomo Aronson,[1] about my father as well, who shot himself in 1944 after there was apparently some danger they would uncover the fact that he'd been successfully aiding Jews to escape from Germany to Denmark using fake passports and the like. My father actually was the first one to become a Nazi, before my uncle. It's quite definite. At the time, my uncle even laughed at my father a bit because he'd gone over to the Nazis. Sometime in '28 or '29. And then my father rejected National Socialism very decisively and, on the contrary, became very active on behalf of the Jews. And when he noticed, or thought he had, that he was just about to be discovered, he shot himself. But that's a story in its own right. Because we suspect that this change of attitude on my father's part is bound up with my uncle's falling victim to assassination in 1942 in Prague. This expression "falling victim to," that's one of those treacherous formulations that sort of creep into one's language insidiously. I mean when he was killed. My father was handed a letter my uncle had written, a very thick envelope, from which he probably learned about what had really been taking place in Germany. I believe my father was very naive as far as everything happening around him was concerned. I think it was not until much later that he really understood and discovered this for himself. Actually, I thought that was terrific—it really helped me a lot later on—the fact that he came to his own conclusions in this matter. But for me, well, all this begins . . . Listen, if I'm talking too fast for you, please feel free to interrupt.

B: There's no need to. Did he ever speak to you about this, or to your mother?

T: I'm sure he spoke to my mother, but not to us. You shouldn't forget that when the war broke out I was eight. Up until that time, these topics had never been discussed. And then my father went to war, saw combat action, '41 I think, and from that time on there was no longer any conversation between me and my father.

B: He was in combat where?

T: In Russia. First in France, then in Russia. He was attached to a propaganda company. They put out a paper for soldiers. He volun-

1. Shlomo Aronson, *Reinhard Heydrich und die Frühgeschichte von Gestapo und SD* (Stuttgart: Deutsch, 1971).

teered for combat. We still don't know why exactly, because he didn't have to. He could just as well have stayed back here. So the figure of my father remained rather hazy and unclear in my eyes. And as I mentioned, no letters—or not very many—were preserved from that period.

B: Can you still remember him coming home on leave?

T: Yes, I can recall that quite clearly. There was always a lot of excitement, lots of happiness, because what was very pronounced in our family was the enormous tenderness that existed between my parents. It was passed on to us too. We children are unusually tender and loving today in our relationships with each other. Not only among us as brothers and sisters, but also in our relationships with others as well— a lot of touching and hugging, all that is quite natural. And this goes back to that period. I think it comes from our experience of the love and tenderness my parents felt for each other. And my mother was a kind of cuddly, loving cat toward us children right until the day she died. She passed away three years ago. But I do have this memory of my father coming home on leave from the war, although the war as such didn't have much meaning for us until the bombs started falling in 1943.

B: Did he seem preoccupied, troubled?

T: Very much so. Before, we'd known my father as someone who was always laughing and joking around, like a Punch-and-Judy show. He was a real joker, life of the party, as they say. All that stopped completely after he went to war. I even believe that he had more leave than other soldiers. For example, he was always home for Christmas. Undoubtedly, this was due to some special favor granted to him for being a Heydrich, for being The Brother. But I can only remember my happy, joking father from a much earlier period. My brothers and sisters, who are all much younger, don't have any recollection whatsoever of a happy, joking father. He was always very despondent, even depressed, at the end. My mother isn't able to explain it. We didn't know either why he'd killed himself. It wasn't until after the war that we found out my father had started this rescue operation with a friend of his to get Jews out of the country. It's all quite definite and certain. There are a number of well-known people who told us about it. For example, the wife of a famous actor got out of Germany because of my father's help. He did it in complete secrecy. My mother didn't know about it either. It only came out after the war.

B: Who was the friend who was involved in it with him?

T: He was the head of his propaganda company. There was a railroad car where they'd print the paper they were editing, and I think the two of them printed the false passports there. These passports then made their way somehow to people who needed them. So in the course of time—we don't exactly know how many people, but we estimate that more than a hundred individuals were helped over a period of about a year. This friend was a journalist. He worked as a journalist after the war too. He was even sentenced at that time, but it's rather mysterious. As I mentioned, I haven't looked into this matter in detail, because the other side of it, the whole thing surrounding the Gestapo head Heydrich, interested me much more than my own father did. I was very relieved to hear that my father, although himself a Nazi, had attempted in his own way to do good. That's the only way you can view it. To help within his limited ways and means—though risking his own life, that's for sure. A man who even went on to commit suicide when he thought they'd found him out. There is a final letter from my father to my mother, a totally confused letter, without a single fact or piece of information, that repeatedly says she won't be able to understand now, but that someday she would, and so on. Then came defeat and the collapse. Naturally, I was a member of the Nazi Jungvolk at the time, and I can recall listening with my ears glued to the radio to special reports about the war—which I didn't understand but was listening to with enormous attentiveness because I was simply fascinated.

At that time—I was maybe thirteen—I was fully aware of the importance of the name Heydrich. I was the oldest in our family, and I think that even as a boy I had a sort of special feeling for the role of the crown prince. I can even recall that I said to someone in 1944: "I'm the oldest Heydrich." Because my uncle was already dead, my father was at the front, and then there were two other sons of Heydrich, my cousins, but one of them had been killed, so only one was left, and I thought he was stupid. And besides, he was younger than I. So I was *the* Heydrich. Now, I didn't have this feeling in terms of anything political, nothing like that, but I was—this can be something psychological, or due to my own nature and character—I felt I was something special. I had no idea at all about the Gestapo, not the slightest notion of what that was. All this had never been discussed in our family. So I didn't have any idea of what it meant to be Gestapo head or the Reichsprotektor of Bohemia and Moravia. I just knew that it was something fantastic, really important.

B: Wasn't it embarrassing for your mother? After all, she did know.

T: Yes, she did. And she placed an enormous distance between herself and all this, dissociated herself. She was certainly careful about this. But there was no explanation about things like the Third Reich or Nazi Germany forthcoming from her, nothing at all. She repressed these things completely, naturally for reasons of self-protection too. She had a husband she loved and whom she'd always considered to be a die-hard Nazi. He didn't have any special governmental job, no special function. I do believe, however, that out of consideration for his safety, she relegated her opposition more to the private sphere. She'd say, "I don't feel like seeing that person" or "I don't want to have anything to do with him." And if it couldn't be avoided, then she might deal with that person in a very angry manner, although, as I said, these aren't things I experienced myself. I just know about them because I was told afterward by other people. They said we used to tremble with fear when my mother would decide to stay away from some reception. There was even the rumor circulating in our family that the reason my mother had had so many children was so she could use her pregnancy as an excuse. She did act that way, that's for sure. She would say, "I'm pregnant, I can't go" or "I have to take care of my small children."

I don't think, though, that it has much to do with Heydrich, but rather, only with me in a very personal way. For example, I was crazy about walking down those stairs. There were these enormous stairways in the palace. You can imagine: this little squirt, twelve years old, comes to the castle in Prague to visit his uncle and is given royal treatment. When I'd go out, the guards at the gate clicked their heels, stood at attention and saluted—and they were serious. They took it very seriously. Naturally, it's quite clear that something like this left its mark on me. So I would put on robes and royal cloaks, and then I'd descend the grand stairway. I was constantly being theatrical. What became my profession later on, I think the seed for it was planted in this early inclination of mine at the time to make an outward impression. Though one can't distinguish very exactly between whether it was an inborn predisposition right from the start or whether it was also shaped and molded by the environment. Probably something of both. My mother was an actress before she married. The Heydrichs were a very artistically inclined family. My grandfather was a famous opera singer; he had two conservatories. My father was unusually musical. Even the other Heydrich was very musically inclined. There'd be these derisive little remarks all the time to the effect that, after he signed the order for the execution of thousands of Jews, he would play the violin. And he played very well indeed. That's true, this is a gift that runs in the family. It comes from both families.

And when the war was over . . . But please stop me. I can go on and on. Speaking this way is a kind of liberation for me, a way of breaking free a bit, because these matters have preoccupied me, as I said, my entire life. I know that when the war ended—we were in Berlin—the day I learned that the Russians had entered Berlin, I secretly put on my uniform and went to the window and started shouting—my mother told me this, I don't remember it myself—started shouting "Heil Hitler!" And I banged against the windowpane and said, "It's not true! It can't be!" If that really did take place, then it's astonishing how superficial it must have been, because just three months later, after the end of the war . . . the Russians entered Berlin in April of '45 and I saw a satirical revue in July of that year, my first important recollection of the theater. It was a satirical revue by Horst Lommer entitled "Das tausendjährige Reich" [The Thousand-year Reich]. It was performed three months after the end of the war in the Artists' Theater in Zehlendorf in Berlin. I sat there listening to it with enormous excitement. Although it was a satirical attack on everything that had just come to an end, it wasn't a feeling of disgust I felt. I left the performance with a feeling of excitement, and I asked myself (at least that's how I tell it today), "Why aren't you upset about this?" It didn't upset me for a single instant, not at all.

B: You were fourteen at that time.

T: Yes, right, fourteen exactly. Even today I see that as a sort of small milestone in my life, my development, the fact that I didn't feel any horror, rage, or anger. I could, for example, have said, "How can some crap like this be thrown at me?" Nothing of this kind. I accepted it, not with satisfaction but at least without any sense of rage or inner protest. My second life, so to speak—the third and fourth come later on—my second life actually starts with the experience of this satirical revue "Das tausendjährige Reich" and with my own astonishment: why am I accepting this? It is clear that I was actually much more mature than other children my age, probably as a result of the chaos of the war, our flight as refugees, and all that. And at that moment, my childhood was over and past, completely. Even my mother started treating me as a grown-up.

B: You were the oldest . . .

T: I was the oldest. The youngest child was one year old, and many of the later errors and aberrations of my own personality can undoubtedly be traced back to the fact that I was forced at an early age into an adult role. This is my first key to understanding developments in my own personality at the time, the fact that at school and so forth, if someone didn't know I was a member of that family, he would have assumed that I came from an anti-Fascist family. Later on, people who'd met me at an early age would always say, "It didn't even dawn on us that you might be from *that* family, although your name is Heydrich. We were occasionally a bit horrified about the name, but the thought never occurred to us."

And at that time I hadn't yet begun to work all this through consciously, but the psychological explanation is much more correct than any others you might perhaps come up with—that there was a very conscious shift in my political attitudes, for example, because *there was no such shift!* It wasn't necessary at that time. And everything I'd learned from the Nazi period couldn't have been important at all, because from that moment, it was over and done with. It wasn't until I found out about what had really happened that I started trying to deal with it. And that proved difficult for me. I believe it remained difficult over a period of some twenty years.

It must go back to the years of 1946–47, when I started to become aware of more and more documentation. Not in school though: nothing at all was done by the school at that time, and anyone who was fourteen, fifteen, sixteen then will know what I'm talking about. Not a damn thing. So anything you knew you had to learn on your own, or others told you about it. Even the teachers who knew who I was, and who I assume had a Nazi past they had skillfully managed to conceal, they never once made reference, nothing. Nothing at all. At a very early age, I devoured information on the matter from books, from newspapers. Initially, I just ate it up. I think . . .

B: Did your mother not try to tell you about that period?

T: No, but there was a totally different reason for that. My mother was indeed probably the only person in the Heydrich family who had been against the Nazi regime right from the outset. She didn't force any ideas on us. And it was my mother, of all people, who was arrested by the Russians in May 1948 in East Germany. At that time it was called the Eastern Zone. And she was convicted and sentenced as a Heydrich—my mother, of all people!—and was placed in a prison camp. So she was there in the camp at a time—I was seventeen— when a confrontation might have been a possibility between the two of us. But this process of confrontation couldn't take place, because my mother wasn't there. We were all alone.

B: Did you visit her there?

T: No, no. I had no idea where she was. She disappeared. She was tricked into going to Dresden—she was actually more or less kidnapped—and then for a whole year we had no idea what had happened to her. We didn't even know if she was still alive. We were taken in by another family at the time. It was lucky for us from one point of view but a terrible blow from another. And this family took us in—my sister later married one of our foster brothers. Nonetheless, it was essentially a stroke of great luck that we were taken in and brought up in such a wealthy, upper-middle-class family. We enjoyed material security, an excellent education. But the fact that this was the worst period of my life was due to completely personal factors. The family was very Christian in orientation, they lived a very explicit *Christian* life—but this family was like ice, without any tenderness or warmth, even with their own children. They had seven children. The youngest was my age. So they had taken in five children in addition to their own seven.

When you talk about this, you always have to be very careful, because what they did was such an incredible thing, so positive it is beyond any description, beyond words. Yet it was also incredibly negative, because this was a family in which, for example, the mother said that she had never given her own children a kiss, never taken them in her arms, seven children . . . and we had been a family in which we'd been smothered in tenderness and kisses. OK, perhaps this was not entirely positive. However, to come into a family that was like a deep freeze, that had a very, very negative impact. I think that all of us children—except for the youngest, who was simply too young—were very seriously hurt, harmed emotionally at the time, suffered serious wounds. But what I wanted to stress is that I had no confrontation with my mother because she simply wasn't around at the time. It was impossible.

B: How long were you there?

T: For two-and-a-half years.

B: What happened to your mother?

T: My mother is a woman of great will and determination, very dynamic. I don't know how she managed to live through this period. I never found out. Actually though, when she returned, although she was still very weak physically, she very quickly became her old self again. She tried right away to initiate something and get it going by herself. Initially she lived with us, in that family. Then she tried to become independent, to get into a profession. After all, she didn't have one—I mean, what woman at that time did? So she learned a profession, then attempted to become independent using money she had borrowed. And she succeeded. She was certain that it was possible to succeed at whatever she put her mind to. That was her attitude. She also got her own apartment and then took her children out of that family, because she sensed the oppressive atmosphere too. She always felt the tension between, on the one hand, her enormous gratitude—because her children were rescued—and, on the other hand, her sense of the danger they were in. Anyhow, my mother coped with all this magnificently. But for whoever knew her, it was perfectly clear that it was quite impossible to break her psychologically, that if she was OK physically, she'd be able to handle it and manage. Right until her death she was an incredible woman. Naturally, I'm my mother's son—not a mama's boy—but most definitely the son of my mother in that sense, and emotionally very much shaped by her . . .

B: Did you try later to confront her with your ideas about the Nazi period?

T: No, I don't think she understood it at all. The need to confront the matter or discuss it didn't exist as far as she was concerned. She appeared to be, well, perhaps this is not one hundred percent true, but she gave the impression of being incredibly healthy and full of vitality. I can well imagine that she wondered why just one of her children in particular . . . I was the only one. The others didn't concern themselves at all with these matters. I always seemed to be years older than my brothers and sisters. Anyhow, I was the only one, and I think she thought I had some crazy ideas . . . [*Pause*] Maybe even why did I bother myself with these notions of guilt? Because I told her that I was terribly bothered by all this, that it was a complex (Komplex) I was unable to break free of. I even had a phase when I was seventeen or eighteen. I had this feeling that I had to expiate this burden of guilt: *my uncle!* Though I never saw it as only a problem with my uncle. It was the feeling that this is my family. Certainly because of the fact that we stuck very closely together in our own half of the family, *family* in my eyes was something special. And this was the Heydrich family. Even if I didn't want to have anything to do with the others; it was still the Heydrich family. So for years I had this feeling that I had to expiate what had happened, that I was responsible for it, yes, *responsible!* Today, in retrospect, the idea appears to me to have been a bit sick, because there was no reason for it whatsoever in rational terms, and there was no one who came from the outside and said I bore responsibility. Never once during my entire life has anyone ever reproached me in any way for being a Heydrich. Never once has there been any such reproach by anti-Fascists, Jews, Christians, or people who suffered . . .

B: The fact that no one reproached you can make your life even more difficult . . .

T: Naturally. [*Pause*] But I was never able to have any argument, any confrontation, because whenever I mentioned it, they'd say, "Come on, stop it, don't be stupid! You're not even his son. What the hell do you want?" And if we did broach the matter at all, then there was a kind of placating gesture, as if to say, why are you worried about this, why do you let it bother you? And I do believe that everything

I've done since I was nineteen or twenty is connected with the fact that I'm a Heydrich. For example, I only realized quite a good deal later that my favorite authors are Jewish. I didn't choose them because of this. Down to the present time, the authors that I like the most—I guess you know what I do for a living—well, they're Jews.

B: Who, for example?

T: Heine, for example, Tucholsky, Walter Mehring, and so on. What is so noticeable in my eyes is that I quite consciously chose this career. I'm doing exactly the opposite of what . . . The Nazis would have locked me up for this, or maybe they would have hanged me, I don't know. I started to do things that amount to exactly the opposite of what I should have been doing in the Third Reich, what I would have done if I had grown up at that time. So I'm quite sure there's a connection there. OK, the fact that I inherited some gift from my family—the ability to be an actor, to be able to present myself on stage, to be interested in having an effect on people, the good voice I have, and so on and so on—that's something else. But what I *did* with all this, that's undoubtedly connected with this confrontation with the past. Initially these were two quite separate tracks, so to speak: on the one hand, my private confrontation with what I felt to be my guilt, or the responsibility I have been burdened with, and, on the other hand, what I wanted to do with my artistic gifts and abilities. Initially these were two separate tracks.

B: I can understand what you say about yourself, but what I find harder to grasp is what you say about your mother. Somehow, in spite of everything, it seems a bit strange to me that, even if she had no direct involvement and guilt, she knows she was close to a person who murdered, who was in charge of murdering thousands and thousands of Jews. And she lived with it without mentioning anything. You have to understand . . . I am trying to make sense of it, not to judge or blame you or her . . .

T: Yes, naturally, certainly. Well, I think right from the start, long before my uncle became the big shot Heydrich, she had quite a personal antipathy toward the man, she didn't like his type, and at that time he was still a nobody.

B: At what point did your mother first have contact with the family?

T: When she married. That's when she met my uncle. And the same natural way in which she loved my grandfather, for example, that's how much she disliked my uncle. Though, as I said, at that time Heydrich was as yet nothing special. So as he gradually advanced to the position he was to occupy, she most certainly didn't know about it initially. And when she did find out, I believe she saw it as a kind of confirmation of the opinion she'd had of him from the outset, her personal opinion of the man: that here was a man who was working at his career with an almost deadly ambition, a murderous ambition.

B: Did you speak to her later about this? Did she know about the liquidation of the Jews?

T: I think only what the average citizen in Germany knew at the time.

B: There was no such thing as an "average citizen," there were different kinds of . . .

T: Well, what I call an average citizen is someone who noticed that suddenly his neighbors were missing, that the synagogues were burning . . . I myself can still remember the burning of a synagogue. Sometimes, when I hear what those who were adults at the time say, I tell myself: I was only seven, it was 1938, we were living by accident right next to a synagogue in Berlin. I used to see that synagogue every day. And suddenly it was on fire. Now, at the age of seven I didn't understand that it had been set on fire, but what I call a "normal" citizen is someone who knew exactly what a burning synagogue meant, who knew that people were constantly disappearing. And who didn't ask, "Who set the fire?" or "Where are they? What's happening to them?" I think my mother was that sort of person.

B: The "inner circle" didn't know about the extermination process?

T: No, that was inconceivable. I think probably what happened is that my father never spoke about these matters at home. My mother told me this plenty of times later on.

B: And he knew about it?

T: He most certainly knew about it. No doubt about that. I believe my mother only knew what many others did as well. And I even think that the few things my mother did know she saw in a positive light. There was this half-Jewish stage designer in Berlin, and my mother had learned that she was in some camp, I believe it was in 1934. So she told my father that this woman had been sent there and that she was a friend of our family. And my father went to see my uncle—by the way, this occurred quite often, that's very clear—and then I guess my father told his brother about this. The two men actually liked each other, despite the fact they were so different. So my father told him so-and-so had been imprisoned, how did they dare to do such a thing? My uncle said, "I don't know anything about it, is she really in detention?" Anyhow, the next day that woman was sitting with us drinking coffee. She'd been released. So my mother, if she did have any knowledge of things, she was able to view it all in a very positive light. Because when something took place that really concerned her, well, she was able to help out, even if this was only via my father and, in the final analysis, my uncle. So I think that then, at least at that time, she didn't know anything. Only later was there this terrible burden.

B: Was the relationship that you describe between the two brothers ever sundered or did it go on until the end?

T: Yes, well, it went on that way until the very end, I assume. As I said, I do know some stories, family stories. When my uncle was appointed Reichsprotektor of Bohemia and Moravia, he said good-bye to my father in Prince Albrecht Palace, or whatever the place was called, in Berlin, the Gestapo headquarters. My father was on leave and went there to say good-bye to him. And later on my father told my mother about this tearful good-bye. I guess that on both sides of our family, there were very strong emotions, we're very emotional. So they said good-bye to each other with tears in their eyes. My father then thought that maybe his brother was worried about *him,* that he might be killed in battle; he spoke to him about this and told him that nothing would happen to him, he shouldn't worry. And my uncle said, "I'm not worried about your being killed. *I'm* not going to get out of it alive in Prague. I'm getting into a hornet's nest. I won't make it out alive." My father was quite shocked to hear this because he'd thought my uncle would certainly survive the war.

Anyhow, I believe that right up until the end they had a very warm and close relationship. And my father would always defend my uncle if my parents ever discussed the matter. He always tried to explain how he'd become what he'd become. There is a whole biography behind this, that's clear. It didn't just happen overnight, it was a development. He would always defend him vis-à-vis my mother. My mother would always say that the only squabbles they'd had in their married life, the only arguments, always concerned my uncle. Later on they apparently tried to avoid the subject. Then came the war. My father wasn't at home much during the final years of his life. And during the few days or weeks he was home on leave, it's certain that such topics were avoided.

Anyhow, I'm quite sure that my mother didn't know very much right to the end of the war. Later on, it could be explained by her character, her personal situation. After all, she had five children to bring up, the youngest only a year old. Now, even for a woman as energetic as my mother this was not an easy task—to bring up five children, and burdened with this name on top of it. I know from my own experience . . . for example, right after the war ended we were living with my grandparents, not with the Heydrich grandparents—thank God, they weren't in Berlin—but rather with the Werthers, my mother's side. And once, when we went over to our old neighborhood, where we used to live, this butcher's wife said—I can see it now as if it were yesterday—she approached us on the street and said, "Are you people out of your minds to come around here? You'll be hanging from the next streetlight! Just get out of here. Everybody knows you around here." My mother was terribly frightened. She didn't understand at all. "Why me, how come? And then my children . . ." So the first few months she didn't go back again. Because others also told her to be careful. "No one will ask what you did personally. Your name is Heydrich—that's enough."

B: So you certainly needed a lot of courage to go on living under this name.

T: Yes, that's a story in its own right. My mother wanted to start using her maiden name again: Werther. This was even before she was arrested, must have been around 1947 or so. So she sat down with me—naturally she used to talk over everything with me, because I was no longer just her son, I was her partner—and said she thought we should discontinue using the name, that it would be better. "We can prove that the new name has as little connection as possible with all these matters. And to go on living with this burden, to have to do that—I don't think it's right." I believe she thought this way in terms of the other children. I can't recall how I reacted, but I do know that my mother eventually rejected the idea and said, "No, I mustn't be such a coward." Maybe at the back of her mind was also the thought that after all, we had nothing to hide. If the others were to change their name, well, that would be understandable, but not us. In addition to this, there was the lasting love she felt for her husband right until her death. He had been a Heydrich and it would look like a betrayal to cast aside his name.

The question posed itself for me personally later on when I noticed I was having certain difficulties in my profession, particularly in connection with the more official types of institutions. So I asked myself why someone with the name Heydrich would choose this kind of career. Someone—a very prominent person—said to me, "Are you nuts or something? Among artists, it's quite common to use a pseudonym, and you, of all people, have to insist on keeping your own name." At that time, I had already gone beyond the period when I was working through this problem, and so I replied, "It's completely out of the question. I've suffered for years because of this, and now I'm finally at a point where at least I can live with this burden. So now you say I should throw away my family name, cast it aside, after all that? No, my friend, now I want to use this name openly." You know, today I feel a sense of great inner satisfaction when I see a poster that says "Heydrich performing Heinrich Heine," or "Heydrich performing Tucholsky," because for me that's the upshot, the result of a process of working through things, of reaching the point where that's possible. The fact that I'm able to perform has to do with my own gifts, but the fact that I can do it this way has to do with what I went through, worked through . . .

B: Emotionally?

T: Yes, emotionally. That's what I think is so important.

B: Did you discuss these matters with your brothers and sisters?

T: No, for my brothers and sisters the problem really didn't pose itself. They were all younger, and the problem of having to deal with this, well, it never arose. Actually, from a contemporary perspective, I'd say that they reacted in a very natural way. They said, "Why should we? We're not even the children of this particular Heydrich . . . We have lives of our own to live!" All four of them are left-wing politically. To what extent this constitutes a conscious turning away from some right-wing political interest or other, I can't say.

B: Did your father ever try to write about how he dealt with this conflict—between his love for his brother and what his brother had done?

T: Unfortunately not. The war is to blame for that to the extent that he didn't have time for such things. I'm certain that if my father had lived, this confrontation, the process of working through and dealing with these conflicts, would have been the most important thing he would have done or wanted to do: on the one hand, the Nazis, and on the other, his own brother, his own flesh and blood. Because during the last two years of his life, he repeatedly said to my mother, whenever they'd talk about the possibility of his being killed in battle, "I really want to stay alive, go on living, because I still have so much to do . . ." This always included writing a book. Now, he didn't mean a novel or anything like that. No, I'm quite certain that what he had in mind was precisely this process of confrontation, which he could have carried out in a far more direct manner than I could have. That's what he wished to do. But he never got around to it because of his suicide—suicide that turned out to be completely meaningless, at least as far as his fear that something might happen to us was concerned. Perhaps not meaningless—who knows what he was spared in this way. Who knows if the Russians might not have hanged him or condemned him or carted him off to Russia. It's impossible to say. But the actual and immediate reason for his suicide—namely the danger that he might be discovered—well, that danger didn't exist at all. It was a pure coincidence that this investigative commission showed up, and he then assumed they'd somehow found out what he was doing, had unearthed something or other, and that his arrest was imminent. So he shot himself.

B: Didn't he speak with his friends, his comrades about it?

T: No, the fellow who worked with him in forging the passports— I talked to him later about this period—and he told me again and again, "For me your father was a committed anti-Nazi." And I later learned what sort of person he actually was. On the one hand, he was one of those romantic Nazis. They actually existed. That kind of inflated and immature (verquast) ideology that he constructed for himself. And then to be confronted with reality, very directly and personally, in the person of his own brother. And then to reach certain personal conclusions that something had to be done. But he never confronted his comrades or discussed these matters with them. Rather, they just did something, tried to do something, that was all.

And the point when all this began for him? Well, according to my mother it's possible to pinpoint that very exactly. When my uncle was murdered in Prague, my father was called back from the eastern front. There's this macabre film they show repeatedly of the state funeral, my uncle's funeral in Berlin. My father was a relatively simple, common soldier. He didn't join the Waffen SS. As a member of the SS, he volunteered for the Wehrmacht and, as far as I know, at the time he was a lieutenant, just a simple soldier. So when you see this film— Goering, my father, Reinhard's two sons, Hitler in between, and all the other puppets and big shots—a macabre picture, totally petrified, frozen. Anyhow, as I said, this point can be determined, because during the few days he was on leave for the funeral he was handed a letter written by my uncle, a letter of maybe a hundred pages. And after the funeral my father went to his room with this letter, locked the door, and read it. He read until the early hours of the morning—it must have taken him ten or twelve hours—and then he burned it immediately. And my mother said that from that hour, my father was a different person. We don't know what the document contained. My own suspicions may be all wrong. Perhaps there were documents pertaining to the Jewish background of the Heydrich family; that's possible. Maybe it was a kind of last personal testament. It is clear that my uncle was a devil, but even devils are made up of various sides and facets. So possibly the envelope contained a kind of testament, a coming to terms, a reckoning with everything he had done. Or possibly all it contained were very personal diary entries, personal notes and comments meant to enlighten my father as to what Reinhard had himself thought and felt in regard to what was happening. Anything is possible. As I said, we just don't know.

B: Was he the only one who read it?

T: He was the only one, and he burned the document immediately. In reply to my mother's question about what it contained, he said, "We won't discuss that until the war is over and past." This is quite in keeping with his approach, the fact that otherwise he never told her anything either in order to protect her, shield her, so that if something came up she actually wouldn't know anything. So we really don't know. So that's the date. What triggered this was the document, my uncle's papers. And that's when this attempt by my father begins—to do something positive, with the forged passports or whatever. But, perhaps also before that, like the stage designer I told you about . . . that sort of thing is supposed to have happened rather frequently. My uncle's adjutant officer told me himself that when my father would phone them up at the palace and say, "I want to see my brother," well, the entire outer office staff knew that there was someone he wanted released from custody. But that too was still at a time when my father was—in spite of everything—a Nazi.

B: These involved personal relationships, nothing political?

T: Yes, personal relationships, not political ones. But it is so crazy: to be a Nazi in this overblown, overromantic way, with the kind of ideological superstructure he'd constructed for himself, and then to go to my uncle and say, "Look, you've got someone in custody"—so he *did* know, he was aware that they were arresting people—"you've arrested so-and-so, how could you, have you gone insane? He's a really nice fellow, she's a really nice woman. So release the person." And this was taken care of immediately. As far as we know, my uncle never once refused my father what he wanted when it was a matter of letting someone out of a concentration camp. And it is certain that his staff knew it: if Heinz Heydrich phones, well, then we're going to have to release somebody. [*Almost smiling, full of compassion*] And my uncle himself must have reacted the same way, because my aunt told my mother later that when my uncle would come home in the evening or whenever and say, "Heinz came by again today," she would respond, "Well, I guess someone had to be let free again, right?" It was obviously a Heydrich family joke.

B: Did you know any of the others who were in the "inner circle"?

T: No. I know that I'm once supposed to have sat on Goering's lap and to have seen Himmler, but I can't remember either incident. That was when I was at the palace near Prague, but I can't recall anything.

B: You had no contact with their children?

T: No. Now that's because after the war, while I was growing up, maturing—and this at a much too early age—well, I quite consciously kept my distance from all these ties or any possible connections. People would often approach me—from the neo-Nazi party, the so-called Reichspartei as it was called then—they tried to establish contact with me in order to get me to become active for their cause. But, I mean, I not only viewed that with contempt, I responded with a scornful laugh. That was quite inconceivable as far as I was concerned.

B: Did you meet young men or women you had known before?

T: Yes, of course. I certainly had friends who had been with me in the Hitler Youth, the Jungvolk—my closest friend at school—though he wasn't Nazi in the least in his thinking and didn't become that way later on either. So that no confrontation over these matters was necessary in that connection either. I mean, there were no Nazis in my immediate proximity, and those who were couldn't have been older than fourteen at the time, so they were never really Nazis. But if they had indeed been influenced in this direction by their parents and their upbringing, apparently they felt very early on—and they not only felt it, they *knew* it—that they couldn't talk with *us* along those lines. That's very clear.

B: Did you have any contact with your cousin?

T: None whatsoever.

B: Where does he live?

T: In Munich. He's an engineer and there are also two daughters, who live close to where my aunt used to live. One of them is an opera singer. All three of them are completely nonpolitical, or you could almost say apolitical. I recall that early on, I paid a visit to them at my aunt's place—my cousins were there, both of them—but a conversation between us just never developed. I know my mother had a bit more contact with the children, and my brothers and sisters did write them now and then. But no confrontation of the past is taking place. It never did, not at all, not in respect to their father or the Third Reich. I don't mean that they bask in the memory of what he was. Not at all. But they've pushed all this out of their minds. I wouldn't go so far as to say they'd repressed it from consciousness. They haven't repressed it. Rather, it just doesn't exist as far as they're concerned, it doesn't interest them at all.

B: Do you have any explanation for why you felt this responsibility?

T: Why I suddenly had this feeling of guilt? It certainly can't be explained in political terms. It should be explained psychologically: my growing up must have had something to do with a coming-to-terms with the family (Auseinandersetzungen), i.e., it was impossible for me to grow up and become an adult without confronting *something*. Maybe it could have been something else. But in any case, when you know from earliest childhood that you're a Heydrich, when you get this with your mother's milk, so to speak (mit in die Wiege gelegt gekriegt), then it's the, I wouldn't say "easiest," but the point of departure nearest at hand in order to prove that you are an adult. Though in quite the opposite way it harmed me or tended to prevent me from growing up, so that basically I became an adult much later, matured much later than might actually have been possible. I mean, there's no doubt that I succeeded in healing psychological wounds and bruises much later than others were able to.

Actually, as paradoxical as it may sound, maybe not to you, but to other people . . . I mean, it's a paradox when I think about it: in order to grow up I confront something, try to come to terms with something that actually *prevents* me from growing up! I think that I've really only been an adult for twenty years. On the other hand, I was fortunate to have been given a talent from birth maybe that made it possible for me to have a certain presence and an effect in public, to do this in a way that was very positive for me, but I hope for others as well. Sometimes I think, well, that's my uncle, he had a public impact. Like a devil in human form.

B: You feel sometimes as though you are still this child walking down the stairs in your uncle's palace in Prague, an actor standing out in front of the world?

T: [*Pause*] I haven't looked at it from this angle yet. I know that the feeling of walking down the palace steps, God, that was a great feeling. There was delight in it. I felt terrific. I feel terrific in my work now—that's true. Though looked at logically, I'd naturally say that at that time I wasn't doing anyone a favor except myself. I simply felt tremendous. I was the magnificent prince. Today when I descend the stairs like that, well maybe . . . I never thought of this comparison before, though it seems to suggest itself. Even then I was a small actor. That's certain, but I don't believe that has anything to do with the situation in the family. Because I was already playing the actor at the age of seven or eight, at the beach and everywhere. A prince maybe—in a royal family it's quite clear that the crown prince will become king. But we had quite a normal middle-class family, one in which there was perhaps a certain musical talent. And then suddenly one of the family becomes such an important big shot.

B: Did your father tell his sister about any of these things?

T: No, no, he didn't. I know that from my mother, that Nazism with its negative aspects was, I believe, never a topic of conversation in the Heydrich family. Naturally, that may be due a bit to the nature of the role that my uncle himself played. I could well imagine that the Goerings and the Goebbels were a lot more open in dealing with this topic than was the case in this rather mystery-laden role my uncle played. I mean, in one's own family it was easier to talk about, well, Reichsmarschall Goering or Minister Goebbels, than it was to talk about the Gestapo, the concentration camps, the persecution of the Jews, and the killing of people. And afterward, I think the other relatives were pleased that they were able to emerge from the whole thing without any damage, at least relatively so. The fact that I had contact with Jewish friends—whether they knew it or not—and got along very well with them, that's something completely different, because that's a human and personal contact. But, for example, to go off to Israel, well, many years ago the idea would have been unacceptable to me, although that's changed completely now. So, if someone were to invite me to go to Israel, it wouldn't be a problem for me any more, none at all.

A Heydrich in Israel reading Heine in German . . . they would kill him! He can't imagine what that name still means there.

B: But you haven't taken any initiative yourself in this respect?

T: No, I wouldn't take the initiative myself. For example, I wouldn't want to go to Israel as a tourist. I'd be able to but wouldn't want to. If I went, I'd like to go as the Heydrich you see in the poster.

He shows me a poster announcing his performance of Jewish poets in the Town Museum in Düsseldorf: an evening of Brecht, another of Tucholsky, Walter Mehring, Heine. He invites me to come to the following Tuesday's performance—Walter Mehring. "Do you know him?" I am embarrassed to admit that I have never heard of him.

T: I'd be very happy to go to Israel this way.

B: I can understand that it is your dream to be invited there.

T: Yes, yes. That's right. For example, the brother of my best girlfriend converted to Judaism, became a rabbi. He dropped over when he was here on a visit—the only case I know of a Christian who converted to Judaism. His father was quite a big shot. He's the son of a Nazi, a bona fide member of the SS, and he said, "I don't want to have anything to do with this family." He converted to Judaism, went to Israel, and even became a rabbi there. He took a much easier and less troubled path for himself. I spoke to him when he was here. I told him that I didn't approve at all of what he'd done and said that he hadn't really confronted the matter at all. I told him, "You said you don't want to have anything to do with them. My father was a Nazi. OK, that's all, I'm becoming a Jew. You haven't even started to work through the whole matter, you've just avoided it." And he just sat across the table from me totally bewildered and said, "I can't figure you out. I even have the feeling you're criticizing me for what I've done." "Yes, I am criticizing you, because you've never really confronted the thing and dealt with it. You just drew a line, threw everything away, made a new start, and that's it." [*Angrily*] He's got four children over there. I didn't even marry—how can I bring children into this Heydrich story? They say that converts are even more Jewish than the Jews, just as we say "more Catholic than the Pope."

B: And what did he say to that?

T: "Yes, part of that's right. I haven't confronted the whole problem the way you did, but I began a new life."

A Heydrich and the rabbi from Jerusalem: two totally different ways of dealing with the past. I try to convince Thomas to give me his friend's address. He is somewhat reluctant at first. Maybe he feels he should have been more discreet. But eventually he agrees to ask his friend's permission.

I return to my hotel with mixed feelings. On the one hand, I appreciate Thomas's warmth and openness. He is perhaps the first nondepressed interviewee I have encountered in Germany. On the other hand, I have difficulty with his theatrical manner.

The following Tuesday evening, I find myself in the audience in the Town Museum. Thomas begins his performance with some old Walter Mehring cabaret songs from the 1920s, overacting Mehring's cynicism and his ridicule of the Fascists. I shrink in my chair and feel very uncomfortable. But after the intermission he presents some of Mehring's later songs, written after Hitler came to power, and ends with one about "two Jewish children."

1.
Two children, curly-headed and small,
off to the butcher's, fat and tall.
So what'll it be, kids? Half a pound of pork?
Sadly the children replied: No!
Well then, you little brats, what are your names?
My name is Esther,
said the little girl.
And mine's Jacob,
said her brother,
The butcher grinned, maliciously:

Haha, hihi, ho-ho-ho—
Esther and Jacob, now, ain't that cute!
God, that's a gas! Jez, is that funny!
I can't stop laughing. Too much, just craa-zy!

2.
Two children, curly-headed and small,
facing the butcher, ruddy and tall.
The butcher bellowed: OK, just gimme a guess or two—
Jacob, I bet you're a damn little Jew!
Hey, people, look! Here's Judah in the flesh!
Come and behold: black Esther and her
hideous little brother Jake . . .
Yeah, lemme take a closer look at him,
An-a-tom-i-cal-ly!
Haha, hihi, ho-ho-ho—
The whole shop stood there, staring stupidly.
They gaped and thought: God, what a gas! Jez, is that
    funny!
Can't stop laughing! Too much, just craa-zy!

3.
Two children praying, you know their name,
Jacob in fear, his sister in shame.
Me, shouted the butcher, I slaughter pigs, slaughter cows,
But you bloody Jews, why,
You slaughtered the Christ child!
So maybe I'll just finish you off now
with one sharp knife or another,
First you, black Esther,
then your miserable brother . . .
Revenge, revenge on Judah!

4.
His bellowing grew, it spread
Like an epidemic.
Jewboy, sheenie! Get the sheenies!
The whole street was shouting,
chasing after the two tiny children.
The townspeople yelled and thought: God, what a gas!
Jez, is that funny! We can't stop laughing!

A young Jewish girl. Dead
By her own hand. Alone.
Motive for the suicide:
        Reason unknown . . . [2]

2. From Walter Mehring, *Staatenlos im Nirgendwo* [*Stateless in Nowhere*] (Düsseldorf: Classen/Econ, 1981).

The small audience applauds, but Thomas does not return to the stage. I like what he has done and go backstage to thank him. I find him crying in a corner of his dressing room. He falls on my shoulders and starts to sob, and I cry too, suddenly feeling the terrible weight of the past on our weak shoulders. It is the only time during any of my visits to Germany that I cry with a German.

We meet again a year later. Thomas invites me to his home for brunch. When I arrive I find a beautiful table laden with every possible kind of cheese and meat, bread and toast. I wonder if I will be able to eat while I listen to more of the Heydrich story. We find a place to set up my taping equipment and return to the issue Thomas spoke about last time: that people usually do not associate him with the Heydrich.

B: And what if you simply told people?

T: Look, sometimes I do tell people. I mean, when it's more than just a question based on curiosity, if I sense that there is a more serious interest involved, if we get into a genuine conversation, well then I tell them. And the reaction, the first reaction, is almost always horror. It's strange, but it's almost always older people who ask me. And there's something touching about that. It crops up with certain people, a lot of whom I've gotten friendly with in the meantime, some of whom were themselves in concentration camps—or their families were in the camps or died there. And after this initial reaction of horror—which they can get over relatively quickly because they can understand, well, *he* had nothing to do with it—the next reaction is almost always, "My God, how can you deal with that?" Quite astonishing, but you never get the opposite negative reaction: "You've got a lot of gall" or "What you're doing is a kind of blasphemy." Things like that. You never hear that. It's always the opposite. And I'm always astonished that they are able to ask that of someone who belongs to the family of a victimizer.

So, while I worked piece by piece, something after all did change in my subconscious. I can't say at what exact point there was that moment of sudden insight when the curtain was torn open. That's not the way it was. For example, I can say that I still have the image in my mind . . . the Third Reich, 1945, in the Artists' Theater in Zehlendorf. I mean, it's crazy that I can still remember the thing. I could even show you the seat—the building no longer exists—I could point out to you the very seat where I sat and watched. That's something I can recall very precisely. That was the key, the first time there was maybe a glimmer or something. And after twenty years, I still can't say to you that the second key was at such-and-such a time. I can't say that. It was just suddenly that way, around 1964. I can only identify it in retrospect, because that was the moment when I broke free of all the ties that connected me to the family, although that was also bound up with the fact that there had been a very great distance between my mother and me for years. I went to Berlin to see her only reluctantly. That was about the time I moved to Düsseldorf, yes, it was already 1964.

That was stage number two, though it's only now that I know that. It was ten years ago, even fifteen, and at the time I didn't realize it, but suddenly I was free of the thing. The difference between then and now is . . . for example, when I read a book then about the Third Reich, or even about Reinhard Heydrich, and when I read such a book today, I know a lot more about what actually happened. I mean, coming to terms with it (das Damitfertigwerden). In retrospect, the path was actually very straight. If someone were to look at my life, knowing everything, and then follow all the turns and undulations, all the detours, false directions, crazy things, chaotic conditions, well, without this reference, that is, my being a Heydrich, he wouldn't be able to understand it at all, never. I recall that when I had the feeling I had come to terms with it, then I asked myself if this path and all those terrible detours were really necessary? Detours that, if you look at it as an outsider, cost me twenty years of my life.

B: This Reinhard Heydrich in you, what did you think about him, what was it that you thought he was capable of daring to do?

T: "Capable of daring to do" (zugemutet) is a good expression. We'd say it differently; we'd use the word *zugetraut*, "attributed to him," though that word *zugemutet* is probably a much more accurate expression. What I thought he was capable of doing. Today I know that I was basically quite correct. There was an even greater discrepancy. I mean, this split, this gap (Schere), these two planes were still quite separate in my eyes, because I knew, on the one hand, what kind of a person he was in my father's eyes and what my father had said about this at home. On the other hand, my mother was the other half of the scissors, so to speak. She hated him for these very same things, and she believed she had reason to do so. My father, for example, said that a man who had such a warm and hearty laugh couldn't be a bad person, but my mother responded, "He brays just like a goat." My father, probably because he was used to it from childhood, thought that way of laughing was something warm and hearty. So here we have the contrast between the Gestapo chief and a loving father, that stupid image that people make use of so easily. But even better, say, perfunctorily dashing off his signature some afternoon on an order to have fifty thousand Jews murdered and that same evening playing the violin in a quartet with Mr. K., things like that. That one and the same trait in a human being can be viewed either with love or hate—I had that notion in my head. That is to say, I didn't make a split personality out of the man—the devil there, and, well, maybe an angel . . . for me it really was one and the same person. And they are still doing it today. When you read about him, well, this split in his personality comes up again and again. And they don't try to explain it, they just present it as a phenomenon.

B: And this same thing could be understood in various ways . . .

T: Right, it is possible to understand the same thing in different ways. And I believe that much of what I do today—though, as I said, not what I do consciously—what I can discuss with people and do even in my most personal and private contacts with others, derives from an insight that is relatively rare for a young person: that my uncle is one person, not two.

B: And that one person can then do all these various things?

T: Yes, as one person. It's a question of being one way *and* another way at the same time, not either/or, but rather a whole and undivided person, *one* individual. And I could imagine that . . .

B: If he is such a person, then you can be such a person as well . . .

T: Right, that's what I wanted to say. This conclusion, this notion of not dividing a human being into a good part and an evil part—and, in so doing, to extend this to society, to all of humanity, to my own person—but rather to see him whole, a single and undivided person. I could imagine that that's a frightening idea for some people. But for me it's not. It's actually something quite possible in my eyes . . .

B: And it took nineteen years for you to grasp that . . .

T: Yes, right.

Over brunch, I find myself telling Heydrich's nephew about the cabalistic approach of Lurian philosophy: within each evil you find a sign for good. Even as I write these words a year after this conversation, I can hardly believe it.

We meet once more at the university. Thomas has agreed to be videotaped with me. It is not easy for him to tell his story to the camera, although he is well acquainted with the stage. Afterward, he waits for me and we meet at the cafeteria. He looks tired and says, "I believed I was over all that, that I had worked it through. But now I see that I only found a way to live with it. There are things one can never finish, get free of. This Heydrich will follow me to the last day of my life."

chapter 7

The Rabbi from Jerusalem

I return to Israel after my first meeting with Thomas and wait impatiently for him to send me the address of the "rabbi from Jerusalem." But six months pass, and only after additional persuasion does he finally identify Menachem and give me his address. Then for another month I do not even look at the information, because first I must consider just what I am to say to this man. "I know you are the son of a prominent member of the SS. I received your address from Heydrich's nephew." That does not seem to be an introduction that would win the cooperation of a man who has been living in Jerusalem as an Orthodox rabbi for many years. I do not even know if his wife is aware of his past. After a while, another idea occurs to me. Perhaps I should conceal my purpose, tell him that I want to do some research on Ger-Zedek, righteous converts to Judaism. Then I think: he is a religious person and I am nonreligious; he will find out that I concealed information from him and it will damage my credibility. I decide to tell the truth. I will tell him a few things about myself, who I am, how I got involved in this research, and then a bit about the project itself. After that, I'll mention the fact that, in the course of my research, I happened to meet Thomas, who gave me his address. I hope that he will respond to this straightforward approach.

When I walk through the narrow streets of the Jewish quarter of the Old City, it assumes a new dimension in my mind: even here, doors conceal the stories of those "others." Until now, the geographic separateness of the children of perpetrators from my own home has allowed me a necessary distance and given me a feeling of relative security. Here, on a Jerusalem street, even this is gone.

I ring the doorbell and a girl opens the door. "Daddy!" she calls in Hebrew, "someone is here to see you." Menachem welcomes me with a strong handshake. The beard, the clothes, and the kipa on his head make his religious identification clear. Only a finely tuned ear could pick up the German accent in his Hebrew (the same accent the other children used to attribute to me as a child, although I was born in Israel), and seeing him here, I would never have guessed his past identity.

We chat briefly, and it becomes clear that he is ready to talk about his past, that he has not kept it in any way secret in his new environment. Without awkwardness I can now concentrate on my main task: to try to find out if this extreme move—from there and them to here and us—makes it easier to live with that terrible past. In my mind, Thomas's words still echo: "Menachem never really confronted the thing and dealt with it. He just made a new start and that's it."

M: I was interviewed in the early 1970s, when I had just finished my conversion. Already then, I stated that the Holocaust was not a central focus in my move. Perhaps it does constitute some sort of point of departure for my path toward Judaism. That does seem reasonable and likely. I was just five at the end of the war, but later on . . . in high school, I started to think about what had happened in Germany. I also obtained a certain amount of information in history classes, in books that treated the topic in a free and open way. I had one teacher who was a converted Jew. He did in fact talk about the Nazi period, from '33 to '45. It is clear that any thinking person has to deal with that whole phenomenon. Because the question I asked—and I think it's quite natural to ask such a question—when I was twelve or thirteen, I started to ask myself: How was it possible for such a thing to happen? And why specifically in Germany? That's a question for which I don't know if there is any answer. How did all that happen in the Germany of Goethe, Kant, Beethoven, Mozart—in *that* Germany? It was a jungle—within the framework of a culture that was so developed. Maybe there is a kind of historical approach to that question: the long development of anti-Jewish religious sentiment, and after that, the more modern phenomenon, namely, racist anti-Semitic opposition to Judaism. It is not surprising that this took place within the context of a Christian world. Christianity from its very inception was rooted in and based on religious opposition to Judaism, such as you find in the New Testament.

B: Do you come from a Christian home?

M: No, basically not. My parents had left the church. Even before the Nazi era, there was no close bond with the church within our family. Officially, they were no longer members of the church. My father didn't return to the church after the war either. Only my mother did. One of the elements is the historical legacy of Christian anti-Semitism,

Christian anti-Jewish tradition. It is clear that this is very deeply rooted: the notion that the Jews murdered the Son of God and that the guilt for having shed his blood is visited upon all the generations. History substantiates this: the Inquisition, the Black Plague. There are those anti-Semitic passages in Luther, for example, in Luther's infamous tract entitled, "The Jews and Their Lies." Initially, he intended to try to convert the Jews, and for that reason, he wrote a very positive book about the Jews in the beginning, emphasizing that Jesus had been born a Jew (although the Jews were a "stubborn" people). Anyhow, he wasn't successful. Later, he wrote the treatise about the Jews that contains all that anti-Jewish theology, and four hundred years later, the Nazi paper *Der Stürmer* made use of those ideas. Things like that don't come about overnight. It was a long process of development.

B: Did you speak with your parents about these matters?

M: No. After the war, my father was interned in Siberia for many years. I remember that we'd just about given up all hope. Suddenly a letter came saying that he was on his way home. I was already ten at the time. I must say, my father and I had almost no discussion about that whole topic.

I think that when we did get to talking a bit, well, I'd say that my father had not broken free from his Nazi background. It didn't just start with Hitler—he grew up in that atmosphere and drank in anti-Semitism as a child drinks his mother's milk. He was born in 1908, and German culture was permeated with anti-Semitism at that time. Books by men like Eugen Dühring, literature like that even in academic circles. Dühring's book, *Die Judenfrage als Frage der Rassenschädlichkeit* [The Jewish Question as a Question of Race Malignity]. It was in the air. So, despite the terrible calamity that occurred, I don't think my father ever became completely free of all that. His views about Jews were always negative.

That was shown not so long ago, in 1969. I had been in Israel on a visit—this was before I came as an immigrant in 1970. I had been studying at the rabbinical academy Merkaz Harav[1] in Jerusalem and was on my way back with a friend. He was returning to London, and I was going back to the United States. We stopped off in Germany on the way, and I visited my sister in Düsseldorf. My parents were on a visit elsewhere and were supposed to come to Düsseldorf. I went to the station to meet my father. When he saw that there was someone else with me, someone he recognized as a Jew, he didn't get off the

---

1. An Orthodox theological center of Rabbi Zvi Yehuda Kuk in Jerusalem.

train but continued on to the next town. That was in 1969. Even before that, when I left Germany to go to the States—I graduated from Hebrew Union College in Cincinnati; that was before my conversion—well, when he learned that I was attending a Jewish institution, it was the end of the world for him.

On the other hand, though, I heard a story from him when I was a child. He told me that there was a Jew by the name of Stern in the neighborhood. My father had learned something about an action the Nazis were going to carry out and he warned Stern. He was apparently the same age as my father. He knew him from the neighborhood. And my father told him to get out for his own good. And he told me this story, although I don't know its significance . . .

B: What was his job in the army during the war?

M: Officially he was a member of the Waffen SS. But I'm not aware that he was involved in anything special.

B: Where was he stationed during the war?

M: In various places: in Italy, after that in France, Belgium. Only toward the end of the war was he sent to the East. And after the war, he was taken to Siberia. I don't think he was involved in anything against the Jews. I don't know of anything.

B: Didn't you ask him?

M: It simply didn't work, because the Jews were a taboo subject. Look, after I began my studies I didn't spend much time at home. I was at various universities in Germany for a couple of years. I spent my vacations outside Germany—in England, Czechoslovakia. Once I even went with some other students on a three-month trip to the Near East. In any event, in 1967 I left Germany and went to the United States, and later emigrated to Israel from there. So for at least twenty-five years there was little or no contact between us.

The last time I was in Germany, seven or eight years ago, it was a very short visit. I was sent as a representative of our Orthodox synagogue. I personally didn't want to go, but it was something connected with the government. I only spent a few days in Düsseldorf, didn't go to my hometown at all. In any event, since I'm a religious Jew, I don't do any traveling on Saturday.

It was my sister's birthday, and generally I phone her on her birthday. We have a very close relationship. She is younger than I am, was born in 1943. She has been here in Israel a couple of times to visit. She has a completely different view of things. She lives in Düsseldorf, quite near the synagogue. She told me she chose this location because "when Jews like you come to visit, they'll have a place to stay," they won't have to go anywhere else on the Sabbath. My mother is seventy-seven. There was no relationship at all between me and my father during all those years. But my mother—well, that's mom, that's something else.

B: Did your mother ever say anything about the Jewish issue?

M: No, basically nothing. Only in connection with one very interesting story. I think it's quite possible that this did influence the path I later followed in life. I recall that once right after the war we had gone out for a walk in town. It had been devastated, turned into a lunar landscape after the American raid of November 1944. It was 80 percent destroyed. So I was out walking with my mother, and we saw this tiny old man sitting in the ruins of a house. My mother remarked, "Why, that's Pastor Ehr!" This is interesting, because Ehr was a Jewish cousin of Franz Rosenzweig. He had been a philosopher in Heidelberg, and at the age of forty or so he converted to Christianity and became a minister in our vicinity.

I heard many stories about him from my mother and my aunt. My aunt was a leader in the League of German Girls. Ehr had been their minister. Look at this Bible here [*points to one of the shelves*]. It was given to them at their confirmation. So they told me about this Jewish man. My aunt had all the usual anti-Semitic feelings toward him, even though he had long before converted to Christianity and was their pastor. Then she became a leader in the BDM, and this influenced her attitude toward him. So that is the way I first met him, because he came back to Germany after the war. I don't know the whole story, but he was among the first to come back. He was in town for a while, and we met a few times during that period. Despite the fact that the Nazis had attacked his house, the home of a minister, on Kristallnacht in 1938, he came back right away after the end of the war to resume work as a pastor. He felt obligated to his community. He passed away in 1958. I knew him for a period of several years, heard his sermons in our congregation. They were based mainly on Old Testament texts. What a person. Even though he was a minister, there was still something Jewish in him. Also from the perspective of his theological views. It is possible that he did influence me in an intellectual sense, even though the Holocaust for me basically remains a kind of point of departure. Dealing with the facts of history pushed me to think in a certain direction: to familiarize myself with the Jewish people and to think about the Jewish people.

B: When was the first time your curiosity about the Jews was aroused?

M: Well, as a result of dealing with modern history, what happened here. The entire matter of the Third Reich stands in the center of the

Jewish question and its solution. As Hitler says in *Mein Kampf*, he appeared on the stage of history to "solve" this problem. Whoever deals with this period must necessarily deal with the Jewish question. I didn't know any Jews personally.

B: Did you perhaps ask whether you yourself might not become a Jew?

M: No, I simply studied history, dealt with that. But at a later stage, when I went on to the university to study theology, then my involvement with historical problems took on a new dimension, a more intellectual significance. I began to develop an interest in Jewish literature, in German-Jewish thought, especially Buber and Franz Rosenzweig. This was a kind of transition from an involvement in questions of Jewish history to an interest in Jewish philosophy. But during all those years, there was no talk or thought of any sort about conversion to Judaism.

I didn't even dream of such a thing. I wanted to become a Protestant minister somewhere. Over the years, though, I . . . you know, theology students in Germany have to learn Hebrew and take an exam in it. So over the course of time, I penetrated ever more deeply into this area. At that time, I also began to be interested in getting to know Jews. So I went over to Dortmund, to the Association for Jewish-Christian Fellowship. I didn't establish any contact with Jews until I was nineteen or so.

But this is a long story. I've been thinking of writing a book sometime, a spiritual report on the long path I've taken. To sum it up briefly, at the University of Hamburg I served as assistant to a professor in the Institute for the History of German Jews. In that way, I began to get involved. And later I went to the United States. I asked the professor for advice, and he told me to go either to Israel or the United States to study, since those are the two centers. So I went to the States, and three years after that, came to Israel. In the end, the conversion—which I underwent in the United States—was the result of a process of thought, that is, the confrontation with Christian theology. I was no longer able to accept the Christian conception, though that's also a long story. So the whole matter of the Holocaust is only a point of departure. In deciding to leave the German people and join the Jewish people, it was not the decisive factor for me in taking such a momentous step as conversion. It was the first factor, the initial factor.

B: When you first decided to move in the direction of Judaism, how did your father respond? Did he regard it as something strange?

M: Yes, because before that I had been working as a translator in a factory, in the export department of a firm in Germany. I had a good salary, a nice office, but I gave all that up because even at a young age, I was more interested in things of the spirit. I wasn't able to content myself with only the material side of life. I wanted to delve more deeply into things, which is why I went in the direction of theology and philosophy. My father wasn't pleased with that, though that is another story. Because it's simply crazy to leave a good job and to start again from the beginning. Before the war he had already owned a factory of his own. So I went my way. I would have been prepared, even after all that, to maintain a certain contact with him, but he didn't want it. So I did what I had to. That doesn't bother me. I took a completely different path, founded a family. I have this feeling that all that is a world very distant from me now.

B: Do people here know about your background?

M: Oh yes, they've made a great deal of fuss about this whole matter here.

B: Oh, I hadn't heard.

M: Yes, it started after I immigrated. It began with an interview in '71. I was a student then in Merkaz Harav. They published a long article on me in the newspaper *Maariv.* It was in a sort of series called "Just between the Two of Us." There was a lot of noise and commotion as a result. I was interviewed on TV, appeared on a couple of programs. I really didn't want to, because it's difficult to explain things like this in public in a few brief minutes, but they talked me into participating. Radio interviews too. Various media contacted me.

B: How did people react, how did they accept this?

M: Well, there were different kinds of responses. In Merkaz Harav I was accepted with open arms. There were very deep and profound discussions. After that, after I left that yeshiva, I studied at the Fishl Institute, a seminary for rabbinical students, and they stressed that their students should go out into the world and be active, and not just sit and study the Talmud until they reached a ripe old age. In the end, I received a rabbinical degree.

About that same time, after I received my degree, the post of rabbi at the Technion in Haifa was advertised. The Chief Rabbi of Haifa encouraged me to apply. I was surprised, but in the end I did apply. I didn't receive any answer for some eight months. When I did it was positive, although afterward, I found out that there had been disagreements behind the scenes for a number of months. First, there was the question of whether a convert can take such a central post. In addition to that, there was my own special background, the fact that I was from Germany, the son of a Nazi. These were factors that played a very important role. In the end, Rabbi Zvi Yehuda Kuk had the last word, and everyone accepted his decision. However, there were many problems after that. During army reserve duty—I served as a medic for several years—and after I got the post in Haifa, people said to me, "What are you doing in the Medical Corps? You're not a professional. You belong among the chaplains." Now in order to join the army rabbis, you have to take a course for officers, so again, there were disagreements behind the scenes. In the end, though, I was accepted and became an officer. Anyhow, today I'm a major in the Israeli Defense Force Reserves.

I emphasize this in particular when I speak with non-Jews. The week before last, for example, I spoke to a group from Germany, theologians from the Protestant Academy in Iserlohn. When I speak to such groups, I emphasize this because they tend to view Judaism as something peculiar, and I'm a living example. What does that mean, "particularism"? Or "racism" and such things? Though there is a particularism in Judaism on the one hand, on the other there is a lot of openness. It is a fact that converts are accepted—not only that—but a convert can even become a rabbi and serve as a major and chaplain in the Israeli Defense Force! That says something.

B: In everything you've said so far, you haven't mentioned much about your mother. I understand that your mother's view of things was somewhat different from that of your father—in respect to the Jews and to your conversion. Did she ever speak about the Third Reich, about her experiences?

M: Mother is not a university graduate. She's been a housewife all her life. In my case, I thought about all this from an intellectual perspective. But this wasn't so important to her. What had happened, had happened; there had been a terrible crisis. However, I don't remember any conversations of any particular significance . . .

When his facial expression shows some sign of pain, he reemphasizes an intellectual view of events. Is Thomas right? Can it be that Menachem is still trying to avoid the emotional side of his own life story?

B: Was she aware of what was happening to Jews in your immediate vicinity? Did she mention it when someone was arrested?

M: Yes, but it was the common excuse we hear all the time. She'd say, "We didn't know. We didn't know anything at all." Then there were those typical stories about the Third Reich, how Hitler had done important things, built the autobahn and all that. Kristallnacht, yes, we didn't live very far from the synagogue. But what occurred after that, beginning in 1940, and the concentration camps, I do recall that we discussed this, yes, and she knew nothing about it. The big excuse . . .

B: You think she did know something and was trying to blot it out of her memory?

M: No, I don't think so. She wasn't interested in politics. I don't think she knew anything.

B: What about your father, did he know?

M: That is possible. He may have, yes.

B: What was his rank in the SS?

M: He didn't have a high rank, he wasn't an officer. He was a non-com and didn't have a key function of any kind, either in the Party or in the army.

B: Did you ever try to find out whether his unit was involved in any actions?

M: He didn't discuss it. Basically, he didn't talk about such things. If I think back now, it may be that he didn't want to talk about it. There was a sort of taboo about such matters. After I had set out on my own path, I began to read certain books, and he said to me, "What do you want with books like that?" He'd say things like that. Then there was the Society of Returned Soldiers (Heimkehrerverband). He headed this organization. It still exists: a mixture of nostalgia and neo-Nazism. There are groups like it all over Germany, of men who had been POWs and who returned to Germany much later. Those circles are quite nationalistic, not really neo-Nazi in the sense of the neo-Nazi party—they don't write neo-Nazi slogans on their flag, so to speak—but the entire atmosphere . . . they used to take these trips and would invite the whole family, children too, in big buses. Sometimes they would organize a "veterans' evening" (Kameradenabend) at a bar, something like that. I never wanted to go along as a child, but they used to take me, they wanted me to accompany them. There were certain kinds of songs, particular statements they'd make, expressions they'd use. All this wasn't in public though, just within the framework of these groups.

His daughter comes in. These are the days of Purim,[2] and she wants to get one of her father's scarves for her costume. She laughs happily while he opens one of the wardrobes, looking for what she needs. Their chatter is so merry that I start to laugh too. It is hard to link this vivid image of a father and daughter in Jerusalem with the story of the family trips of ex-Nazis.

B: In your path toward Judaism, was your decision to make *aliyah*,[3] to join the State of Israel, a reaction to your father's attitudes?

2. Carnival festival celebrating the rescue of the Jews in Persia, as recorded in the book of Esther.

3. In Hebrew, *aliyah* means "going upward"; it is the Israeli term for immigration to Israel.

M: I don't think so. That's too . . . The entire question of conversion arose much later on. I didn't convert formally until I was twenty-eight. And I mentioned that in the beginning I had no such intention, even later, when I had studied theology and knew Judaism better. I studied the theological thought of a nineteenth-century rabbi who developed the notion of the "Law of the Sons of Noah." He was a Talmudic scholar who taught that there was no need to convert, because the Law of the Sons of Noah does not require formal conversion.

So there was a period in which I almost came to the conclusion that theologically, this rabbi's position was my position too: there was no need to convert. It would even be possible to remain in a Christian framework in some sense, but as a "son of Noah." All that is expressed in Jewish tradition. I wanted to be satisfied with that. But I was, nonetheless, so far removed from the center, in a metaphysical sense. I was in a Jewish college for three years, and then there was no alternative, although it was quite late in the process. That decision was much more intellectual than it was personal.

B: When did you change your name? Was it at that time?

M: No, that also came about in stages. In the beginning, well, Jewish tradition requires that you change your first name when you convert. That's when I chose the name Menachem. My last name, though, I kept for several years. Only when I immigrated to Israel, well, then I wanted to express the notion that a person's name is not just "sound and smoke," to quote Goethe, but also has meaning, especially here in Israel. So I wanted to give expression to the fact that the step I had taken was a serious one. I wanted to link my change of name in some way with this complete and total change and the fact that I wasn't returning to Germany.

Because I believe that the path I've taken and all the decisions related to it are a coming-to-terms with German culture in its broadest sense, not only a reckoning with what happened between the years '33 and '45, but rather, from the perspective of dealing with that entire legacy of Christian culture: two thousand years of Christianity, in which I see a long path of development that led to the ultimate "decline of the West," something like that. I'm not alone in thinking this way. There are others, colleagues of mine in theology, who also are no longer able to find their place either within the church or within the entire complex of German culture. They are colleagues in theology who went off in another direction, pursued philosophy. I don't know if that's any kind of alternative.

B: Were you thinking of your father when you made the decision to change your name?

M: No, I wasn't thinking about him, though I'd have to examine my own thoughts on that now. Maybe subconsciously there was . . . But if you ask me in this way, then I really do believe that the path I've taken is a highly intellectual one. It is not some sort of *response* to anything. Some such factor may play a role in it, but not a central one. I really left that culture in an intellectual sense, in contrast to Pastor Ehr. It's hard for me to understand him. Maybe the explanation is that he never recognized how Judaism was attacked by Christians.

B: He became a Christian . . .

M: Yes, he did. Though that entire circle—Rosenzweig . . . Rosenstock-Huessy also became a Christian. They were liberals, felt more German than Jewish. Even Franz Rosenzweig considered converting.

B: Yes, I'm familiar with this phenomenon even within my own family . . .

M: Right, it was something characteristic of the times, to the point that Hermann Cohen wrote his famous essay in 1917, "Deutschtum und Judentum" [Germanicity and Jewry], in which he spoke about the wedding between the spirit of Judaism and the liberal Protestant spirit. The great Hermann Cohen, writing that only fifteen years before Hitler came to power!

B: Do you know any others from an anti-Semitic home who took a step similar to yours: becoming Jewish and immigrating to Israel?

M: Because of my background, during the fifteen years that I've been here all sorts of people have contacted me asking whether I could help them in their conversion. Many Germans in particular, though only young people. I was recently asked to help prepare a German for conversion; he had passed the Abitur exams and left Germany at the age of eighteen. You might want to speak with him yourself. He converted at the age of nineteen, which is much younger than I was at the time of conversion. His father was a judge during the Nazi period, a district court judge. So I gave him lessons in preparation for conversion. He also studied at Merkaz Harav. A very bright boy.

There were others, some girls too, but all from the generation born after the war. The notion of the State of Israel influenced them, it was some sort of challenge. Some of them worked in kibbutzim, then returned. Sometimes there's a certain counterconsideration (shikul-neged) that is a factor. The most important figure in this connection is a professor who was an important authority on the Old Testament. He was the editor of the journal *Zeitschrift für die Wissenschaft des Alten Testaments*. Upon his retirement at age sixty-five, he and his entire family, his wife and three children, converted to Judaism. He was an adult during the Third Reich, but we've never discussed it. He is a very closed person. People seek me out for help in their conversion but never go to him. A few months back, he was attacked by Arabs late in the evening in front of his house. They didn't take any money or anything, just attacked him. He was slightly injured and felt depressed after that. Later I asked him, "How do you explain that? They didn't *steal* anything." He said, "You know, that's what happens to an old Jew," as if it were some manifestation of anti-Semitism. [*Laughs*] It might be interesting to speak with him about this topic in particular. I'm from the generation after, but he lived through that period, though I don't think he would be willing to speak with you.

B: I want to ask you a difficult question. How is it possible to comprehend a situation in which people took part in a program of liquidation on a daily basis, in camps such as Auschwitz and Treblinka, in the Einsatzgruppen? They were involved in liquidation and then went on home to their wives and children as if nothing had happened?

M: That's a question that must be dealt with. It's difficult to answer . . . that entire cruel and violent framework of the war. It was a calamitous tragedy for Europe, a jungle . . . people have forgotten what was done. I have asked myself that question. After I learned what had happened, when I would be sitting in a streetcar, a bus, a train, opposite people of a certain age, I'd look at them and ask myself, "A man who is now so polite, so clean . . . maybe he was one of *them*?" Perhaps the German soul is divided into two parts: a bright side and a dark side. Two sides of the same coin, so contradictory—all that culture, and then what took place! It is difficult to explain, difficult to explain. Perhaps obedience also played a role. It's so very characteristic of the Germans to obey orders. Eichmann used that excuse: he was under orders . . .

B: Imagine then that a father returns and doesn't talk about all this. What happens between him and his children? Does this have an influence on them? Can they feel it?

M: [*Moving uncomfortably in his chair*] Let me tell you, perhaps I was too young at the time. Just a few years, that wasn't much time, because after that I went off to other places. But I did ask myself that question in regard to Eichmann. They searched for him, and when they found him he had quite a normal family life, a wife, children at home. Maybe you need to ask Eichmann's children what they think today. It's difficult though, I don't have any answer . . .

B: Did you know the children of any such people back in Germany—children whose fathers were in Treblinka or in the SS?

M: Well, Thomas Heydrich. I met him only seven or eight years ago at my sister's home. She introduced me, said she would like me to meet Heydrich, and I immediately thought to myself: Heydrich! After all, it's not a common name, not Stauber, Lehmann, or Meier. And he spoke about his uncle . . . But I don't really understand him, even though he went off in another direction and expresses this in his work. Why doesn't he change his name? Maybe he plays a bit with it in some sense. After all, he is an actor. He even asked me to help prepare a tour for him here. He wanted to come and do a reading of German-Jewish authors in Israel, Heine and Tucholsky. "Heydrich reads Heine." I was shocked. That's impossible. I spoke with a professor in Haifa, a German Jew, about it, and he was shocked too.

The interview is over; he has to go to evening prayers. We walk together in the Old City of Jerusalem. It is a beautiful early spring afternoon. There are local Arabs, tourists from just about everywhere, religious Jews en route to the synagogue, and ordinary citizens out for a stroll, savoring the atmosphere of this sacred city. Into this "potpourri" a new element has been introduced: the son of a former German SS member and the son of a German Jew who are trying to make sense of what happened.

We meet again six months later. It is just after my second visit to Germany, and on the phone, Menachem tells me that he too has just returned from a short trip to Germany, where he attended his father's funeral. This time we meet at his university office not far from Tel Aviv, where he comes each week to teach a course in German-Jewish philosophy. It is a tiny room filled with books and papers, and I feel somewhat awkward about putting my tape recorder on his table. What if one of his Israeli colleagues comes by in the middle of our conversation? Menachem, however, is at ease, and we start almost at the point where we left off last time.

B: Have you had any doubts on the difficult and unusual path you have chosen?

M: That's not a proper question, because I didn't experience any pressure in this regard. It is an interest that stems from all those factors we spoke about in our first conversation. Put briefly, from the perspective of the events of German history and from the point of view of theological thought. It's not a question of history in the sense of what happened and how.

B: What I asked was whether you've had any doubts that the path you've taken is the right one . . . ?

M: Actually, the path back then was not planned as one that would lead to such a goal. I had interests, and I searched quite naturally for frameworks that would afford the possibility simply to study and pursue those interests. At first, of course, I studied thinkers who wrote in

German. Then I reached the point where that wasn't enough either, because I simply wanted to be able to live within a Jewish framework. Now how can you find a Jewish framework today in West Germany? That's very difficult. So I went to the United States, to Hebrew Union in Cincinnati. As a nonmarried student, I lived in the dorm with the rabbinical students and spent the evenings with them. This despite the fact that I was a goy [gentile]. There were two or three Ph.D. students in the dorm, and the rest were Jewish rabbinical students. Then the time arrived when I took stock of things, after having come down that long path. All sorts of considerations were involved, though I'd stress that they were *theological* considerations. I came to the conclusion that I should become a real Jew, not just a "son of Noah." It was so *natural* in the end, so obvious. It was perfectly clear that this was the decision I had to make—to become a Jew in a formal sense. So that's what I did. This course of development had started when I was thirteen. I was twenty-eight when I converted, so there was a period of some fifteen years leading up to this formal act. Yet I must emphasize that in the beginning I did not have any such intention.

B: Yes, but that's true of other people's lives too. We walk down a path and don't know where it is leading us. My question relates to later stages of the process, after you converted. Did you have any doubts later?

M: Did I ever regret what I had done? Look, that is *the* question. You're aware that Orthodox Jewish law states that converts are not received under compulsion, and no effort should be made to influence their decision lest someone regret that decision and find it's too late. Because once a Jew, always a Jew. You can't alter your nature, at least in respect to the Halakic concept. There have been instances in which individuals converted and regretted what they had done. Therefore, there are certain reservations in this regard. Sometimes people are not all that enthusiastic about preparing converts. However, almost twenty years have passed since then and, on the contrary, what came after that was a continuation on the path, climbing higher.

When I arrived in the States, I thought that maybe I'd go back to Germany later on. It wasn't clear to me. Everything was open. But immersion in Jewish thought brought me to the decision that my true place was in Israel. This led me to decide to leave the States, even though I'd begun to put down roots there, both in respect to a career and legally. I came to the conclusion that it wasn't for me. I had been to Israel several times on visits, and one day I decided that I should become an immigrant. So I bought a ticket, got on a plane, and came here. It was the continuation of the path in the form of *aliyah*. Then I married, and now I have five children. Doubts? None, none whatsoever.

B: Yes, but weren't there moments when you asked yourself, "What am I doing here?"

M: Look, nothing in this world is perfect. Not in Judaism either. Because the realistic approach within Judaism says: "*Be* holy!" Because you are not holy, it's put in the language of the future imperative. An objective, a task that you can never realize. All this talk about the holiness of the land and the people—though there are those who support such a view, I don't. I accept those currents in Jewish thought that view this as a task you must aspire to as much as possible, yet knowing it is impossible to attain such an ideal in perfect form in this imperfect world. Because that's the way it is. Certainly there are problems in this world, and in Judaism too. That's obvious. On the other hand, in comparison to all sorts of other ideologies and religions—to the Christianity I grew up in, European philosophy, the Holocaust—in contrast to all that darkness, Judaism is, despite everything, the light. Sure, there are shadows in that light, undoubtedly. But the light has greater power. I know with certainty, and I say this after nearly twenty years, this is my place, where I belong.

B: Did you try at all to influence friends in Germany to take the path you have taken?

M: Not intentionally, no. By the way, I was in Germany just a short time ago. I hadn't been back for some eleven years, but my father passed away. It was right at the end of the semester here. My sister phoned from Düsseldorf saying that he was in bad shape and she was very worried. After that she called and told me he had died and said, "You must come, you have to!" I told her I couldn't, it was the end of the semester, exams and all, but that I would try to come afterward, during vacation. Three minutes later she phoned again and pleaded with me in tears, saying that I simply had to come to the funeral for the sake of my mother. OK, two days later I was there. That was the external factor that brought me back to Germany. I was there three weeks and took care of many important academic matters. Since I went without my family, I was independent. Because of this opportunity, I was able to have many conversations with my friends. Heydrich was there too. He gave me a record on Ringelnatz that he had done. Satire. My sister has a large circle of friends from Düsseldorf and beyond. Every evening there was something else going on, in her apartment and elsewhere. All the conversations were a chance for people to get "firsthand" information on what is happening in Israel, and, of course, on the "Jewish question." All those matters.

So I had a chance to voice my views, but they asked questions and wanted to argue with me. They were very anti-Israeli. Maybe they weren't even aware of it. I would dare to say that this was a new, more sophisticated form of their old anti-Semitism. Intellectuals too, teachers, people like that. Heydrich was there, but he's philosemitic. But after several discussions, I regretted that I had stooped so low as to speak with them, that I had given individuals with such negative ideas the chance to talk with me. I felt insulted and hurt by these conversations. I regret that I talked with them, because the very fact that I did conferred on them a certain respect and honor.

There were certain other more serious people, including theologians. That's something else; such groups sometimes come to visit here. I live in the Old City, and they want to hear a lecture on what Judaism is, what Reform Judaism is, Conservative Judaism. So I tell them what I think. But there is no motivation there to be any kind of missionary. If someone *decides* to take this path, has that intention and then comes to me for guidance in order to prepare for conversion, well, that is something else. We talk with them, teach them, give them books so that they can pass the test at the Rabbinate. Beyond that, I'm not one of those missionaries for Judaism.

B: How was the visit with your sister and mother?

M: My sister has already been to Israel several times. My mother has never been. The last time I had seen her was when I was in Germany eleven years ago. It was a bit strange, despite everything. Imagine: suddenly I must take part in his funeral. My father wasn't in the church. Back then, he was involved more or less in the Party. And the Waffen SS. He didn't return to the church, he was against it. So that everything I did ran against the grain of his view and was against his will. He had all sorts of functions in various organizations that were quite nationalistic. This was reflected also at his funeral. There was this fanfare, flourish of trumpets. I was standing way at the back. People don't know me because I left so many years ago. It's some thirty years, a generation already. Of course, the entire family was there. The whole family stood at the side of the grave. People expressed their condolences. But I was way at the back, as if I wasn't one of the participants. I came just because it was the right and proper thing to do.

In regard to my mother, that's something else. She was never against me. She's not ideological. She came to accept what I did over

the course of time. Whether she is happy about it or not I don't know.
After the funeral I went to my parents' home and stayed there for
several days. Over the years, they had told the neighbors I was in the
United States. Of course, I *was* in the United States for three years.
But I've been in Israel for nearly sixteen years! "He's still over in the
U.S." They simply concealed the fact that I was in Israel. However, I
made a stupid blunder, a faux pas. Some neighbor suddenly came
over to me, and I started to talk about Israel. Then the cat was out of
the bag. So there was no alternative left but to tell the truth. It wasn't
very pleasant.

B: How was the relationship of your sister with your father?

M: It was good. His views about Jews apparently didn't have any
influence on her. Her children attend the Jewish kindergarten. There
were certain friends, however, who still have a German nationalist
perspective, with all that implies when it comes to Israel. Also the Jews
themselves, they became worse than the goyim. I walked out of the
synagogue wearing a kipa and they said, "Why are you still wearing a
skullcap? It's dangerous!" And that was even before what happened
in Istanbul.[4] An armored car of the Border Guard watches over the
synagogue during the entire Sabbath. Strange things after being away
for eleven years. So I was happy to return home, to get back to Jerusalem.

B: Did your father have any contact with you before he died?

M: There was none, because . . . OK, I did write occasionally, there
were letters, but only to Mother. I phoned my sister on her birthday,
once a year. And sometimes he would get on the phone too, though
there was no connection between us. Interesting thing, my sister told
me a story. He was near death and one of his friends came to visit him.
Now that friend looks a bit like me. Afterward, he told my sister that
I had been there. That apparently gave him some sort of inner re-
pose. I don't know if it really happened, but it is what she told me.

B: She didn't correct his mistake?

M: No, she let him believe it. If the story is true, maybe it reveals a
certain connection between us despite everything. [*Pauses, very agitated
for a second*] But in actuality, there was no contact.

B: Did she tell you about any arguments they had?

M: Yes, but only arguments that took place within the framework
of the relationship between a father and his daughter—a daughter

4. The massacre in the Istanbul synagogue in 1986, in which twenty-five Jews were
killed during Sabbath prayers.

who loves her father, a father who loves his daughter. Their relationship was a good one down through the years. There were conversations of that kind, but none that were political. In actuality, there was no change in his opinions.

B: Do you talk to him in your imagination, try to examine things, make them clearer?

M: Look, if that had been feasible and would have resulted in something, perhaps I would have been pleased. Maybe. On the other hand, I know his background. I know the anti-Semitism he had grown up with as a child, an entire milieu that was saturated with anti-Semitism. It didn't start with Hitler. To the point that at his death—and then at the funeral—I felt nothing at all. Felt as if nothing had happened. In Judaism we have Yahrzeit, Kaddish, the seven days of mourning, the thirty-day memorial. But it was as if he were someone I had no relationship with whatsoever. Somebody had died, my sister had phoned and asked a favor of me . . . it was really cold, cold. And I know that in Judaism even a non-Jew, according to Halaka, can, if he chooses, sit the seven days, mark the thirtieth day, just like a Jew, even though it is not his obligation. Yet I didn't think of doing any such thing. It was as if nothing had happened. It was an act of politeness on my part. That's all. Really. After the funeral I . . . I went back to taking care of my affairs.

B: I think you're very angry with him . . .

M: [*Angrily*] No, no! It doesn't interest me at all! I'm not angry with him. It's not a significant factor in my life. Besides, I only got to know him after I was ten years old because he had been in Siberia. And I left home in 1959. Not for good, I would come back during vacation, visits.

B: You don't remember those first years with him?

M: [*Hesitates*] Only in Czechoslovakia during the war. The children were evacuated because of the American bombing of the Ruhr. I remember that he returned once during vacation, in uniform, for a day or two. It was a very brief visit. I was four years old, I can remember. He was in Sudetenland, a German territory. That was the first time I saw him. As if some stranger had arrived, someone I hadn't known as a child. No anger, no regret. A stranger who then left the stage of life, departed.

B: What do your children know about him?

M: Nothing. They have my wife's parents as grandparents. They are from Algeria and are very warm people. They have nothing to do with my parents . . . They do not exist for them. My sister does, because she visited us a few times, but my parents don't. When they become teenagers, maybe then I will tell them the background, but today it means nothing to them . . .

During the bus trip back to Beer Sheva I try to make sense of my own feelings: Heydrich's nephew and Menachem the Jewish rabbi—to whom do I feel closer? Both were open with me and shared their intimate thoughts and feelings. With both I spoke in my two mother tongues, German and Hebrew. But one remained a gentile, while the other stepped over to "my" side, to Judaism. One, an actor, presents Walter Mehring in Düsseldorf, so that the younger generation will not forget its Jewish poets, while the other teaches Jewish theology and philosophy to Israeli students at the university. The first devoted nineteen years of his life to keeping his last name, while the second gave up his name after a fifteen-year journey to Judaism. One loves his parents, even recognizes his diabolical uncle in himself, while the other "can't feel anything" at his father's funeral. One unmarried, no children; the other married to an Algerian Jewish woman, five children. I cannot make up my mind: I feel close to both of them in exceedingly different ways.

chapter 8

Freedom and Responsibility

I meet Bernd during my third stay in Germany. I know about him during my first stay, but I am not sure then whether I want to interview him: he is the son of a prominent Nazi leader extensively discussed in the media. I am afraid I will meet a person who has been influenced by all the publicity. Then I am informed that he himself never appears publicly; it is mainly his sister who has been approached by the media. Beyond that, he is a former priest, and I am looking for "confessional settings" as part of my research: did victimizers approach priests (or physicians or psychologists) to confess the atrocities they were involved in during the war? During my first and second stays in Germany, I got in touch with some eighty priests, physicians, psychologists, and psychiatrists, but none could inform me of such a confession. Only two, a psychiatrist and a physician, had heard from their colleagues about such an experience. Can Bernd help me in this respect?

I call him about a month after a television program on children of victimizers in Germany. A book on the subject was published earlier in the year and another is on the way. I feel a new tension in the air—very different from earlier visits, when I gathered my data quietly. Then I worked in a kind of vacuum, which seemed peculiar, since I was in a country populated by hundreds of thousands of descendants of Nazis. I wonder if this new development will affect Bernd's willingness to be interviewed. He listens to my introductory remarks and reacts hesitatingly, "So many years have passed, and so many people do not understand." "It is difficult for both of us to meet, even after all these years, but let us try," I say. There is a long pause, but finally he agrees. We arrange to meet at my university office several days later. I hope he does not change his mind in the meantime.

When we meet, I am stunned by his likeness to photographs I have seen of his father. It takes me a few minutes to realize that the Nazi era is over; I am meeting the son, who had nothing to do with those times. A strong hand-

shake, then a long silence. On the way upstairs, we chat about universities and schools. He is teaching religion at a high school. We are both a bit shy.

Br: I was born in 1930 in Munich, and I grew up in southern Germany as well. I entered primary school in 1936 in F., where we were living at the time, and then we moved to Berchtesgaden. Maybe you're familiar with that place because of its famous name. I continued on in school in Berchtesgaden. That school was something like the college-preparatory high school (Gymnasium) we have today. But things didn't turn out very well for me there. I guess I played hooky too often. My father wasn't at home at that time and . . . So they gave me this blue slip to take home, a warning that I might flunk out of school. My father's reaction to this was very extreme: he sent me to a Nazi boarding school in Volkerdingen on Lake Starnberg. I was there until the end of the war. So I was at home only during vacations. That, in brief, is how I spent the time we want to talk about.

Maybe I should say right at the outset that I don't have much to tell you about your topic—the question whether I had any experience at all with the persecution of the Jews, since at the time we moved to Berchtesgaden there weren't any Jews living there. And certainly not on the Oberkarlsberg, where we were. The place was a kind of ghetto with three interconnected zones of protection. Zone A was the inner zone, B and C formed the outer circle. We were living in Zone B. Everything was under the security protection of the SS. Only the families of top people in the leadership lived there, along with everyone needed to maintain this relatively large settlement. I mean, there was an entire battalion of SS troops stationed there, along with officers and service vehicles. Everything necessary for a headquarters. It wasn't just military. No, it was organized as a place you could go back to in order to rest.

I can recall only one incident from that time connected with my starting high school. It was Easter 1940. There was a copy of the newspaper *Der Stürmer* on display in a case next to the entrance to the school. It contained some terrible news [anti-Semitic propaganda], and I told my mother. She tried to calm me down, but after that, *Der Stürmer* wasn't put in that display case anymore, probably because it was in nobody's interest to shock young people in that way. Especially because it wasn't a relevant question in Berchtesgaden. I didn't see or hear anything at all in connection with Kristallnacht. It wasn't mentioned. I was eight years old at the time, and it wasn't talked about at home. Maybe in the papers it was possible to read about it. But an eight-year-old child doesn't read newspapers yet, so I can't remember anything in that connection. But my confrontation with the persecution of the Christians by the Nazis was much worse. That was the real problem for us. I had a very strong and direct experience of that. I didn't think that was so terrible. But it was the actual counterpart [to the persecution of the Jews] because the Catholic church was presented as being an extension, so to speak, of Zionism. The confrontation with the Jews was considered to be over and finished, taken care of more or less.

As far as I can recall, I never, ever saw anyone wearing a Star of David. But my wife had quite a different experience. She was from Upper Silesia. And she has terrible memories, of Kristallnacht, for example. Her mother cried bitterly, because the shop of a family they were friendly with had been smashed. The persecutions affected almost everyone who was of any importance in the world of business. Naturally, no one spent much time criticizing these things, but they knew about it. Then they took in a Jewish girl, and she stayed on for many years—she left in 1940 or '41, I'm not sure. She never had any problems. She was well taken care of there. She even participated in the BDM youth movement, the League of German Girls, though that was more a kind of cover for her. So she survived that whole period.

The confrontation with the Jews was considered "over and finished, taken care of more or less."

B: Maybe we could go back a bit. You were the oldest son?

Br: Yes.

B: What are your earliest memories of family life?

Br: Well, when we moved in 1936 from F. to the Oberkarlsberg, and then building the house up there. Before that, I remember a little about school. I have one memory from F. that stands out from the rest: I had to leave religion class. I wasn't allowed to take part. My family had formally left the church. "Pious and God-fearing" is a terribly deceptive label people use. Then there's another, similar memory: My sister, who died in 1947, went along to church services on Ash Wednesday, which is quite customary in a Catholic town. When she came home and ran over to hug my father, he saw the black cross of ashes on her forehead. He was really furious. That was in 1939. I was about nine years old.

It's very difficult to recall anything definite. I used to ask my mother—I can't remember exactly how old I was—what the crosses were supposed to mean. I noticed them at some point there in Bavaria. But my mother didn't give me a straight answer, she avoided the question. Then I asked one of the drivers, and he explained to me what they meant. Then he walked away. He said you shouldn't talk about things like that with kids. It was a taboo subject. I can't recall much. When we moved there, they still had the heads of the church communities. They hadn't been disbanded yet. There was still a Catholic church community. But then it was dissolved. They had to leave the settlement up on the Oberkarlsberg. Only later on, after the war, did I find out that a few of the girls who were working for us at home used to go down more or less regularly to attend church services in Berchtesgaden. They didn't have any problems with my dad because of that. He permitted them to go. He apparently was of the opinion that the whole matter would take care of itself with time. There was a religion class in Volkerdingen, but that was more Germanic ideology. It became more and more radically anti-Christian during the years 1940 to '45. And the confrontations with the population living there ... For example, in 1944–45, we were only allowed to go out in groups. We weren't permitted to go around in the village alone, because occasionally some of our young people, who were in uniform, were attacked, and there were fistfights. Perhaps it had already been influenced a bit by the resistance movement and the White Rose group.

B: What are your earliest memories of your father?

Br: [*Hesitates*] A trip through Germany. That must have been in 1936–37. Once I was allowed to go along, to Thuringia. That's the first time I remember meeting my grandmother. It must have been 1936 or '37. She lived in Weimar. He was often away. Yes, after the war started, I mean, how often did we see him . . . And on top of it, I was in Volkerdingen. He visited me there a couple of times. Otherwise I would go home during vacation, but he usually wasn't there then. He was at home only a few days during the whole year. My memory is that then he would pack the entire family into the car and drive out somewhere and then walk with us in the woods. And we went to visit the place where he was building something.

B: Did you like that?

Br: Yes, it was a little exhausting at times because he used to walk faster. Especially so for the younger children.

Bernd looks at me as if he has noticed my presence in the room for the first time, and smiles. His expression is a tender blend of love and pain as he recalls this early memory of his father.

Br: After the war I tried very hard to meet an uncle, my father's brother, and learn something about the reasons why my father was so very clearly and evidently against the Catholic church. But I was able to find out very little. My father left home at the age of fifteen, ran off during the First World War. His father died when he was three. His mother remarried, and his stepfather, who also had children from his first marriage, mistreated his second wife and his own children, as well as my father and uncle, but mainly the older boy. So that's what led to this conflict. And then when my father was a teenager and left home, he wanted to enlist in the army, but he was too small, too weak, so he worked in an oil press until he was drafted in 1917. Then he told his mother he wouldn't come home as long as his stepfather was there. He didn't return home until 1923, after his stepfather had died. My uncle, my father's younger brother, says that his stepfather whipped Christianity right out of my father, so to speak, because he was pious in a very narrow-minded way.

So this piety on the one hand and the rough way he treated my father on the other led my father to think—much more so than in the case of his brother—that the whole thing was a pack of lies. He was still very young at the time. He got involved with the Freikorps [German nationalist groups] at the end of the war, knocked around with them. Then he moved to Munich, became involved with the top leadership of the SA, and moved very rapidly up the ladder.

B: As a child, how much did you sense of what was happening at the time? What was National Socialism like at home? What did you experience?

Br: We lived very cut-off and isolated. You could only get in with a proper I.D. It started pretty early on. Even before the war, these guard posts were in existence, and they expanded them more and more. The farmers were transferred to other areas. Anyone who wasn't part of that circle had to leave. So you had the feeling—OK, not that you were actually locked up—but that you were living in a special area. But we could leave and go down to visit our school friends in Berchtesgaden whenever we wanted. Then they opened an elementary school up on the Oberkarlsberg, so we didn't have to go down into Berchtesgaden anymore. There was an increasing isolation from the rest of the population. When there were big receptions or visitors, the guards were there. I can recall when Chamberlain visited. We were able to see via telescope directly from our house up onto the mountain. Everything was remodeled and expanded at our house. When that was finished, we also received foreign guests. The Italian ambassador and people like that stayed at our place, they were put up there.

B: And they were important people to you?

Br: They were important people. This made me someone special then, but cut me off at the same time.

B: And what impressed you especially, what was discussed?

Br: A big change came for me when I was sent to that school in Volkerdingen, above all else because I wasn't sent over there in the normal, regular way. Normally, this was a school for a special, select group of pupils. In my case, I was sent there by my father, and they were told to make a decent person out of me, since I had cut school, played hooky before that.

B: Was there a personal confrontation between you and your father?

Br: [*Hesitates*] No. He wasn't at home. He was at the Führer's central headquarters at the time. That must have been his headquarters in the west. This was right before the campaign in France. My mother phoned, wringing her hands because I'd brought home a blue slip. So on May 10, the day the invasion of France began, I was taken with my luggage to F. It was very difficult for me at first, somehow a hard pill to swallow. The others had already been there for four weeks when I arrived. I came there not as the result of a process of selection, the way the others had, but rather because my father at that time was also the person in charge of this school. This fact served to isolate a person more than to integrate him. So I had to try hard to adapt to the strict rules there. I was only ten years old. It was like a military academy with a lot of emphasis on sports. And I wasn't very athletics-minded. So I had to make up for that in an intellectual way and through friendships. I was successful at that. Things worked out, but at first it was awful, mainly because there were such strict, draconian rules.

B: Were you given recognition?

Br: Recognition, well, I was known, but, well, nothing special. On the contrary, because of the fact that I'd gotten in there as a result of my connections. My classmates didn't know anything about the blue slip. But I hadn't been admitted there through the normal process of selection. And initially I wasn't able to keep up with the others when it came to sports. So I made a kind of negative impression. My academic accomplishments were quite good after a short time. Yet I had my problems blending in with the others. It was no advantage for me, having been sent to the school in that way. On the contrary, it was a disadvantage.

B: Did you get back home frequently?

Br: We were able to go home three times a year: at Easter, during summer vacation, and at Christmas. [*Bitterly*] My father was very strict during the vacations. I always had to do something or other, so the summer vacation wasn't really a vacation. I was sent to work in a garden nursery during the first summer vacation, and the second summer, I had to work on a farm. The third summer, I was sent to Mecklenburg to work on a farm during the harvest. There was a nice side to all this as well. I learned how to ride a horse, and the last summer vacation, 1944, I learned how to drive a car. So I was always busy with something. I had very little free time for myself.

B: How did your mother react when you, as the oldest son, left home?

Br: We wrote each other regularly. We didn't telephone much at that time. I had been sent there by my father—and my mother too—to sort of keep tabs a bit on the school, make sure it was running smoothly. I was a kind of informant, so to speak, in a positive sense. For example, there were certain problems. The menu that was issued every week didn't correspond a hundred percent with what we were actually served. Once I innocently mentioned this in passing when I was home. After that, my father asked me to send him the menu every week, with commentaries. The upshot was that once he came unannounced and checked up on what was going on. Then he set the place in order, and a few of the staff were sent elsewhere, because they had clearly—and he'd caught them in the act—been stealing. They used to steal things from the pupils and then sell them. It was corruption. So this didn't help my standing much with the teaching staff. We weren't permitted to send a letter without first having it cleared by a teacher, but I had my stamps from my father, and naturally they couldn't say anything against that. Or do anything. It definitely helped all of us there, the fact that more attention was paid to make sure certain things didn't happen.

B: As a result of this, did you have a positive feeling toward your father? A feeling that he could help you when you needed him?

Br: [*Smiling*] Yes . . . although he only offered his help in connection with matters that he regarded as being correct. He would take action if something was being done improperly.

B: How did your mother react to the fact that you had been sent to this school?

Br: I don't know. No one spoke to me about that. And I didn't think that the school was bad for me. I still think today that the school didn't harm me. If I had been singled out too much as the son of my father, that definitely wouldn't have been good for me.

B: What influence did the fact that you were away from home have on your relationship with your siblings?

Br: Well, we definitely didn't become strangers as a result. I would say that I was kind of the big, older brother. The fact that I was always running around in uniform didn't matter in this respect.

B: And how do you feel about them? Having younger siblings while you were not around?

Br: That didn't bother me at all. On the contrary, when the bombing raids started, my mother took in fifteen children from the Ruhr during the vacation, children who were still too young to go to school. Later on, she took in children in a second house in the Black Forest that her father had bought for her and which was renovated as a place for the children. When the end of the war came, she was brought, together with my siblings and the children she'd taken in, to the South Tyrol. And she declared the house there to be a home for children. Many of them weren't even six years old.

B: Had you already returned at that point?

Br: No. I was in school and didn't come home anymore. My school was disbanded. The fourteen- and fifteen-year-olds . . . Maybe there were about 150 . . . no, not even that, maybe 120 boys, were sent marching south, and the idea was to use us as home guard troops (Volkssturm) on the southern front. Luckily though, the weapons didn't arrive, and so we were disbanded and sent to the countryside to escape the bombing raids. When the school was disbanded, it was a very chaotic affair. Because we had to draw sketches from the school atlas, and we were given food and ration stamps for a week along with a hundred marks, and then told that each of us would have to make his way home by himself. I got a special assignment. First they said I should try to reach my mother in the South Tyrol, but that was cancelled after a short time. I wasn't sent away. Then they sent me to Salzburg, where I was supposed to be taken care of by the Nazi District Director (Gauleiter).

Since I felt that everything was very uncertain down there, I decided to join the people I knew who were in this convoy of trucks. But when they moved on, I fell sick and stayed with a farmer in the mountains, who took me in. I told them I was from Munich, and I used a different name. I knew from my father's brother that everything in the center of town had been burned, that the town hall had burned down, and the registry had been destroyed. So I assumed a fictitious name with a fictitious address in Munich. It was impossible to check it. Since I was sick, I was literally unable to walk, but the farmer and his family just took me in. I was accepted by them as if I were their own son, at the age of fifteen. I used to spend every morning up on the mountain pasture, though I would have relapses because of the food poisoning I'd had. Gradually I recovered, and I did the work as well as I was able to.

B: When did you see your mother again?

Br: I didn't see my mother again. She died in 1946 of cancer. I had my first very short, but not direct contact with my siblings in 1947. Maybe as a result, I was caught and deported from Austria. Because of all those interrogations and whatever, I had already been in touch with the religious order I later entered. I had contacts in the spring of 1947 with the Catholic church in Germany, and they took me in. They were the ones who made it possible for me to return to school. I finished high school and entered the order in the autumn of 1951.

B: I'd like to go back to the year 1945. Did you sense at school that a collapse was in the offing?

Br: That actually started with us in 1944.

B: In your family?

Br: In the family and at school too. But it was stronger at school than at home. In our family, my father had ordered everyone to be optimistic.

B: How did he put it, what did he say?

Br: "Even a dying lion can still strike out." That was his optimism in the face of fear. I can't say to what extent he actually believed it. I got the last letter in March 1945. He still had the same view then, that victory could not be taken from us, but he certainly no longer believed it himself. When school started again in September, we had to miss classes in order to strengthen the fortifications in the area. That was quite conspicuous and unusual. In addition, the fourteen- and fifteen-year-olds were trained to use infantry weapons, all the way to anti-tank weapons, and were organized as a battalion of the Volkssturm home guard. All that was an indication that things were deteriorating.

Once I was caught doing something. I had gotten a radio as a gift for my fourteenth birthday—there weren't any transistor radios back then—but I'd been given a small portable. That was quite a special thing. We would listen to the Allies at night. And once we were caught in the dormitory by one of the teachers, but he stayed to listen too. From that time on we would listen, although with a bad conscience. We were also able to locate other stations for soldiers, Allied forces stations broadcasting in German. From the grid locations they gave, you then had to figure out the real line. That was a crucial matter for a number of us, since the students came from all over the German Reich. Then they would hear that their hometown had been overrun, and they would wonder how they'd ever find their families again as the Russians broke through into East Prussia, then Silesia, and gradually started pushing westward.

B: And you would talk about this?

Br: Naturally we discussed it. In a hidden way, carefully, since you wouldn't dare say anything that would have been interpreted as defeatist. The mood got worse and worse. Once we were assembled and they asked who would volunteer for operations such as one-man torpedos and exploding boats. And a number did volunteer. But the papers apparently weren't sent on or just stayed on someone's desk, I don't know, but nothing else happened to us. Then on April 23 we were transferred to Steinach. Very late. The road was broken, the railway destroyed, and we still didn't have any weapons. We stayed there until April 28 or 29. Then half of us became sick, probably because of contaminated food. About seventy boys had come down with a bad case of diarrhea. And that's when we received the order to disband. I spent the night from April 31 to May 1 in Lenbach in the Tyrol. I had been taken there by someone from the Party Chancellery, a man who'd been assigned to take care of what was left of the school. That was the nearest Party headquarters in this area. They were a small group of diehards. Then, at 2:00 A.M., we heard on the radio that the Führer had died in the circle of his loyal people. The mood was one of despair, the end of the world. During the following two hours, eight people shot themselves in Lenbach. I was almost ready to do so myself. Then I met a friend and we talked each other out of it. And cried. It was terrible.

The next day I returned to the Oberkarlsberg. My mother wasn't there. She was with the children in the South Tyrol. I met my father's secretary—I still had my own papers at that time—and he said, "Are you insane?" and arranged for me to get false papers: a piece of paper with a stamp, the stamp blurred so that it was impossible to read. Then he sent me on. He told me I should try to disappear someplace. What we feared most was that we would be caught. We had been taught, it had been drilled into us, that if they caught us they would finish us off. It would be terrible.

I sense the excitement of those days in Bernd's short sentences and breaking voice, even now, forty-two years later, although he tries very hard to control it.

B: Do you know whether your father tried in any way to rescue you?

Br: I don't know anything about that. I only know one fact. The last radio message my father's secretary got he didn't pass on to my mother. But after that he sent my mother in a big bus with the children to the South Tyrol. He never told me what was in the radio message, but there is reason to believe it may have said that my mother should commit suicide together with the children, the way Goebbels did. Apparently my father was no longer able to contact her, it was only possible via radio. The telephone lines were all cut, and the telegraph was no longer operating.

B: Did someone speak to you about this?

Br: No, I only found out about it later on.

B: So what happened then in that place in the Tyrol where those people committed suicide?

Br: At 4:00 A.M. the leader had us assemble and then made a speech. He said the cherries would bloom again. "Your women and children are waiting for you. Whoever turns a weapon against himself is running away from life, running away from his responsibility toward his family." In this way, he gave the people there a kind of moral pep talk. Then I said I wanted to get out.

B: What did you think would happen?

Br: Initially, I didn't know. But I ended up with farmers and survived by living with them. First of all, it was just simple survival but then also the feeling that things would get better. I sat with them at the same table, was fully integrated into the family, without their asking a lot of questions. I was also able to help out, since the farmer's sons were still away in the army. Two of them returned in 1945. Another one didn't come back until 1947, from Yugoslavia. But they were weak, their health impaired. I'm still in contact with them—not with the old farmer and his wife, they died long ago, but with the farmer who has the place now, the son who returned from Yugoslavia. And I am in touch with his children. This experience of living as a Christian—the complete and total opposite of everything I had heard at home—was ultimately influential in my becoming a Christian, in my becoming a priest.

B: Had you begun at that time to doubt everything your father believed in? When did you start having doubts?

Br: [*Hesitates, agitated*] Not yet. I didn't know anything about the Holocaust then. We only found out after the war. And my doubts arose in the course of the year 1946–47, when there were more and more reports, when there was an organized network of newspapers again. When I had time to read newspapers, in the winter of 1945–46. Evenings are long in the winter and there isn't so much work. In the summer, I was taking care of the animals up on the mountain and didn't hear any news reports at all. There was no radio, no newspapers, nothing. The only ones who repeatedly upset us were the Americans. They'd come on up and try to shoot wild goats. When they didn't find any, they'd shoot the cows or calves of the farmers. In liberated Austria! So that was a difficult experience for the farmers in Austria. That was the first thing.

When the media gradually started to operate again—we didn't have any radio receiver at that time on the farm, and there wasn't any electricity, all there was was the newspaper—the farmer would get the *Salzburger Nachrichten,* a weekly. That's still a leading newspaper in Austria, a leading daily. There was an editor by the name of Naumann who wrote the editorials. He's someone I still admire today. I must say that his editorials and the reporting in this paper, which always tried to be honest and fair, gradually enabled me to recognize the truth and face that truth.

B: Were you able to speak with anyone about it?

Br: No, that was the other half of the bad situation, because I couldn't tell the farmer who I really was. They didn't know anything, and I was afraid. I lived there in a rather isolated way and didn't become friendly with anyone. I just kept to myself as much as possible. For example, I told the farmer I was Protestant. They were all Catholics. And their reaction was beautiful. They inquired at the nearest Protestant church and got me a schedule for church services. They wanted to help me make some contacts there. But I went up into the mountains. I went off alone whenever I had free time. Under certain circumstances, being alone leads to a process of thinking about things, pondering matters.

The most important things for me were the first pictures. Those photographs from Bergen-Belsen, for example. Who could have thought such a thing was possible? We had a work company from Dachau at the school in F. I think that was '42 or '43. In any case, for a period of two years. They worked in construction because our school campus was still being built. We saw the people from the concentration camp, but they were over in a barracks camp surrounded by barbed wire with a watchtower and SS guards. The people would come to work singing. They didn't look hungry and emaciated at that time, they looked relatively well fed, maybe because as an external construction unit, they belonged to a better group anyhow. We never witnessed any attacks by guards directed at prisoners. We only saw some being mistreated by two Kapos who were there. The Kapos were taken from among the prisoners. Under certain circumstances, they would beat their fellow prisoners, would threaten them or throw stones at someone who had stopped to rest. "Concentration camp" was a concept we were familiar with, but we didn't believe it was anything worse than a jail or a prison, that it was something other than a punishment for people who had done something wrong. We weren't familiar with that. We did learn what the various triangles in different colors meant. The green triangles were for the criminals. Red was for political prisoners; political prisoners were against National Socialism, they were enemies of the state . . .

B: And what about the Jews?

Br: They never came up to the school. I never saw any Jews there. I don't know either whether there were Jews in Dachau. There were a lot of Christians in Dachau, but they weren't allowed out either. Then there were red badges with a P on them. Those were Poles, Polish political prisoners. Homosexuals, for example, also weren't permitted to leave the camp. We only heard about that from the guards. We were allowed to talk to the guards, and we asked what the badges meant. Black, green, red—that's all there was. Religious groups weren't allowed out either. Jehovah's Witnesses. So all those who were regarded as dangerous because they might establish contact with the population were not let out of the camp. I don't know when the death camps, the extermination camps, were introduced. But I think that the extermination camps, in the true and horrible sense of the word, were set up in connection with the overcrowding in the concentration camps, and that probably wasn't until the war started to go against the Germans (als der Krieg sich wendete).

Extermination was begun because of overcrowding in concentration camps, when the war turned against Germany.

B: But the first death camps were established as early as mid-1942 . . .

Br: [*Tense*] Sobibor, Treblinka, yes. In the east. That was another point. The death camps were all in the east.

B: How did you understand or what did you think about those first pictures of Bergen-Belsen or Auschwitz?

Br: I didn't comprehend them at all. That is an abyss I can't explain. As a Christian, perhaps with the concept of what is called "the mystery of evil." The satanic dimension becomes visible and manifest for me in this somehow . . . Please don't misunderstand me. I don't mean satanic in the sense that I'm looking here for something supernatural, something beyond man as a scapegoat. But the terrible abyss, the horrible depths that can open up in a human being (die fürchterlichen Abgründe, zu denen Menschen fähig sind), the concept of sin—this became clear to me at this point.

B: Were you still in the mountains then?

Br: It started a little then as a result of what was being published. I can recall, for example, once when I had to go to the next district town, I accidentally met a former fellow pupil at the train station, and I didn't tell him where I was living. He didn't want to know either. What you don't know you can't blurt out to anyone else. We talked about the future. We were both completely uncertain about what the future would bring. But at that time, we were still of the opinion that, in terms of those first horrible reports, the people who'd been involved were criminals, outsiders. We thought then that National Socialism had been an exalted idea, one that had been misused by a handful of criminals and outsiders. That this was immanently a part of the system, that it was in the final analysis rooted in the ideology—insofar as one can even talk about a National Socialist "ideology"—that came only later on. Dr. Buchheim[1] in Munich tried very hard to clarify precisely that point. I think he is right in saying that what is called National Socialism does not, in reality, have any unified ideology. Rather it's a hodgepodge with a few common points: exaggerated German nationalism; excessive racism; and then the insane notion, based on this racism, that there is a chosen German people. Maybe way down deep somewhere, this is also a very fundamental reason for virulent anti-Semitism. The chosen people of the Bible, the Jews, recognized in Christianity as the chosen people, over and against this notion of a Germanic race. All that actually started long before National Socialism. Richard Wagner, Chamberlain . . . if you look into the roots of it . . .

B: What did you feel about your father? He was no longer around. Did he know about any of this? How did you confront this matter?

Br: [*Looking me straight in the eye*] I'm pretty certain today that he knew about everything, or almost everything. I'm also pretty certain that he approved of it all, more or less. I can only explain it by the fact that he grew up and into (hineingewachsen) this ideology as a young man. And that Hitler apparently represented for him a kind of father figure. That is all I was able to learn, from others who worked with him as well: he must have regarded Hitler as a kind of father figure, an absolute master. In the final analysis, all I can say about it is that God alone knows all the reasons, he alone can deal justly with a human being. There are so many influences that turn a person into what he becomes. So I am always very, very careful in every respect when it comes to blaming a person, placing guilt. Though on the other hand, I must state unequivocally that this absolute crime, these depths of human inhumanity, you just can't rationalize it, explain it away. You can't "psychologize" it either. Rather, there is no doubt that there is guilt involved here. And I believe that when something like this takes place, a person is conscious that he is not simply entangling himself in

1. Hans Buchheim, "Die SS in der Verfassung des Dritten Reiches," *Vierteljahrshefte für Zeitgeschichte* 3 (1955).

guilt, he is committing a sin (in Schuld sich nicht verstrickt, sondern dass er eine Schuld begeht). I believe that man is never so unfree as to be forced to commit a sin. Rather, responsibility presupposes the concept of freedom.

B: Did your father ever express any doubts about what he knew about the exterminations? Did he ever mention that he thought things would turn out badly?

Br: We never discussed the matter at all. I can't say whether he ever talked with my mother about this. She never spoke with us about it. Those were areas that had probably been made a taboo subject, maybe in an attempt not to burden children with matters that might indeed become burdensome. I do know in retrospect, though, that Himmler was once an eyewitness to such mass-shootings in the Baltic countries and that he himself was unable to stomach it. So that somewhere, the human quality breaks through despite it all. And that as a reaction to this experience—Himmler himself was unable to stomach these brutalities, the shooting of women and children in a pit—he then ordered the shootings stopped. He had heard from the commander that the soldiers couldn't stand doing it, that it wasn't combat duty befitting a soldier, it was murder, the murder of women and children. And the murder of women and children is something a normal person cannot stand, especially on this scale. Then apparently he also wanted to see for himself, to take part in such a shooting or to watch. And he felt sick. He couldn't stand the sight of it.

There is a thesis, a suspicion, that the gassings, these techniques, were basically a means of distancing the murderers from the killing, of making it more bearable for them. This is even more horrible. Perhaps it is an analogy to the Vietnam War or to war today: the greater the distance over which these horrible weapons operate, the less the person sitting at the trigger knows about the misery and murder, the death and suffering he is causing. Someone who drops his bombs from an altitude of thirty thousand feet doesn't see what is happening down below. Or say, a pilot in Afghanistan: he doesn't see what the explosives he drops actually do, the harm they cause.

B: If your father had seen that himself, would he have reacted differently?

Br: I don't know. I'm very uncertain about that. I don't know. Look, what do I really know about my father anyhow? Basically it is embarrassing, so very little, because he lived with us so little of the time. I occasionally saw my father when he was terribly angry. But those were always spontaneous outbursts over some trifling matter. I never experienced him being brutal with anyone. He was a farmer, a human being, a person who liked to be with other human beings. I saw him celebrating with other people at home, with guests. I saw the way he was on the farm, the way he dealt with the workers. I saw how he would act with animals, with the cattle. He loved farming and actually always wanted to return to it. After the war, he wanted to cast off all that political rubbish (den politischen Plunder wieder abgeben). [*With considerable pain*] What do I really know about him?

B: Can you say in retrospect that maybe he was in actual fact burdened by what was happening—I mean, by the extermination?

Br: Burdened? In what way? Psychologically (Vorbelastung) burdened right from the start . . . I don't know. I only suspect that his hatred of the Christian church was conditioned and caused by his unhappy youth with his stepfather. Somehow that seems to make sense. I can't say anything about the other matter. I can't recall a single instance when my father ever dealt at all with the problem of the Jews . . .

B: You mean he never even made any of those anti-Semitic remarks that were so common at the time?

Br: I can't recall any at all. I do know that he had had a complete falling out with his father-in-law because of his attitude toward the church and toward Christians. My grandfather had fired the leader of a Party branch from his office, and somehow my father agreed with him on this. In that respect, they were on the same wavelength. But when my grandfather started to defend the ministers and the churches . . . It went so far that we were no longer allowed to visit our grandparents, and they weren't allowed to visit us. But in respect to what you're looking for, I don't know anything.

B: Do you know other children from Berchtesgaden? I mean other children of prominent Nazis—Himmler's daughter, for example.

Br: We had no connection with them. I think I saw Pippi Himmler once—she was seven or eight years old—when we visited the Himmlers at Lake Tegern. Himmler came to visit us frequently, but always alone. Maybe he came once with his family when I was away at school, I don't know. Himmler was the godfather—not the baptismal godfather, but according to the code of the SS—of my brother. But then they began to go against each other more and more, and at the end, my father and Himmler were quite bitterly opposed rivals. But those are things I found out about only gradually after the war, the sorts of intrigues there went on in this top echelon of leaders.

B: How did your siblings deal with this part of the past?

Br: That's also something I can't say much about. Because I was in a religious order, I had very little contact with them. Yet it was only after the war that we became distant—I mean distant not only in the spatial sense. They are, well, we stick together, but there was very little discussion about such matters. Perhaps I talked the most with my oldest sister, who died in 1957. I think that she was the one who most came to terms with all of this, or at least tried to. She was married then to an Italian engineer. My second sister—she was born in 1934—has evidently suppressed (verdrängt) everything. And she doesn't want to think about it either. A purely defensive attitude: what I don't know, I don't have to deal with, to work through. In the spirit of that motto.

The most extreme instance of denial I experienced was with my youngest brother, but he doesn't bear sole responsibility for it. You also have to take into account the education and upbringing that shaped him—he was born in 1943. He went so far once as to say—how far he would go in that regard today, I don't know—but once he went so far as to say, "My God, my father, listen, what connection do I have with my biological father? He didn't shape and influence me. Look, I'm not responsible for what he did!" He simply cut his father out: it's a biological fact, a given, but no more than that.

Maybe when it comes to anti-Semitism, my father actually did have a different view. Although when it comes to foreign forced laborers in Germany, I do know that he was implicated in some very bad things: in exploitation of workers from France and from the eastern territories. He was certainly responsible for some terrible things in that connection. My father wasn't able to establish formally who his own great-grandfather was. His background wasn't in accordance with the stipulations of the Nuremberg laws on race because he wasn't able to complete his family tree. From 1932 until February 1945, my father had repeated correspondence with a whole series of people in the Office for Race and Settlement. He engaged a number of individuals in the search for his great-grandfather. He wasn't successful in locating him, and this must have upset him a great deal. Somehow this was traumatic for him. The first wife of my uncle worked on the staff of Rudolf Hess as of 1924, and it turned out that she did not have a pure Aryan family tree. When it was discovered, my father saw to it that this marriage was destroyed, more or less forcibly.

Hitler himself attempted to bring these two hostile brothers together again. My father refused even to say hello to his brother—he was a nonperson in my father's eyes. Once I tried to find out from my uncle, with whom I have a very good relationship, something about their childhood and youth that might have been a possible negative factor influencing all this. But he wouldn't talk about it. After 1945 he just withdrew into a kind of total silence, so to speak. About the first

half of his life, his childhood and youth, well, he just won't say anything. Absolute silence. Now that's something I just can't understand.
I mean, it would be very important for me, my brothers and sisters,
yes, and maybe their children, to arrive at a genuine clarification of all
these matters, to work them through in a full and thorough way.

*We take a short break. When we sit down again, I find the look in his eyes
warmer than at the beginning of our conversation. I tell him about my
interest in "confessional settings."*

B: Did anyone ever confess to you, or to one of your friends, about
the atrocities he was involved in in carrying out the Reich's extermination process?

Br: [*Hesitating*] No. I can't recall any such instance . . . Wait a minute, yes, there is one instance, although I am not sure if you are looking for this kind. He came to me shortly before he died. He told me
in his confession that over the years, the brown eyes of a six-year-old
girl had never let him rest. He was a Wehrmacht soldier in Warsaw
during the ghetto uprising. They were clearing the bunkers, and one
morning a six-year-old girl came out of one of these bunkers and ran
over to hug him. He could still remember the look in her eyes, both
fearful and trusting. Then his commander ordered him to stab her
with his bayonet—which he did. He killed her. But the look in her
eyes followed him all those years . . .

Bernd's voice breaks and his eyes fill with tears.

Br: And he came to confess this to me before he died. He had
never told it to anyone before.

*There is a long pause. Neither of us can go on talking. It is as if both of
us are seeing the imploring look in that child's eyes.*

B: [*Crying*] Tell me, maybe you can help me understand: how come
only those eyes? Why didn't he remember the eyes of all the others he
had probably killed? Why was he the only one to confess? What did all
the others do about the eyes of the children and women who looked
at them helplessly before they were killed? Maybe you can tell me how
he kept this memory to himself all these years?

Br: I don't know . . . I have no answers . . . I can only assume that
they all had some feeling of guilt, at some moment . . . to some extent
. . . But I really have no answers to your questions. I did not meet any
similar cases but can guess there must have been others.

*The tape records a long silence, during which I try to regain control over
my emotions. I feel I must conclude the interview in some reasonable way
but find it hard to do so.*

B: What can one learn from that period?

Br: Well, what can one learn? I think there are two things. First of all, I believe there are depths within a human being (Abgründe) that one is incapable of imagining as a normal person under normal circumstances, depths that can open up when a person gets into some sort of exceptional situation. Let me give you an example of such an exceptional situation quite aside from our topic. Take a situation of hunger in a camp, say, with prisoners of war or whatever. Now it is well known that people will start to eat each other, turn cannibal, in such a situation, even people who would never in their lives have thought it possible. For this reason, it is almost presumptuous to say, "It could never happen to me." The second side of it is that if you recognize this, then you have to train yourself—gear yourself mentally and imagine yourself in such situations in order to gather strength so that, in an emergency, you'll be able to resist.

As I see it, this is closely bound up with what kind of meaning you give your life and the way you view death. The moment death loses its horror, its sting . . . I believe I have discovered a key with which I can prevent my being amenable to extortion, to getting involved in such situations: the moment you are able to decide that you prefer to suffer an injustice yourself rather than to commit an injustice you have found a way out, one that can protect you, although I can't cancel the first thing by means of this. I can well imagine that torture can be so terrible you literally collapse. But it was my own personal experience during the civil war in Africa that this kind of training could be very useful. So it's a question of your inner freedom.

B: Could you give an example?

Br: Yes. I was put in front of a wall for execution three separate times as a priest in Africa. But it no longer frightened me. I was still able to stick by my values. And I told myself, OK, if they want to shoot me now, I won't be destroyed. Death is not the worst horror. And being shot is certainly not the worst horror. We trembled in fear of being tortured, yes . . . during that torment and torture, which exceeded the limits, well, I lost consciousness, but I was lucky. You reach a point at the boundary of the sensation of pain, a point beyond which you no longer feel anything. They marched us seven kilometers barefoot. We sat for three days in a swamp, our feet completely raw and exposed, because it had been raining all the time. Then they gave us rubber boots. You can imagine the condition the soles of our feet were in. They forced us to walk for seven kilometers over broken stones, and they whipped us. The stones pushed right up into our feet, but we didn't even sense the pain because of the lashes and blows we received on our backs. Somewhere there is a boundary to pain, a limit. Either you lose consciousness and collapse at that point, or one pain cancels out the other, so that you survive the experience.

B: What were your thoughts then?

Br: I thought it was the end.

B: Did you see any connection between that time and this?

Br: No, no. We were placed up against the wall three times and were rescued three times by our fellow Christians. They came on through and said we had to be spared because we were good people. The Zumbas took us as hostages because the white mercenaries had gone off with the army on the other side. They hadn't done anything to us earlier. This torture was certainly an abyss that opened up, but I don't think it had any ideological underpinning.

B: Do the students in your religion classes ever ask you about your personal past or about the Holocaust? What do you tell them?

Br: Yes, they sometimes do. It's something that doesn't remain hidden. Some are not interested in it, and others occasionally ask about it out of curiosity. I see no reason to deny it. I try to look at it positively and make an effort to advance things just a bit further. I must say that in the past three or four years, far fewer problems have been raised in this connection. I mean, today students are less politically oriented. This is connected with the fact that they've all had no—or very little— history in school. As I see it, this is a deficiency. It isn't the way to deal with these problems. Though naturally, when people come . . . For example, I got myself Hilberg's book, *The Destruction of the European Jews.*[2] I have no direct occasion for using it in teaching, but once I did try in my classes to teach students something about other religions. And when you start talking about Judaism, then naturally you have to deal with the question of the persecutions, the Holocaust. Where are the roots, what is the problem? You have to go back a long way in history. Where were the first pogroms? Why did they occur in Spain and Portugal? Why did they happen repeatedly during the Christian Middle Ages? Why did Christian princes brutally persecute Jews, again and again? What were the underlying reasons? Because the Holocaust is the endpoint in a development that began way back, some time during the Jewish wars or maybe even before that, if you want to go as far back as the Babylonian Captivity. For me, the history of Israel is the history of salvation. And it is a mystery to me to this very day.

---

2. Raul Hilberg, *The Destruction of the European Jews* (Chicago: Quadrangle, 1961).

We walk together to the local bus station, still preoccupied with our thoughts and emotions. We decide to meet again in a week. Bernd has agreed to be filmed in the video studio and will ask his wife to join him. I watch him as he walks away. He seems to carry a heavy weight on his shoulders, a great burden in his heart. I sense his deep commitment and his feeling of responsibility for what happened in his father's time.

It suddenly occurs to me that Menachem and Bernd share a common denominator: both have sought a spiritual refuge (whether Jewish or Christian) to help them cope with the burden of their parents' involvement in the Third Reich. Menachem has dissociated himself completely from his people; Bernd did so only temporarily during his missionary work in Africa. Did his own confrontation with his father's past or his life-threatening experience in Africa enable him to receive a dying man's confession? Or is it just a coincidence that he is the only priest who can report such an experience? I can still hear him say, "Responsibility presupposes freedom."

chapter 9

Small Hills Covered with Trees

Rudolf answers my ad in the local newspaper: "Children whose parents witnessed or took part in the persecution or extermination of Jews and/or Gypsies and who are willing to participate in a research project by an Israeli psychologist at the local university, please . . ." He calls and says he will speak only to the Israeli interviewer. We set up a time for the interview, and I agree to meet him at the bus station.

Compared to the interviewees I seek out, about whose parents, and their role during the war, I have detailed information, the ad respondents are a mystery to me until they tell their stories. I usually reach the meeting place a few minutes ahead of time in order to see the person arriving—how he approaches the station, what he looks like, if he seems troubled or at ease, if his expression changes when he recognizes me. But Rudolf is already waiting, glancing impatiently at his watch (although I am not late). He is tall and looks like a manager in some local firm. A strong handshake. I can sense his excitement. He starts talking immediately, but I steer him into small talk because I want to reach my office, where the tape recorder is set up. When we finally reach my room and I invite him to sit down, he pulls a yellowed sheaf of papers from his briefcase.

R: I was born April 4, 1930, in Wuppertal, the son of an unemployed textile worker. My father was out of work at the time. Before he lost his job, he was employed as a master craftsman in a textile plant. But there was a great deal of unemployment in the area, and he was laid off too.

B: Are you the only son?

R: I was the only son until 1940, when my brother was born. He's still alive. He was born on January 14, 1941, in Wuppertal. I spent those very early years more or less pleasantly until my dad found work again. He found a job later, I'm not sure exactly when. We were living in quite a primitive little house. Although he was out of a job, my father built himself a small house in a garden. He was very enterprising, but the thing about him—right up until he died he was a very pious and believing Christian. And that has accompanied me through my entire life—Christianity, being a Christian. At home we would pray— have a Bible hour and sing together. There were also others who'd come over to our place in order to read the word of God together.

I experienced National Socialism right from the start. OK, not from the very beginning, the years before 1930, but after Hitler came to power in 1933 it began to be a reality for me. For me it was something I was born into, I couldn't question it. It was something quite normal. When I'd see the soldiers marching outside, the Hitler Youth marching past, for me that was something: I wanted to march too. My mother would say to me, "Just wait, see what happens, you don't know . . ." "Mama, I'd like to be in the Hitler Youth too!" "Just wait and see first." Well, I joined the Hitler Youth in 1940. The war had already begun. I advanced through the ranks very quickly, went to a leadership school, and became a squad leader (Jungenscharführer). Later I became a platoon leader with a group of thirty boys under my command. That's one side of it. I experienced all that directly and with a feeling of joy. Now I finally had what I'd been longing for. Now I was a leader, I was able to command, although I was still just a child.

There is something very theatrical in his way of talking. I wonder if this is his usual manner or if it is due to his excitement in recalling and relating the events of the past.

B: How old were you then?

R: I was only eleven when I went to the course where young leaders were trained. I was twelve when I became a squad leader and thirteen or fourteen when I made platoon commander. In any event, something very peculiar happened at that time . . . well, not peculiar, but something that had a powerful formative influence on me. My father had found work again even before that, but he wasn't happy. He tried to find a position that was more challenging. So he went to work with the railroad. It was called the Reichsbahn then. He laid track at first, then he was a station conductor, and later on he worked with the signal box. He always felt attracted to the track gang, the guys who laid track, but he was also preaching sermons as a member of a Protestant congregation of the Free Church, a congregation that was independent but still Protestant. So he was a preacher. The railroad was his job and being a preacher his love. And his family—his children—were his pride and joy, his great love. He did a lot of Sunday school lessons with small children, taught them about the Bible. Actually he lived just for the family, for his congregation.

Naturally he had to work, and he had this enormous garden. My father was a very believing and religious person, as I said, and he was filled with a great deal of love. I felt protected in his love. Whatever my father said was right. Then the day came when my father was approached by the Nazi Party, by the National Socialist German Workers' Party. He was already a member of the NSV, the National Socialist Welfare Association. He collected money for the Party and distributed ration cards—those cards were quite common at that time. So he was already active in the NSV and was asked to join the Party. I can recall that this had been discussed once at home. I had listened and thought about it. I myself was in the Hitler Youth and my view was "Dad, you have to join the Party!" First he resisted. Then he thought that maybe it would be a good idea after all if he joined up: maybe he could advance more quickly, make headway in his profession and—just maybe—be in a position to shield his congregation. At that time, they didn't want such Christian congregations—I think it was a passing phase for National Socialism at the time. After the war they would have done away with the church congregations anyhow. I oscillated back and forth between the Hitler Youth and the congregation. I was undecided and psychologically unfulfilled. I loved the Hitler Youth more and more. Religion became more and more unimportant to me. I felt invigorated and full of life. They knew how to do that. The Hitler Youth leaders were good at animating young people, motivating and preparing them psychologically for tasks they would carry out later on. It went without question in my eyes that what the Führer said and did, that was the truth. He was almost more of a god for me than the real God . . .

B: Could you give an example of how the leaders did that?

R: We used to have evening get-togethers when all the boys would sit in a large room. The room had black wallpaper, completely black. The benches were dark red. Up front there was a picture on the wall, not of the Führer but of a famous Germanic king, along with two lamps that shed a dim light on the picture. It was quite dark in the room. Then we were told stories about the ancient Germans, our Germanic forefathers. The Aryan race, which has the sole right to lead. We would sing songs in a minor key. It penetrated very deeply into our souls. We felt this very deeply. We believed everything, and we were very proud to be members of this Germanic race and leaders to boot. Young leaders, tribal leaders within this race, this new Germanic race. Young people who were now setting out to rule the world—they really wanted to rule the world. So for us what was predominant was what engaged our feelings. That wasn't the only thing though, not just such evening gatherings. Marching out on the street, marching like soldiers . . . we youngsters already felt like grown-up soldiers. The music that accompanied us, played by the Hitler Youth, with flags and drums through the streets—everyone had to salute our flags, and we were proud to be full members! The fact that we were children was used to prepare us for what was to come. I say for what was to come, but what was that going to be? We were as yet unable to grasp what "later on" might be. We didn't know what was really involved. Who had told us? No one spoke about it.

[*Sighs*] But now I have to return to the subject of my father. My father was inducted as a railroad man and sent to Russia, to Poland. To be more precise, my father was sent to Parafianovo.[1] That's between Vilna and Smolensk. He worked as—what they called during the war an adjunct work-squad leader. He had a section of track to take care of. It was between Parafianovo and Smolensk, maybe three hundred to five hundred kilometers. I can't give you a definite figure. It was his job to maintain this section of track, which was frequently attacked by partisans. They blew up the tracks so the trains would be derailed. But the most important thing, the thing that had such a formative influence on him—which is why I'm here—and on me, was an experience he told me about after he returned. He came back earlier than expected. There was a Jewish ghetto in Parafianovo. A lot of Jews had been brought together and concentrated there in one area, where they were allowed to live. These Jews also worked for the German railroad. A large number were used to help maintain the tracks. For example, there was—I just can't forget their names—there was Aaron Katz, Maria, and the cook for the men my father worked with. This cook was Jewish. I can't recall her name. I think Dolla was her first name, or people called her that. My father could go into the ghetto and speak with the Jews there.

Since he was a convinced and religious Christian, he also spoke with them about the Talmud and the Scriptures, our Holy Bible. And they saw that they both believed in a common God, except that, for the Jews, Jesus is a kind of strange chapter inserted in between. In any event, they understood that they were equal. And basically, we Germans are also a tribe of Israelites. If you assume that certain tribes

1. Placenames appear in their Russian form; these are small villages in Belorussia, between Vilna and Smolensk.

developed up north and that the Germanic tribes, the so-called Germanic tribes, are a conglomerate of many peoples, they are also a tribe of Israelites. Not that this is important, it's something secondary. [*Very agitated*] Well, the day arrived when the ghetto was surrounded by the SS. They asked my father, "How many do you need?" And he told them, "I need all of them." "No, I need a few heads," the officer said, "they're all to be shot." So now you have this Christian, with a soft and childlike heart. He stands there and can do nothing! What should he say, "Shoot me too"? He had children and a wife of his own . . . What was he to do? [*Almost shouting at me*] He didn't have such great courage. He couldn't resist. He was unable to save *his* Jews—after all, they were his brothers, he had lived with them. First, a woman was shot. She had given birth the day before. She was tossed down into the grave. [*Crying*] Whether they also shot the baby, he doesn't know, he didn't know that. Then he ran away and cried bitterly. And a young SS soldier ran after him and said, "I can't go on either! I've killed so many, I just can't go on!"

In any case, he was criticized after that. I could read you a letter written by my father to make things clearer, a letter he wrote right after the end of the war. He became very ill and was released from service too, following this experience. He wrote the letter only after the war because he was afraid to put anything at all down in writing during the war, during the National Socialist period. Let me show you. It's an old letter, and here is also the confirmation that my father was in the east and had been given an early release.

His hands shaking, Rudolf hands me the two documents he has brought with him. He is sweating. I can see that the documents are old and have been carefully kept in a nylon bag. I can also see that they are written in an old-fashioned hand and that on one, the words Our Guilt appear at the top. I offer Rudolf a glass of water and suggest that he read the documents to me himself, since I would have difficulty with his father's handwriting. He starts with the one that carries the swastika, a formal certificate of the Nazi railroad authority. Then he reads his father's letter, dated May 16, 1945.

Our Guilt

Finally now, after many weeks of a serious illness that almost robbed me of my senses, I find myself able to commit to writing those things that (so soon) made me ill and have so completely shattered my nerves. I intend to narrate events one after the other in the course of writing and to present a reason for having chosen the above title.

Until 1941 I had been active for many years as the director of a Sunday school for children. Our parish served in external and internal missionary activities in China. It was my favorite task to be involved in service to children. Since I generally had a great many friends (through my work with the children), the Party believed it had found the right man for its National Socialist Welfare Program (NS-Volkswohlfahrt, NSV) activities. At the same time I was working for the National Railways (Reichsbahn) and had a very low income. On the basis of my work as block chairman of the NSV and as an employee of the Reichsbahn, I became a member of the National Socialist German Workers' Party on June 1, 1941.

I was also promised that I could retain my faith, but shortly after I became a member of the Party, I was forbidden to hold Sunday school classes. That was the first blow. I had to keep silent and put aside my favorite activity.

I was transferred to the town of Parafianovo in Poland to work as head of an auxiliary work squad on February 9, 1942. Among others, there were also some 247 Jews—men, women, and children—living in the town. The Jews were put to work at all kinds of jobs but generally lived in a closed ghetto. We Germans (four men) were assigned a Jewish cook by the name of Dolla, a sweet young girl with red hair, who was very, very clean. My fellow soldiers did not treat her with much respect, since she was, after all, Jewish. But she soon noticed that there was someone there who treated her with love, and we became friends, though no one was supposed to notice. I became sick one week, a bad cold, and Dolla called the Jewish pharmacist Belzik, who procured excellent medicines for me. My fellow soldiers began to taunt me about this friendship with a Jew, and even started to criticize and complain. When I regained my health, I visited the ghetto for the first time. Visiting the ghetto was forbidden and a punishable offense. Due to my illness, I was allowed to go to the pharmacy that was located in the ghetto.

So I visited the pharmacist in the ghetto for the first time, and I was pleased to meet several wonderful human beings: the Jewish women Maria (Mr. Belzik's daughter), Rita (a teacher), and Lilli (a piano teacher), as well as the Aaron K. family. These people proceeded to tell me all their cares and worries. I was confronted with one tale of woe after another. These Jews, whether young or old, were each given a ration of three hundred grams of bread week after week, this and nothing else, month after month. The great misery among these poor people now became evident to me. I then tried in every possible way to help them, and since I knew that they were God's own people, I began to beseech him and to help where I could.

I was very happy when we were joined by a new fellow soldier who shared my view, Mr. S. from Munich, who faithfully pitched in, helping these poor people wherever help was needed. We had to go about it very cautiously and could only pay visits to people late in the evening, though each time, the Jews were overjoyed when we came. I noticed, however, that their troubles were growing from day to day, because everywhere there was talk about Jews being shot. Their questions became ever more pressing and urgent: What will become of us? I tried then to explain to them that the living Lord would not abandon them, and at home, in my room, I myself engaged in a fervent struggle with God and asked him for help. Yes, in my distress I said, "Lord, I will serve you faithfully forever, but please let these people live." As a result of this terrible distress and misery, our relationship became very, very close. It went so far that we even knelt down together to ask our Father for strength in all these matters. One evening, when I was visiting them again and we were all sitting together, I quietly sang the song "Guten Abend, gut' Nacht" [Brahms's Lullaby], accompanied on the guitar. When we came to the words "Tomorrow, God willing, you'll be awakened once again . . . ," Rita broke out in sobs and said, "I feel so strange." The rest of what she said was lost in sobbing. That was the last night of her young life.

Rudolf is crying and searches desperately for his handkerchief while continuing to read.

Early the next morning, we suddenly heard that the ghetto was surrounded by the SS. The Jews were herded together and forced out of the ghetto into an open area. There they had to take off their shoes, coats, and jackets, and they began to weep loudly. A boy of about fourteen tried to run away but was shot immediately. In response, a Jewish man became extremely angry and began to rebuke the SS; however, he was brutally beaten on the spot, so that he had to be transported in a vehicle. The men of the village were forced to dig a large hole, and everyone—children and women, young and old—had to lie down face to the ground. Among these miserable creatures there was a woman who only the day before had given birth to a child. That woman was the first who had to stand up and go to her grave (and the grave of all). I saw how this woman tottered and reeled, clutching her almost naked infant and crying bitterly, asking for her life. She was pushed brutally into the hole and then shot.

Rudolf is unable to go on reading and sobs heavily. I am stunned, distressed, and wait until he regains enough control over his tears to continue.

I went as fast as I could to my room, heard shots again and again, and collapsed at the foot of my bed. Now I lost everything. I had followed the Lord faithfully for twenty-eight years, and now this horrible thing occurred. I had believed right to the last hour that the Lord would preserve these people as a result of my prayer, but then I cursed God and all men.

Rudolf stops again, bursting into tears.

I wanted total oblivion (ich wollte von nichts mehr wissen). Apparently abandoned by God and all of humankind, I carried out my duties in total apathy and hardly knew in subsequent days what was happening.

My fellow soldiers—except for S.—called me a coward and a "lover of Jews." Jews were being shot everywhere, in Glubokoe, Dokshitsy, Vileika, Budslav, and Krulevshchyzna. I had one small consolation when I came to Dokshitsy ten or twelve days later and met the captain. His first question was, "Where is Maria?" (Maria was the pharmacist's daughter in Parafianovo, liked everywhere as a result of her universally respected love for human beings.) I said, "Maria is dead." The captain began to cry. He grabbed my hand and said, "It's a rotten shame!" (Schweinerei). I didn't see him again after that, but I knew that his heart was also bleeding with grief. Eighteen hundred Jews had been shot in this village. There was great commotion and shouting. I ran over to see what was happening, and to my horror I saw Jews emerging from subterranean caves, some eighty to a hundred people, a terrible picture of misery and suffering. They were crying for water, emaciated, their faces white as chalk. Hardly able to utter a sentence, they dropped to their knees and begged for their lives. Without receiving anything, they were pushed and herded into a barn. I watched as a girl about the age of ten, who had hidden herself in a hay shed and was now almost completely emaciated, was carried past me. This poor girl looked more like a pile of bones than a human being, and this bundle of misery and agony, it too was carried into the barn. As long as I live, come what may, I will never forget this horrible sight. I can't help myself. It was just too horrible and made me sick for the rest of my life. I just can't comprehend how human beings can be such beasts. These images haunted me day and night.

After a few weeks I was sent to a field hospital in Vileika because of hypertension. But then I collapsed completely, since I was not allowed to tell anyone of my suffering. And this suffering became even more intense when I realized that I was a member of such a band of murderers and criminals, a band that would not have spared my life if I had objected. So I got sicker and sicker and was sent to Vilna. There, for the first time, I had fainting spells and mental disturbances. They didn't know the cause, and they asked me all kinds of questions, but I didn't tell them a thing, since I couldn't trust anyone, including the doctors. After that I was released and sent home to Germany accompanied by a soldier. Back home my condition got worse, to the point that I could hardly walk without someone to accompany me, since I was suffering from the enormous weight of the events I had experienced. After some time, I was reproached by the local section of the Party for not having (as they saw it) a National Socialist outlook on things. My general outlook was more religious in orientation than anything else. When I subsequently wanted to talk about my experiences, I had to be so careful and cautious (pretending as if I thought this and not that) that I became very sick and Dr. D. considered it advisable for me to be placed in an institution. I was afraid they were going to get rid of me there. Shortly after this, I had to enter City Hospital for observation. It was there that I revealed all my suffering to Dr. L. and explained everything to him. Dr. L. did not belong to the Party. He understood me completely and advised me to try to forget things—something that was, and is, impossible.

On April 14, 1945, I was suddenly approached by a man in the street, who came up to me and said, "We know who you are. You've been undermining the work of the Party now for some time. You're a dirty saboteur and that's going to cost you your life!" I didn't know what was happening. What had I done? I took a few steps and must have collapsed on the spot. Witnesses say I was going on about "common murderers, brown bandits, and shootings of Jews." People thought I was insane. I remained in this condition for several days. I had, in any case, been sick and unable to work since December 17, 1944, but now I was completely finished. Dr. G. and Dr. S. were at my bedside. When I regained my senses a bit, I asked myself, "What have I done!"

I had confided in several families and told them about this crime in Russia. Whether they remained silent I don't know. In addition, I had also not given away the presence of a man who had been living away from his unit for a year and a half, about whom I was often questioned. I covered for him whenever I could. I couldn't allow him—someone who quite early on had seen through all the lies—to fall into the hands of that pack, who wanted to build a so-called "workers' paradise" on the blood and bones of the dead.

I can't understand that there are those who wish to kill me because of this, since anyone who has a fairly just view of things must admit that if we had won the war, then there couldn't be a just God in heaven, one who could give his blessing to such bloody deeds.

On May 3 or 4 when he visited me I told Dr. S. about everything, particularly about Russia. And I can say that he cried bitterly and was ashamed of his . . . [document illegible]. When I asked him, "Can God . . ." [document illegible], he replied resolutely and with determination: "Never!"

I doubted God in Parafianovo, but ask him today for forgiveness. He was not on the side of those who perpetrated such injustices, and he expiated those bloody deeds.

R: So that is the end of the letter. That was the experience. And let me tell you that this man suffered right up until the end, until he died, and if you want to know when that was, I can tell you. He's been dead now some eight years. He wasn't able . . . and was given early retirement. He was a bit absentminded. But you must understand: the thing that shaped and molded *me*, what influenced me, was that I was unable to comprehend what my father was talking about. I had been so fanatic about this idea of National Socialism . . . But when he returned from Poland and told me these things—I was able to understand various things by this time—I was unable to go on believing in it. A cause I was ready to sacrifice my life for—these people had done such a thing? First I accused him of being a deserter! I did not believe his story, I could not believe it. [*Agitated*] So then I was bothered by doubts. What should I do? I was a leader in the Hitler Youth, but what should I do? I lived in a constant state of inner tension. I didn't know what I should do. Though I must say that in the course of time, that feeling disappeared, it dissipated. My father spoke less and less about it, he withdrew more and more into himself. More and more, the only person he spoke to was my mother. He turned away from me, because I was unwilling to take off that uniform. He turned away from me, and I could see that he was extremely ill, seriously so, because of it. Yet I couldn't follow in his direction. But then there was an experience that actually opened up once again the wound he caused in me by what he'd said.

B: What was that?

R: Well, it was in '43 or '44 I think. They showed the movie *Jud Süss*. It was a film against the Jews, but I didn't recognize it as an inflammatory film. For me it was a simple fact: that's how Jews are. The film portrayed them as the dregs of humanity. So there was this contradiction in my mind. There was "Jud Süss," this carefully polished character in this horror film—that's the expression you could use today—

which destroyed young people spiritually and prepared them to . . . something they could never vindicate: to pass judgment on a people I had never experienced directly or seen. [*Gets up and walks around restlessly*] OK, I had seen some Jews with yellow stars. For me they were just people wearing a yellow star—the Poles had a P and the Ukrainians a U—for me these were second-class people. And I used to hear remarks, during those years you could hear again and again shouts of "Jew!" "Lousy Jew!" "Criminals!" "Vultures!" "Bloodsuckers!" Or "The Jews are responsible for the war!" The Jews were guilty of everything. There was *nothing* the Jews weren't responsible for. Then this film *Jud Süss* was made.

I forgot one thing: Kristallnacht in 1938. I hadn't been a witness to that. I didn't see what happened, I only heard about it. I heard them talking about a shoe store, a Jewish shoe store—I think it was called Rosenthal's—and that it had been smashed and shoes were lying all over the street. They carried out a child wrapped in a lamp shade. Everything was gone, the Jews were gone. But those events occurred on the periphery of things as far as I was concerned. At that time, for me the Jew was someone so small and inconsequential . . . They weren't an independent people, didn't have an independent state. Jews were nothing, just nothing.

Once my father came to me and said, "Rudolf, Rudolf, listen." He noticed that we were drifting farther and farther apart. I was also aware that we were growing more and more distant. Then he said, "Rudolf, we have to sit down and have a serious talk." That was during the war, but at times he had very clear, sane moments (lichte Momente). "We've talked so often about the Bible. You've read the Bible yourself, and I've read both the Old and New Testaments. You know that the Jewish people are in fact a people in their own right, God's chosen people. It is so and will remain that way. You can't, we can't deny that. No matter how many Christians curse them, the Jews are the chosen people. The Jew is the hand on the clock of history: whatever happens to him, from that you can read the course of history and time. Just remember one thing: if you lift a finger against the Jews, you can cut off that finger because you are going to lose it! Never attack a Jew. Be careful, cautious, and have respect for the Jews." Then he told me a few more things from Jewish history, from the Old Testament. After that I was filled with a sense of fear. He said to me, "Do you believe in Jesus?" I said, "Yes, Dad, I do believe in Jesus Christ." "But you know who he was, don't you?" and I said, "Yes, he was a Jew, right?" "OK, so do you believe in Jews now?" and I said, "Yes, Dad, I do. I'm sorry." And then I started to cry. I cried a lot. I was so sorry that I had been so blinded by this idea, that I had been led astray, led astray again and again. But even what my father said to me—said to me in tears, and I noticed that he was sick—even what he said to me, I didn't believe, so profound was the influence of the National Socialists, of their propaganda.

A long pause. Rudolf sits down and wipes his forehead with a handkerchief.

And then I was apprenticed in 1944, I got an apprenticeship in the railroad, the Reichsbahn. I wanted to be a locomotive engineer and in '44, I was sent as an apprentice to a plant where locomotives were repaired. This plant had its own fire brigade, since such plants were often attacked and bombed during the war. Now because I was the only one who had been in a leadership position in the youth movement—I was the only Hitler Youth leader among the sixty apprenticed trainees—I was given the job of getting them to assemble in formation in the early morning; I had leadership status once again. I also had to join the fire brigade at the same time and went out with this brigade a few times after heavy air raids.

I was involved during the last big raid—it was the end of '44 or the beginning of '45, I can't remember. There was a raid and we were called out to see what we could save. The buildings were on fire. And then I saw something. As a young man, I was a runner, a messenger— we didn't have any radio equipment. I had to supervise the inspection of hoses, make sure the hoses were laid properly and weren't leaking. And I noticed that under a hose lying on top of some debris, there was something dark red, shining there underneath. I said, "Mr. B."— he was the chief at that time—"Mr. B., there's something over there!" He had the debris cleared away and I could see a woman lying there. She had run downstairs and out the front door, and a bomb had exploded right in front of her. Shrapnel and a lot of debris went flying, and this woman was killed. They lifted her out, and then I felt sick: her lower body was ripped open, and everything inside came tumbling out. Now I had seen a great many dead people those months, but this was the worst thing I'd witnessed. I started to feel sick, and Mr. B. said to me, "OK, go on home." Well, that was the end of my activity in the fire brigade. That was shortly before the end of the war. What I did after that was . . . But I was no longer filled with such conviction. Now I understood what my father had told me at the end: you can't justify and accept it.

During the last half hour, Rudolf has been very agitated, and I actually start to worry. But he wants to go on, as if a hidden volcano has finally erupted.

R: Though I must admit that I felt split and divided. After the Americans marched in, people said, "Now the Hitler Youth is finished." I felt a certain sadness, not because of the fact that the Hitler Youth was done for, but because I was no longer able to meet all my friends. That camaraderie was something I missed.

Those were actually the main experiences. I wanted to tell you that, well, that a family can be destroyed during a war by these things. My father passed away, but before he died, he lived in a kind of twilight, a constant twilight, psychological and mental. He would only work with clay. He used to have this clay brought in and . . . Now I want to mention something that once again concerns those two religions, where you can see the schizophrenia . . . He had a board, and on this board he fashioned and shaped mountains and small hills covered with trees. Down below, at the foot, he made a crèche with Jesus lying there inside, and there was a path that led up to a synagogue above. So he wanted to make this connection (in his unconscious) between Christianity and the Jews. He was unable to cope with the notion that a Christian had been able to do such things against a Jew. In his state of mental twilight, he wanted to restore this connection. And he died with that. He didn't die as a Christian or as a Jew: he was something in between.

In front of me I see the son of an exceptional father, the only person I've heard of who lost his mind because he could not go on living a normal life after he witnessed the massacre of Jews. I hug Rudolf and thank him for talking with me. As we walk out, he says that he has never told anyone about it before, but when he saw the ad in the newspaper, he knew the time had come to bring his father's letter out into the open, to tell his father's story— which is now his own.

We arrange to meet again a few days later. Rudolf arrives with two heavy folders in which he has carefully collected the songs from his days in the Hitler Youth. He looks more relaxed, ready to go on.

R: I had certain other experiences in the Hitler Youth that were especially memorable and important for me—for example, when I was promoted. Those were moments when my soul was lifted up again. They'd make a campfire in the evening, although it was prohibited on account of the air raids, but they would let us know: OK, no enemy aircraft in sight. Promotions were usually announced on Hitler's birthday, April 20, and on November 9.[2] It was all done in a very military atmosphere, with torches and songs . . . [*Singing*] "Holy Fa-

2. November 9 marked the anniversary of the failed 1923 Munich Putsch; it was a sacred day on the National Socialist calendar.

therland in danger, your sons gather in around you . . ." And this was sung in a minor key, which makes you feel a bit melancholy, and it would rouse our spirits. Then they would announce the promotion: Comrade so-and-so is now promoted to the rank of squad leader, effective as of such-and-such a date. They would pin on the special ribbon, and you'd go home through the streets swelling with pride. You already felt like a young representative of National Socialism.

Later on—I have to say, not at that time but later on—I had this thought: What would have happened if *my* generation had been sent to carry out these murderous acts? OK, people were killed during air raids, but we never killed, we didn't get that far, thank God. But just imagine, what if this generation, which had been psychologically trained and geared up for it, what if this generation had been let loose on mankind? Then what occurred with the Jews, why it would pale in comparison—it would have been nothing. So that's what I have to tell you: we would have been worse. We could have done it without any doubts whatsoever. [*Agitated*] We were trained to hate from a very early age.

B: Did you have any friends at school who were Jewish, or were there any Jews in your school?

R: No, no, none. Wait a second, there was one: she was half-Jewish. I started school in 1936, and there was a girl—we didn't know this at first—who was half-Jewish. She told me after the war that they had— I was no longer at that school then—that the other children had stripped her naked in the street, because they heard she was half-Jewish. Even young children had been indoctrinated to the point where they could pull the clothes off a classmate and shout, "Jew! Jew! Jew!" She told me this after the war. She still lives here. She's married to an Englishman. She said she wouldn't want to marry a German.

And there was something here in town, not very long ago, at the zoo. I don't know whether you heard about it. There's a large hall at the zoo where meetings are held, and it was hired out by the police. The police had a celebration there, and a police officer, who was functioning as a kind of master of ceremonies, said, "What do you answer to 'Sieg'?" And a few young men shouted, "'Heil'!" That was the salute the Nazis used to use. The policeman really didn't mean any harm by it, I know that. They had all been drinking a little . . . But this Jewish woman was there and she filed a complaint against the policeman. He was temporarily suspended from service, and then there was some sort of punishment. I don't know exactly how it turned out. Anyhow, it was in the paper. She was a classmate of mine. Her brother and father—or her brother and mother, one of them died before that—

were murdered in the camps. Aside from that, I had no other Jewish classmates. There weren't any left. It is astonishing, but I didn't actually have any direct experience of Jews being sent to concentration camps. I didn't know about it. I only knew that Jews had to wear a yellow star—I knew that later on—a yellow star. They were marked and singled out so that you could recognize them as Jews. Though I must emphasize again and again, it was also true for the Poles, the Ukrainians . . . it wasn't anything . . .

B: After your father told you his story, did you ever discuss it with friends?

R: I wasn't able to discuss it with my friends. That would have endangered my father.

B: What happened between you and your friends after your father came back?

R: Actually, there was no break, no rupture between me and my friends. I think you have to view it in this way: the overriding, all-embracing concept was the Hitler Youth. National Socialism was a phenomenon that accompanied this organization. Only in a subconscious way was all this hammered into us: National Socialism and Adolf Hitler. Basically, in terms of our behavior, we remained young children, only that, via our subconscious, they attempted to prepare us for the later phase. After all, we were still immature, still under the age of eighteen. You couldn't get rid of our childlike character. That was something that remained.

Maybe I should tell you about one more experience. I told you that I was a trainee with the Reichsbahn, and that I was a youth leader there. I wasn't all that good as a student, and I wasn't the best among the apprentices, but I was the leader. So we young guys—you can see from this just how young we still were—we got up on a hill during recess and started throwing stones, as boys sometimes like to do, a kind of game. There were two sides, two groups, and we were throwing stones at each other. The winner was supposed to get a bottle of soda water or something. So I heaved a heavy stone and hit a boy right in the stomach. He got really angry, and he shouted, "You goddamn Nazi pig!" And that was during the war! I ran over to him and said, "What did you say?" "You goddamn Nazi pig!" Whammo, I gave him a left and right to the nose, and he dropped to the ground. Then I told him, "Just you wait. I won't forget this." I told this kid, "You watch out!" Now what comes is like the seed that has been sown in a child and begins sprouting unconsciously . . . [*Stands up and walks around the room waving his arms*] I threw a stone at him and hurt him, he felt pain and shouted at me, "You Nazi pig!" His father had been in a concentration camp as a Communist, and he always stressed the fact that he wasn't a Nazi. He said this spontaneously, even though the Nazis were in power. And I told him, "Just you wait, I won't forget this!" Now that tiny seed began to sprout. It was still very small. But if it had grown, I probably would have turned out to be one of those who could have killed someone for saying such a thing . . .

[*Sits down again, trying to calm himself*] I recall that when I was a leader in the Hitler Youth, I . . . in Germany we have people who, as you would say in slang, are "brown noses," people who want to make trouble. Well, I loved to go around dressed in my uniform. I even went to school in uniform, to work—I was very proud. And at that time Russian civilian laborers weren't allowed to drink any alcohol. Then an incident occurred that I have to tell you about. There was this Russian civilian laborer. I was out with a lot of boys, and this drunken Russian laborer came along. I asked him, "Where are you coming from?" Me, just a child. And he stammered something in his drunken stupor. I said, "Do you want to have a fight?" He said, "Yeah." So I slugged him. He smashed his face into the big window of a grocery store. There was a pointed grille covering it, and his whole face was cut and scratched. No one did anything to me, though. After all, they couldn't hit me. If anyone had done such a thing to me while I was wearing that uniform, he'd have ended up in a concentration camp. Terrible, right? Anyhow, my father found out about this incident and he gave me the worst spanking I ever had. He really walloped me! It was the right punishment. But, as I said before, the small seed had started to germinate, to grow and sprout: "I won't forget that, you'll see!" "You Russian, listen, you're not worth a damn thing! I can do something to you, even though I'm much smaller, and you can't defend yourself, you can't do anything!"

Rudolf is in a kind of trance. He is staring at the ceiling, trying to bring out the memories that have plagued his conscience all these years. I listen carefully, wishing I had a camera to film this interview. The stories continue to pour forth, however disjointedly, one after another.

R: Then there was this Frenchman . . . My uncle lived between Brandenburg and Berlin, and he had a fruit farm—he made a living growing strawberries, apples, and tomatoes—and a Russian, a Pole, a Serb, a Frenchman . . . these were the people who had to work for him. Early in the morning there was the "funeral procession." That's what we called it. There was this old German soldier who could hardly stand on his legs, and he led the French POWs off to the various fruit farms. And when they would pass a farm where one of them worked, he'd leave the group and go on in. They walked very slowly, took a lot of time, this German soldier and that French POW. Once I spoke with the Frenchman, whose German was rather good. I was actually quite surprised that I didn't react differently. We were sitting together between the rows of strawberries, and he told me something about his attitude toward the German people and National Socialism. I let him talk and didn't react at all, although I was very bothered by what that Frenchman was saying. He said, "Pay attention to your own history, the history of Germany. Don't always go on carping about the Jews, the French (because the French had been our archenemies). Just take a long, sober look at your own history, without rose-colored glasses. Take your history as it really is, what really happened, and then form an opinion. How much hatred do you Germans have in yourselves? How far do you expect to go with it? How many more do you plan to exterminate in the name of this hatred?"

So, as you can see, that idea stayed with me, what he said, though I myself was deeply indoctrinated. OK, if you place all these little piles of impressions one next to the other, you can understand my reaction—the way I experienced it later on, the way I reacted to myself. I almost felt like Judas in the Bible, that disciple who committed suicide. Yes, well, more than that I . . . I have such a modest heart, wouldn't harm a fly . . . But they had swelled up my heart. They were able to deform a person's heart.

Then the war ended. If it hadn't ended, I don't know, I'm not sure I would have forgotten all that. I mean, it's especially easy to manipulate children at that age, and where you can get at the children, that's where—at least this is what I think—that's the history of the people. If you can drill the notion into their heads: you are from a tribe, a race that is especially valuable. And then you tell them something about the Germanic tribes, their loyalty, their battles, how Germanic women let themselves be hitched up to carts to fight against the Romans. You, you're a child of this race, a people that dealt the Romans a destructive blow in the year 9 A.D., all that sort of thing. Then there were the songs. I'm especially affected by songs. When they would sing those songs glorifying the deeds of the Germanic tribes, such as [*singing*] "The sons of the people ride on silvery stallions, born from a divine multitude, warrior of the Nordic people, they ride in silence to the far fields of the northern lights, on secret paths they greet elves at the shore of the pounding sea." Or "Holy Fatherland, your sons crowd in around you." How does it go on? "What we swear is written in the stars, he who directs the stars will hear our voice . . . before the foreigner robs you of your crown, O Germany, we would prefer to fall side by side." Or "The flag is dearer than death." Death was nothing.

The flag, the people—they were everything. You are nothing, your people everything. Yes, that's how children were brought up, that's how you can manipulate a child . . .

He is singing, talking, and crying, shifting back and forth between one memory and another.

We meet again a year later. Rudolf is willing to be interviewed on video-tape: he will do it for me, for the research, for humanity. When he reads his father's letter during the filming at the studio, he cries again, and this time too, he does not seem able to find his handkerchief.

We walk out together when the taping session is over, and I thank him for coming. He tells me that his own children did not want him to come. They do not want to have anything to do with this chapter of the family's past. Their motto is "past is past." They want a life of their own. Outside the studio, we shake hands warmly, and Rudolf walks slowly away into the darkness. I suddenly realize how lonely he must be, carrying his father's letter: "Our Guilt."

chapter 10

The Divided Self

Dieter and I become acquainted through mutual friends. They are able to tell me some of his family story but nothing about his father's role during the war. I go to see him on a clear autumn day. His house, not far from a river, is surrounded by woods. Living in the Israeli desert as I do, I am overwhelmed by the beauty of the European forest at this time of year.

As I climb the house's staircase, Dieter approaches from the upper floor holding a wolfhound on a leash. The dog looks alarming at first but soon becomes friendly. Dieter shows me into his large study: two sizable swords hang on one wall and a large picture on another. "That's Napoleon returning from the Russian battlefield," he says with a smile. While he prepares coffee, I look at some of the books on the shelves, many of them on the Crusades and medieval history. On his desk I notice a photograph of an SS officer in full uniform. Later, as we sit drinking our coffee, I realize how much he resembles one of my students in Israel: the small, silver-rimmed spectacles, the pipe, the intelligent gaze. Dieter belongs to the academic stratum of German society. My friends have told me that on the previous day, he celebrated the acceptance of his doctoral dissertation, which dealt with a Mamluki sultan who conquered Egypt in the twelfth century.

D: I was born in 1949. My father was born in 1896, so he was relatively old. Quite old. It was my father's second marriage. He got married during the war.

B: Are you the oldest?

D: Yes, my brother is two years younger. My mother also had two daughters by her first marriage. My two half-sisters are nine and eleven years older than I am. I remember very little about my early childhood.

B: Where were you born?

D: I was born in L. on the Main River. We lived there during my first year and I still have this image of a café. Then this memory, at the age of two or so, of an argument between my parents about who should take the child out in the buggy: my father ended up taking me out in the buggy. A very early memory. What I don't remember well is that my mother used to give me to an aunt to be taken care of when I was quite small. The reasons aren't very clear to me. My mother always said she did it because our own apartment was too damp, but I have a suspicion it was because she couldn't deal very well with babies. My two older sisters, for example, were taken care of by my grandmother on my father's side. My brother was placed in private children's homes. And we moved a lot. I noticed as a child that we moved every year or two.

B: With your aunt?

D: No, no, that was this one year when my parents were living in L., and that year I guess they gave me to her to take care of. Six months later I was back with the family again, and I didn't even learn about the birth of my brother. I can't recall, but he must have been sent very soon after birth into a private home for children. I was already four, and I remember my mother saying, "You have a little brother. We're going to get him now from the children's home." I was really happy about that. Well, we picked him up and he had a very bad case of rickets. And there was jealousy between us very quickly, because he went for my toys. But I'd been so happy to hear I had a brother. Actually my mother always favored me. I was her big favorite. The situation became polarized, so my father took my younger brother a bit under his wing.

Dieter suddenly stops and asks if this is what I want to hear. "Yes," I say quietly, "please go on."

D: Well, all this frequent moving from one place to another—I found it strange, though we sometimes had very beautiful houses, often a bit outside of town. It was a problem for my two sisters to get to school. My older sister is a little weaker physically, and she suffered a lot because of this. She was ill later on, was in a clinic for nervous diseases for eight years because of schizophrenia. But I'm getting off the subject. Because of all the moving around, my older sister had trouble in school. She couldn't handle it. High school had become too hard for her. She was sick a lot, was in a commercial high school for a while, and then my father arranged to get her a job as a secretary at an army school in Munich, with the German Federal Armed Forces (Bundeswehr). I don't know if it's all true, but the story is that she fell in love with some military doctor. He was married and wouldn't consider a divorce. We lived far out of town at the time, and she had to leave on the 6:00 A.M. bus in order to get to work and didn't come back until 7:00 in the evening. So she did this for a few years, and then she had a nervous breakdown. It was awful. She'd get these attacks, these fits of rage. She smashed all the military pictures we had at home, and my father was outraged that my brother and I should see the way she treated him. We had to leave the room. But she smashed his things. And my brother—I was fourteen, he was twelve— always got wind of the reason for the argument, although it wasn't too clear to us; my sister was much older than we were. But it upset my father a good deal. My father had a lot of memorial photographs, mainly pictures of officers from World War I and World War II.

So my sister had had this affair with a military doctor, it had come to naught, and she developed an animosity toward the military. These were very unpleasant arguments, though she was still healthy. Then there was all the strain of traveling back and forth to work. On Sunday she liked to sleep late, until noon or 1:00 P.M. And my father would say, "Breakfast's at 10. Let's get her out of bed. She has to come down to eat." I have one extremely unpleasant memory, that my father tried repeatedly to encourage my brother and me to hit my sister if she didn't behave properly according to his notions, if she didn't come down to eat. Anyhow, my sister subsequently had such a bad break-down that she was no longer capable of taking part in family life. She stopped washing herself. So my father said that she ought to be sent, as he put it, to a "loony bin," that the situation was impossible. So he contacted the clinic in K., and the doctor in charge had been on the staff during the Third Reich. And he told him, "Bring her in and we'll take a look. Once she's here, she's here. Try to get her over here." But it didn't work. My mother refused to have my sister placed in a clinic, because she said she'd become familiar with a psychiatric clinic near L. during the war, and she'd seen the way people were taken from the clinic; she knew they never came back and the terrible conditions they were kept in. So there was this terrible conflict, my mother refusing to let her daughter be put in a psychiatric clinic. She still had the notion that German clinics were what they'd been in 1943.

So it went on until I finally went to Tübingen to study. I met my wife there—she was studying political science—and she tried to convince my mother to put my sister in a clinic. My father, in the meantime, had passed away. So she was there for some eight years; even now, she hasn't regained her short-term memory. She can't remember what day it was yesterday or what we had for dinner, although she has recollections of things very far back and long ago.

B: Her father had died?

D: No, they got divorced, my mother and her first husband. I can only reconstruct it on the basis of what my mother has told me, but it must have been a terrible marriage. They only married because he forced her to. He'd slept with her, she'd become pregnant, they'd talked about an abortion, and I think she really had an abortion but was very frightened, worried she would get into trouble in the Third Reich for having had an abortion, and so she tried to have her husband sent to the front. She met some commanding officer, and he gave his signature for her husband to be sent to the front.

During the war, she met my grandfather, my father's father, an old Prussian general, and through this connection she met my father. She was told her husband was missing. But then he returned after being released as a POW. So she tried to get a divorce, asked a girlfriend to sleep with her husband, which she did. Then she claimed he'd deceived her and got a divorce. He was found guilty. So my mother got out of this marriage and then married my father. Then I was born, and my brother.

Somehow my mother liked K. very much as a place. My father was also in a field hospital in K., because he came down with TB. Then he was confined to bed in K. convalescing. He mentioned that a former soldier-friend of his had come by and said that if the Russians were to come to K., he'd have to get out of there, because he'd been sentenced to death in absentia in East Germany. As children, we were never allowed to go to Berlin either. If there was a school trip, for example, well, we weren't allowed to go along.

B: What did your father do that the Russians were after him?

D: My father had already taken part in World War I, and then helped set up a paramilitary group to fight against the Bolsheviks in Russia after the war. Then he started law school and worked for the customs office. Hitler came to power, and he reentered the military when Germany started to rearm. My brother and I were confronted a great deal with all this military past. My father was a soldier through and through, and he talked about a lot more than just World War I. He said in a reference to World War II that he was a Prussian soldier and he didn't want to have anything to do with Hitler and the Nazis. He also told us that he'd made derogatory remarks about the Party and Hitler, and had been released from the army in 1936 or '37, although he was drafted again for the Russian campaign because of his experience in leading a paramilitary unit in Russia after World War I. But as children we knew very little. We didn't know, for example, that my father had had TB. That was hushed up, kept secret. Everything was kept secret. We didn't know, either, why we were always moving, what the reason was. Everything was kept secret, hidden away.

B: What was the reason your parents were so secretive?

D: I think my father was always afraid people could bring charges against him. At some time or other he told us he'd had villages burned in Russia. He'd come into a village, and there was some farmer who cursed the troops, made a face at them from a window. This happened after a German soldier was killed near that village. So he gave an order to have the village surrounded and burned down. The villagers weren't allowed out. Then some Cossacks killed a few German officers, and my father had the whole Cossack section shot. So my father was afraid this might come up and he would be held responsible, have to answer for his acts. He always used a false number for his regiment too, different from the one he had served in. It's a certain irony of fate that my father—he was very intellectual—felt himself to be an officer faithful to the Emperor in World War I; he didn't like the Nazis and he didn't like Hitler, that "Bohemian corporal." But his section got involved in fighting the partisans and securing roads for the army. Probably he simply got caught up in the course of certain events that basically caused him to become an active agent in what was taking place, an active agent in all the crimes.

It is the first time I hear about a father who has told his son about the heinous acts he was personally involved in.

B: Did he tell you all this himself?

D: Well, a bit. We have these photo albums from World War I, a lot of photographs, and he told us stories. There were some from World War II as well. I asked him things. My brother wasn't much interested, but I asked him a few questions, and he said that he'd been with the tank corps. But there were photos in which he had a completely different hat on. So I asked him why he was wearing a different hat and what his regiment was. Then a letter came, something about his officer's pension; it mentioned regiment so-and-so and there was a discrepancy. So I asked more questions and became suspicious. The older I got, the more pointed my questions became. And then you could notice that he was trying to evade. And sometimes with friends of his, well, they'd get to talking about the Third Reich and forget that we children were around listening. It's quite a peculiar situation. Once we read something in the newspaper about a young man having raped a girl, and my father said, "That never happened in our regiment during the war. I had a noncom hanged right away after he had raped a Russian woman." "How come," I asked, "wasn't there any court martial?" "No," he said, "we just went ahead and did it ourselves." So a person starts paying special attention when he hears things like that. Of course many things, even today, remain unclear. My mother keeps a suitcase full of papers in her basement, my father's papers. And my mother has strictly forbidden us to touch it. Things from World War I addressed to the Honorable Lieutenant and citations for World War I service. I don't know if there is anything from World War II.

And then suddenly, in 1965, my father was indicted to stand trial. And I recall that my parents went looking for a former friend and officer who was supposed to testify to the fact that my father had refused to join the SS. Apparently when my father was discharged from the army and the war broke out, an SS officer came to my father and asked him whether he wanted to serve in the Waffen SS. And he said that under no circumstances did he want to joint the SS. He also said he knew he'd been discharged from the army because he wasn't a faithful supporter of the Party line. The SS officer replied that that didn't interest him, that they were simply looking for people who'd had experience in Russia. Since my father had said he didn't want to join the SS, he wanted it confirmed before a court that he'd refused. But the man said he couldn't remember. Then the trial was stopped. My father was sent back home after a few weeks because he was found to be unfit for detention due to his tubercular condition. When my mother accompanied him to the prison in B., a man got on the train, identified himself as belonging to an SS support group, and offered my father money and false papers so that he could flee whenever he liked. And my father—he was very old already, more than seventy— refused this offer. But he was released from prison and sent home because of his serious illness.

There is a short pause. Dieter lights his pipe, and I think that, compared to other families I've come to know, this is hardly a "secretive" one.

D: I once told my father that he should have become a big shot, somebody more important. I asked him, "Why did you stay a colonel when others reached the rank of general? You were in World War I, and almost all the officers who served in that war later advanced to a higher rank. You could have become a group leader in the SS if you hadn't acted so stupidly." And my father looked at me and said—he didn't get angry, or anything—but he said, "You just don't know what you're talking about."

Dieter looks at me and cleans his pipe.

D: Two years ago a new book appeared about Frederick the Great. I told my sister, who is a teacher, that the book was tremendous and she ought to read it. And she said, "Look, leave me in peace, I don't want to have anything to do with Prussia, Frederick the Great, and all that." My brother is the same way. I have very little contact with people in the family, just with my brother. And he has no interest in anything military, or in history. With him, it even goes so far that, well, to give you an example: I told my brother I was reading Goethe's *Elective Affinities* and he said to me, "Read something recent. Why all this old stuff?" Probably it's due to the fact that my father as an old man lived a lot in the past and that my brother somehow, in reacting to this, doesn't want to have anything to do with the past in any way, shape, or form. Although I, as a historian, am constantly involved with the past. History can't hurt because it's already past . . .

Dieter smiles as he says this, and I ask him if history does not hurt him, especially the details he has just shared with me. He hesitates for a moment, and his smile fades. "Yes, it can hurt, it does hurt sometimes."

B: What happened later on to your father? Was he ill in the hospital?

D: Yes, he was. He came home from prison and lived at home. Then suddenly he came down with a cold during the summer, the flu, and was treated by a village doctor. His condition deteriorated more and more. He had trouble sleeping nights, he was constantly calling my mother. During the day he'd sleep. He was too weak to get up. He needed transfusions. I took my high school finals, and then I was working. We used to get up very early in the morning. My mother would get up early to make breakfast, and then she was on her feet all day and night taking care of my dad. I was afraid that somehow my mother might have a breakdown too. So I insisted that my father be brought to a hospital nearby. A new doctor came, and I asked him to drop by and convince my father to go to the hospital. He had to send my father to the hospital, which he did. Then they wanted to transfer my father to a lung sanatorium, but he didn't want to go. So he came home again. But I said, "No, you belong where there are doctors." I was very insistent. He said, "I don't want to have anything more to do with you, you're not my son, you're cruel and terrible, you just want to get rid of me!" So he was put in the hospital again, and then the doctors discovered that his sick lung was seven-eighths gone; only one-eighth was still intact, the rest destroyed. They said there was little hope, and a week later he died.

B: Did you have a chance to talk with him?

D: Well, the head doctors said his condition was so bad that he was dying. He had quite bad pains because his system was poisoned, kidney failure. And my mother said, "Dammit, can't something be done? You just can't stand there and let a person die!" And a nurse said,

"Maybe someone from the family should be with him in the evening. It's hard to watch him all the time, and something might happen." So I took my mother home and returned that evening. I went to his bedside. He probably knew his time was almost up, and he told me I should always be there if my mother needed me. I guess I started to cry or something, and he said, "Come on, pull yourself together, stop crying." Then he fell asleep. During the night the nurse came in and said he needed a shot. And a few hours later he fell asleep for all eternity. That was all.

He stops and lights his pipe again, very tense.

D: At one point a clergyman wanted to come, and my father said he'd gotten along all his life without clergymen and didn't want to see one now.

B: Did he have any nightmares?

D: No, not in the hospital or when I was with him.

B: Did he mention anything else about the war?

D: No, nothing else. Nothing at all. I don't know to what extent my father felt he was guilty, I don't quite know.

B: Did you try to find out, or are these your own reflections?

D: I don't know. [*Hesitates*] Listen, he was a person of extreme contradictions. For example, once my father said that the attempt on Hitler's life had been senseless because the Allies had waged war against Germany, not just against Hitler. Probably the SS had done it against the regular army and it had been too late. He also said it had been done in a very amateurish way. And my father taught us very early on to hate Americans. They had played the decisive role in both wars— World War I and World War II. My father even said derogatory things about Hitler as a "Bohemian corporal." But, on the other hand, there was this imaginary entity "Germany" for which he'd fought, for which it had been worthwhile to fight. So that maybe somehow this faux pas in Russia had left a bad taste in his mouth, as it were. And he didn't have a feeling—when he had set fire to a village, for example—of horror or disgust. Instead, he was rather sober and clear-headed. But when that Russian gave them such a dirty look, well, sudden anger arose in him. He said that once he'd sent out a platoon on patrol, and partisans had nailed the men to a barn door, cut off their genitals, and then buried them alive in a pile of ants. And he wanted to take revenge for that. So he was torn this way and that, though he didn't speak about it very often. He was afraid of being discovered. He had this disgust for the Nazis, yet, on the other hand, there were these acts he committed during the war.

B: So what was the actual reason he was brought to trial?

D: We were never told. They simply said my father was standing trial because he'd had villages burned down and because many civilians had died in the process, and that according to our laws of court-martial that was a crime, a war crime. But unfortunately it was the case that nothing could be done against it, and he was actually found guilty unjustly. Suddenly he lost his pension, and we had terrible financial problems. Both my brother and I reacted by thinking: This is an injustice. He was a soldier, he'd been ordered to do this, and now we are burdened with these difficulties as a result.

B: Did you try to find out later on? Or to get hold of the trial documents?

D: I spoke to my mother about it, and she said that while she was alive, the papers she had would remain in safekeeping. And I thought, I have a great deal of influence on my mother and if I really asked her long and insistently enough, maybe I could get the papers. Though I don't know whether maybe I myself don't really want to have the papers. OK, my mother says she wants it that way and I respect her wishes, but maybe that's actually just an excuse for me to avoid it. Maybe I really don't want to know the extent. I have a friend who's doing some research, working on a Ph.D. on similar matters, and she has trouble sleeping at night. Now imagine if you read reports about your own father . . . So maybe you try to push it away from yourself.

B: But if you don't really have the facts, maybe your fantasies exceed the reality?

D: Yes, that's right. Sometimes I have fantasies about Mengele. What if I found out I was his son . . . his experiments on victims. And this family, the son knew where his father was. They sent him money, that animal in human disguise. Well, is it possible that a father can act that way and that you, as his son, still stick by him, support him? And I thought to myself, well, if Mengele had been my father, OK, at best I wouldn't have given him away or betrayed him, but I wouldn't want anything to do with him. Though I wonder. Maybe I would betray him, I just don't know, you just don't know.

[*Pause*] In any case, I am sometimes seized by a tremendous feeling of horror and disgust. My father, for example, loved dogs more than anything. When his dachshund died, he was disconsolate, he cried terribly. But then he told about hanging people from trees during the war, told this without any emotion whatsoever, indifferent, insensitive. As a child I would hear from him things like, "Dammit, you mustn't cry, you have to be tough, you mustn't cry." And today, in my relationships with others, often I don't show enough warmth. I have this cold exterior, or unconsciously I remain very cold and hurt other people very much through this sort of behavior. So you don't show feelings.

Dieter seems very irritated and uneasy. He busies himself with his pipe again, and I take a short break on his balcony. When I return, he is looking at some photos and puffing on his pipe. I ask him who the person in SS uniform in the photograph on his desk is, his father?

D: No, not at all. This man lives just around the corner. I like him very much. He was the head of an Einsatzgruppe in Russia, someone I met when I came here for my studies. He said that Hitler was the one more or less responsible. He was a Nazi through and through. He had sat at the same table with Hitler and would tell me how educated Hitler was and what a magnetic effect he had on other people. He said he'd taught at the SS academy as a political officer, and that for him the entire Third Reich and war were a great adventure: in terms of personal power, he could do whatever he wanted, drive a car drunk, and no policeman would stop him . . .

B: He simply told you all that?

D: Yes, he simply told me about all that. Though he never intimated to me in any way that he'd had someone hanged, or shot, he never talked about that. He only told me he'd been in Russia, that he "took care" of some Cossacks, that it was an incredible adventure, and that he'd sat at the same table with Hitler. But he never talked about real details pertaining to the war, only sporadically. He's still alive, lives right nearby. He's eighty-five but still in the best of shape mentally and physically.

B: And who is this person? [*Points at a photo Dieter is holding*]

D: This is my father. And this is my grandfather.

B: Your father's father?

D: Right. My grandfather was a very dynamic personality and incredibly strict. Until my father was fifty, he had to keep careful accounts of all his money because my grandfather had charge of the financial side of things. In World War I, my father served in a first-rate regiment, but his salary wasn't enough, and my grandfather gave him what he needed to live in accordance with his proper social class as an officer. My father would buy something and send the bill to his old man. He was so domineering that my father didn't dare come home late at night, he had to be home by eight sharp. He lived to be eighty-six. Throughout his entire life, my father was unable to deal with money, he was always dominated by his father. It was the most natural thing in the world for my father to obey.

I wonder how Dieter's father, a high-ranking officer in the German army, could be so powerless when it came to his own father. Dieter takes out his family album and starts going through it systematically.

D: My grandfather was in World War I, on the General Staff. This photo is from World War I: there's Ludendorff, Hindenburg, here is my grandfather, and that's my father's brother, the one who died in World War II. This is my father as a nineteen-year-old lieutenant. Here are pictures from World War II. These are the ones I asked about—who these people were, what kind of tanks, and so on. They weren't pasted in when I was young.

B: It sounds to me as if you grew up in a family where many things had to do with the military, with wars. In what way did it affect you?

D: [*Hesitates*] I decide many things alone or do them alone, independently. Only if someone else tells me it's a rotten thing on my part, tactless, do I begin to think about it and say, "That's right." Well, the woman I live with is two-and-a-half years older than I am. And when she asks me how much I have in the bank, I don't answer; or I tell her I have to go to Munich, it's urgent, without saying why. Maybe I'm not an open enough person in a relationship. When an argument arises, I try to avoid getting involved. My parents used to fight a lot. It was really terrible for me as a child when my father started hollering like some madman and my mother was half-hysterical. I think people should try not to argue and fight. If you argue, things fall apart. When there's an argument, I don't get involved, I keep quiet; it's easily interpreted as arrogance on my part. Then there's this matter of being tough, the hard exterior. When I feel hurt, I don't say anything, but rather bury it inside myself and then become very cold. People tell me I'm callous. I married in 1975; we separated in '81, still see each other occasionally, still talk to each other. Probably both of us were too young when we married. We had very different interests. The woman I live with told me I'm like a piece of ice. She says it's hard to get close to me, I'm so withdrawn. I often feel so alone. As a child I always felt very alone.

B: Did you try to talk about your father with your wife, with friends?

D: Yes, with my wife I did. And she said, "It's not your fault." For both of us, our difficulties stem from our childhood upbringing. My wife was a child born out of wedlock. Her mother was a very proper Swabian housewife and always felt it was a terrible disgrace to have had an illegitimate child. And my wife had a lot of psychological problems. She was in psychotherapy for twelve years, developed a compulsive neurosis. I didn't go into therapy myself, but I believe that our problems, hers as well as mine, stem from our upbringing and our parental environment. Once she said to me, "You know, I'm *doing* something, going to see a therapist, but you don't do anything, you push it away, try to conceal it with this cold exterior, this arrogance, though you can't help it. Still, you should understand it and try to change. This being a lone wolf, this distance you maintain, you only suffer from it." This cool aloofness, which my ex-wife criticized me for in our marriage, is also a problem now, in my new relationship.

Dieter pauses and fiddles with his pipe again, somewhat nervously. He looks at me for a second and continues.

D: I have colleagues, but it's difficult for me to form closer friendships. One friend I've known for many years is Jewish. His father was in a concentration camp just before the outbreak of World War II. He booked passage to Australia and was taken by surprise by the war while traveling there. They were taken to the Hong Kong ghetto, where my friend grew up. He returned to Germany, still looking for a homeland, I think. He started to delve into Chinese culture and language, never really lived inside Jewish tradition, had no Jewish upbringing. And then, two or three years ago, he started to learn Hebrew, began to devour Jewish culture. I think that he's found some sort of home now. That's a man who wakes up screaming at night, afraid that what happened once could happen again.

He looks pale and tired. I put out my hand to stop the tape recorder and end the conversation, but suddenly he resumes his monologue.

D: Then there's another aspect: I can be very cynical in conversations. Sometimes I put forward a certain opinion or say things about the Third Reich I don't really believe. Opinions that, well, those who didn't know me very well could believe I was really an enthusiastic and unreconstructed Nazi—for example, if I talk with some colleagues and say that it was politically stupid to murder the Jews. This expression "politically stupid" can be interpreted to mean that the killing was unimportant, that it was only a stupid thing politically. Or sometimes I tell jokes from the Third Reich—there are such very good ones that really criticize the government—and a colleague will say, "Be careful. Someone who doesn't know you might think you really like the Third Reich. What you're saying is very provocative."

B: Do you miss your father very much?

D: Strangely enough, I often dream about my father. He died twelve or thirteen years ago, but I still dream about him at regular intervals. I always dream about him as a dear person, a good father. I dream that he has to die, I start crying in the dream, then I wake up and I'm crying, as if something I wish were good and whole—a family life that's intact—has fallen apart. In dreams he appears to me as a dear person, a loving person. When I met the woman I'm living with I told her that, actually, I'd had a very happy childhood; we'd lived in wonderful houses. But then I also told her terrible things: That my father was irascible, that I had to sit straight as a candle at the table. That when I didn't eat properly, my father used to have a fit of rage— he'd throw a potato at me or something. Or when I'd throw up, he'd force me to eat my own vomit. That there were terrible arguments and fights with my parents. Then it becomes clear to me that what I long for is to have had a beautiful childhood, that maybe my childhood wasn't all that wonderful. As a child, I always suffered from the fact that my father was already so old. We'd go out somewhere and he'd be mistaken for my grandpa.

B: I can well understand your wish to have had a beautiful childhood, a good father. That's quite natural.

D: When I think back, for so many years as a young man I wasn't permitted to do things. All I had were my books. I read a great deal but just suppressed many other things, like active sports. I guess there was no real interest on my father's part.

B: Do you ever remember playing with him, having closer contact?

D: No. I can recall sitting on my dad's lap once, when he asked me what I wanted for my birthday. I said a stuffed lion. Anyhow, I remember going from store to store with him looking for a bow and arrows. And once I wanted a sword, and he ordered one from a cabinetmaker's shop, made especially for me. So from the time I was four or five, I always got war toys to play with: new tanks, small figures of Indians, cowboys. My father took time to explain to me that the Prussian army had one kind of uniform and the other army wore such-and-such a uniform, things that are useful to me even today in my research. Though I never played with my father. He was already sixty years old by then.

My father once told me he didn't want me to serve in the Bundeswehr. There's definitely a break in tradition when it comes to me and my brother: neither of us served. Ever since the seventeenth century, our whole family has served as Prussian officers. But my father was very active in trying to figure out some way to prevent our having to serve in the Bundeswehr. He said, "That's not an army anymore. They're all a bunch of milksops. The officer used to be some sort of ideal, an example to society. I don't want you to become an officer in *this* kind of army." He had strong feelings about it. Actually, I'm quite happy I didn't go into the army.

Some people say it can never happen again. But I believe that people like *that* live on, they're around all the time, they won't be extinct. Given certain structures of command, it could all repeat itself. Some people fall prey more easily than others. Perhaps the Germans have a certain tendency toward violence and strict obedience. They're politically unenlightened. Though I must say I talk a lot with this Jewish man, and these conversations mean a great deal to me. As a result, I leave my military-childhood memories far behind me. Family traditions are handed down if you live within them. I guess they master our lives. We can't really move away from them . . .

My father, for example, was definitely an anti-Semite. He accepted as truth those terrible stories that Jewish women were unclean. My father looked rather Jewish. It was quite horrible: My father was buried under rubble during World War I. When they dug him out, his hair had turned white. So he used to dye his hair. Here, you can see him in the photo: a hooked nose and black hair. Once during the Nazi period, he was in a restaurant in Hamburg and the waiter refused to serve him. He asked why and the waiter said, "Jews are not served here." So he went home and put on his uniform and returned to the restaurant . . . My father was furious that people mistook him for a Jew. Yes, I remember that my father always spoke of Jews in a derogatory way. In the Prussian army, a Jew couldn't become an officer. When my brother and I expressed a contrary opinion, my father used to shout and curse. There was simply no basis for a conversation. It's embarrassing for me to say this. I feel ashamed.

B: Ashamed about what? The fact that your father was an anti-Semite?

D: I simply can't understand it, I have no prejudice of that kind. I mean, that a person can react that way, and later on, even after all that had happened, have such a view. I myself have problems with Jews; for example, I attended a conference in Spain on medieval history, and there was a historian there from Israel, an Austrian Jew who'd emigrated to Israel. I knew that he spoke German; he used to publish in German, though he doesn't nowadays. I wanted to ask him something and spoke to him in German. He became very upset and answered in English. I suddenly felt embarrassed to be German. I mean, if I feel ashamed in Turkey because of the rotten way the Germans treat the Turks in West Germany, or because of the tactless way German tourists behave overseas, that's one thing. But when it's a Jew, and he's suffered at the hands of Germans, I can't . . . For example, I've never told my Jewish friend that my father didn't like Jews. I did tell him, though, that it was quite terrible, that my father was in the war. My father disliked the Jews, but he always thought the Russians were

OK. They were good soldiers, he liked them, liked them a lot. But Jews and Poles, "Polacks," expressions like that . . .

My mother was no different in this respect . . . There was a movie about Mengele on TV. She usually watches any lousy program, but she didn't want to see the film on Mengele. She just can't stand seeing that sort of thing anymore. And then she talks about how the Americans and Russians treated the Germans, about how many women were raped, murdered. She says it sickens her to see all this now, it disgusts her. I have to protect and shield her a bit. She's very old, in ill health, and perhaps she doesn't understand any longer. [*Suddenly very agitated*] It's also incomprehensible to me that my mother could say she wanted to get rid of her husband and get involved with the local commander so that he would send her husband to the front! You can't hate someone so much that you cause him to be sent to the front, perhaps to die out there. Those are things that are so terrible I actually can't tell anyone about them.

Dieter is carried away by his emotions. It is the first time during the interview that he is really angry.

D: My mother never says anything negative about the Third Reich. The only terrible thing was that the Allies bombed German cities. That was terrible. But nothing else. And she knew all kinds of people in the Party and so on. When we were small children she used to threaten us with the withdrawal of her love. She'd say "If you don't behave, I won't love you anymore." Or she'd say, "I won't look at you," and for two or three days she wouldn't look at us. She'd just pout. I wished very much at such times for a mother who'd give us a good spanking, so that the matter would be over with and forgotten.

On the other hand, she was overly protective. I'll tell you a story. Two years ago, at Christmas, the woman I'm living with went with me to my mother's place to celebrate, this very emotional and intimate holiday celebration my mother likes. I took my friend around the area, showed her the castles, the landscape and countryside, and we arrived at my mother's at the appointed time that evening. But my mother thought we'd already eaten. There was a terrible fight between the two women, and they started shouting at each other. Then my friend said, "I'm leaving." And I said, "If you leave, so will I." My mother thought that was really awful. "You're going along with this woman, you stick by her and not by me? I just can't believe it!" My mother was despondent, simply staggered. She was angry with me for weeks. Even today, she reproaches me and says that I stick by "this witch" instead of her. That's what she thinks. Every other woman is bad in her eyes. Ever since my days in school, any girlfriend I had was no good as far as she was concerned.

The interview is over. As we walk down the stairs, Dieter suddenly mentions that in a couple of weeks he is going to Israel for ten days. In his research on Crusader castles, he has always avoided Israel, claiming that he'd need a second passport or that there are no interesting castles there, unlike Syria. But he has discovered that it would be useful in terms of his research to go to Israel, although he knew that three years before. He is very excited and looks forward to it. We decide to meet again when he returns, and I wish him a pleasant journey.

I walk down to the river and along its peaceful bank wondering how I would feel if I were the son of a father who cried when his dog died but told emotionless stories about the villages he'd set afire and the people he'd ordered hanged, of a mother who arranged for her first husband to be sent to the front in order to marry another man—who happened to be my father . . . Would I not also wish for a beautiful childhood?

We meet at his home again three weeks later, at almost the same hour of the day. The leaves in the forest show stronger reds and yellows, and a few trees have already lost some of their foliage. Dieter is back from his trip to Israel, and I am curious about his impressions of my homeland. He introduces me to his friend, and we wait for her to bring in some tea.

D: Well, I've been in Syria, in Jordan, in Egypt, and I found people friendly everywhere. But in Israel it was just the opposite experience. Both of us felt that way. The strong impressions began at the check-in in Munich, all the strict security measures. Sure, I understand it's also for my own security. Then they started questioning me about why I was going to Israel. I told them I was doing a historical survey, and they wanted some proof that I was at the university. I had this book from our Institute, and it had a historical map from the Roman period with the name Palestine written on it. The security officer said, "It's Israel, not Palestine." And I said, "But it's a historical map." Anyhow, we flew with El-Al, and the stewardesses were anything but friendly. Of course, that can all be just a coincidence.

Then we went on into Tel Aviv. We'd booked a hotel from Germany because I didn't want to look for one, don't know the town. And the man at the reception desk was not particularly friendly, he was very morose and sullen. The next morning, though, the people who were friendly were all the Arab help in the hotel dining room. We took a bus to Jerusalem. I'd picked out a hotel in an acceptable price range, and a taxi took us there. I noticed that a lot of signs were in Arabic; it is run by an Arab. I spoke to him in Arabic and he became very friendly. We stayed there three days and I had a number of conversations with him. This Arab is not particularly radical, but he said he wasn't comfortable in the State of Israel. It wasn't democratic in his eyes: Arabs didn't have equal opportunity there. The second day there was an Indian group, forty people, and they seated all the European guests in the hotel at one table and the Indians at all the others. There was a French couple, Jewish, and they said they wouldn't sit at the same table with Germans. We felt quite upset and annoyed. I mean, we were born after the war, and we found that rather narrow-minded. We went to the Old City, and I bought an Arabic paper, because I was curious to see what can be published in an Arabic paper in Israel, and if you carry an Arabic paper, well it's useful. Then the tradesmen warm up and invite you in, you feel more like you belong.

We went to a modern luxury hotel and asked if we could have a drink. They said the bar was closed. Then I asked whether there was a room vacant. The man at the desk looked me up and down, saw the Arabic paper, and said no, they were full. Then we went back to our hotel and I phoned and asked whether they had a room, and he said yes, they still had some vacant rooms. So it became clear that they had rejected me earlier either because I was German or because I had an Arabic newspaper with me.

There is a pause while Dieter fills his pipe. I feel as if I am under scrutiny.

D: Then we left Jerusalem and traveled north into the West Bank. We walked through an area with ruins, and the children came over. There was a small village, and we were greeted with a very spontaneous friendliness—of course, people are curious, we were Europeans—but it was a kind of friendliness that I experienced among the Arabs everywhere. So we went up to Tiberias, looked at a spot where the Mamluks defeated the Mongolians; drove from Tiberias toward Zefat to Ma'alot, where we walked to a place where there are a great many poorly identified ruins from the Crusader period; then back to Ma'alot and on to Nahariyya. And in Nahariyya we stayed at a hotel run by a woman from Czechoslovakia. After dinner we were sitting in the hotel, and there was a couple sitting across from us, the man about sixty, the woman forty or so. We chatted and they asked us how we were spending our vacation, swimming or what. I said I was interested in Crusader castles, and it turned out that the man was from the Department of Antiquities in Jerusalem. So I took out my maps and showed him the places we were planning to visit. And his wife then asked whether they could come along. I said that the car was a bit small, that I wasn't sure whether we'd all fit in. Then her husband said he'd have to think it over. I asked for his calling card, which he gave me. And from that moment on he didn't look at me again. The next morning I was at the breakfast buffet, and the man treated me as if I didn't exist. He didn't react in any way. Then we were gone all day out in the field and when we returned that evening, I thought he'd ask what we'd seen. Nothing. I just didn't exist as far as he was concerned.

Then we spoke with the hotel personnel and asked for cigarettes. One of the hotel workers brought us cigarettes and asked why I spoke Arabic, what I was doing, and so on. And he told me he didn't feel comfortable in Israel as an Arab but wouldn't want to live in Syria or Jordan, because those were dictatorships. We spoke for about an hour, and then he left. Our room was located in another building. We had to go through the garden, and suddenly we were confronted by a man who identified himself as the son of the owner. He asked us why we had talked such a long time with this Arab. "How can you just sit down with my employee and talk, what can you talk about?" I was really nonplussed by all this, didn't quite know what to say. He thought I hadn't understood. Then I said I was French. He continued speaking to us in English but suddenly became much friendlier and warned us about the way the Arabs whisper things, that you had to be very careful. After that we went up to our room. And I had this feeling again and again: my God, it's like being under Stalin or Hitler. Fear of the secret police. I thought maybe the man could report us, have us deported. We simply didn't feel free in the areas under Jewish control. Out in the countryside we walked around, exchanged friendly words, felt more freedom. And always there were questions from Arabs, but people would look to see if anyone was coming and speak quietly, with lowered voices, full of fear.

We saw a few older people with concentration camp numbers. I felt a cold chill. But these people were very friendly. An old woman who'd been in a camp—she had a number on her arm—said that she hates the Germans, but that's acceptable, understandable, a natural feeling. Another woman watched her mother, brother, and sister being taken away in Auschwitz, and her mother called to her. Later she escaped with another inmate. She was very nice, asked about Germany, and also said something about her difficulties, that it was so difficult to learn Hebrew, that she couldn't completely forget German. So one can have experiences with people who react quite differently.

In connection with the massacre[1] in Lebanon, I read something in *Der Spiegel,* an Israeli psychologist who wrote about the Israeli army,

1. At the Palestinian refugee camps Sabra and Chatila in September 1982.

the officers. An essay, maybe a book, pointing out that among Jewish officers there were certain tendencies toward a cult of masculinity such as had been observed in the Waffen SS: a contempt for death, a disregard for one's own life and that of the enemy, incredible courage, readiness to strike a heavy blow.

Something else I'd like to say in connection with Egypt. The Egyptians have known two hundred years of tourism and colonialism, the people have little money, and in Cairo you can sometimes get into terrible arguments, say with cabdrivers. You can have a really heated argument. If a cabdriver in Cairo wants to cheat me, then I tell him he's a dirty louse. You can have a nice argument. Well, in Jerusalem we were sightseeing down around the Cardo, and a young man came along and asked if he could show us the Jewish Quarter. I told him that we weren't interested, we could find our own way around. But he was insistent, so we agreed. Then after a very informative half hour, he wanted money. I gave him two thousand [old] shekels,[2] and he said it was too little, he wanted more. I said I hadn't asked him to be our guide and assumed that he wanted to show people around because he was interested. Then he got angry, and I gave him three thousand and said that was all. He looked at us, and my friend asked if he was Jewish. He lowered his eyes and said he was, although we thought he was an Arab and had just said he was Jewish to get a more positive reaction. I wasn't sure if he was Jewish or not. I didn't think he was, but . . . As a German I had this feeling that I couldn't really have an argument. In Cairo, you can have a good argument. You know, if an Italian policeman upsets me, I can argue with him. But I can't argue with Israelis.

B: Why not?

D: Because in a general sense, Germans are persecutors in Israeli eyes. And we are the children of the persecutors. And so we wouldn't get the same reaction as others would get in a similar situation. Though I must admit that there was one incident. We were robbed near Caesarea, of things that the thieves couldn't use but that were important to me: my camera, research materials, scholarly books. A thief can't do anything with these things, he'll simply throw them away. The police in Hadera were very friendly, the detectives we spoke to there. They made a report, were really cordial and nice. This theft really didn't influence our experience in Israel. I mean, it happened there, it was upsetting, all my papers were gone. But something like that can happen in Germany, in Spain, it can happen anywhere. Still,

2. About three dollars at the time.

what I associate with Israel is an unpleasant feeling of a lack of freedom. You can tell me that I was particularly interested in and attentive to hearing only negative things in order to exonerate myself for being German. I don't know.

B: This example of the Cardo, where you weren't able to have an argument. Did you ask yourself why it was so hard for you to have an argument?

D: When I say to an Arab taxi driver who wants to cheat me, "You're a dog, you're a pig," for an Arab those are just swear words. But if I had said such things to the fellow who was our guide, he might have gone to the police and said, "These Germans here cursed me." And I thought that the police might help him, say he was right, that he went to a lot of trouble showing us around and we had to give him a decent fee for his services: what do you think you're doing as a German insulting a Jew this way here in Israel? So it was probably a kind of personal insecurity. And because we didn't quite believe in the objectivity of the Israeli authorities under the rule of law, we also felt a certain fear.

B: You couldn't evaluate if there was any real threat—aside from the fear that you'd be taken to the police and they'd say that as a German you couldn't bring a complaint against him because perhaps he'd been in a camp? The likelihood of this occurring was quite minimal.

D: [*Long pause*] I'm not sure. That incident with the Arabic newspaper in the hotel made me furious. I thought they were against me, but I didn't argue. If it had been anyone else, I'd probably have said, "Why are you looking at me that way?" But I felt an inner block, I wasn't able to argue with him.

B: You felt an inner block, which serves to increase your suspicion of the other fellow. A German with an Arabic paper: I don't get the response I expect, then I react and my suspicion is even greater. Under other circumstances, such situations can easily be cleared up. Maybe you actively look for situations where you can be hurt . . .

D: I mean, in France I had arguments in a hotel. In the Arab section maybe I was more open, more normal toward Arabs, so a conversation developed.

Dieter refills his pipe.

B: What was your reaction to the conversation we had before you went to Israel?

D: After our last talk I dreamed about you for several nights. I also dreamed about my father. All this had a strong emotional impact on me. I thought constantly about statements my father had made, and then this trip to Israel, the personal experience.

B: What did you dream about?

D: For several nights I dreamed about freight cars. There weren't any people, just freight cars. And you appeared to me in these dreams as a helpful person, someone who helped me. Another thing I recall is seeing my father set fire to this village. That's an image that haunts me anyway: a village surrounded, everyone in the village being killed. I've often had dreams in which my father is a very nice person, very sweet. I experience his death, am sorry he's dying, sometimes I cry. But in these latest dreams my father is always dressed in a black uniform, hard, and you and he are sort of changing roles. I can't describe a particular dream to you in detail, but I know that these dreams kept recurring for days, and that the following day I was haunted by it. It really haunted me in a powerful way.

Actually, what I wanted was to be able to talk to you, to tell you about Israel and that at the moment I have a certain anger toward the State of Israel. That for me there's a big gap between Jews being persecuted in Europe on the one hand, and the State of Israel today on the other, or the victims of concentration camps I met in Israel and unfriendly policemen or soldiers. I told you I have a Jewish friend. Well, he went to Israel once and came back and told us how nice it was. He really liked it. He felt secure and safe there. But I personally found some things shocking. I didn't feel secure and safe at all. No matter where you were, there were always soldiers around with automatic rifles. You felt very uncomfortable.

Dieter takes a second pipe from the shelf. He hesitates for a moment, fills it with tobacco, lights it, and returns the first one to its place.

D: As far as I recall, that wasn't the case in the dreams. In Israel and during the trip back, I had this feeling: you mustn't hate, you mustn't let any feelings of hatred arise inside you . . . this inner fear that you could try to excuse the sins of the fathers on the basis of these experiences now. I said to myself, you can be upset about the government but not the people. You can be upset the way you might be about the United States or South Africa, but you shouldn't be upset about the Jews. And I suddenly noticed something very much under the surface, maybe coming from my early childhood upbringing, a sort of anti-Semitism deep down inside me. Something you tried to overcome all your life, saying it's idiotic, criminal, it mustn't be. And when some of this diabolical material surfaces in me . . . [*Pause*] Though I have the feeling that I still have to sort it out a bit . . . but there is a certain sense of disappointment.

B: These two sides of you—being strong and weak, feeling love and hate—did they also come up in your relationship with your father?

D: Yes, very much so. My father came down with TB in Russia so that finally, he had only half a lung left and was extremely ill—the older he got, the weaker he got. I often said to him, "Pull yourself together, you can't let yourself go like that, be tough." Sometimes he would be given to tears. And he told me he would never have spoken with his father in that tone, and if his father were still alive he would have told me his opinion in no uncertain terms. I told him I thought I would have gotten along beautifully with his father and that I couldn't understand how an officer could be so weak, just let himself go like that. I wished for someone who was stronger. How can a person be an officer, command several thousand soldiers—and at the same time he has to be home at seven or he won't get dinner. He's cowed and frightened of his father, so soft at home, unassertive. There was a sort of mixture in my father's case: on the one hand, we were spanked if we didn't eat what we were supposed to; on the other, he was soft, not strict enough, and this upset me. I thought you had to have self-discipline, you shouldn't let yourself go. I saw my father crying a few times, actually something quite normal. But I couldn't stand it. I can still remember that, as a youngster, I would stand in front of the mirror, and I'd say something funny and try hard not to distort my face. I wanted to be impregnable, never show any weakness or emotion. I tried to exert a very strict self-discipline and control.

B: Maybe your father understood that his weaknesses helped him after all?

D: Actually I've never been able to understand his contradictory reactions. In school there was this discussion about the death penalty. At sixteen you give things less thought, you're often more radical. So I came home and told him I'd written an essay at school on the death penalty. And my father said that no human being has the right to take another's life. I was absolutely astonished to hear that from a man who'd been in the war and who'd told me he'd had a soldier hanged. As a child, I wished that my father was stronger, because he was sickly. Since his death, in all my dreams I've seen my father as a dear and caring person or as a sick person. Or I dream he has died and then I cry. Only since these talks with you does my father wander around in my dreams dressed in a black uniform. [*Suddenly looks very sad*]

Sometimes I feel that I'm longing for an inner peace I don't have. I often sense that I'm not focused, anchored enough in myself. Merely being nice to others doesn't satisfy me anymore, but when I do something else I'm still dissatisfied. I actually find it terrible that I have these sudden feelings of brutality, aggression, that I could even wonder how a battle between the SS and the Israelis might turn out . . .

Dieter and I meet again a year later at his home on the edge of the forest, and again the first leaves have begun to change color. Nature is cyclical, I think as I approach the house. Are people's life experiences cyclical as well?

B: Has anything new come up over the course of the year?

D: You gave me the name of a colleague of yours in Frankfurt, a psychiatrist. I thought about it for a while, and then I decided not to contact him. I just set it completely aside for various reasons. For one thing, I really don't know how I could pay for it, whether I'd have to pay out of my own pocket. And if I had to finance the thing myself, well, at the moment I'm not able to. So naturally that was an important reason. The other thing was that when you shelve something, put it away in the drawer, then somehow you don't think about it. And I've got so much else on my mind at the moment that to get involved in confronting myself—that's something you push aside again and repress (verdrängt). You say to yourself that things always went along somehow, that life will go on. But the conversations we had did shake me up (aufgewühlt) quite a bit. I certainly haven't forgotten those talks. And maybe they stimulated me to think more now about these matters than I did before. Perhaps, for myself, I'd like to try to work these things through in a more intensive way, devote more time to them, although it does involve effort on one's part and, like a coward, one would rather just push the thing away, avoid confronting it.

B: In what ways did you get back to this topic during the year?

D: I spoke with my woman friend about these things; there have been certain moments when we got to talking about it again. Or when I met B., I asked her about her research. I know her dissertation has been published, and I asked her to send me a copy. And when we speak about these SS leaders, what she found out about what they'd done in Russia, then I do start thinking. Of course, what's involved there is on a different level, another scale, you understand. But nevertheless, it gets one thinking. Or I see something on TV about the Third Reich, the Holocaust, and then it comes back, I sense it very strongly.

B: Have you tried, in the meantime, to find out from your mother what happened at your father's trial?

D: I visited my mother a month ago, and I told her I'd like to look at the documents she has. She started up, told me she didn't feel well, who knows how much longer she's going to live anyhow, and that I should be patient a bit longer. Then I'd get the suitcase with all the documents. She didn't want me sniffing around in those documents while she was still alive. And I also asked my sister. She was at home with my mother for a few weeks too.

B: Your mother's daughter . . . ?

D: Yes, my half-sister, from my mother's first marriage. And she told me, "What the heck do you want with all that junk? Come on, let it be. Leave it alone. It's done and past." She categorically rejects history, prefers to be a person without history.

B: In any event, she wonders why you should want to see these documents?

D: "Just let it be," she says. Actually I don't know whether my father's past—about which admittedly I don't know very much—whether my being involved with it is simply a certain kind of curiosity, wanting to know what really happened, what really took place, or if it is a result of the feeling that it does, after all, have something to do with life here and now?

In connection with this, they showed a film made about the life of Rosa Luxemburg here. Now, the movie wasn't all that good, and it was very much focused on Rosa Luxemburg as a person, a woman with feelings and hopes, though not necessarily oriented toward making the viewer feel sorry for her or take her side. Yet historically, what happened is that Rosa Luxemburg was murdered along with Karl Liebknecht by officers of the Guard in Berlin. These officers are presented in a very negative way. Now, I know that my father knew about this murder, this assassination, that he was involved. Not that he was among the ones who killed her directly, not that. But he arranged an escape vehicle for the officers who did it so they could flee to Thuringia from Berlin. And my father always used to say, "Those left-wing swine, we got rid of them!" So this was the thought that came back to me: it was my father who . . . Sure, he was little more than twenty at the time, still very young, but totally inside this tradition of the Prussian Junker in terms of his upbringing. These people must have been so thoroughly indoctrinated that they weren't even aware, they just accepted it all without any criticism.

B: Do you have some sort of total picture of your father's activities during those years, this early period in his life, when Luxemburg was killed and later?

D: Well, my father was on the Western front during World War I, in France; he was buried alive in Verdun, partially paralyzed for a certain amount of time apparently because of a bone pressing on some nerve. And as I said, his hair turned completely white. So he returned home and then went through the revolutionary riots in Berlin [in November 1918]. He saw two fellow soldiers from his regiment thrown off a railroad bridge by a group of soldiers who had mutinied. And he himself had this experience: He suddenly found himself in the midst of a riot in the streets. A band of angry soldiers pushed him up against the side of a building, and he was afraid they might kill him. He really feared for his life. Then he spotted a sailor in this crowd of soldiers, someone who was wearing a sailor's cap, and he said to this man, "Hey, you over there, you're a good sailor, how can you stand by and watch an officer being murdered?" And this sailor, apparently because he felt personally addressed, helped push my father through a door to safety. He managed to get away and ran immediately to the soldiers of the Guard Corps. My father had contacts with these extremely reactionary circles of officers. They sealed off the street and proceeded to shoot the rioting soldiers.

Then he went and built up a voluntary corps in Russia, and they fought against the Bolsheviks in the Baltic on the side of the White Russians. I think it was 1922 when the unit was disbanded due to British pressure on the German government. Then the situation became less tense in Germany. I don't know much about that period. I only know that my father studied law somewhere for a time after his adventure in Russia in the 1920s, and that he joined the army, the Wehrmacht, in 1933, as soon as Hitler came to power. There was rearmament, Germany was being rearmed on a grand scale . . .

B: He entered the Wehrmacht with what rank?

D: I think he joined as a captain. He was on the General Staff in 1934 and '35, working on early preparation plans for the invasions of Czechoslovakia and Poland. They started planning these operations very early on, and many officers were informed about them, they knew.

B: How do you know about this?

D: From my father, from the stories he would tell. He was assigned to the central area of the front as part of a unit involved in combating partisans.

B: What was his position?

D: My father was a colonel. But then his unit was placed under the command of the SS and he received a rank in the SS: he was a regimental commander (Standartenführer).

B: And he was there until the end of the war?

D: No, no. My father was transferred to France when the Allied invasion began. They transferred his entire unit through Czechoslovakia to France. I don't know whether it was in France or in Russia that he developed TB, and he wasn't captured but was sent to a military hospital near K. shortly before the end of the war. My friend B. once told me she knew that certain units were transferred from Russia to France. So this only confirms that it was indeed possible. I mean, otherwise he might only have been lying. I suspected this for some time, because my father had faked and changed the number of his regiment.

B: Do you think your father had any afterthoughts about his activities in World War II?

D: No, but his rejection of the death penalty and his reply to me, "You don't have the slightest idea what you're talking about" . . . I do think my father, well . . . I don't know whether he had nightmares, I don't know whether he suffered because of this, or to what extent he worked through and dealt with it. I don't know whether it oppressed him at all. Maybe the training he'd had, maybe its influence was just too powerful. Perhaps he simply told himself it was an order that had to be obeyed. Then you're not really responsible. I just don't know.

B: What you tell me about your father is very interesting. You're the only one of my interviewees whose father said anything at all about the war at home.

D: None of the others?

B: Not a single one.

D: Well, if my father spoke about it, this could be a sign that he actually was bothered about it, although he didn't talk a lot about all that. He was constantly moving from one place to another, but somehow it did trouble him. When our dog died my father started to cry, and I said to him, "Dammit, come on, how can you cry because of a *dead dog?* Sure, he's our dog, we love him, but you saw so many people dying during the war, constantly." And he said, "You can't compare the two. That was war, it wasn't of my making. But this is *my* dog." So I asked myself if perhaps deep down, my father was really a very soft and gentle man. Did he get swept up into this machinery? On the other hand, if a man is so soft, I mean, when partisans killed some of my father's men, he had an entire Russian village surrounded and set ablaze, and he knew that a large number of the villagers were Jews. But he remarked, "This one Jew, he grinned at me in such a dirty way." You might be able to tell yourself that it was necessary from a military point of view, that the area had to be made secure, or that they were Jews, and maybe it wasn't so terrible after all . . . [*Long pause*] Sitting here talking with you, though, I would say that there were quite simply a great many facets . . . You have these contradictions. My father would speak, on the one hand, about the virtue of honor and his rejection of the death penalty . . .

B: A lot of details that don't fit together, don't mesh.

D: Don't fit together, right . . . [*Long pause*] It's almost similar in my own case. For example, I can't stand the sight of another person's blood. When it's my own, for example, when I go to the doctor, it's not a problem. But when someone else is bleeding, that's a terrible thing for me. Whenever I see animals being sent to the slaughterhouse, for a couple of days afterward I'm unable to eat any meat. Yet, at the same time, I'm so intensely interested in military history. It fascinates me. Sure, you could say that history is a chronicle of human stupidity and cruelty . . .

Dieter can go on endlessly, but he finds no solution, no peace. That evening, B., our mutual friend, tells me she could not find Dieter's father's name listed in any of the regiments he has mentioned. She suggests that perhaps the mother does not want to reveal the details of the trial because the father was indicted for nonmilitary crimes. Maybe he had only been a simple private and told his son stories he had heard from combat people in his unit. "How terrible. What you're telling me is that the son might be torturing himself with fictitious stories? Wouldn't he be happier if he knew his father had lied?" "I'm not sure. Perhaps, deep down, he knows the truth but prefers dealing with a hero-perpetrator rather than an insignificant liar." I wonder if Dieter represents a new mode of coping with the past in the repertoire of the post-Nazi generation. Would he be relieved if he knew for sure that his father bore no direct responsibility for wartime atrocities?

When I see Dieter again several months later, he tells me that there was a fire in his mother's basement. Although he succeeded in rescuing some of the papers in his father's suitcase, the documents from the trial were burned. Now he will never know for sure why his father had been tried.

chapter 11
—————

Gathering Evidence

Renate comes to me through a friend, whom I have interviewed a few weeks earlier. They are taking a bicycle trip into France the next morning, and they arrive at the house where I am staying dressed for their ride. Renate and I go into another room so we can speak privately, and while I set up my taping equipment, I ask her if she is familiar with my research. She smiles and says, "More or less." Through her friend I already know that Renate's father had been an Einsatzgruppe commander during the war and that she herself is a lawyer and active in a leftist organization.

R: We remained in this village in Thuringia, in East Germany. My mother and I lived there, and her brothers and sisters. I always was told that my father was a soldier. And in 1948, when I was about five years old, we left this village and went to the Federal Republic—at that time it was called "going from East to West"—because my mother had learned that my father had returned from the war. He had been a POW in an American camp in Italy. He didn't want to come to the East; we were supposed to go over to the Western zone. And so my mother got us, one after the other, over the border. It was already against the law then, but it wasn't so difficult. Somehow she managed. I know that we paid some people in the business of getting others across the border, and they got us across. Once they just left us in the lurch and pocketed the money. But we made it across, and then we were in a refugee camp near Hannover. That was the first time I consciously saw my father. He visited us there. I was six at the time. Then we waited until my father found an apartment for us. The first was a one-room apartment, also near Hannover. We were given quarters there, forced to live there. All refugees from the East were required to live in such quarters. I remember quite vividly that people were very nasty to us children. They had large gardens and fruit trees, and we weren't even allowed to pick up an apple from the ground. If we did, a man would run after us, a man with a whip. We were living five in one room, the whole family. Then we got an additional room, and I started to go to school.

It was very important for my father that we should go to high school, we girls too. My mother was always of the opinion that we didn't need to, that we were going to get married anyhow. That's something I'm very grateful to my father for. We were not well off. It was very difficult for my parents to send all the children to secondary school. But my father, as in other matters, insisted on it. My mother thought we could go to work somehow. And my father tried to get set up again in a job. I know that in the beginning he was out digging peat. Later on he worked in advertising for a company that made neon signs. He was always on the road. Then we moved to Hamburg—I was twelve—because my father had found a better job, though at the moment I can't remember what sort of job it was.

And then I found out some time or other that he was trying to get a job as a civil servant once again. I found out that he had once been with the police, though I wasn't particularly interested in why he wasn't on the police force any more. So we were in this place in Hannover, and my father moved to Hamburg. It took a few years until he got an apartment, and then we moved there too. We lived for a few years in Hamburg, and then he moved on to Düsseldorf. The family was actually separated quite frequently, which I didn't mind so much, because my father was very strict. And he would come back once a month, or every two or three weeks. We kids had much more freedom when he wasn't around. I recall that I started going to dancing school in Hamburg. I was maybe fourteen at the time. And I went out with a fellow I'd met on a date. My mother said, "OK, but be home by ten." So I came back, it was a little later, and my father was already home. He made a tremendous stink about it, the fact that my mother could allow me to, well . . . And then he said that he knew about everything that was going on, that my mother was just naive, she had no idea of the dangers that were lurking for young girls. So my experience of my father was of someone who was very authoritarian, very strict.

B: How did your mother react?

R: Well, that was in Hamburg, and I just can't recall. I was sixteen when we finally moved to Düsseldorf. That's when it began, we were with him all the time then. I think I really enjoyed the freedom my mother allowed me. But when my father was around, I didn't want any trouble, and so I used to behave, to conform somehow. And in Düsseldorf my father was back on the detective squad of the police there. That's when I found out that he had been with the criminal investigation department before, and that now he was finally back at his old job. So we were together in Düsseldorf, and there were a lot of conflicts, because I was at an age where I enjoyed going out with guys on dates, and that was difficult. I recall a scene, the breakup with my father, when I was seventeen. We had this apartment, and upstairs was a small attic room. My sister had her room there, and since she was in training at a hospital, it was my room, a great little private room just for me, so to speak. Once I was upstairs in my room, and a friend came by and whistled up from downstairs. We'd agreed on a certain whistle whenever my friends would drop by so I'd know it was them. So I went downstairs to talk with him, not to go out or anything. And my father got wind of it. When I went past his door on the way back up he came out, slapped me on the face, and said, "Girls don't run out into the street when you whistle for them!" Well, that was something I really resented, that slap on the face. I thought it was very unjust.

[*Very emotional; long pause*] Actually, my sister was always my father's favorite. She was always the most well-behaved. My father used to tell about how ashamed he'd been when he took me out in the baby carriage because I was always awake, I cried, I wasn't very sweet. My sister was always sweet and loving, and somehow she continued to be that way later on. My brother was the one—he's two years younger than I am—he was the one who rebelled most against my father. Also the one who was treated the worst by him. He used to hit my brother, but except for that slap, he never hit me again. In my brother's case, spanking as a means of education was applied quite deliberately as a matter of principle.

Anyhow, in Düsseldorf I felt quite OK in the family because somehow we three kids spent a lot of time together, and our parents didn't have much of a say-so. We were on our own a lot, and I found ways of getting around things that were forbidden. Somehow it was all pretty nice. And my father gave me recognition because I was the smartest. My sister didn't graduate from high school, she dropped out a couple of years before the finals. My brother didn't get a high school diploma (Abitur) either, which is something that somehow triggered a lot of aggression toward my brother on my father's part. I guess he couldn't accept that his son had failed. He was intent on seeing accomplishment, it was a fixation. I was successful that way, so it was OK, he couldn't say anything. We would always get a reward for bringing home a good report card from school. There was a certain amount of money. I was successful at school, and that's why he accepted me. It was possible to sort of butter him up if you wanted to get something from him. So somehow I discovered the means to get what I needed.

I had a circle of friends, many more than my brother and sister had, and I was with my girlfriends a lot.

B: And your father got the job he'd had earlier.

R: Yes, and I recall that my dad was promoted, made a chief inspector or something. That was quite interesting. He used to talk about the case he was on, things you'd read about later in the paper, though I was only marginally interested in all that. Then, in 1962, I'd been out on a date at the movies a few weeks before final exams for the high school diploma. And when I came home with my friend, we started to neck a little downstairs at the door. And then some man entered the stairway and asked whether I was so-and-so. I said yes, and he said, "I'd like you to come upstairs to the apartment right away. Something has happened." I didn't know the man, but I said good-bye to my friend and went on up. And they were all sitting in the living room, my mom, my brother, my sister, my father, the whole family. In addition to the one who had spoken to me downstairs, there were two other detectives. They'd come to arrest my father.

B: When was that?

R: That was in 1962. And they'd been waiting for me, because I wasn't at home, so that he could say good-bye to me. They'd been there a long time, and my father had asked them to wait until I got there. And not much was said. I don't know if that evening . . . in the presence of those men we didn't talk much. So my father went along with them. And only after that did I learn from my mother what was up. Nothing specific but something about my father's activities during the war. My mother knew that trouble was approaching, she knew that an investigation against my father was in progress. He had also expected to be arrested. I remember that a short time before, my father had gotten passports for all of us, something that seemed unnecessary because we never traveled abroad. I found it strange and later asked my mother about it, and she told me that my father had been thinking about going with all of us to some country in South America. Because he knew he was going to be arrested. But he knew that it was impossible because we had no money, no capital.

B: But he was in the police. Didn't he find out earlier what was going on?

R: Yes, that was a few weeks earlier . . . I don't know, I can't say if he knew officially, or whether he learned via connections somehow. Anyway, he knew that an investigation was under way, and he expected to be arrested. Then we tried to get information from my mother, but she refused to talk about it . . .

B: Did you ever hear before that day about what your father had done during the war?

R: No. It was like a bolt out of the blue for me. We never spoke, there was never any talk at all about it. I never asked about it, never asked what he did. I knew too little about recent history to make the connection. I only learned later on that he'd been in the SS. He'd always said he was a soldier.

B: He never said anything about what he'd actually done during the war?

R: Well, he talked about being in captivity as a POW. He was in Rimini in Italy, in an American POW camp. He told us it was terrible. That's why we never went to Italy—because of his recollections of this POW camp and the fact that somehow he escaped.

Well, I was coming up for the big final exams in high school. It was important for me to make it, to do well, and I did. Then there were reports in the papers, and we would get anonymous letters from people who knew somehow that the reports referred to my father. My mom would get them but she didn't show them to us. I took my diploma and then studied at the university in Cologne, but I kept living off and on in Düsseldorf. At that time I know I didn't much concern myself with all this, didn't want to maybe. I guess I thought that something had descended on me that I just couldn't deal with or handle at all. In the course of time I've learned a bit from my mother, though actually very little. My mother just said, "He had to do it, had to shoot people." She always talked about the necessity of obeying orders and only spoke about the whole affair from the standpoint of defending him.

B: What did she know?

R: I don't know whether she knew. Though, yes, she did say to me later on that only when she heard about the investigation that was under way did she know that maybe he would be arrested. Then he told her what he'd done, what was involved. But my mother had known beforehand that he'd been in the SS. She knew he'd been with an Einsatzkommando group operating in the Ukraine. She did know that. But what he'd done and why he was later convicted—up to that time she hadn't known that. Though my mother is the kind of woman, well, my father could have done anything and she would have stuck by him, she would always have defended him. And I don't think she ever asked him a question later on that he hadn't already answered for her before. I can still recall the first time I visited him in prison—I think it was just after my Abitur exams—and he said right away that they were watching us to see whether we'd want to talk about these things. But then he only complained about how bad things were in jail, the fact that he had to be in with common criminals. I remember very distinctly his expression, that he, "a decent and proper German civil servant, was locked up along with criminals."

Then he was tried and sentenced to four years in prison. The charges were that he had taken part in a firing squad unit involved in executions and had also been its commander. They had executed Russian partisans. I don't know any of the details. My father had a second trial in Stuttgart. I was studying in Tübingen and went there once. And I got permission to speak with him. He was acquitted in this trial in Stuttgart; there were similar accusations. What he did, I can't quite recall. I think he served three years of the four-year sentence. It's hard for me to remember that period. Actually I wasn't around much anymore. I was in Tübingen, then I spent some time in France and visited him only very infrequently. Yes, and then I got married.

Renate stops and searches for a cigarette. From her forced smile I realize how tense she has been.

R: Later on, in retrospect, I thought maybe I'd broken free of the family by doing this, because I never actually wanted to get married. Anyhow, I married quickly in Tübingen and had a child, and that was sort of halfway accepted by my parents. After I had a family of my own, I didn't really belong to them any longer. I guess I put a certain distance between us. I had my own family and maybe this served as an excuse not to have any time to come home. And when my father was out of prison I had some contact with him, occasional visits, but we always got into terrible, heated arguments whenever the topic of his trial was broached.

B: Do you remember any discussions with your brother and sister?

R: Yes, I know that they had exactly the same point of view as my mother: it was a terrible injustice, what had been done to him, and that he'd only done it because he'd been forced to. The necessity of having to follow orders, that had been his line of defense too, I know that. So they thought you simply had to stick by him in this situation. I wasn't able to. And what I found so awful in the conversations I had with him after his release—because when he was in prison hadn't been much communication between us—was that he actually felt sorry for himself. I had always hoped he might say something about the victims, find a word of some sort to say about those he'd killed. But it never happened, never. He pitied himself, he thought it was completely unjust that he had been found guilty, that he had been made responsible for the deaths of the people he had killed. Or for those he'd ordered to be killed. He moaned and complained about himself and his lamentable fate but never once found a word to say about the victims. I believe I could have made myself speak to him if that had been different, because I was indeed prepared to recognize that he was suffering, that he'd been in prison three years, and I was prepared—maybe not then, but now—to acknowledge that it had been difficult for him to avoid the situation he'd gotten into. But I could not accept it unless he acknowledged at least once the fate of his victims. [*Cries; long pause*]

B: He seems very dear to you. Were you looking for some kind of justice?

R: Well, the contact between us was always very intermittent. Sometimes I thought maybe I should break off contact with him. It was a bit difficult always avoiding this subject, but then I had our child, their grandchild, and I thought it would be cruel if I took that away from them, cruel to my mother. So I had this loose contact with my parents. I'd visit them during vacation, or they would drop over to see us, generally when they were passing through town. As long as my father lived, I didn't speak with him about it. Then I studied law. That's another point, which is also connected with my father. I started out studying Germanic and Romance languages for a couple of semesters. And I believe it was the impact of my father's trial in Stuttgart, which I'd gone to one day . . . Actually, I don't think I quite understood what was going on, but I had the feeling I wanted to understand it. I think there is a connection, that I studied law to understand more. During this entire period I learned nothing about my father because I was considered something of a traitor in the family. I was the one who hadn't given my father unconditional support and had even said to my mother that I thought it was right that he'd been found guilty and sentenced. That one had to deal with these matters in terms of law and to use the excuse "obeying orders" was not enough. That was seen somehow as a kind of personal betrayal of the family, which is another reason I was cut off from information. When I would ask something, I would be told nothing. They always said, "All you want to do is tell your dear friends about it."

On the other hand, I believe I could only have learned more directly from my father if I had told him that I was on his side, that he'd been unjustly sentenced, and so on. That was the price. Then I might have learned something. But it was impossible, and so I was cut off, excluded. Sometimes I think that—my father's been dead for three years—that now I'd like to deal with this matter, because now it can't influence and burden my personal relationship with him. And when

I'm at home alone in my mother's apartment, I sniff about simply to see what I can find. And I have found things—clippings from newspapers, trial reports, things about my father—that are, in part, very positive. And somehow this has given me a great feeling of relief. For example, there was one day at the trial when all the witnesses testified that my father had tried to be transferred, that he had tried to get out of this firing squad execution unit. It was good to look at these things, I found it positive. Though I can well imagine what his arguments were, let me tell you, I can imagine precisely how he defended himself before the court.

[*Angrily*] And I must also tell you, something I always found so terrible was that my father said he'd done it all for us, for his family. He said that if he hadn't obeyed these orders they would have shot him, and then his family would have remained helpless and alone. That's what I thought was the worst thing of all: he said he had done it out of love for us!

B: You mean he said he killed all these people out of love for his wife and children?

R: Well, somehow I think he didn't really mean it that way. But I thought, my God, he did it out of love for us—that implicates me even more. I thought it was a terrible argument. And I told myself that there's not a single case in which someone refused to carry out such an order and was executed for this refusal. Ever since my father died I've been trying to get hold of all the documents and papers. There's a whole suitcase full, but I don't have access to it. My mother gave it to my brother when she moved and asked him to destroy it. But I asked him not to and he didn't. So the suitcase is still there, although my brother won't let me have it, because he thinks I would do something with it, publish things. My brother bears my father's name, and he's worried that they'd associate all this with him. He says I don't really care because I have a different name now, my married name. My brother doesn't want to be associated with anything.

The longer my father is dead, the more I'm actually interested. And naturally, the whole trial . . . I mean, I know from what I read in the newspaper clippings that he was involved in the shooting of Russian partisans and that he ordered the execution of people who had dug graves, possibly mass graves, for the burial of partisans or Jewish prisoners. But I hope I can find out more.

For the first time, Renate says "Jewish" prisoners in referring to her father's victims. She looks at me with some apprehension as if to gauge how I will take it and lights another cigarette.

R: The relationship between me and my father was very tense.

When we would talk, he was never able to admit to me that he had suffered because of his involvement. But I know from certain papers I've seen that that was in fact the case, that he suffered a great deal because of it and tried to get out. He applied for a transfer, which was denied. So he stayed on and did what he did. I remember a discussion we had when I said I understood it had been difficult for him to resist, but if there had only been something more than just the application for a transfer. I told him, "If you had only said you wouldn't do it!" And then once he said, "You'd be happy to have a father who had done that and been shot for it." Yes, maybe I would have preferred such a father. [*Cries*]

Actually, in my personal life, I've tried to draw certain conclusions, politically, but I've never really tried to deal with this whole story, I've never dared. Though I think I should, because I am no more guilty than those who are as old as I am. Maybe their fathers were also implicated in situations where they had to do something similar. I don't know whether I'll be able to cope with it if I really get seriously, intensively involved with this material. I notice, for example, that when I see movies of German troops, shootings, concentration camps, well, my reaction is quite different from that of my friends. My friends go to the cinema, see all of this as historical fact, and are moved, disturbed. But in such situations I react personally in a much more emotional and powerful way than those who may look at it but don't have this personal involvement, this sense of being bound up in these events (persönliche Verquickung).

B: How far did you manage to get in these conversations with your father?

R: Well, somehow we got around to discussing his involvement during the war, although there was this silent agreement never to argue, and that's why we would avoid political topics. My father did tell me that he had joined the Nazi Party at a relatively late date, and, as he said, under duress. He always referred to himself as being "German-national" in orientation, which, in terms of his farming background, is probably correct. When he joined the police force he wasn't even a member of the Party. He claimed that the criminal investigation department was forced to join the SS.[1] He eventually joined the Party, not to further his career—that would be exaggerating things—but in order not to have any disadvantages on the job. But we never had quiet discussions. More often than not, they would end with him

---

1. This is partly true. All Kriminalpolitzei, at a certain point, became members of the Gestapo; those police officers sent abroad were assimilated into the SS.

shouting and me crying in anger or misery. Our conversation would be over, and the topic wouldn't be broached for months on end to avoid triggering another confrontation.

With my mother I notice that the longer he's been dead, the more critical her comments are. It's very interesting to observe. Only now does she allow herself to ask how he got involved in this situation. She says this herself. She told me recently that in "those days" she thought Hitler was just terrific, that she would run out into the streets shouting "Heil, mein Führer!" And that my father criticized her sharply for it, because he found her behavior so impossible. He didn't like it. There was also this SS school for brides, the wives of SS members; my father was in the SS, but he avoided all of this by some trick or other. At the same time, my mother tells me she's beginning to wonder whether it was all as compulsory and under duress as my father described it, which she had believed to be true. I can well imagine that my father simply didn't tell me his thoughts because he didn't trust me. He didn't think I was sympathetic to his position—and I wasn't at that time. Too bad my father is dead. Now we'd be able to speak to one another without my attacking him in a personal way. I think I could be more sympathetic and understanding toward him. Though maybe that's just an illusion that's arisen in my mind since his death, now that the chance no longer exists, I don't know.

B: Was your father more open in his relationship with your brother and sister?

R: Yes, he didn't have to convince them. They accepted the notion that he had been implicated in these matters without any guilt on his part. They somehow accepted that. However, about the more difficult issues he didn't talk with them either. My sister often criticized me and said that in such a situation I should have stuck by him, I shouldn't have attacked him, shouldn't have asked him any questions. Though he didn't confront these matters himself. Basically the whole topic was a taboo subject in our family. My father didn't want to discuss it. He was also very busy trying to establish himself in a new job, since he'd been dismissed from the civil service after the trial. He was trying to get various jobs and work his way up again.

The last big argument we had was provoked by my daughter—a political argument. My daughter has been brought up in quite a political way; her father and I are politically active, and she's well-informed. The last time I was with her at home when my father was still alive, my daughter criticized my father, reproached him because he hadn't learned anything, something like that. And he shouted at her, called her a little brat. That's how discussions on this topic would end. He said he wouldn't stand for her trying to tell him anything.

B: Do you have any sense that he felt guilty because of his actions?

R: [*Hesitates*] No indication of that whatsoever. That's the only thing I'd really like to ask him today. And I also believe—insofar as I can assume this on the basis of my mother's hints—that even if he felt any guilt he was afraid his activity during the war would come out, be made known. He had trouble in connection with de-Nazification proceedings and wasn't reinstated as a civil servant right away. I don't know how it came about that he was reinstated later, I mean, politically, I just don't know. I do know that at that time, when we moved to Düsseldorf—I found out about this later on—many of his former colleagues, who were with him on the police detective force and who were in the SS, were arrested and put on trial. I think it all started in the mid-1950s. Documents were discovered, certain types of material. I think he was afraid early on because of his record, because he'd been a member of the SS. What he really felt . . . nobody knew what he really felt.

My parents only knew how to complain: it was unjust, nothing happened to many who did the same things he had done or even worse things. Even today my mother thinks it was very unfair, and I do have to agree with her that in many cases, people were not brought to justice, though that has nothing to do with his own personal guilt as far as I'm concerned. I'd say—not that I know what my father did—it was right that he was sentenced, though I also feel that physical punishment does not help, because it may even free a person from feeling guilty. This is bound up very closely with my own work as a criminal lawyer. Now that I'm active as a defender, I want to keep every person out of jail, no matter what his offense. Really, no matter what he did, I want to keep a person out of jail or make sure he is sentenced to as short a jail term as possible. I don't identify at all with the notion that the government, the state, has a right to punish offenders. On the contrary, I think this notion is wrong. I know that people suffer when they're locked up in jail, that they are in even greater danger when they get out afterward, all that sort of thing.

I don't even think it's important that my father was punished. That's no satisfaction in my eyes. I think it would have been easier for me if he had told me what he had done, how much he had suffered, what he had learned from all this. For me that's an important point: this feeling I have that he didn't learn anything at all. Nothing from his own personal fate, nothing from the political developments that transpired, nothing from history—that he learned nothing at all. [*Angry and agitated*]

B: Are you sure?

R: Yes, from the way he talked about it. For me it would have been important if he had . . . well, he never uttered a word to me about the people he'd ordered killed. Never. Never, in any way. The victims were simply not a subject worth talking about. All he would talk about was the injustice he'd suffered. And for me it was always the victims who . . . especially when I think that twenty or twenty-five million were murdered by the Germans and that maybe a few hundred of these can be charged to my father's account, then I have the feeling that the weight of history is somehow on my shoulders. And that a person who was personally responsible for this is unable to find a single word of pity and compassion for the victims—that's what alienated me most of all from my father. The three years of suffering he spent in prison, well, for me you just can't compare the two. There's just no way of equating the two.

B: Did he never make any remarks, for example, when watching something on TV?

R: Yes, but only in the sense . . . I recall the remark my parents would make sometimes: "That old topic, they're bringing it up again." I think they ignored programs on the Nazi period, books, and the like. Somehow they always felt that they'd suffered enough themselves because he'd been in prison. They didn't want to look at these films about the atrocities on top of it. My father was a convinced anti-Communist and anti-Semite. It came up once in connection with your country. [*Looks at me, upset*] Though he always claimed he wasn't anti-Semitic.

I myself was very critical of Jewish policies in the Middle East. I took part in demonstrations against Israeli policy toward the Arabs. We always talked about this and once my father suddenly agreed with me enthusiastically. Yes, he said, he thought that was right. And he said to me, "Well, you're finally wising up," something along those lines. And I thought, my God, now I'm on his side. It was clear to me that it was the old anti-Semitism in a new guise, provided with new fuel.

B: Could you talk about your father's past with your husband, with your daughter?

R: With my husband, yes, I spoke to him about it. Surprisingly enough, he had a very uncomplicated relationship with my father on a kind of buddy-buddy level. Somehow they hit it off well. Naturally he knew what my father had done during the war. But I had not told my daughter because I always thought I would tell her when she was older.

B: What happened?

R: When my father died, my daughter was vacationing with her father. We were already divorced. And he chose this occasion to tell her that my father had been in prison. A friend of my daughter's was along, and I just didn't like the way he . . . I would have preferred to tell her myself. She was sixteen and at an age when you could certainly do it. But somehow I resented it terribly at the time, the fact that he'd taken this from me. My daughter is exceptionally interested in the whole matter. She says it's good for me to get at the documents. I believe the historical documents are really valuable. I'd also like to know who my father was, what kind of man he was in this particular situation.

Otherwise, maybe I've told this to three people since my father's death. While he was alive I didn't speak to anyone about these matters, because if they ever met my father, I didn't want them to see him as a Nazi war criminal. I'm not sure how all this has influenced my relationships with other men. I do have difficulties when it comes to long-term relationships with men. I don't know if it's connected. Two years ago I had a client who was Jewish. He'd been in prison. I fell in love with him, very much in love. I had a very intense relationship with him. But he's from South Africa. I didn't follow him there, because I can't live there—he's a white South African. Then I thought, well, this is no mere coincidence. I chose to fall in love with one of my father's victims who is a victimizer of others at the same time . . .

B: In what other ways might your father's story have affected your life?

R: [*Thinks for a moment*] Just what occurs to me. I can't bear to see violence, people being beaten. My sense of pity, of compassion, is very strong. I can't stand seeing people suffer, can't stand it when people are tortured. Verbally either, any kind of violence. I get involved, I interfere. I think I have quite a pronounced sense of social justice. I always think I have to be on the side of those who are weaker, who are disadvantaged or in a weaker position. Maybe my chosen profession has something to do with it: a small personal contribution, a form of reparation, the fact that I help people and protect them as far as possible from misery and suffering. I see my profession very much in terms of a struggle against authority and the exercise of power, state power.

I do think that my divorce has something to do with my wish to be free from the control of my husband's authority, because I always felt he was intellectually superior to me. In the beginning he was quite superior, but somehow I caught up with him a bit during our marriage. I'm also very grateful to my husband, because he helped wake me up politically. My father always wanted to marry me off to one of his associates, his cronies, and I'm really happy I got away from all that politically through my husband. I probably looked for someone like him for that reason, but I think he helped me come a long way too.

B: And your sister and brother, did it affect their lives as well?

R: No, I don't think so. My sister is married and very devoted and obedient to her husband. Like my mother, she voluntarily submits to his will. I think she's afraid that if we talk together about my father I'll try to turn her against him, that the image she has of him will be tarnished. That's what I used to feel when I was at home more. When there were discussions in the family, she'd always take my father's side. At some point I just gave up talking to her. And she, well, she suffered a lot because of his death.

Renate picks up a cigarette but prefers to play with it rather than light it.

R: For me it was no great loss. I've gone through three funerals in recent years, my father and two close friends. A very close girlfriend and then a friend who was a mountain climber—he was killed in an avalanche. That shook me up much more than my father's death. The death of my mother would be a terrible blow. But my father's . . . It actually came quite unexpectedly. He was very healthy and strong. He died suddenly, had a stroke out on the street.

B: And your brother?

R: I really don't know. I only had occasional contact with my brother and sister during visits home to my parents. My brother is the one who suffered the most from my father. For a time, he must have hated him terribly, the way my father treated him. And he was the one who rebelled the most against my father. My brother was married for a short time, a year and a half, but his wife left him. Then for several years he traveled around the world. He used to be an athletic coach and soccer trainer. I think I get along with him now almost better than with my sister. It's difficult with her, because her husband is always present and she always pays attention to what he says. My brother has the temperament of what we call a "jovial Rhinelander," though he isn't one by birth. His philosophy of life is: we'll work it out, no problem (das kriegen wir schon). He hides his problems better than I do. I don't know whether he thinks about all this. He doesn't communicate much of what he's thinking.

My brother and sister and I, well, the contact between us is not like that between friends. There was some closeness when we played together as children, but now what keeps us together is the support we give our mother. She's been having a bad time of it. My mother's been in psychiatric clinics four times because of depression. Last year it was very bad. She finally realized that my father was dead. Initially, she didn't react to his death in any way we could notice. They had known each other since early childhood and had spent their entire lives together. She was extremely depressed, so I had her brought to a clinic. We all see to it that someone is with her at all times, as much as possible, or that one of us goes off with her on a trip somewhere. So contact between us is very much determined by "how mother is doing" and what we can do for her. At the moment, that's generally what we talk about. We don't exchange our own thoughts much at all.

Undoubtedly, all this has some connection with the fact that my mother has been very ill on occasion. She tried to kill herself when my father was released from prison. Last year, when my mother was here and worked through her whole case history with the doctor, it became clear to me that it all began when my father was released from prison. Before that she couldn't allow herself the luxury of illness, she was too busy. She was a woman who, on her own, was always really terrific. She kept things going through the entire period of the war with three small children and all. My brother was only a few weeks old when we fled as refugees. We were on the brink of starvation in East Germany. She was on her own with us there too, and I think it's absolutely terrific what she did, the way she took care of things. And when my father was arrested, she went to work in a store. But after that, whenever he'd come home, she'd always submit to his will again immediately. He was the boss. And all the independence she'd gained during the time he was away just vanished. Perhaps it was something she forced upon herself. She really didn't want to be so independent. She was happy to slip back into her old role.

B: She just went back to being dependent on him?

R: I think my father treated my mother in a condescending manner much too often. He made her feel she was inferior to him. That upset me very, very much. On the other hand, it bothered me a lot that my mother was just a good little housewife who never contradicted him, someone who always yielded to him and always accepted everything. I would have preferred a stronger mother.

Our conversation is over, and we join the group in the kitchen for a late-night cup of tea. Renate seems tense and does not take part in the discussion. I, too, am immersed in my thoughts. Hers is a normal life story, with the usual family tensions and confrontations. Only . . . her father had ordered that a few hundred partisans and Jews be shot after digging their own grave. He would have remained a hero in the eyes of his daughter had his past not come to light.

And here sits his daughter, the only one of his children who did not accept his point of view. She waited for some expression of guilt or remorse for his deeds, even a single word that would allow her to understand him and go on loving him. Instead, she heard more anti-Semitic remarks, which became interwoven in an ironic way with her own political reaction to Israel's relationship with the Arabs. Renate writes to me a few weeks later to let me know that our conversation has made a deep impression on her and that she has decided to see a therapist. She wants to confront the unfinished business of her father.

We meet a year and a half later in a small restaurant not far from her office. It is a beautiful, warm day, and we decide to sit outside, under a big chestnut tree. I can see that Renate is happy to meet with me, and I imagine that, had the situation been different, we would hug each other. But both of us bear too heavy a burden to be able to do what we feel, so we shake hands and sit down. I let her order for me: a soup she claims is the specialty of the kitchen. Before I have a chance to turn on the tape recorder, she tells me she has finally gotten hold of the suitcase in the attic, but we come back to it only later in our conversation.

B: You remarked that since the last time we met, you've thought a lot about these things, that they've preoccupied you . . .

R: Yes, and the conversation with you, which was actually a great surprise for me, very unexpected, I wasn't prepared for it at all, well, that conversation really shook me up.

B: Was I the first stranger with whom you discussed these things?

R: Yes, you were the first stranger, yes, I think so. I've never spoken about this before with someone I didn't know beforehand. I do think, though, that it happened because of my friend D. She is somebody I've often talked to about such matters. She's been interested in questions like this, she's been dealing with them for a long time, quite intensively too. And she was somebody who always suggested to me that I do something about it. I think she felt this need a lot earlier than I did, so she sort of rushed me into going to see you. And a sense of trust was established pretty quickly. I felt so shaken after our talk, and that's when it became clear to me that my father's story troubles me today much more than I ever thought it did. The way I went about solving the problem—by being very active politically, in anti-Fascist organizations and against racism in South Africa, for example—well,

I felt that that way wasn't actually the right way, it wasn't enough in order to grapple with the entire personal problem I have with my father, or to clarify it.

Then some other things happened that also had a big impact on me in this connection. During the trip I took to the Soviet Union, in Moscow, I laid a wreath in the name of our tour group at the monument to Soviet citizens who perished in the war. And that left me very, very upset. Yes, somehow this gesture of ours—actually, what it was was a political gesture of friendship—meant a lot more than that to me. I had the feeling that somehow I was doing it for my father's victims. Then, about two years ago, my daughter moved out. Looking back now, I think that since then, I've actually been thinking a great deal about what my father did, about who he was as a person. I think this is bound up with the fact that when he was in prison, I left home. I established my own family and tried in that way to break free of the burden my old family and my father had been to me. And I think I was successful to some extent for the next twenty years. But when my daughter moved out of the house, I was thrown back into the situation I had been in twenty years earlier. It led me back to my point of departure, my own original family . . . That's why I went into therapy, and what comes up again and again is my father, or his guilt—the guilt I've taken over.

B: Why does your father appear? Is it because of what he did or in connection with your relationship to him?

R: Well, it has to do with what he did, but mainly it's my relationship with him—and I also think my relationships with other men, relationships in which he plays a very important role. I have the impression that because of this—and what I'm telling you now is a result of this therapy—I believe that it was a tremendous disappointment, what I went through with my father. After all, I was already twenty when he was arrested, and I didn't have any idea at all about what his crimes were.

B: Weren't there fights with him earlier on?

R: Yes, but I think those fights had to do with authority, which I think was quite normal. Or maybe it was normal for my generation; since then, a lot has changed in the way kids are brought up. My father was very strict, yet he also worried about us a lot. He was a father who took very good care of the family, provided for us. Now what he did as an Einsatzkommando leader, where he shot so many Russians, mainly of Jewish background, well, it didn't fit that picture. Until then I hadn't asked myself questions, and I hadn't put any questions to him either. So when he was arrested in 1962, I was quite uninformed. I don't recall if I even knew that my father had been in the SS. Yet even if I had known, it wouldn't have meant much to me.

At school we didn't deal at all with that entire period. It was customary back then that high school kids would get as far as the beginning of World War II. And then the war was talked about very briefly, just touched on, but the period of National Socialism not at all. So I had no awareness that there was a problem at all. Otherwise maybe I would have asked questions. But I was also such a conformist and I'd been brought up in a very conservative family atmosphere. So it was really a bolt out of the blue, a total surprise when I came home that evening and my father was being taken away. And I think that's one of the reasons why I've had difficulties in my relationships with men, as if I'm afraid I might experience another disappointment like that. I mean, to love and trust a person who later turns out to be a criminal . . .

B: So you can no longer rely on men?

R: Yes. I often felt very sorry for my mother because my father was so domineering. And because she was so dependent, she was very vulnerable. I wanted to avoid that in my own life.

B: She was vulnerable, easily hurt, but she didn't react.

R: But there is a story about my brother that I may not have told you last time we met. One time my father wanted my brother to have a haircut. They had a terrible argument, and my brother said he would rather leave home. And then my mother intervened—for the first time in her life. She said she would leave with my brother if my father didn't stop tyrannizing him. Basically, she tried to help my brother and stick up for him. I don't think she seriously thought he would be leaving, and maybe that's what gave her the strength to become so self-assertive and rebellious. He was the only one of the kids still living at home. Maybe she sensed somehow what might happen to her if this child too were "chased away" from home. Also, my father was very strict with him, stricter than he was with us girls, and my brother resisted, he wouldn't obey. He was often punished. He wouldn't be allowed to eat or would be sent to bed without dinner. Then my mother would secretly bring him food. But never before did she dare to confront my father openly.

B: What was your father's reaction?

R: I don't know, I wasn't around. I can only imagine. Based on what I know about him, I think he was completely and totally shocked. He must have been. Because at no time in their entire life together did she talk to him like that. He apparently thought she really would make good on her threat. So my brother was allowed to keep his long hair.

B: Suddenly the big man had turned into a small man?

There is a short pause, and I regret my remark. Perhaps it is too strong for someone still trying to feel her way between love and the disturbing truth.

R: Yes.

B: Do you sometimes think of things you would like to speak to your father about now, things you didn't discuss then?

R: When he was still alive, somehow we never talked much. And I also believe that simply to maintain his position as head of the family, he had no other choice but to tell his children he was innocent, the judgment in the trial had been mistaken ... Sometimes I wonder if he'd say that the guilt he felt [*speaks very emotionally*] was too great to be admitted to us, whereas I always used to think that he had no sense of guilt at all. That's what made me so furious, the fact that he never expressed it. I simply thought he felt no remorse for the people he murdered or their relatives.

B: And lately you think he did feel guilt after all?

R: Well, the way I see it now, because I'm able to have these "dialogues" with him in my mind, is that if he admits his guilt, then it can be lifted from me. I'm certain that back then I would have given him a lot of support if he had admitted his guilt to me and his remorse for his victims. In the imaginary conversations I have with my father now he always does. Maybe because I hope he would see what a terrible thing he did, what a terrible burden it is for me, my brother and sister, and my mother.

B: It's interesting that he left the suitcase.

R: Yes, that's true. I've also asked myself why he put this suitcase away for safekeeping when it contains such ... For example, I discovered that he was a member of the Gehlen organization.[2] It was a very secret organization. No one was supposed to find out anything. But maybe he also wanted us to find out. And he was very pedantic and well-organized, he never would have dreamed of throwing away such important documents. It certainly does have some definite meaning, the fact that he left them behind, that he didn't simply throw them away. Maybe he wanted to give us a hint too, some indication ...

B: Yet aside from this one example, nothing is known about his inner conflict?

R: No. But I do have the slight hope that perhaps the prison chap-

---

2. An intelligence service organized by the United States and directed against the Soviet Union that hired former war criminals.

lain knows something about it. I could well imagine that, being in this situation, he might seek out another human being to whom he could talk openly about it. Maybe it was this chaplain. Somehow I think I would be happy—or relieved—to know that my father had any inner conflict whatsoever, and that he talked about it with someone.

B: Didn't he leave anything in the suitcase that . . . ?

R: I haven't read everything yet. I have to go through it bit by bit.

B: What have you read already?

R: I read the judgment and the preparation for the trial, the protocols that were used in preparation for the trial and by the defense. Naturally, it all follows the official line: the catchword is always "acting under duress" (Befehlsnotstand). Sworn statements about this were obtained from various people. But there are definitely no notes dealing with any inner conflict, if a conflict actually existed as such. But I don't know whether he would have been able to live so well, keeping up appearances the whole time down to 1980, if he had been living with an inner conflict. Maybe he really did succeed after all in internalizing the defense strategy he used in court and became convinced it was true. But I don't know how it is possible for someone to live with a conflict like that if he can never allow it to surface.

B: How long was he in that Einsatzkommando unit?

R: It was a comparatively short period, one month, I think.

B: And what did he do after that?

R: It had always been his wish to be assigned to a unit fighting against partisans. Apparently, he had certain "special qualifications" for that sort of thing. Then, after a few months, he was transferred to another Einsatzkommando unit, which had other duties, what was called "combatting partisans." It had been the job of the first group to which he was assigned to follow up on the heels of the Wehrmacht and engage in "mopping up" operations (Säuberungsaktionen). To "mop up" meant to kill people, Communists or Jews.

B: What rank did he have?

R: He was a captain (Hauptsturmführer) in the SS. At the trial he defended himself very vehemently in this regard, saying that he had been assigned against his will and given the same rank he'd had when he was a police officer, which is probably true. I really do believe that these men had no clear idea of what was going to happen to them. And they were placed in a situation that surprised them, a new situation. But that doesn't explain why everyone—or almost everyone— then did what was demanded of him. People like my father. I think the others were just as much people who . . . for example, the three men who were found guilty along with my father were people who had lived a very proper and orderly life . . . lawyers, these men had all studied law, and my father had too, although he didn't finish his degree. So these people were . . .

B: Educated?

R: Yes, very proper . . .

B: Normal people?

R: Yes, normal people.

B: Who lived a normal life thereafter?

R: Yes, right. And afterward they lived a completely "irreproachable" life, as the expression goes (untadeliges Leben), without ever committing any act that was illegal or a crime, people who lived in a very correct manner. My father was such a correct and honest official. A man who definitely never cheated, even just a little, when he handed in a bill for travel expenses or that sort of thing. Incredibly honest and correct when it came to little things. With such a Prussian sense of duty, a quality that can be quite positive, too, in certain situations, but which, in the situation where he found himself, led to his doing what he did. He testified in court that he knew it was unjust and wrong, but that anything else would have been absurd, that it was impossible to refuse to carry out the orders he received and was obliged to pass on. So it was that same sense of duty, otherwise such a positive quality, that made him do the wrong thing in such a situation. The notion that if the state orders me to do it, I will, no matter how criminal the deed. I'll simply carry it out, because I'm a conscientious bureaucrat.

B: What else have you managed to read of the documents in the suitcase?

R: Well, what I mentioned before, that after the war my father worked for years in the Gehlen organization, a kind of secret service, and always told us he was working for an insurance firm. We were living in a small town in Lower Saxony at that time. He was somewhere else during the week, came home only on weekends, and he always said he was working for an insurance company. But during that entire time he was working for the secret service, which is reputed to have continued anti-Communist spying, maybe even killing, after the war with the support or tacit approval of the Americans. And there are those who went from that outfit right into American intelligence organizations, because people found their anti-Communist attitude, and then most definitely their practical knowledge and skills in respect to the Soviet Union, quite useful. What terrible cynicism! [*Crying*]

So he lied to us about more than one period in his life . . . Actually, up to now, that's all I've read about. I've only looked into the suitcase a little and put back, for the time being, a number of items I just glanced at. I have to take my time and read all these things bit by bit. I don't think I'd be able to digest everything all at once anyhow. And since I've taken so much time for this whole thing, I can allow myself a few weeks with the suitcase too.

I sense Renate's bitterness. She looks in the suitcase for hope, something that will confirm her father's humanity, but all she has found so far is evidence of his ongoing need to be on the side of the powerful.

R: I think a person always stays that way, that's for sure. But what I imagine, what might perhaps be my ultimate goal, is to be able, with the help of therapy, to live with these two conflicting images of my father and to reconcile one with the other to a certain extent. What I've noticed recently, or actually in the last few years—and people have pointed this out to me—is that I never mention my father when I talk about my childhood. I mention things about my brother and sister, my mother, but never mention my father.

B: So you've removed him from your past?

R: Yes, I've tried somehow to eradicate him, even as the good father he was for twenty years. At the same time, I find it quite impossible to recall a "good" father without also remembering the criminal. It's hard to do. And I do think I've tried to push my father as criminal, as perpetrator, from my memory, although with the result that my father—as a Nazi criminal—has forced himself more and more into my consciousness.

B: And now you can see that . . .

R: Yes, now I don't freeze up when someone asks me about my father. I'm able to say who he was and the difficulties I have with that. I also see that it is not only a question of my relationship with my father. What is also important for me in all this is my own future. I've discovered that it's impossible to eradicate one's father from memory, to try, maybe via political involvement, to make up for or compensate for something. It was difficult for me in therapy to accept that this is really a case of transference of guilt. I have taken over the guilt my father didn't feel, or didn't show me he felt. In rational terms, it's absurd, I mean, I had nothing to do with it. And I used to think that because I had nothing to do with it, I was untouched by it.

There is hope in Renate's eyes that was not there when we first met. We finish our soup and chat for a while. She tells me that she has tried to convince her sister, who is becoming more and more bitter toward life, to go into therapy. But her sister's husband does not want to hear about psychotherapy;

he thinks that psychiatrists and psychologists are all sick people. Renate smiles.

We shake hands again when we part near her office. As I walk away, I say to myself that next time, I will give her a hug. A few months later she writes me a note. She has spoken to the prison chaplain, who reports that her father never approached him for any kind of confession. She concludes, "But I've learned not to give up. Someday I will find evidence that he did feel something for his victims."

chapter 12

My Father, My Self

It is pouring rain the day I go to interview Monika for the first time, and I arrive at her door dripping and sneezing. A small table is already set with coffee and cake for three, and I am introduced to her friend, who sits quietly on the sofa. I would prefer to discuss these difficult issues in private, but I do not object, because I sense that her friend's presence will make it easier for her to tell her story.

I was referred to Monika by B., a historian who is doing research on the leaders of the SS and the police during the Third Reich. Because her father was tried and hanged in Riga when she was a child, Monika has no actual memories of him, but lately she has become more interested in learning about his involvement in Nazi atrocities. When B. asked her if she was willing to be interviewed for my research, Monika was hesitant at first but finally agreed to talk with me. When we sit down, I note the frank, open expression on her face.

B: Perhaps you could start by telling me when and where you were born, what your earliest childhood memory is . . .

M: Before I say anything else, I should say that I didn't know my father . . . I'm an illegitimate child. I was born in 1941, and by then he was in Russia and had been there for a long time.

B: What are your earliest memories from those years, the war years?

M: Well, I can remember a few things. We had been evacuated out to S. Now that was from 1944 to early 1946, when my mother and I moved to D. I have certain recollections bound up with that year and a half in S. Vague memories, even dreams, of sitting in the air-raid bunker . . . There were a lot of Poles in S. at that time. It's a small town, with the usual biases and prejudice—"that's dirty, that's full of lice." My mother is like that too, which is why I can still recall it so vividly, but I know about those years mostly from stories I heard from her later on. I can recall that an American stopped me in the street—it was after the end of the war—and gave me an orange. And my mother went home with me to eat the orange. I've also tried to find out about things in a little more detail. My mother says it was a terrible time. She's only told me about a few things, for example, when the Americans came into S . . . Suddenly they were just there. My mother didn't go outside. They entered the houses, asked for valuables, cameras. My mother handed them over. To her it was something important, it was weighty in some way, that's probably why she remembered. Then she told me that the Americans burned bread right in front of the local population, bread that had been left over and that the Germans, of course, would have been very happy to eat. It was destroyed before their very eyes or thrown into the mud or something . . . It was a direct provocation. I have some very vivid memories of that time, but not of anything involving the political background then.

B: What sort of memories?

M: Well, the house—our house was a former mansion, and a few years ago we went back to see it again—it had a gallery. And people had come there from different areas of the German Reich, they'd been evacuated or had fled. And they formed this group living together in that house, a very nice bunch of people. They made puppets together, wrote a skit and then performed it. I still have a vague recollection of that. And then—my mother told me about this—people would sit around together in the evening and read fairy tales or plays aloud. They had all kinds of books . . . I can still remember that well . . . we still have that play. It was very much a part of daily life, along with gathering wood to burn, or berries. We'd go out in the forest for hours looking for all kinds of berries. I can recall sitting up on top of a cart. My mother and my grandmother would get the things we needed to survive. And it was very nice for me. I still have a few images of all this in my memory . . . going out to gather wood and pinecones.

I can also remember all the stories about food. Probably nowadays no one would eat food like that, but to me back then it was delicious. Or eggs. I can remember that once for Easter I was given a nest of eggs, and I ate all the eggs right away. I ate them all, one after another . . .

B: When did it occur to you for the first time that your father was not around? When did you first ask about him?

M: I can't recall when I first asked. At the time, my mother claimed that he was "missing." But I do recall that there was a very intensive period in my life, in my first and second years at school, when I saw that the fathers of other kids were coming back from the war. We were already living in D. then, on a busy commercial street. There was a lot of life and noise. It was also a street that served as a route going north out of town, so it was one of the main streets. I saw a great many POWs returning. I can remember once there was a POW who'd fainted, he was lying there, and a few women were standing around him. And they gave him some food. Now I had a carrot in my hand, and I thought about whether I should give it to him. I can still remember that those women asked him, "Where do you have to go?" and then discussed among themselves what the shortest way would be.

Then there was another guy who fascinated us children. Unfortunately, kids can be pretty brutal. This fellow had some sort of difficulty walking, he just staggered along, couldn't walk normally. And a whole bunch of kids, including me, would trail behind him. Not that we made fun of him, but simply . . . I can recall that I thought about what could be wrong with him and asked my mother a lot of questions, though it was clear that he was a released POW.

And yes, in school too, you'd hear that someone's father had come back. I can still recall quite well that I was waiting too, but my mother didn't pass on any information, although she already knew. She left me in the dark about it. She said he was reported missing and that it wasn't known whether . . . Then she said he was probably no longer alive. And she didn't understand that it was the stupidest, the worst thing she could have told me. Because as a child I had been very optimistic, and I had dreamed up all kinds of stories—that he was still alive and would come back. And I started to think that maybe he really would come back. For a long time, actually every day . . . I had this definite notion that it would be in the afternoon. So when the doorbell would ring in the afternoon—I can still see myself standing there—I would stand at the top of the stairs (we lived on the top floor) and look down, thinking it could be him. Or my mother's brother—it was clear that he would be coming back. He'd written us that he was soon to be released. And I had this very definite notion about when I would see him . . . because there were thousands of such stories, and I myself had seen some men going around asking and looking. You'd also hear a lot of stories about someone who was going around here and there, asking questions, searching. So I imagined more and more that . . . I would dream up all these stories about how it would be if I were to see my uncle on the street, and I had thought out how I would explain to him where he would have to go, where my aunt lived. I had thought all this out . . . how I could best explain to him where . . .

I remember, for example, that my mother had a special way of baking cake, a cake that consisted of separate pieces, and I would leave a piece, just in case, though she didn't say anything. It was probably very unpleasant for her, the fact that I did that, but she never told me anything definite. I didn't wonder about her silence either. We would get food at school, and there would be something extra for the kids who—I can't remember the expression they used—for kids whose fathers hadn't returned (die Hinterbliebenen). I was somewhere in the middle, I don't know why, and as a child I didn't ask. I never asked. It was known that I was growing up without a father, that it was difficult at home. But I wasn't officially registered. Anyhow, there would be this extra bonus, chocolate or cookies. Actually I had no right to receive them, but if something was left over, or if a child was absent, I would always get something extra. Or when the Red Cross would distribute something, clothes or food, I would always be asked, and I would have the choice: should I be a child who is needy, a poor child, or not? I recall that I couldn't make up my mind . . .

B: Sometimes one way, sometimes the other?

M: Yes. Once, I remember, we had to—I'm not sure in what connection—anyhow we had to tell something about our fathers. I was supposed to say what his name was. That must have been back in first or second grade. But I didn't know his first name. My mother always said "Daddy."

B: Hadn't she told you that your father's name was such-and-such?

M: No. When she talked about him, she always said "Daddy." I can recall that it was something of an embarrassment too, because the kids would say, "Ha ha, she doesn't even know her father's name!" So I said my father's name was Friedrich. It sounds a bit like *Friedhof* [cemetery]. And I knew exactly what I was saying in using that name. I remember that the teacher didn't say anything, even though he was quite conventional and middle class. For the children too, it was a cover story. My mother had built up such an image of this man, he was like a deity to me, a terrific man, a tremendous father . . .

B: What did she tell you about him?

M: Not facts, at least I don't recall any facts. She would just rave to me about him, tell me how wonderful he was, how much she still loved him, that he was the only man in her life and that no man even came close to him. I can't quite recall now, but she would stick to these things: he was a courageous man, a good man. She never said much that was concrete. Though she did say, when I got older, that I was very much like him, for example, when it came to looks, behavior, things like that. She kept on saying this for a long time, right up into my teens. There were also things she viewed more ambivalently, but she would forgive me for them because my father was that way too. For example, my dislike of formalities—she actually felt critical about it, but because he also had this tendency, she didn't say anything.

B: That's why she accepted it?

M: Yes. Or my love of nature—it was always quite clear that I'd gotten that from my father . . .

B: How long had your mother known him?

M: Eight years. I have this stubbornness, this determination about doing something or sticking to an opinion. My mother is very conventional, very much so. She's really a product of her times. Even today, she gets upset if I don't conform, if I say what I think and occasionally upset other people, that sort of thing.

B: Like your father?

M: Yes, though now she no longer says it. In any case, during my childhood and early teenage years, whenever I would be very lively or full of energy, it was all quite clear: I was taking after my father. My father had four sisters, and he had told her that if anything happened she could turn to his mother. This is how she developed contacts with one of his sisters, who helped us a great deal. A genuine friendship developed. And this aunt always said that there was a certain similarity in the way I moved . . . when I was a child and would roughhouse and make lots of noise, she would say that I reminded her of her brother.

B: Did you see any photographs of your father?

M: Yes, certainly. I have a lot of photos. And that aunt tried repeatedly to get my mother to tell me the truth about him, although my aunt didn't like him—politically her views were different from his— and she had always avoided talking about him. She felt inhibited because she knew my mother never said anything about him. Anyhow, she didn't succeed in getting my mother to tell me.

B: How did you view this discrepancy between your aunt and your mother?

M: My aunt died fairly early, and at that time I still didn't know. When I was fifteen or sixteen, my mother told me there'd been a report in a Berlin paper: he had been found guilty and executed, the sentence had already been carried out. I didn't know any more than that, although then this vague feeling became stronger in me that there must be something fishy in this story. For a long time, I simply didn't accept that he . . .

B: Do you mean his activities during the war?

M: No, the job he had. I thought that when someone has such a function . . . though I didn't know exactly. My mother only told me about it in very vague terms. Only much later did I try to put it all together in a systematic way, to reconstruct it using books and letters. When I was fifteen or sixteen, I finally convinced her—and it took a lot of persuasion—to hand over my father's letters to me. There were eighty-three of them. And it was written there that he was a general. So I thought, of course, when someone in a position like that, who has had such a function, is caught by the other side, then it can happen that that person is sentenced and executed.

B: You were very upset about this then, you resented that the other side had executed him?

M: No, no, that wasn't it, and strangely enough, my mother didn't feel that way either. That was never a factor, and such feelings are completely alien to me now. In school, in high school, we never dealt with the Third Reich in our history classes. We only got as far as Bismarck—twice. And in my study group, I once picked the topic of National Socialism, but the group only met a few times. I volunteered to give a paper, and I would always do some reading about it on my own. At that time it was separated in my mind. We were the guilty ones. That was one aspect. The fact that he'd had that function, that position, that was something else. Afterward, I noticed that whenever people would ask me about my father, I never told them what he'd been. I had a complete and total block whenever I was asked. I would say that he was missing in action. That was a very familiar thing for me to say, because it was something I had believed officially for quite a long time.

B: Did other children say anything to you about your father's being in the SS?

M: Children?

B: Yes, other children.

M: No, no one knew, no one.

B: The secret of your being an illegitimate child?

M: Well, I don't think it became known because only our family— my grandmother, my mother's mother—knew about it. He'd been in D. a couple of times and had visited the family, but he would never appear in public and be noticed. They'd always arrange to meet at different places. So there wasn't even a suspicion . . .

B: Did you know about your half-sisters or half-brothers?

M: When I learned about them I was fifteen or so, and it was quite a shock. Fifteen-year-olds today think differently, but back then we didn't have such liberal views about marriage. I was very idealistic. So for me, the shock was that he'd had other children. I thought a lot about meeting them simply because I viewed them as being brothers and sisters. Then, for a long time, I didn't. But recently, in the past few years, I've sensed this interest again. I've thought about it repeatedly and even searched through telephone books, though now I'd see it from quite a different perspective, not as a question of meeting brothers and sisters. There's something else motivating me: maybe I could find out more about my father from them, in particular about the end of his life. Because there's nothing left. I don't know if you're familiar with the book *Die Truppe des Weltanschauungkrieges* [The Soldiers of the War of Weltanschauung].[1] Anyway, I met a number of times with the author and he didn't know anything either. He wanted to ask me the same questions I was asking him! So I feel this inhibition, not about asking questions about the past but rather about suddenly appearing, presenting myself.

B: Did you have any contact with his family?

M: As long as this one sister was alive, I knew a bit. There was only a very, very loose connection with the family. His wife withdrew very quickly. It was very difficult to maintain contact with her. My aunt also knew very little, only how many children he had, their names, when they were born, a few such stories. No more than that. Though they do know something, they must have been there when he was arrested. They were also in prison for a while.

B: Was he arrested at home?

M: According to my aunt, yes. He was arrested here in Germany. The front was moving closer and closer. In his last letter, or the next to the last, he wrote: "There are just a hundred km as the bird flies from here to home." So it's certain he was arrested here, he must have been. Then his whole family was under arrest. They were even arrested with another family, one with many children, and there is this terrible story that they all got themselves capsules of poison. The other family really did have poison. And his children watched as the other family died right in front of their eyes. When they were released, my aunt was brought over to take care of them. But I knew it was useless even to try to find out more about his activities during the war, simply because she knew that I knew nothing, that I wasn't aware of the extent of his atrocious activity. I probably wouldn't have tried to tell a young child the truth either, if I'd have been in her shoes.

B: When did you begin to become interested in what your father had done, what his job was?

1. Helmut Krausnick and Hans-Henrich Wilhelm, *Die Truppe des Weltanschauungkrieges: Die Einsatzgruppen der Sicherheitspolizei und des SD, 1938–1942* (Stuttgart: Deutsch, 1981).

M: [*Pause*] That's hard to say, because I had been brought up from childhood with this very positive attitude. It was only quite slowly that I . . . the first shock was when I learned that he'd been married to another woman. I wasn't bothered by the fact that I had been born out of wedlock, though I did suffer a lot because of it. Back then it was still considered a disgrace . . .

B: Did your mother suffer from it?

M: Yes, she suffered too, because some of our relatives were almost brutal. We were really the doormats in the family, that's how we were treated. My mother was quite suited for this role. She didn't put up any resistance. It was fun for them to run my mother down, and me too, and my mother suffered a lot because of it. For example, she didn't receive any financial support because I was illegitimate. And a guardian was automatically appointed. That was also rather difficult, when I got my first guardian. He was Jewish, and he tried to get information from my mother, he had this suspicion. And the way she describes it, he really tried to torment her a little. He locked the door and told her he wouldn't let her out of the room until she told him who my father was. But you have to know my mother, her character. She provokes such a reaction, she's such a grateful little victim. Anyhow, he found out, and he simply (es ihr ungeschminkt hingeknallt) told her off in no uncertain terms. After that she got another guardian. In the beginning the situation was such a mixed bag she didn't want to say anything, not to anyone. It was the same when it came to the question of finding a job. When it came to the question of family . . . Naturally, in government offices there was always some difficulty . . .

B: What about that first shock . . .

M: Well, I was fifteen or sixteen when I learned about the concentration camps and what had happened there, not at school, but from other students. I still recall that my mother denied it . . . She repeated all the usual excuses: the photographs are forged; it never happened. She was very resistant to all this. However, I can still recall that after I had delved a bit myself into the question of the mechanisms that operate in a dictatorship, I tried to convince my mother that all this had been wrong. Because when you stamp out the opinions of others, when you ban art and muzzle the press—a government that is really good doesn't need to resort to such methods. So I would talk about it and afterward, I always thought she must have understood. My arguments were so good, she must have finally understood! Then she would disagree. After that I stopped talking with her about these matters. I gave up.

Much later, after I had left school, I came across a book of photographs: all those terrible photos from the camps, those starving, emaciated people, the piles of corpses. The way I see it today, unconsciously I knew there was something there somewhere about my father. For many years, whenever I'd come across a book about that period I would always check the table of contents and the index. I felt this sense of uneasiness, and it got worse the more I read, the more knowledge I acquired . . .

B: Did you find anything about your father in these books?

M: Yes, oh yes. I found the first relevant point in a small brochure. So for a long time I thought, well, with a position like that, he must have been involved in persecuting the Jews or in murders. I just couldn't repress this idea any longer. The first things I came across were selections from reports that had been gathered in Czechoslovakia, the original documents, or excerpts from them, with statistics. And my father was involved in all that. I started to look through all the books I came across at the university and in bookstores. I looked in a focused, systematic way, but found nothing. Then once, quite by accident, I came across a notice in the paper for the book I mentioned before, *Die Truppe des Weltanschauungkrieges*. It contained a lot, including material about him.

B: How did you feel when you read that book?

M: Well, it wasn't easy . . .

B: How old were you?

M: I was much older by then. This first bit of concrete information I discovered just seven years ago. I recall that at the time, I felt a very strong desire to tell my mother about it. I spoke to a number of people and they all advised me not to tell my mother—she'd just turned eighty—that I couldn't do that to such an old woman, that she would become ill or have a heart attack . . . But I wasn't prepared to protect and spare her. In the meantime, it is clear to me that my mother really wasn't able to understand anything on the basis of her conversations with him or the letters. He was very clever about it. You would be quite convinced that he was "the brave soldier, standing in the front line of battle, standing by his men, going through thick and thin with them. A man who is there for his men, an idealist," rather than a man who had lost his way, who could no longer see things clearly, who simply had not grasped that the war had become something senseless.

As she speaks these last sentences, Monika mimics Nazi propaganda films. She is tense, determined, unsparing.

M: Actually, for the woman who loved him, he really was the only man in her life. There are two points that deserve mention here. My mother was always a conformist, very much so, and as a result, she simply adopted a lot of his ways. At the same time, for example in respect to politics, she can see quite clearly and sharply what is happening today. I think it's terrific, really admirable. Her approach is quite left-wing. I have to ask myself how she's been able to develop a position like that, because she has a circle of friends who are all quite conservative. She's the only one [who has left-wing views], and she's also criticized for her stance. So on the one hand, you have this stance, and on the other, there are these really terrible things—her National Socialist ideas. I think, though, that it's simply her way of being faithful to my father. After his death, she was never involved in any way with another man. She was no longer prepared to consider marriage, although she had plenty of opportunities after the war. She just didn't want to. She wished to remain faithful to him.

B: Ten years ago when you wanted to talk about these matters, what was her reaction?

M: She said she hadn't known anything. Let me give you two typical examples in this connection. She tells this story about her experience on Kristallnacht. And you can see that she's not a person who would say something just to please me. She tends to have a cautious "watch out" approach toward me. Anyhow, as she recounts it, she went to work the morning after the Kristallnacht disturbances and walked through the central downtown area. She says she felt terribly ashamed. She thought what they had done was terrible, really despicable. Well, when she arrived home, some members of the family were over visiting, and she mentioned that she thought it was terrible and started shouting, asking how such a thing was possible, how people could do such a thing. But the others disagreed with her. One aunt said to her that if that was the way she thought, she should be reported to the authorities. So my mother figured she was going to have trouble. When she talked about it with my father later, he told her— and whenever she starts telling this story she mentions this, quite relieved—he also thought it was a terrible thing. That he had said he couldn't understand it at all, not at all. Yet in that book I found out that *he* was the one who actually directed the operation! That's the most recent thing I've learned. He was, for all practical purposes, the man who directed the entire operation. But she clings to her story very strongly. She says he thought Kristallnacht was a terrible thing too.

The same thing happened in respect to the campaign against Russia. Recently, for example, after the Chernobyl disaster, she told me it was terrible that the Federal Republic was not ashamed to demand damages from the Soviet Union. She got very excited about it and said, "That's a country we attacked! A country we ravaged! And now we want damage payments from them? Don't we have any sense of shame?" Back then, she had told my father that she couldn't understand it at all: first there was the nonaggression pact, and then we were suddenly at war. You know by the way she tells it that she must have been very upset. And she says that he told her he couldn't understand it either. Yet he had known about the plans a long time before that . . . he was practically a part of it.

B: Does she know today, is she aware that he directed the Kristallnacht operations?

M: No, she doesn't know. For example, once we had an argument. She said it wasn't true and told this story again. I was terribly angry, but I hesitated, wondering whether I should tell her or not. I find it very difficult to take this last illusion away from her. Yes, I pity her in this respect. She's so totally convinced of the truth of what she remembers about him. The first time I told her about his activities during the war, she retreated a little. I noticed that she turned white, felt weak in the knees. But she said no, she hadn't known about it and didn't want to know either. At that point, I put the book I was reading down in front of her. And she never spoke about it again.

Recently, in connection with that book, I asked her about it once again, and I also asked a lot of other questions. She started to cry, said I was trying to pressure her, to grill her for information, and that she couldn't stand it. In order not to shut her off for good, I told her I wasn't interested in making him look even worse now. I said that what was important to me was to understand how a person could do such things. All she said was that I shouldn't think she had a false and distorted view of him. These were simply two different sides to his personality. He was very sweet and charming, a caring individual, that was true, but there was also this other dimension, I said. And the question for me was how a person could come to that point. Well, then she was prepared to respond and told me to let her have the book for a while, which I did. She kept it quite a long time, and she says that she read it too. But she wouldn't say anything else about what she had read.

Monika leaves the room for a few minutes, and her friend, who must have heard this story before, looks at me searchingly, as if to discover what effect Monika's monologue is having on me. I am amazed by Monika's courage in asking these questions and in ferreting out the answers but feel incapable of uttering a word, even when Monika returns.

M: Two years ago I went to Riga because I thought I could get documents about my father there. But normal mortals can't get hold of documents. You have to request them in connection with some research project. For my mother's eightieth birthday, I promised her a trip. She could choose to go wherever she wanted. I had told her about Riga, my experiences there, and she said she would like a trip to Riga. I asked her if she realized what that meant, and she replied that she hoped we weren't going "to go digging back into the dark and distant past." But I told her, "Look, I'm not planning to traipse with you through a lot of churches and museums." She's very interested in art. I said she should realize that I would try to establish further contact with people there. A friend of mine was invited there as a historian, and he met a Russian who'd been at my father's trial. So I asked her if she wanted to go anyway, and she said she did.

Some weeks ago, my friend and I attended a social gathering and my mother was there. We discussed the past, the Third Reich, and my mother didn't say anything the entire evening. The other guests were upset. Then my friend said to her, "You haven't said anything all evening. I'd like to hear what you think. Why aren't you talking?" And she replied, "Why should I say anything?" She said she'd loved a man who had incurred guilt, and she felt she was also guilty. If you know my mother and realize that she is capable of saying very different things, for an eighty-year-old woman, that's quite remarkable.

She stops and sighs, almost in tears.

M: Yes, it's very hard for me. It comes in phases. Every time I find out something new, I'm preoccupied, it's difficult to digest it. And when people keep telling me how like my father I am, it's very difficult . . .

Monika cries. There is a long pause.

B: What did you find out during your visit to Riga?

M: I met two women in Riga, one of whom was present at the public hanging. She told me about the execution. And the other woman I met had been questioned over a long period of time by my father. In fact, after I read the book that contained the text of the interrogations, I went into therapy. It was triggered by that. Often, what happens is that people attempt to minimize matters. They say, "What can you do, you're not responsible. You didn't even know him, you were just a small child." The therapist I went to had that point of view. Several times she tried to make me "talk" to him. I did it, but it was very artificial. In the last analysis, however, it has provided the impetus for me to delve into things—hoping to discover a certain awareness in him after all, certain breaks or ruptures (Brüche). Or maybe a pious wish that in the last year of his life, the monstrous character of his actions became clear to him. But I've found nothing like that. Instead, there were frequent instances of hiding, of covering matters up. So I asked myself how I would have behaved if he had come to me asking to be hidden? Perhaps I would have turned him over to the authorities—or maybe just the opposite. So I live my life, on the one hand, all the similarities, on the other, the fear that someone might know I'm *his* daughter. If someone were to know that I'm the daughter of the person who did all that . . . [*Cries*]

B: Didn't you try to let people know who your father was?

M: You mean that anything should become known that would connect his activities with me? No.

B: Why not?

M: Because then I would be afraid they would place me on the same level. That people would despise me, find me detestable, because of him. Yes, it's quite an extreme experience. He killed quite a few people. And they said that it was his own choice, that he was responsible. My father, for all practical purposes, was another Eichmann. He just didn't become as well known because he was condemned right away.

Neither of us speaks for a few minutes.

B: Have you had any contact with Jews?

M: In Riga we visited the former Jewish ghetto with a Jewish woman. We went with this Baltic group. Let me tell you, no history book, no lecture could have presented the Baltic problem to me so clearly. It was terrible, though quite fascinating at the same time. But it was impossible to get any information from these people. Half of the group consisted of people who had lived in Riga [before the war], older people, who had spent part of their adult lives there. But they were not prepared to answer any questions about the former ghetto. The grounds of the concentration camp in Riga have been made into a large memorial square. There's a small museum. We accidentally met the woman who takes care of the museum, and it turned out that she had been interrogated by my father. And she told us where the grounds of the former ghetto were. Initially, we'd simply tried to ask people on the street about the ghetto, but no one wanted to answer. Even if they spoke German they wouldn't answer. We went with this large tour bus, we insisted on a big bus with a state tourist guide.

B: What is there to see there?

M: What was left of the camp has been torn down. You have this enormous expanse of open land surrounded by forest. And there's a small museum with a few photographs. In the ghetto itself, a lot has been destroyed. A few houses are still standing, but you can see that much has been destroyed. There are gaps, and new buildings have been erected in many places.

B: Do the Russians acknowledge that the place was a Jewish ghetto?

M: No. The Russians say there were Jews too, but mainly they talk about the patriotic war of the motherland. The problem of the Jews is played down a lot. So we were in the ghetto, and a woman spoke to us in a café. She told us right away that she was Jewish. We started to talk, and I asked her some questions. She told us that living with the Latvians was very difficult at that time, that they had given a great deal of support to the Germans. And when it became clear that the Jews would have to leave the ghetto, the Latvians took up positions on the rooftops and started shooting at the fleeing Jews. She feels terribly isolated there, terribly alone. She has little contact with other Jews.

Anyhow, this woman explained everything to us, and we went back again, secretly this time, because in the Soviet Union they don't want you to go anywhere on your own. It wasn't recommended, but we went anyhow. The Russians were all very friendly, though, and led us part of the way on foot. Then we went again with the official guide to the museum, and I asked about a photograph there, this photo of the court proceedings of the Nazis after the war. She didn't answer. I wanted to know who the people were, whether they'd been condemned. I asked her four times, but she wouldn't give me an answer. She spoke excellent German, so language wasn't the problem. Otherwise they just spoke about the Russian people, or the Latvians. But they don't speak about the ghetto or about the Jews. That's all glossed over.

B: How does your generation relate to this period? Do they try to confront and deal with it, or do they repress it?

M: Well, I'm a schoolteacher. At school, some of the students are very interested in this period, very open to hearing about it. I've talked about it several times, although initially it's a bit difficult to get beyond a certain point. The persecution of the Jews, students are very interested in that, although there are many other aspects. But parents soon start to complain. They ask me to let this period of history rest, to let it be. They say you can't go on talking forever about those things, and that I bring up only the negative side. They say there were also good things about Hitler. Those years weren't all that bad . . . they mention building the autobahns and solving the unemployment problem, that crime wasn't as serious a problem then as it is today. A typical complaint is that I don't talk about what the Allies did [to the Germans]. "How about Dresden?" So the parents have been protesting, saying I should stop.

B: How old are the parents, what generation?

M: A number of them are younger than I am. Most of them are. I'm quite old in comparison. But there's been a big shift since last year. The commemoration of the fortieth anniversary of the end of the war didn't provide a way of working through the problems or dealing with them; rather, it was a kind of cover-up, covering them over (ein Zudecken). There was something different [on TV] every day, but it was really an attempt to whitewash the issues. Since then, it's become a problem at school. Students say, "Stop, stop, I don't want to hear any more about all that!" And they're right in reacting that way. It was the same old thing over and over again, no new insights whatsoever. A lot of people were put off by it. They're no longer interested. You have to awaken interest, ask questions, wake people up.

So that's one group of people. Then there's another, much smaller group: the intellectuals. Their approach is to make everything seem black and white. They have a large fund of historical knowledge, but they say, "I'm interested in this as a historical topic." There was this woman who had heard from someone else that my father had been somebody, and she was quite interested. She didn't know exactly what his job was, but she knew that he'd had an important function. And the first thing she said to me was, "Are you still able to talk to your mother? Is it possible at all?" Now that's the sort of thing I mean. I tried to explain a little to her about how sometimes I am incredibly upset with my mother because of her rotten ideas (Scheissansichten). But I told this woman I would never dream of telling my mother that I just couldn't talk to her anymore. And I tried to explain a bit about my mother's situation. How something like that can come about, and how she deals with it now, what sort of process of development she went through. And then this woman said, "She must have known. She just must have known." I replied that it was necessary to see this in a more open-minded way. It is simply not true to say that she knew. So that's the approach: black or white, no gradations in between. In our family there were Nazis, in theirs there were Communists . . . She's really a very intelligent woman, well read, very alert and bright. We work together in a team, and once she wanted to let us know that a new student had arrived who only spoke English. We hadn't heard anything about it yet, and we asked her who had arrived. She said, "The Jewish girl!" We said, "Who?" "Why, the Jewish girl. Haven't you heard?" So you'll notice that there is a lot of *knowledge,* but feeling, or whatever you want to call it, is lacking.

I identify with her sensitive approach.

B: Actually, what did your mother know? Did you try to find out again later on, after she had read that book?

M: I've tried repeatedly, and I've also had a number of conversations with my mother. But at the point where you have to say, "That's how it was," at that point she avoids the issue. I had an argument with my mother two weeks ago and I thought, she has to continue to describe things as different from the way they are to hold onto her illusions—and in the craziest ways imaginable. As a child one tends to see parents in a positive light in any case. It's the drive for self-preservation. And then, if one discovers that this same person had some really terrible convictions and held on to them . . .

B: How is it possible that in one and the same person there can be these two sides?

M: That is pretty much the crucial question. How is it possible for people to do such things? How is it possible? And later on, how is it possible for an entire people simply not to come to terms with it? They just don't want to take the risk of even thinking about what happened, they don't want to allow such thoughts to creep in. Then there's also the argument: What right do you youngsters have to talk? You weren't even involved, you don't know! That's quite a typical argument. You have no right to talk, all you know is what you've read in books. It's all just theory. We were there. We're the only ones who can talk. Such a complacent attitude: you only have the right to say anything if you were there yourself . . .

I can't emphasize it enough: it is not a question of accusing someone, it's simply a matter of thinking about all this afterward, of asking how it was possible, what sort of processes were involved. My interest is not in accusing people or reproaching them. What is important to me is the process of confronting these things. But it is always interpreted as a reproach, as an accusation. You can explain to them as many times as you want that it's not a matter of looking for guilt, that you simply want to clarify things.

The rain has stopped at last, and I walk to the train station. I want time to digest our conversation. Monika is the first person I have met in Germany who is asking the same questions I am asking—she who is the daughter of one of the Reich's most vicious murderers. I wonder why she is the only one.

As I walk, I can still see Monika's face and feel the tension between her love and respect for her mother, and her deep anger that her mother is incapable of understanding the true identity of the man she loved. Monika's persistence in trying to find out who her father was and what he was like is understandable in view of his insubstantiality during her childhood. How comforting it must be to discover that the father one never knew died for a noble cause; how terrible then for this particular child to learn otherwise. I feel very close to her, and what is strange is that it does not make me uncomfortable.

We talk again a year later in the identical setting: the somewhat darkened room, the table set with coffee and cake for three, her friend sitting on the sofa, attentive but quiet. I say "Hello" when Monika comes in as if I am meeting a close friend. But she is restrained. I sense that for her, there is still a barrier between us.

B: What things have occurred since I last saw you?

M: Well, after our talk, I started to get very intensely involved with all this. Our conversation was a very powerful emotional experience for me. Then, suddenly, it was over. That was hard for me, because the thing was sort of left in the air as far as I was concerned. Would there be a continuation? Why, I couldn't even remember your name, because I have such a bad memory for names. So for me, it was like a sudden cold shower. It was broken off in a very abrupt way.

B: Didn't you look into it or inquire about me? Didn't you try to find me or find out how to continue with this?

M: No, because as I saw it, it would have to be on your initiative. I mean, even if I'd had your address, I wouldn't have gotten in touch with you. As I understood it, you had a certain plan, you were looking for certain information. So I wouldn't have done that on my own.

B: Why not? Wasn't it important to you?

M: Yes, it was important that I could talk about these things with someone, specifically someone Jewish. I sensed the need to discuss it more generally, but I'd never had the opportunity to do so. That was the first time. I mean, I did talk with others about it, but never with someone who was directly involved and affected (einem Betroffenen).

B: What topic or aspect of what we talked about before do you want to discuss further?

M: I think it's important for me to understand a little better this strong need in me to expose myself to a situation like this. I tried to do this in psychotherapy, but what I discovered was that my therapist didn't want to deal with the matter directly. I repeatedly tried to get her to discuss it. And at the last session we had, she said that for next time, I should try to ask myself what I actually expected from a confrontation with this problem and how important it was to me. I got upset. I had to think theoretically about what I wanted to achieve, what goal I wanted to set for myself.

B: Did you go to Riga with your mother?

M: No, actually I decided not to, because I would have felt too restricted, too hemmed in.

B: Maybe you were also a little afraid of going to Riga with her . . .

M: Well, I was afraid in the sense that perhaps the anger I feel would surface, that it would be a big effort for me. I would have to behave toward her in a way that would be very exhausting. I would have to be on my toes and not say anything wrong. It's possible to do that for a period of hours, let's say, but in such a situation, when I know she has certain expectations, it would be unbearable. In addition, there's the fact that my relationship with her has actually deteriorated since I've been in therapy.

For a long time I told myself that I wouldn't hold it against her that she put me in a *Lebensborn* children's home[2] initially. I would try to excuse her: that's the way things were back then, she was stupid, she didn't know any better. But gradually, because of therapy, I'm also able to allow myself to have other feelings. Often I feel such rage welling up in me. I was three when she became my mother; she got a "finished and ready" child, so to speak. She never really learned how to understand me or tried to deal with me. So now, when this rage gradually starts welling up in me, I let it happen, let it flow. For this reason, my willingness to be considerate when it comes to this old woman, with the idea that she will change and that I should invest a lot of effort and energy in the relationship, is a lot weaker now. Two years ago, maybe I would have been more willing. I think it's less that I'm afraid and more that I simply don't want it. Occasionally we even have a terrible argument. It happens quite often. But she knows that I'll simply go home, and after a few days I'll call again, calm her down, smooth things over. She's quite an expert when it comes to repressing matters. So when I call her up, I know the matter's been laid to rest.

Monika smiles. I try to remember if she smiled at all during our session a year ago.

B: Did you try to get in touch with any of your father's other children?

M: No, but every now and then I think I should. I've always approached the matter as if I wanted to get to know a half-sister or half-

2. The *Lebensborn* or Well of Life Society was established in 1935 and financed by the SS to care for the illegitimate children of SS members and their mothers. Eventually, it provided lying-in homes for married and unmarried women and an extensive adoption service for placing both illegitimate children and "Aryan" children from Poland and other territories, largely in SS officers' families.

brother, but it was really connected with the desire to find out more about my father. Everything else was pushed into the background. Did you try to get in touch with them?

B: No. I wouldn't like to do that before you . . .

M: Yes, but with them it's something quite different, because they had a conscious, direct experience of him.

B: Do you know where they are now? Do you have their addresses?

M: No. But I heard a story from my mother that goes back to the days when my father was still alive. One of his sons had the job of taking out the dog. This was his regular chore at home. And once, when my father asked that son whether he'd taken the dog out, the son replied that he had. But it turned out that it wasn't true, he hadn't been out with the dog. The upshot, apparently, was that for days my father refused to speak to him. The boy was about ten years old. Then my father had to leave, and the boy came to say good-bye to him, but he just walked on past the kid without saying a word—and never came back. My mother said it wasn't right, that he shouldn't have acted that way toward the boy. Probably there were a lot of incidents like this that would shed a great deal of light on certain things. Even if you don't have all the tiles in the mosaic, a vague picture will nonetheless emerge.

B: Did you find out any more about your father?

M: I've come to the point where I'm no longer looking for further details about what he did. But what I am intensely interested in is his last year, the period between his arrest and execution. I ask myself why. I'm sure there is something driving me, I mean, *I'm still searching*. Though as B. told me, "You can look and look, and all you'll get is a slap in the face (eine Ohrfeige); you'll just be disappointed again and again when it comes to that man." And she's right. Those matters— what happened during Kristallnacht or what took place after the invasion of Russia . . . Nevertheless, it keeps bothering me, this hope that when he was taken prisoner, maybe it clarified something for him. And I would like very, very much to know just exactly what he was really thinking then.

B: Whether any doubts arose in his mind . . . ?

M: Yes, or when it comes to all the documents, the court protocols, which I find so fascinating . . . It's possible to interpret the material in various ways.

B: How, for example?

M: Well, if you'd like to retain certain illusions (man sich gerne was vormacht), then you could contend that he honestly admits, and he says it too, that he is guilty of this or that crime. Such formulations appear quite often, though you could also conclude that he was undoubtedly tired of life. I'm pretty certain he didn't have any courage left, any desire to go on living after the collapse. He was devoid of hope, no longer saw any meaning in life. And he probably thought that no matter what he said, whether he tried to talk his way out of it or not, he wouldn't be able to save his own neck. So maybe for that reason, in my eyes anyway, it would be too simple just to accept as true what is written in the protocols of the proceedings. It contrasts too much with what went on before. It can't represent a process of understanding and insight, a truly genuine rethinking of what he had done. That's impossible. There must be other underlying reasons. Maybe it was partly a sense of resignation, or of hopelessness.

B: There are some who committed suicide because of that.

M: Yes, I know from my mother that my father was planning to. The year before he told my mother that if things went wrong . . .

B: What would go wrong, the German Reich or what he was doing?

M: Well, that isn't clear. I assume he meant both. They were interconnected. You couldn't have had one without the other.

B: Nonetheless, he didn't do it . . .

M: Yes, that's the question I've often asked myself, whether he tried to take his own life. I visited a friend in Berlin who had been to Riga after my trip there, in an official capacity with a delegation of historians. They talked with a person there who had been an official observer at the trial, and that person said—how did he put it?—that my father had been the only one who had retained his dignity (Haltung bewahrt). He said it had been very impressive. He had accepted responsibility for what he'd done (dazu gestanden hat). I asked my friend what that meant, but he said the man hadn't been more specific. He retained his poise, his dignity—maybe in the sense that he didn't try to deny what he'd done. He didn't refuse to testify or to make use of whatever possibilities were available to him.

B: And does this seem to you like a "slap in the face" (Ohrfeige), as B. says, or is it something else?

M: In the beginning, it made the thing seem more understandable to me. From what I have learned from B., I found the relationship Himmler developed with his vassals quite interesting, and the influence he was able to have on them. The psychology involved, how you had to be [in psychological terms] in order to be able to have an exchange with Himmler on that level. I think I took all this in at a distance, relatively speaking, as a bit of interesting information. Later, when B. called my attention to one of my father's letters to Himmler, it was like a "slap in the face": "In October 1944 my house was destroyed by bombing, and all I had was turned into ashes. However, my wife and four little children are safe at her parents' home. And now just the more!"

What I was thinking of more were things like his psychological makeup and how it might have affected me. Because it would be very easy to accept it as something that could be used to excuse a person. I thought about whether perhaps it had precipitated something in me. [*Long pause*] Those are aspects of his personality that have become clear to me now, and I don't like them. Yes, that's what's behind it, what helped make it possible.

That's the kind of man he was. It makes it more understandable, but not any nicer, or better, or even a little bit more pleasant. This special mission he had in connection with partisans—he had been given a special mission because he was so especially thorough and painstaking, so ambitious, so "one hundred percent." Still, the worst blow was really the one in connection with Kristallnacht.

B: Which you heard about from your mother?

M: Yes. [*Crying*] If only he had kept his damn trap shut. Yet he said he thought it was terrible, that he couldn't understand it either. That's actually what's so awful, that's the worst thing. He made a game of it on top of all the rest. He didn't have to go that far. All right, he didn't want to say anything, that's clear. He wouldn't have been allowed to and he didn't want to have to stand there in front of my mother . . . But he didn't really have to do it in that particular way. He could have said, "I can't condemn it" or something. But to go along with what my mother was saying, well, I thought that was the lowest . . . The same thing when it comes to the Russian campaign. That really disgusts me. To keep my mother in the dark, not only not to tell her but actually to encourage her. My father must have thought it over carefully. He must have known what he was doing . . . And he was already very much a part of the operation. It is probable that he knew much earlier that he would be taking part, but he went along with her, played along, said he'd been taken totally by surprise, that he hadn't known about it beforehand.

And the most terrible thing in the witnesses' statements, although I'm prepared to believe that maybe the witness was exaggerating, was that when there were shootings and one of the men had trouble pulling the trigger, my father would laugh along with the others and say, "Oh, he's thinking about his kids back home." That's when I realized I had reached a limit in being able to think about him as a human being.

I do think that something has changed for me since last year. One of the reasons I went into therapy was this feeling that I was identifying too strongly with my father. Abstractly, I know you can't simply equate being biologically related to someone with what that person does, but I kept thinking: What do I harbor deep within me? What am I capable of? That somehow there must be something evil in me. This feeling has now lessened, I think, because during therapy, other matters have been brought up and dealt with. As I've gained more self-confidence, that sense of something evil has faded a bit. It's no longer such a tormenting thing.

Although I'm still not so sure . . . When I saw that program about the "Final Solution" on TV last year, I asked myself whether I would have been capable of doing such a thing. And I don't think it's clear to me yet, I mean, whether I might not say, "No, I'd rather die!" [*Crying*] As a teacher, there are many people I know personally, and certainly a number of my students, in connection with whom I think how terrible it would be if they knew about this. I have the feeling that I'm stigmatized. I would be very, very afraid they might see in me some kind of offshoot of something evil.

B: And evil is forbidden, unacceptable?

M: Yes, well, I mean that symbolically. I don't mean that in the usual sense of the term. But let's just take an example. As a teacher, you could easily get into a situation in which you feel that your students are incredibly angry with you because you have demanded something, or maybe you were really nasty (böse) on some occasion, or ill-tempered, or acted in an unfair way. I believe I could liberate myself from the fear that my students might say, "Of course, she's someone who *would* do something like that."

Her friend asks if she actually feels as if she is a victim of her own father.

M: Well, "victim" . . . if I have to define it, "victim" would mean that I suffer unjustly for something. No, this element of unjust suffering is not part of it in my case, I'm certain about that. He had *real* victims, and I didn't have anything like their fate. This wasn't an individual phenomenon. It has a historical background, an educational background to it connected with upbringing and with everything that was happening at the time. So that I don't have any feeling of being a victim of injustice, or that I've been made into a victim, because I can see that people have not worked through this period of history. That also interests me a great deal: to find out how people approach and deal with this period. As a teacher, I hope I can bring about a significant change in my students. This period of history hasn't been dealt with properly. It's still unfinished business.

Several days later, I call Monika to ask if she would be willing to participate in a videotaping session at the local university. There is silence on the

chapter 13

The Narrow Bridge

When I return to Germany in June 1987, I find that, in terms of my re-search, the situation has changed considerably: a book reporting on his en-counters with children of Nazis has been published by an Austrian-Jewish journalist, a German television program has presented a series of interviews with children of Nazi leaders only three weeks before, and several articles have appeared in the local newspapers. Suddenly the children of the Nazi era are in the news. This shift means, among other things, that I can now locate other potential interviewees through their letters to newspapers and magazines. I come across one letter from a man in a town not far from where I am staying, in which he tells his father's story and expresses his relief that the subject has finally surfaced. He has been torturing himself with this heritage for years and has felt very lonely in a postwar society that is silent on these matters.

When I telephone his house, a woman answers. "No, Fritz is not at home. What do you want?" I tell her who I am, what my research is about, and that I have read her husband's letter to the editor and would like to meet him. There is a short pause on the other end of the line, and then she speaks in Hebrew, "You can talk to me in Hebrew. I am from Israel." An Israeli married to a Nazi's child! I don't know what to say, but she is more relaxed and tells me her story. She was born in the Ukraine and during the war was hidden on a small farm by her gentile grandmother. After the war, her mother located her, remarried, and they went to Israel, where she grew up and lived on a kibbutz. Because of an unhappy love affair, she went abroad and found work in Düsseldorf, where she met Fritz. They have been married for the last twenty years. Yes, her mother still lives in Israel, but she does not know anything about her son-in-law's father. "And," she adds, "we have no children."

* * *

We arrange to meet on a Friday afternoon. At my own home in Beer Sheva, it is time to put on white shirts and get ready for the Sabbath. We are not religious, but we like to have a traditional, festive atmosphere on Friday nights. All the family members who are present sit together at the dinner table, light candles, and sing traditional songs. Before Yariv died, my wife used to bake Chale, the special Jewish bread for the Sabbath.

Here in Germany, all that seems very remote, but by going to see Fritz and Maya, I feel I am closer to home. We meet at the train station: a brisk, warm handshake, and then, a few minutes later, we are at their home, sitting around the table drinking coffee. Two Jews and a German, all about the same age. I decide to start the interview with Fritz.

F: Through the articles and the book that appeared this year I had a chance to take a look at the documents I have and to recall what I know about my father. But I still don't know the full story. I've begun corresponding with a historian in Braunschweig, and I hope to learn a great many new things. But the precipitating factors were first, my mother's death, and second, an article in *Der Spiegel* earlier this year. As a result of these recent developments, I've decided to continue with this. For example, I've been corresponding with a woman in Berlin who found out that her father was an active Nazi. I simply think that we have to get together, work together on this, and put an end to our silence, although for me this was really a process of development. I mean, it wasn't a quick decision. I felt mild curiosity and then was pulled into it more and more. A process of development. Why, three months ago I was still saying to myself that I didn't want to get too involved. And now I've reached the point where I know that it's possible to handle this, to deal with it, and I want to take it all the way. That's a kind of brief preface to the interview.

B: Let's start with a question: When and where were you born?

F: In Hamburg, 1940. That's where my father had a job. After the heavy bombing raids on the city, we moved to Braunschweig. He got a promotion there. He was made head of the Gestapo and put in charge of the Braunschweig area. The fact that this included the Goering plant was something extra, an added dimension.

B: Are you an only child?

F: Yes, I am. A sister was born two years after me, but due to the terrible medical situation at that time, she died a week or so after she was born, I believe, in the hospital. My mother never talked very much about it. I heard about it from my uncle.

B: What is the earliest memory you have of life at home?

F: I can only remember four encounters altogether that I had with my father. Which is to say that he didn't play any decisive, formative role in my life at all. Even as far as these four times are concerned, I'm not sure if one of them isn't just a dream. Maybe it was a dream I had as a child—I was sleeping and then I saw him. Once we were short of food at home, and he came home wearing his uniform—that was an exception; he never wore his uniform off-duty. I put my little teddy bear on the wastebasket because he had to go to the bathroom . . . and afterward, when we looked in the basket, lo-and-behold there was a big sausage! At that time, that was something sensational, really. Then I remember a long trip in a car, a lot of checkpoints, roadblocks where we were checked. It was dark and there were soldiers. Then I recall a visit to the POW camp, when he was interned in the British camp near Hannover. That was at the time of the trial regarding Camp 21;[1] it was as a result of that trial that my father was arrested. We were allowed to visit him there, although it was very difficult to get permission to see him. That must have been shortly before he was executed. All I can remember is that he was wearing a British uniform. They had given him some sort of job. He knew English well, was a trained lawyer, and he had been given some sort of position. He gave me a box of crayons as a present, and I made a drawing. That was the last time I saw him. Basically, I saw him just those three or four times. That's all I recall.

B: The first time you saw him, you were already three or four years old?

F: Yes.

B: Do you recall ever having seen him out of uniform?

F: I only remember seeing him once without his uniform. He was in the car. I'm not sure what he was doing, but he didn't have a uniform on. He was probably wearing a dark suit. Then I remember him in that British khaki uniform. The khaki material used to keep people nice and warm. It had a typical British-style jacket.

B: Yes, I know what you mean. My father was in the British army, and I remember him in a similar uniform. Do you have any memories of your mother at that time?

F: Only later. Let me see . . . we were in the Black Forest. It was our first vacation trip after the war. It was in 1948, around Christmastime, and my mother told me that my father had died in British captivity. I believed it at the time. As much as a child can tell, when I saw him he

---

1. A "reeducation" camp where Germans and others were sent because of some "act of treason."

hadn't looked very well. He had lost a lot of hair and wasn't the man I remembered. I didn't ask any questions about it, because it seemed believable to me. Aside from the fact that at that time there were many people who . . . someone had even shot himself in front of our house, things like that. As a child I knew that men were dying all around us. So I accepted what she said. And I was only enlightened about this whole matter—"enlightened" isn't perhaps the right term, but . . .

B: How did she tell you the news? Did she cry?

F: No, I don't think so, but I can't exactly recall. We were sitting alone together in the room, and she said, "You've always said a prayer for your father to return, but he won't be coming back. He's dead. You'll have to live with that, and I must live with it too." If she cried I . . . It's true that her voice sounded very troubled. I assume that she had been crying, but I don't know for sure. In any event, when she told me, she wasn't crying. So I accepted it and didn't miss him either, because I really hadn't known him.

I did have a grandfather whom I met around this time. After the war we moved to L. We didn't have a house—everything had been destroyed—but my grandfather had a house in town. The Americans had been quartered there, and when they moved out, we were able to move in. There was plenty of room. I came to like my grandfather a lot. He was my mother's father. He had never approved of my father. My grandfather didn't have much in common with the Nazis either. Rather, he was a monarchist in orientation, pro-Kaiser. He was very liberal in political terms, very upset that the Nazis had outlawed his Liberal Party. He was a real and genuine factory owner. A manufacturer body and soul. He didn't have much to do with all that. I came across his diary later on, and he had written that he didn't approve of my parents' marriage, wasn't very happy about it. He expressed his opinion in two sentences, and that was it. My father's father—I also knew him of course—was an old high school music teacher. I didn't like the man. Whenever we would go to visit him, I was always glad when it came time to leave. The only nice thing I recall was that he gave me a pocketknife. Otherwise, he was pretty much nonexistent as far as I was concerned, not important to me.

B: Why is that?

F: Today I understand why. He was a rigid, old-fashioned old man who would talk enthusiastically about the First World War. Maybe "enthusiastically" is the wrong word. Anyhow, he would talk about World War I a lot, and it didn't concern me. When he would tell some story for the fifth time, it used to bore me too. Somehow I had the feeling that something was wrong. Children notice things but aren't able to explain why. We used to visit him once a year, and then he died. After his funeral, we didn't have any more contact with my father's side of the family. He has a sister, but we never heard anything again. Contact was broken off completely.

B: Did you grow up with your grandfather and grandmother?

F: Yes. My grandmother was a very independent-minded woman. She didn't have much to do with the church, with the Nazis, with anything in fact that smacked of ideology. She was very self-confident, which was just what my grandfather needed: someone who would contradict him, stand up to him. Otherwise he was pretty obnoxious as a person. Actually, she had a very formative influence on me, because my mother would be away at the plant all day long. She would come home in the evening exhausted, with a headache. So as a child, I stayed with my grandparents, and later on, with my grandmother.

M: His mother later was in a kind of therapy down in Bavaria with a very capable psychologist. Probably back at that time the connection between all these things wasn't so clear. Gradually, however, as we've looked through all the papers, the letters, it has become evident why her condition had developed.

F: Yes, my mother apparently wasn't able to deal with the situation. An additional factor was that my grandfather's company, in which my mother was a partner, went bankrupt. My grandfather had passed away, and my mother was responsible for taking care of matters after the bankruptcy. There was this double strain on her, and she wasn't able to handle it. The result was that I spent a lot of time alone.

B: The fact that she was under great strain, how was it reflected in your home life?

F: I don't know. I tried hard not to let any feelings affect me. Actually, I was very happy with my grandmother. My mother was a problem for me.

M: There was an adversarial relationship between them. They used to fight all the time. Naturally, that was bound up with his father. She was so supersensitive whenever . . .

F: Yes, for a time I had a good relationship with her. After she had finished dealing with the bankruptcy, when she started all over from the beginning again, well, that engendered a feeling of great respect in me. She was living then in a small student's room—this as a woman over forty—and had started to work at a psychological advisory service as a secretary. Soon she had advanced to being executive secretary and was running the place. During that period, our relationship was good. I was living my own life, but I had decided that if I couldn't love my mother, I could be fair and try to be a buddy to her, a friend. And above all else, if someone wanted to do her harm, I could protect her. I was old enough, and that was the basis of our relationship. I wasn't afraid that my mother would have any influence over me. And at some point she no longer tried to. She was opposed to our marriage, but it was because she didn't want to see any woman at my side, anyone serious. Whenever I had a girlfriend, she used to think that was great, but when it got serious, then . . . I know it has to do with the fact that I was an only child, that my father died . . . all those things. In the end, though, she accepted Maya too. When she retired she moved in with us. And then she made an effort to bring me closer to my father in a kind of indirect manner. Naturally, this met with my severe opposition, and as a result, we had some pretty bad arguments before she died.

B: How did she try to do that?

F: How did she do that? Well, it's hard to recall exactly.

M: Well, whenever there was a birthday, or some kind of celebration . . .

F: Oh yes, right . . .

M: . . . she would start talking about Fritz's "wonderful father." She would tell all these beautiful stories about her engagement, her marriage.

F: How happy she was.

M: And he would be presented as a very lovable, sweet, and harmless person, and . . .

F: She would quite consciously talk about that early period in their lives. But I heard from one of my uncles that once the honeymoon was over, there was a lot of tension between them. And probably they would have separated very soon after if I hadn't come along . . .

M: When he was in British captivity, she . . .

F: . . . fought for him tooth and nail . . .

M: . . . fought on his behalf. It is astonishing what she did to try to get him out of there.

F: She went all the way to Holland, tried the ambassador, tried Adenauer and everything feasible; she tried all the avenues she could think of to get that man set free. Still, I assume that if he had gotten out, she would have left him.

M: She had this notion that he had atoned for his sins with his death. That you can pardon the dead, find forgiveness. Something like that . . .

F: But she tried to get him out of there alive.

M: Yes, afterward it was clear, because he had more or less paid for his sins. And she was definitely of the opinion that those who had committed worse crimes had not been brought to justice.

F: Yes, for example, in that trial concerning the Hermann Goering Works, fifty-one were acquitted. She was furious about that.

M: Despite all the reservations she had, she thought it was unfair that they hadn't taken anything into account and had shot him as a scapegoat, because they hadn't been able to catch the others. Although they assured her back then—she told me this—that he would not be released but that a death sentence was out of the question. It was a big disappointment to her, because she had been assured by all kinds of people that he would not be executed.

Fritz and Maya's words interweave with such harmony, I can hardly make out who is saying what.

B: Before your mother moved here, where did you grow up, where did you study?

F: After the bankruptcy, we went to Düsseldorf. We lived there, and that's where I met my wife. I studied in Bonn and Münster. I'm a schoolteacher. In Düsseldorf I also underwent supplementary training as a shop teacher. When I decided to become a teacher, I was still traveling to Düsseldorf. I continued to live in L. and would sleep at my aunt's. That's when I met Maya.

B: What happened after that?

F: She went back to Israel for a while. And then she returned with the idea that we should get married. First we lived together for a while, and then I said we should get married.

M: In the beginning, my family broke off ties completely. Well, they didn't exactly break off ties, but it was . . .

F: Nobody came to our wedding. And the first one who established any ties was her stepfather. He wrote a very nice letter. He had lost a finger in an accident, and he joked a bit about it. So the ice was broken. We traveled down there.

M: Fritz only saw my stepfather once. He died a year later. When they met, they struck up a very close friendship right away. They hit it off beautifully. The ice was broken. They hadn't known each other, hadn't seen each other before. Naturally, for my mother it was strange to meet a German as my . . .

F: Your mother held back longer. Your father, in contrast, was quite different.

M: Because of the blockade in Leningrad and all that, my mother was very reserved toward us during the first few years of our marriage. My stepfather worked with Russians and Germans after the war. He tried to make sure that the German workers would not be discriminated against or taken advantage of. Because he had worked so long together with Germans, he was able to deal with our marriage more easily. And he is from Galicia, so maybe he'd had more to do with Germans in the past. I don't know what the reasons were, but he was more ready to accept it. Perhaps also because I'm his stepdaughter; with a mother it's different.

B: We'll get back to your wife's story in a little while. Let's go on a bit. Was your family's past ever mentioned by your mother, or your grandmother and grandfather, was it ever brought up?

F: No. My grandparents accepted the fact that my mother had told me nothing. That's what I assume. They never talked about it on their own initiative. Grandmother could tell vivid stories, both about the Nazi period and about the years after the war. It was hard for me to picture a lot of those things. And then we were always finding bullets and ammunition in the garden. There were also some strange wires hanging in the trees. Naturally I used to ask about that. Or some objects would turn up that weren't part of the family property, things that soldiers who'd been quartered in the house had left behind.

My grandmother told me that there used to be a restaurant and pub downstairs and that the Brownshirts had taken it over. Once they were having a meeting. My grandfather was sitting there along with all these brownshirted Nazis. They were making a big racket, and my grandfather got upset. He told them, "Because of you I lost a son, you idiots!" I don't know what he said, but he cursed them. The District Head of the Party came to my grandmother and said they would overlook it this time out of respect for my grandfather's age—he must have been seventy then. He said they wouldn't do anything, but that we should try to restrain my grandfather and make sure he didn't show up any more in that restaurant. And that he should shut up or he'd be in for a lot of trouble next time. So my grandmother told him to be careful. He also wrote down what he wanted to say in this regard. That, for him, was very rare. He wasn't politically oriented. Rather, it infuriated him as a human being. My grandpa wasn't political in the least. He came from a very simple background and had acquired a certain education by reading books. But he never learned how to think politically. He had his viewpoint, and it wasn't compatible [with that of the Nazis]. He would always ask, "What did I do to deserve this?" Naturally, I didn't understand. I was only twelve. Or sometimes they would speak about Jews. Apparently my grandmother had had Jewish friends in Berlin, where they'd been living when she was first married. But what had *really* happened—that she didn't tell me about. She probably thought I was too young. Later on, I wasn't able to ask them: grandmother was over ninety and grandpa was dead.

Fritz opens the window. Maya, who has been very quiet for the last few minutes, goes to make some more coffee.

F: I have some family in Holland. They went to Holland after World War I and had a very strange time during the Nazi period. They sided with the Dutch, and so they had problems, big difficulties. My uncle didn't have a son. He always wanted to be a father to me. But it didn't work out because he was too pious, too religious. I couldn't stand it. I was religious at that time, but I wasn't pious. So one day he decided to tell me what my father had really done, and that he hadn't died but had actually been executed.

B: What exactly did he say to you?

F: How he told me, I can't recall, I just can't remember how he put it. But he told me very directly, without beating around the bush. And he added that, although he didn't think my father was innocent, he felt that the sentence had been too harsh. He told me that he'd taken up the struggle on behalf of my father for that reason, that he'd done everything that was humanly possible in Holland via the Red Cross. He said, "I want you to know that. But he was with the Gestapo, and that wasn't an outfit a person could cooperate with in any way. You should also know that." I already knew then what the Gestapo was. He didn't have to explain it to me. I was nineteen or twenty at the time.

So everything came to a head: my matriculation exams at school, the bankruptcy, my mother's breakdown, and then this story to boot. And I was . . . well, on the surface I always seemed cool as a cucumber, but inside I must have been in bad shape. So during the vacations I used to see a homeopathic doctor in Bavaria for treatment. She worked with dream therapy, massage, verbal therapy, and she would also use herbal remedies. And it turned out that various other people were going to her, including a Russian woman who had spent the war hiding out in Berlin and whose health had been affected by it. All these people came together at a farm that had been converted into a kind of small hotel. My mother had also spent some time there. And they got me back on my feet again. I really wasn't completely aware of what was happening to me. I think my mother was very wise. She simply got me into that place (die hat mich einfach da reingezogen). Today it's clear to me that I had probably been very negatively affected by all these things. They were able to put me back on my feet and give me enough strength to cope with life. This is only clear to me now, yet maybe it's good it happened this way. Later on, the first therapist was replaced by another doctor, who took over without a break. Maya also made her acquaintance and was treated: she'd developed a cramp, and there were tensions here at home, so I sent her there for treatment. Right after that we got married.

Fritz takes a deep breath. I can see how tense he has become in relaying this information.

F: Then, because I was aware from my mother's stories that the sentence had been unfair, at least in respect to the harshness of the decision, I got in touch with a lawyer. I was acquainted with a doctor in Düsseldorf who knows just about everybody important in Germany, and I asked him if he could refer me to an attorney who handled such cases for the government and whether I could hire him to work for me. And the lawyer said, "OK, I'll take care of it." But six months later the doctor called me and said, "Listen, he refuses to continue working on it. Various things occurred in those Goering plants. He just doesn't want to go on working on the case." I asked him what happened, but he had no idea. So for the time being, the case was closed as far as I was concerned. I wasn't able to find out anything more about it. I had no access to any documents, in part because such documents and files have only been released to the public quite recently.

Somehow, I simply wanted to enjoy my life at that point. I wanted to have my girlfriends, my studies, and nothing more than that—I was sick of the whole thing. I led a very intense life, sort of nonconformist in certain ways, although I think it was all in reaction to this. I wouldn't let anyone tell me anything. I went my own way. I didn't want to be dependent on anyone, either financially or in any other way. I used to work during vacations selling jewelry because I had no money. I made business deals wherever and whenever I could, didn't want anything from anybody. In this way, I more or less managed to forget all about it.

M: Yes, but it would resurface whenever there were birthdays, for example.

F: Well, first I should stress that I didn't want to have anything more to do with all these matters. Then I met my wife and married. She's more of a family person, and she told me I shouldn't behave in that way, that I shouldn't just cut off my mother, my aunt, my uncle and adopt the attitude that I didn't want to have anything to do with anybody. She simply forced me to pay people a visit, to come around when there was a birthday. For me, all that had been finished.

M: There's a story worth telling. Before your mother died last year, the November before her death, there was something on TV having to do with terrorists. I was standing downstairs and I said to her that what they were doing with the peace protesters was really awful. Then we started talking about the new ID cards that were being planned. And she remarked, "Some people, well, they're simply the ones who are always getting stopped." She went on, "The police can do that because they have experience. Under the Nazis Father was once taken down to the train station and taught how to pick people out of the crowd." I stood there speechless. I thought to myself, my God, who was it they were fishing out of the crowd at the train station in Braunschweig back then? I said, "Mother, what are you talking about?" Then I went upstairs to Fritz and told him, "Look, we have to clear things up, set them straight. Otherwise we're always going to have these stories." So we decided to clarify things, for her too, in order to clear the air once and for all. But she wasn't feeling well, and I had invited a friend over that evening, so I suggested to Fritz that we wait until after the holidays, and then, at the beginning of the year, we should take a trip with Mother and corner her. Now, maybe she had a certain feeling that she would have to face the facts . . .

I wonder what "clear the air once and for all" and "corner her" mean for Maya and whether they have the same meaning for Fritz.

M: Fritz's mother had constructed a world for herself and didn't want to venture beyond it. The older she got, the more she would talk about his father and always in a positive way. She would talk about all the beautiful things from earlier in their life, and never about the war. Naturally, we never got around to clarifying matters, though she did preserve all of his correspondence, all his papers and letters. We looked through them after she died. There were many things that were really very shattering. Too bad she hadn't done that before, I mean, if she had said to us, "Children, take this . . ."

F: Wait a second. I must say that in part I *did* look at this material myself early on. She told me I could, but I laid it aside. I didn't want to because I'd noticed that I couldn't get anything out of my mother. When I looked through it I saw once again just what sort of a position he'd had, all the affidavits he had collected, those testimonials attesting to his clean record (Persilscheine). For example, there was this actress by the name of Mye, and my father was definitely supposed to have saved her life. But the papers didn't say anything about what he was really responsible for, why people were sent to the camp, or what was actually going on back then. All that was only slightly hinted at. It didn't give me the picture I was looking for and I laid it aside.

M: Yet after we'd read through everything, or most of it, because a lot of the material is completely irrelevant, it became clear to us what had happened.

B: What became clear to you? Can you give me an example?

M: Well, for example, that his mother was a fighter by nature, and that she had been ruined, for all practical purposes, by this entire thing. She was never able to cope with it. Actually she was the one who was the positive factor in the marriage, yet for whatever reasons, she was never able to liberate herself and get out.

F: I have a letter my father wrote in which he talks about his ideal when it comes to a wife. His notions are so narrow-minded, antiquated, and petty-bourgeois, it's really awful. My mother wasn't that kind of a woman at all. So what did he really want? Did he want to change her and remold her completely in keeping with his tastes, or did he simply fall in love with her and accept her the way she was? It's not clear to me at all. I would have liked to ask her about this.

M: They used to have terrible fights, especially about this sort of thing . . .

F: Yes, right, because I assume that the marriage was some sort of enormous mistake. They approached it with completely different outlooks on life.

B: When did your father join the Party?

F: He did his exams in . . .

M: In '33.

F: No, it was much later than that. I have his doctoral dissertation here. His goal was to become a judge for juvenile offenders, because he thought he knew how to deal with youngsters. I don't know if he really did. But all that was impossible because of his low grade on his degree exam. Now, why did he do so poorly on his final exam? I mean, he wasn't stupid, you don't just . . . Then I found out that my grandfather had forced him to study law. He didn't want to study law at all. Anyhow, he got a sixty on his law exams, so the only way he could enter the civil service was through the avenue of the Party. He joined the detective force, which was later integrated for the most part right into the Gestapo. He was given a rank in the SS, and then he continued on in his career.

Once he tried to volunteer for duty at the front. When my mother first told me this, I thought it was just one of her stories, but it turns out that it really was true. Naturally, he was refused, because it was already much too late. He decided to apply for duty at the front after things began to heat up in Braunschweig. Before that, he'd somehow been able to deceive even himself. Maybe he never was very clear about what he was doing. But when things got hot, he tried to get out, and they rejected his request. I've often wondered what my mother said to him back then. Did she argue, "Look, you've got a wife and child, hang in there. You can't just abandon me to live here in poverty!" Or did she encourage him and say, "Try to break loose from that bunch!" I just don't know.

M: She never talked about it either.

F: No, and I was never able to ask precise questions because I never knew exactly what I should ask about.

B: Did he ever speak about what he was involved in?

F: People noticed that he was very tight-lipped, that he almost never said anything, although he was critical of the Party, of the "crummy big shots," as he put it when he got upset. He had a real dispute once with the Party because they were sending people to him who were supposed to be put in the camp, and he thought it was completely stupid, ridiculous, since they hadn't done anything. So he went to Gestapo headquarters and was able, in part, to have the orders changed, although some of his requests weren't granted. At that time it was hinted that he should cool it a little, that this wasn't the way to go about things. There's written proof for this. It's true. In private company, though, he almost never talked about these matters. And he would almost never wear his uniform off duty. He wanted somehow . . . he doesn't appear to have been very comfortable. Yet he didn't draw any conclusions.

I think I've discovered what may be the essential point. I asked an old uncle of mine and he told me that my father was a rigid bureaucrat of a man, that his position was "This is where I stand, this is the job I've taken on, this is my task and I'll perform it." I can't find the slightest trace of any political analysis, or of any political opinion or position in the letters he wrote or in his diary—nothing.

M: Especially if you read his defense statement, there's nothing you can say in reply. He claimed that the Gestapo wasn't so bad after all . . .

F: That the Gestapo was a government agency like any other, there were excesses, but these occur in all wars . . . It was the most stupid sort of defense you can possibly imagine.

M: There is no sense of repentance. Instead, he makes excuses: "I was caught up in the machinery and . . ." His defense is based on sheer ignorance and blind stubbornness. It would be interesting for you to read it.

B: Braunschweig is not far from Bergen-Belsen, right?

F: He didn't have anything to do with that. And this camp was not under his direct authority. It was an external branch camp. There were more than ninety such camps. One was located in the former Salzgitter plant. It had been set up provisionally. They'd built a road on pillars, constructed a wall underneath, put up five buildings for living quarters, a canteen, a clinic, and set up a fence. That was the camp. A few kilometers farther on was Camp 21. This one was for slave laborers, concentration camp inmates who were forced to work. Camp 21—and this is really awful—was also considered a so-called "reeducation" camp. A lot of Germans were sent there—those who were disliked by the regime. One, two, and suddenly you found yourself a prisoner there! There's lots of literature about that place, documents from that time and from the trial later on. I read recently that in that Hermann Goering camp there was no way of preventing contact between the prisoners and the German civilian personnel, so there was a strict regulation: don't talk to anyone, don't give anyone anything. They'd been forced to work there under compulsion. And yet they would go against that rule. They did talk to prisoners. This is an aspect that gives me pause. Several of them were punished and sent to Camp 21.

And then when I think that people were sent there for listening to a foreign radio station! That used to be handled by the Gestapo, and my father was involved in those sorts of things. No doubt about it. Exactly what his involvement was, and the extent of it, I still have to find out. As I mentioned before, I am working with this historian. Though of course, my father wasn't responsible for the conditions inside the camp, the fact there weren't enough beds and so on. Everything was so terribly provisional, so temporary. It was organized so stupidly. There were constant complaints about not having enough skilled workers, but they used to let them starve to death there in that camp! If you simply look at this from an economic point of view—leaving aside humanitarian considerations—just from that point of view, the thing was *so* stupid that today I just stand here dumbfounded, completely unable to understand. I just can't explain it to myself, it's inconceivable. A lot of the inmates were individuals who happened to have a Jewish grandmother, something like that, or they were accused of "defiling the German race." And then there were female munitions workers. As I said, I'll get the facts, we'll find out the truth. When someone was beaten to death in the camp, it was the responsibility of the camp commander, the Commandant, and he was under the command of the District Commander. Those who were no longer able to work were also sent to the district headquarters and were usually killed there.

B: Does it ever disturb you that you have continued to use your father's name?

F: Yes. Because my father never had any importance in my life—in respect to my education or the way I think. So yes, it used to disturb me. Not because of his own past. The tragedy of that has only recently become fully clear to me. I wasn't aware before that he was so high up in the Nazi hierarchy. My mother added her maiden name. She never used his last name alone and she was always against being called "Frau Doktor," as is the tradition. She didn't want that. So there were signs, expressions of her position on this and her inability to come to terms with it. And first I thought, I'm a part of that tradition, I'm proud of my grandfather, so maybe I'd prefer to have my mother's maiden name, maybe I should change my name altogether. Then I thought, what's the big fuss? I don't have any children. We're going to die anyhow. If I'd had children, I might have changed my name or simply used my mother's maiden name.

There is a look of pain in Fritz's expression. "I don't have any children. We're going to die anyhow." He is the last in his family.

M: On the other hand, I think that just as a people has to accept its own history, a person has to stand by his own father.

F: [*Angrily*] Yes, but my father was meaningless to me. He provided the semen, that's all. So I don't see why I should have to bear his last name.

M: [*Sighs*] How simple that all seems today . . .

Maya looks exhausted. I wonder how she can listen to these stories, endure this legacy.

M: Well, I don't think children should be punished for the sins of their fathers. I think every person should be given a chance.

F: [*Looks straight into my eyes*] There was a certain perverse quality in our relationship, and I actually only became conscious of it much later. I had successfully managed to put Maya's whole thing to one side, out of view. And the fact that I am dealing with all this today is not in order to learn more about myself. Rather, it is because I want to be more effective in my struggle against the neo-Fascists (die braune Sosse). And I can only do that by stating openly that I am a child of these criminals. That is precisely what legitimatizes what I must say and am permitted to say because of it.

In the meantime, I've started to think more about it. An old friend of my mother's said to me, "Listen, you still haven't come to terms with it, you haven't worked it through for yourself." I recognize now that it's true. At first I didn't understand what she meant and wondered what it was I had to work through. But now I'm clear about that. Today, just before you came, I thought of what she said. In reaction to the letter I published in *Der Spiegel,* a few old Nazis asked me how I could talk that way about my father. And someone even said I had insulted him. But today it is very clear to me that I haven't insulted him. I'm the one who's insulted. Everything I stand for—my ideas about women, the music I love, my politics—why, for each of these things alone, I could have landed in a camp. Under the regime my father represented, I'd have been arrested if I'd opened my mouth. And because I've never been a man who could blend in with the crowd, my life would probably have been pretty damn difficult. And maybe because I used to be quite naive and trusting, I'd have landed in a camp. That's why *I'm* the one who is insulted. My father represents something that is disgusting in my eyes in every respect. In any event, if he had lived, I would have been constantly fighting with him, because I can't approve of anything connected with his system of values. Nothing.

M: [*Looking worried*] Until recently he had great difficulty in dealing with people. But there's been a change for the better in that regard.

F: Yes, you taught me that. I wouldn't have been able to do it by myself. I had nothing in common with men. I had women friends almost exclusively. And a certain sort of man, those who have "principles," who are somehow authoritarian . . . I got into a bad relationship with a professor at the university, though he had nothing in common with the Nazis, and I didn't suspect anything in that regard. But in my eyes, he was simply representative of a generation I found disgusting.

M: That is undoubtedly connected with the fact that you felt yourself opposed to those authoritarian types. It takes a long time for a person like that to find his own way.

F: I don't regret the fact that I had trouble with him. In some ways, it was very productive.

M: In any event, it's possible to contend that his father's shadow was actually a disturbing factor in his life for a long time.

F: I can recall many details specifically from the years 1944–45.

B: What do you recall?

F: Well, the nights we'd spend in the bunker. For years after the war I couldn't stand to hear the sound of a propeller-driven airplane. The sound meant that in an hour there would be an air raid. For a long time I was afraid of that, until at some point I got over it. Then I have this clear recollection of April 1945. We had been evacuated to a farm near Lüneburg Heath. You could see flashes from the artillery far away and hear explosions. It was awful. And some character was constantly climbing up a tree trying to see what was happening. Then a group of prisoners came by guarded by German soldiers. Today I am almost sure that it was the evacuation of Bergen-Belsen, because that was nearby, although I didn't know anything at the time. Then there was the terrible noise of explosions again. And the farmer's wife ran outside to hang up a white flag. Suddenly somebody shouted down from a tree that she should put the white flag away because the SS were coming. So she put the flag inside, trembling and afraid. When the SS had passed by, out came the white flag again. Then the British came—they finally arrived a few days later. The British marched through with a group of German soldiers. Prisoners. Now, I assumed they were soldiers, but they may have been personnel from Bergen-Belsen being taken away, because the British liberated Bergen-Belsen and the camp personnel were taken to a prisoners' camp. Geographically it's possible that they passed by there. There weren't as many roads back then as there are now.

M: We went to Bergen-Belsen last year.

F: Yes, and I said, "Hey, that's where I was as a child, only seven kilometers from here!" So we stayed on this farm, and there was very little food. One day I went down into the farmyard, and they had killed a deer and were dividing up the meat. When they saw me, their faces turned as white as chalk. After that, the daughter gave us a big hunk of meat. My mother asked me if I'd seen them and I said yes. We had two months' supply of meat because of that, because I'd seen them. Nobody was allowed to have a gun.

Then I can recall a long trip overnight to L. And I can remember many other details. We used to find all kinds of medals and things from the war, Party badges. Someone would say we should throw them away. And weapons. It was awful. A playmate of mine got blown up because he was playing with some shells he'd found. Farther down there was a settlement with people from East Prussia and from L. too, living in barracks. Awful conditions, just terrible. One day someone shot himself. And another guy hanged himself in the woods opposite our house. So, as I said, I was used to men dying, and when my father died, well, it seemed quite natural. There was a lot of dying at the time. And I had a pretty wild, magnificent, carefree childhood. Because no one could really look after us, they were all too busy. My grandfather used to come looking for us in the evening, and we'd come home completely scratched up, dirty, bruised and banged up. It was a crazy childhood. Yes, and then school, 1947. School, the teachers, saying prayers, standing at attention. And there was this old lady teacher. She was very nice, very friendly. But now and then, when there'd be roughhousing and noise, she'd say, "This is not a Jewish

school" (Judenschule). And I asked my mother what that was supposed to mean, but she said she didn't know. I can still recall that she
would say that.

And then came the 1950s. It was by reading people like Heinrich
Böll, Paul Schallück, and others that I started to delve into that period.
The play *Andorra* by Max Frisch was put on at the theater, and then
Schramm came and read from his war diaries. He cleared away some
favorite phony notions with that line of his: "You'd better believe
this!" He was terrific. He'd tell people about really unpleasant things,
let them have it, no holds barred. And then there was that movie *Die
Brücke* and all those earlier films about the period—I saw them all.[2]

I knew that I didn't have a father. When they would ask me at school
what my father's name was, I'd tell them "Günter." "What does he
do?" "I don't know." "You must have known him." "No." It simply
didn't play any role.

B: And nobody accused you or said your father was a Nazi?

F: No, no one knew that either, because fortunately those things
had taken place in Braunschweig.

M: Yes, and here—and this is ironic—here people thought he was
one of those who had been involved in the attempt on Hitler's life, July
20, 1944. There was even a story here that he'd taken part in that
attempted coup, because no one here knew anything.

F: Yes, and because of that story about Mye, who was arrested after
the attempted coup. It was known that he got her out of jail, and
people thought that he had been involved somehow. Nothing else was
known. The big disappointment for my mother was the fact that all
his fraternity brothers abandoned him, because, naturally, they all
had something to cover up. And when they were trying to get a clean
bill of conduct for themselves, they all refused to come to his aid. I
have some letters to my mother in which they say things like, "Well,
you know that I myself was involved in wrongdoing and that I can't
appear as a witness for Günter." Or "I haven't seen him since we finished university, and what happened before that is not relevant." So
nothing, just pages of stuff like that. Of course, for my mother, it was
a moment of truth . . .

M: At the same time, she would always talk about her husband's
"comrades" (Bundesbrüder). And Fritz would always become very an-

2. Percy Ernst Schramm, a German historian, was in charge of the official diaries of
the Wehrmacht during the war and later became a professor at Göttingen. *Die Brücke*
(The Bridge), released in the 1960s, portrays a group of Hitler Youth defending a
bridge early in 1945, when the war was almost over.

gry, because in the background was the fact that when these men were really needed, they weren't around.

F: And I have always had something against all these fraternities and organizations.[3] For example, I refused to join the sports club. I have a horrible aversion to any kind of club where men get together and fraternize. It's intolerable in my eyes. I can't stand it. When I was a student, some old fraternity veterans approached me—suddenly they were around again and active—and I wrote them an angry letter. When my father was having a rough time, they hadn't come to his aid, and I told them to stay away from me. After that I didn't hear anything further from them. And when I saw those masquerade parties in Bonn, with fraternity men—there were a few of them at that time—I asked them what they were up to. They gave me a hostile look and I had nothing to do with them. And when my mother started asking me whether I wanted to join a fraternity, I wasn't interested, and she accepted that too. At least, she didn't bring it up again.

M: In recent years she really changed her views on things, she really did. Earlier on, she was much more conservative. But when she started to live here with us, many things changed. She became a lot more tolerant.

F: She also changed her friends and her political sympathies.

We take a break. Maya goes to prepare supper, and I go out for a stroll in the garden. I sense in Fritz an enormous need for love and warmth. I wonder how Maya has been able to handle a difficult situation: to support her husband and help him come to terms with his mother while having memories and feelings of her own. Fritz joins me in the garden and shows me some of the letters he has received since he wrote to Der Spiegel.

> Dear Fritz, the Jew lover,
> Your father died too early to let you know how the Jews made it in the Weimar Republic. If you don't believe me, look how they're doing it again in the U.S.A. now! Perhaps, as a real democrat, you would like to invite me to your class in L. Your students have probably not yet had a chance to meet a real enthusiastic and anti-Semitic Nazi.

> Dear Fritz,
> You are a poor pig, ugly, characterless and should be pitied. What do you know, you nosey type, about the battle of the German people? How world Jewry tried to kill us. Only Hitler understood the real danger. The German army was one of the

3. These fraternal groups were not necessarily Nazi in orientation. Some were German-national, often with a very Christian emphasis.

last human and noble armies, especially during the last war. But all this you probably can't make sense of, not the way your father did anyway.

Dear Sir,

As an Englishman living in this country for many years, I have to comment that you can't be a very sensitive person. I have many friends here, and see myself as a German; however, what you published here about your private nest is real shit. My children grow up here as Germans, and you want them to revolt against the roots of your, now their, own nation? Could you imagine such a thing happening in my country or in France? I must tell you that if the majority of your people thought the way you do, I would regret having become a citizen of your country. Thank God that this is not the case. The broken pride of the German people is rising again. It is a slow process but a steady one, at the end of which I can imagine they might exterminate people like yourself. You are a rootless person, like many others in our era; I pray to God that you will regain a healthy soul and body.

Maya calls me in when supper is ready. She has prepared a variety of German and Israeli dishes and remarks as we sit down that I'm "probably used to eating fresh salads, not like those they make here." We are all very quiet during the meal. When we sit again at the coffee table, I turn to Maya.

B: I'd also like to hear your story.

M: That's a long one: 1940, the ghetto in B., not far from Chernobyl.

B: How old were you then?

M: I was born in 1938.

The year I was born; later we discover that we share the same birthday.

M: There was a synagogue in B. and everyone was called together to meet on May 20, 1941. And the shootings were in B. There were eighteen hundred Jews, and of these only two remained alive: my cousin and me. She was eleven years old at the time. The grave was forty-nine paces across. After liberation, there was no fence there. My mother noticed that and made sure a fence was put up.

F: There were cows grazing there . . .

M: Yes, it was a pasture. So briefly, that's something about the ghetto. As I said, it's not written about anywhere, and it might be interesting for you to learn more about it. My mother doesn't know very much. There was a very large Jewish congregation in the area. There was also a kibbutz in the region, and that's where my family comes from, the Ukraine. Actually our family was living in Leningrad, and only because we always spent our vacations in the Ukraine . . . My mother married a gentile Ukrainian from B. By then, they had already divorced, but we still went there for vacations. So my cousin and I had come to B. from Leningrad for the summer vacation. We came to visit our gentile Ukrainian grandmother, and we were surprised by the war while we were there—even though trains had been standing ready for the Jews for two weeks so they could go to central Russia, no one believed it would happen, and so they all stayed.

F: Your mother said once why so many had stayed. Because a lot of them were from Vilna . . .

M: No, that was something else. There had been a lot of pogroms there earlier. Then the Germans came in '19, and that was a kind of salvation for the Jews, because the pogroms came to an end. They treated the Jews very well.

F: So when someone wanted to leave, the others would say, "When the Germans come, nothing will happen. On the contrary. So you can stay . . ."

B: Where was your mother at that time?

M: My mother was in Leningrad, she lived through the blockade there. She was only in Leningrad a year, though, and when the camp there was frozen over . . . My uncle was a high-ranking officer in the Russian military, in supplies. So he arranged for my mother, my grandfather, and my sister to travel with the transports to Russia. Then they went on the train to Alma-Ata. My mother didn't know I was still alive. She had already heard that the Germans had come and about the things that were happening. She only learned about it when she came to B. after the liberation. We were in the ghetto nine months and then there was the liquidation. My grandmother's sister was the only one who understood what was really happening. And since the column of people was very long, she took me along. Then we separated from the column and she left me on my grandparents' farm. They said she should come when it was dark so no one would see her. But the whole area, everyone around there, knew that she and I were there. Then my grandmother took me and went to the Gestapo, and she told the officer that my Ukrainian father was in Vilna and that he was always for the Germans and for the liberation. She told him this story. She started to cry and asked him to let us stay. And he said, "OK, if you manage to bring her home without being seen and if no one reports it, that's your affair. I haven't seen a thing." So she waited until it got dark and brought me home in a sack of potatoes. There was a small room, and she hid me in there under the Russian bed they had. Shortly after that, Italian soldiers were quartered in the house, and my grandparents were terribly frightened that I might be discovered. At the same time, they were pleased that the military was there, because then no one would think that anyone might be hidden there. For me today, it's pretty hard to understand how a small child could be quiet for such a long time so that no one noticed.

There was an aunt living with my grandparents, Aunt O., and she was a teacher. She became friendly with a German officer who was very nice, a very fine person. He was also a university graduate. She did this in order to cover up the whole affair, but when the war was over, she was arrested as a collaborator. And that German officer did a fine thing. When the Germans were forced to vacate B., he came and said, "Listen, I'm leaving the storerooms open. Make sure you get all the food and supplies, as much as you can. The others will be busy, so make sure you get food for yourselves." Then Aunt O. asked him whether they would be back, because if you do something like that, it could go wrong. But he said, "No, we won't be back, thank God, this is the end." So they did as he directed, and as I said, when my mother came, Aunt O. was in jail. My mother got her out of there because she had proof of her innocence. But Aunt O. never married, because she was still considered a collaborator.

Then my cousin also came to my grandmother's, but my grandmother told her she couldn't stay there because I was already there, and she wasn't able to keep two girls. She told her to go to the next village but not to say she was Jewish. Rather, she was to go to the mayor of the village and offer herself as a servant girl, which she did for a family who collaborated with the Germans. So at the age of eleven she was responsible for everything. She worked very hard, and when the Russian army came, all collaborators were hanged, two families and everyone connected with them. And the family she was working for had also been hanged. Now she was a child who had never heard any Yiddish. She knew just one word in Yiddish, "Mamele." So she sat there in the corner crying, "Mamele," "Mamele," and an officer passed by, a Jewish officer, who asked her what she was saying. And she said, "I'm not one of them, I'm just a servant." So he asked her who she was and took her along. She was with that company of soldiers for two months. They moved on through Russia and took her along as a kind of mascot until a higher ranking officer said that it wasn't right, and they put her in a home for children.

When the war was over, my uncle immediately went to the farm and accused my grandmother of not having saved his child. My grandmother wasn't able to make him understand that it had been impossible, that it would have meant the end for both of us. She sent him to the other village, and he learned that my cousin was still alive. She's in Russia now, both of them are in Russia. She survived, and as I said, only the two of us remain alive of all the Jews from B. The rest were killed. And when my mother got there after the war, no one wanted to say anything. It was as if there were a wall around the thing. Nothing could be learned, there was nothing she could do. They only said—and my grandmother told me this too—that when the Jews were taken out to be shot, many had sung the "Internationale." It was probably very tragic. And then the people had thrown their jewelry into the water. This was the only thing my mother could find out about what had happened in connection with the synagogue and the ghetto.

B: What are your recollections of your mother? You were seven years old at the time . . .

M: I didn't know her, and I must say that for some of this time I have no memories whatsoever except for one thing that happened, something horrible. We had this big dog we kept out in the yard on the farm where I stayed. And two soldiers were living it up one evening, and one of them went out to the toilet. Now this dog was chained up, he couldn't get loose, but the soldier was drunk. The dog started barking and the soldier shot him. I still remember that, because I was terribly afraid. But they told me it was nothing. My grandmother was afraid I would start screaming, although there was a lot of noise, so probably no one would have noticed.

Maya talks quietly, as if reporting very ordinary events. Only the pinched corners of her mouth reveal the depth of her feeling.

M: Yes, and then my mother came and took me to the Ural Mountains. I was sick for the whole trip, initially because I was afraid. I probably hadn't wanted to go along. Yet I have so few memories from this period, perhaps because it was such an awful time. It's like a break in the film. I don't recall anything. I can't even remember my grandmother very well. I only recall that when the war finally ended, well, there was really beautiful weather. I recall that grandmother bought some small chickens and showed me how to feed them. She would knock with her fingers, and she told me that's how they knew there were grains of corn, that they should eat. Aside from that I can't remember anything at all, even though I wasn't so little any more. Then we went to Molotov and lived with relatives. Grandfather worked, but we were very poor. I can remember that my mother had to carry me in her arms to the kindergarten that first winter after the war because I didn't have any shoes to wear. And that's when my mother met my father.

B: Your father?

M: My stepfather. My real father, well, she had divorced him even before the beginning of the war. She met her second husband in Molotov. Things were good after that. He was a tailor and made clothes for all sorts of prominent people there. Tailors then were even more important than doctors. So he met my mother, fell in love, and they married. Then they looked hard to find a husband for my mother's sister, and they finally found someone. Then the two of them emigrated with my grandfather to Poland, because both men were from Poland. My aunt's husband was from Cracow.

B: Your stepfather, where had he spent the years of the war?

M: He was a Communist and had been the mayor of a town for a short time. When the Germans came in, the Communists were all in danger. So he went on to Russia with a few other people, not knowing what might happen.

B: What town was that?

M: S. in Galicia, in southern Poland. He was in Russia when the war broke out. And he heard that all the people back home had been killed, transported to camps or killed on the spot, I don't know. Anyhow, we went to Poland. My stepfather had had a family, a wife and two daughters, and they'd all been killed. We traveled for a long time. I think we were on the road two months from the Urals to Poland. But my mother didn't want to get off anywhere. She said she wouldn't get off anywhere there weren't any Russians. Then we arrived in Lvov. That's where my uncle's garrison was stationed. And really, all there were at the station were Russians. So my mother said we should get off, and we did. A lot of Jews got off there.

Later on, there was a very large Jewish community in Lvov. It was a good time. They organized a Jewish school, first in one building, then in another. Initially there wasn't enough to eat, but then we got all kinds of food packages from America, so we had a chance to regain our health and strength a bit. There was a very active Jewish community life. My stepfather took part in drama courses, they put on plays. There was a very strong group of Zionists active there, the League and the Shomer Ha-Tsair too, so as a child I learned about that as well. We used to go to the Balkans on vacation. Israel didn't yet exist—that was in 1947, no, 1948, and there was a camp of the Haganah [Jewish defense army]. Jewish soldiers were being trained. I can see it before me as if it were today: there was a Jewish flag in the camp and a great many young men in training for the liberation struggle for Israel.

I personally never had any interest in going to Israel. As a child I always said, "No, I don't want to go to Israel. I want to stay here." But my parents visited Russia just after the doctors' trials,[4] and when they returned, my stepfather said, "We've decided to go to Israel." I had just started attending art school, and I said I didn't want to go to that "capitalist country." But there was nothing I could do. We went to Israel. When we arrived, we got off the train in what was really a kind of desert. Today it's Herzeliya, but back then there were just barracks there without any roof, without anything, just the skeletons of some barracks. My stepfather told us to get off and said I should help. I said, "I didn't want to come to Israel. You can carry your own damn suitcases!" He slapped me and told me to help carry the suitcases. So we ended up in these half-finished barracks. We had to clean out all the furniture and benches because the workers were going to come. The barracks didn't have windows or doors. Yet it was very beautiful, and the trip to Israel had been fantastic. Because we were going to Israel, we were given all sorts of exaggerated information. My mother went from Legnica to Breslau to buy a washboard, because they said there were none in Israel. The Jews in Legnica had bought all the washboards and soap and potato flour and candles. My mother knew a Russian surgeon who was associated with the hospital and he got us some candles. And that good woman brought ten kilos of candles with her to the station! When we arrived in Israel, the only thing we could actually make use of was those candles, but they'd all melted during the trip.

Yet when we got here, it wasn't so serious, because we found we could get everything we needed; there were special ration cards. My father was out of work, it was hard to find work at the time. And so I decided, "OK, I'll go to a kibbutz. This damn corrupt capitalist system, to hell with it!" I went to a kibbutz up in Galilee, and those were beautiful years. Then I felt I wanted to see a bit of the world, and so I left. That's when the first Syrian attack on our kibbutz occurred. Luckily, no one was hurt, but there was a lot of damage. Somehow they'd had trouble with the accuracy of their bombs, and a lot of shells fell into the pond. People were down in the bunkers, the shelters. I was so touched by all that I returned to the kibbutz and volunteered to stay on. I was there another year and a half, but then I left, because I found the whole thing a bit too narrow and constricting.

B: Before you came to Israel you spoke Ukrainian and Russian. Did you learn Hebrew after that?

---

4. In Moscow, a number of physicians, most of them Jewish, were accused of treason in 1952–53. The charges were dropped and the physicians released when Stalin died in March 1953, but the incident was an ideological crisis for many Jewish and Israeli leftists at the time.

M: Yes.

B: And when did you learn German?

M: Here. I came for personal reasons. I'd had a love affair that came to an end. I thought I needed some time to recover, and so I came to Germany because I had an opportunity to get a work permit here. I thought I would stay a year and then see what I would do, maybe go back to Israel. But then I met Fritz and he had interests similar to mine, he thought like I did about many things. I really couldn't live with anyone who wasn't socialist in outlook. Since our views about the world, about art and life, were very compatible, we decided to get married, a move neither of us regrets. It was very important for me to be living with Fritz in order to deal with the past. Probably it was important for him too. It has been a very personal way to get over those terrible events.

Though you don't get over it. I still feel very involved. The day before yesterday we got a crank letter. I read it and I'm still very upset. I get very upset when I hear that sort of thing, it still affects me a lot. I can't stand above it and say it doesn't affect me. On the other hand, I think there are a great many people here who are worth knowing, and I personally haven't had any negative experiences—as a Jew, none at all, but very few as a human being either. I can say that my years here have been very pleasant. The first few years were hard because I was treated in such an exceptionally friendly manner, something I didn't like at all. It took a very long time for people we were close to, friends and acquaintances, to stop seeing me as a Jew, to see me simply as a person, a human being. It took a long time.

F: Look, maybe you have an exaggerated view of all this. You have such a friendly way of being with people, it makes them accept you right away, and you have probably reacted by thinking that it was some advantage, some bonus you were being given because of your Jewishness. I didn't sense this so strongly. Of course, sure, everyone is a bit embarrassed, that's quite clear, especially that generation. But much of this is completely normal, in response to positive feelings people feel from you. But you thought they were being so nice to you because you are Jewish. That's definitely not the case.

M: Well, I worked for two years in a home for problem children. And the funny thing is that the children didn't relate at all to the fact that I was Jewish. It meant nothing at all to them. But there was a boy there whose grandfather had been a medic in a concentration camp. He'd been a convinced Nazi. He probably did some pretty terrible things. Later he maltreated his stepdaughter with all kinds of medicines. And this grandfather would listen day and night to old Nazi records, and he also tried to influence the boy, who visited our home a bit, although it had precisely the opposite effect. The boy despised them all. When I came, he asked me not to say that I was Jewish because he didn't want me to have any problems. He told me that his grandfather was so fanatic it was possible he might show up at the home. But even there, I had a very good relationship with everyone—with the housemother . . . we also had a lot of young people who were in training, they came and went, and the relationship between us was excellent. I never felt in any way that I wasn't accepted.

B: Who told you the story about the war period?

M: My mother.

B: When was that?

M: At a very early age. That's also a bit of a story. My mother told me that my stepfather was my real father, who had come back from the war. But you know how people talk. Anyhow, there was this woman I knew, and she told me one day that he wasn't my real father, he was actually my stepfather. So naturally then I started to ask questions.

B: How old were you then?

M: I was eight. I started to ask questions, and my mother said my father had been killed in the war. Only later did I find out what had really happened. When my mother told me he had been killed in the war, well, we had this enormous cemetery in Lvov. There were Russian soldiers buried there, Polish soldiers, all sorts of people. When I heard that he had died in the war, I went with my girlfriend, she managed to swipe a bit of money at home, and we went and bought flowers and a wreath. I took all that to the cemetery. Then we cleaned up the graves, one after the other. I thought that maybe my father was buried there too somewhere. And then I learned that they had gotten a divorce in Leningrad. Can't remember how I found out . . .

B: Was that in connection with the war?

M: The divorce? No connection with the war. It was a personal matter. My father knocked around a lot, and at some point my mother—he was something of an artist by nature, not very settled or stable—at some point my mother said they couldn't go on, and they got a divorce. There was no connection with the war. After the war my father wanted to get back together again with my mother, but she didn't want to. I know nothing about him after that.

B: When did you learn that your father had not been killed in the war?

M: Oh, I was already grown up by then, I must have been fifteen or sixteen already. But as a child, well, for two or three years I used to go to the cemetery and take care of the graves. That went on for a long time. But later on, when I found out that it was a definite fact that they had been divorced, I was very upset. For a long time I had arguments with my stepfather, fight after fight. All that ended when I was about twenty-five. Because I had always felt I was at a disadvantage. I thought the other children in the family were being treated differently. Then I saw that it was just in the nature of the situation. He treated his own children the same way. Only later did I discover how much he liked me, how attached he was to me. When I was sick, he'd be the one to run to the doctor, not my mother. Or when I came home late, he'd be the one who was still awake, not my mother. And they had a very good relationship, even in the last year. My stepfather was a good storyteller. He had a terrific memory and told us lots of stories. We'd have a story hour every Saturday. All the aunts would come over—friends of the family who called themselves "aunts"— and he would start telling his stories. Today I regret that I have retained so little of all that. He was one of those men from Galicia who knew a great many tales, beautiful stories, the kind no one knows how to tell anymore. I saved all the letters he wrote to me because they are filled with the humor of the small Jewish shtetl, full of that way of life. He never really lived in the modern world. He always lived in that other, older world, and he passed it on in his stories.

F: That was the basis of our close relationship, the reason I struck up such a good relationship with him right away—because he was a piece of living history to me. I knew a bit of Yiddish. And it was suddenly all so full of life, so vivid and palpable. He would tell these stories from the old Austrian monarchy about impoverished country squires who lived out in that area. It was a terrific and powerful experience for me. And he noticed that I was very receptive. So that was the basis of our relationship, the understanding that developed between us during our first few days together. Then there were the jokes he'd tell. We laughed our heads off together. I really regret that I only saw him for those six weeks.

M: Something else, and it's a very interesting thing. When I was in Poland and later in Israel, I didn't deal much with Judaism, things Jewish. It was only here that I started to become interested in Judaism. Only here did I understand for the first time the full scope of the things that had transpired: my stepfather's behavior, my mother's. I only then began to understand all those stories. Actually, it's a shame, because if I had known all that back then, probably many things would have turned out differently.

Maya's face reveals her sadness. I wonder what she means by "things would have turned out differently."

F: But that is only against the background of these experiences.

M: You can only know so many things on the basis of these experiences. In recent years my mother has begun to tell a lot of stories. I've made a short tape of her. She knows that period between the revolutions very well, remembers it well, the pogroms, all that Jewish life in the Ukraine. And she can talk about it so well. And I wanted this to be preserved for the children, because, thank God, I have a relative, a boy in the family who is very interested in history. At the moment he's interested in other things, in Peace Now. Yet it's worthwhile to save these things, since he has such a strong interest in history. But I've only been able to make one tape so far, about the time in the Ukraine before World War II. She can recall that very well, things about the Jewish school and everything that was going on in that area.

B: Are you still in contact with your cousin?

M: No, it's not possible. She has a very important job in the Ministry of Justice. She's in Moscow at the Military Academy. With my uncle I do have contact, though in a roundabout way. When he was in Germany a few years ago, we spoke on the phone. But now he's with his daughter in Moscow. It's very important to me, but I can't do anything about it at the moment.

B: Is she married?

M: She was married to a son of the district attorney in Leningrad, a man who was in a camp during the Stalin purge, who was very maltreated. He was later released, but he was already so weak physically that he died. The son was allowed to study in Moscow as a kind of compensation for all this, and later worked there. But he died in the 1960s of cancer. They have a daughter, and she hasn't remarried. So, anyhow, that's my story.

F: Well, it's rather crazy when two people talk about their fathers. The parallels are what I find striking, crazy parallels. What you recall and what mothers try to keep quiet about. The underlying motives are different, but the behavior is very similar.

Fritz and Maya drive me back to my hotel. It is close to midnight but I find it very difficult to fall asleep. I want to call my wife but words seem shallow and remote. I think back over the evening. Maya is a Jew who owes her life to a conversation between her gentile grandmother and a Gestapo officer in the Ukraine. She did not want to go to Israel because it was a "capitalist" state. Her husband Fritz is the son of a Gestapo officer who was executed by the British for his treatment of Jews and other prisoners in Camp 21. The son learned about his father from a pious uncle in Holland, who, for humanitarian reasons, tried to help his mother prevent the execution.

What else? Maya feels at home in Germany since their friends have stopped being nice to her just because she is Jewish. She is childless. Fritz couldn't get along with men before his wife helped him learn to trust others. Maya's cousin cried "Mamele," after the family she had been working for was hanged by the Russians and was rescued by a Jewish officer who happened by. Maya's stepfather, who cared more for her than for his own children, told his stepdaughter and her German husband beautiful Yiddish stories that gave them a glimpse of a wonderful, lost world. I want to tell my wife that I have seen the fragile bridge of trust constructed by this couple with loving care over a sea of hatred, denial, and suspicion. I fall asleep wondering if anyone else could follow their example.

In my dream, I am in Fritz and Maya's home. They have invited Peter, Gerda, Helmuth, Manfred, Shlomo, Naomi, and little Andre for a Christmas-Hanukkah party. Fritz and Maya have arranged the program. They pair Shlomo with Manfred and Gerda with Naomi and send them into another room to tell each other something from their personal history. When they return, they tell the group the stories they have heard from each other. It is a long and difficult process, but they handle it beautifully. I sit in the corner all evening mumbling to myself, "Mamele, Mamele . . ." When I wake up, I am soaked in perspiration. Will Naomi, Gerda, Shlomo, Manfred, and the others ever be able to sit together in the same room?

chapter 14

The Dark Side of the Mind

When I return from my fourth trip to Germany in October 1987, I feel a tremendous need to try to "analyze my data." As a social scientist, I am trained to look for patterns that might be useful in future research. By this time I have interviewed about fifty children of perpetrators, mostly members of the SS, and a similar number of children whose parents had no direct involvement in the Holocaust. I find myself grading my interviewees for every possible distinction I can think of: How old were they during the Third Reich? Were they the first or the last child in the family? Were they daughters or sons? Was the mother loving and warm or cold and distant? Did they come from a religious family? Did they live in a small village or a large town? Did they move around a lot or stay in one place? Were both parents members of the Nazi Party and for how long? Did the father die during the war or right after and why? When and how did the children learn about their father's wartime activities? Were they active in finding out and if so, why? Did they form families of their own? What did they tell their own children?

I sit at my desk night after night constructing tables on background, process, and outcome, trying to summarize my data on every possible variable. I find that children of perpetrators have married less and are more often childless than children of survivors in the same age group. I see myself lecturing about such findings at conferences and sending articles to scientific journals. But I know I am doing something wrong. In such a small sample, I cannot possibly uncover answers to all my "hypotheses" because there is too much variability. Nor can I claim that the sample is representative, since I know nothing about the population as a whole.

But there is a more important problem: I am distancing myself from my interviewees, looking at them from the outside as if I had not been present during our conversations. Although a researcher needs a sense of professional detachment, I feel that my prematurely analytical approach is overshadowing what actually happened during my encounters with these people. I wonder if this is a result of my ongoing ambivalence about the research: am I afraid that if I look too closely I will see ordinary human beings?

I went to Germany to learn about the effects of the Holocaust on the children of its perpetrators. As an Israeli, I know that, aside from a number tattooed on an arm, there are few external signs identifying survivors or their children. As someone once pointed out to me, "We are all playing the game of trying to look normal." Yet in Germany, I discovered that I was looking for some sign in my interviewees—a "working through process." I felt "at home" when I discovered it and upset when I could not.

It was not easy to unravel what I was looking for from my subjects' complex lives. It was even more difficult to be aware of the processes going on as I sat with them asking questions. I had to keep reminding myself of my own assumptions and preconceptions. In a way, my interviewees and I became involved in a common endeavor to confront the truth.

The interviewees can be classified according to their parents' place in the Nazi power structure. The fathers of Gerda, Thomas, and Bernd belonged to the inner circle of the central government, while those of the others were assigned to various levels in the extermination and concentration camps, the Einsatzgruppen, the euthanasia program, the SS, the Gestapo, and the transportation system. Although one cannot assume that individual experiences are typical, I wondered if children of high-ranking officials could reveal something of the atmosphere in which key figures in the Third Reich functioned and if children of lower-echelon Nazis could provide more information about the attitudes of the more informed Germans of the time, especially toward the extermination process. Above all, I was interested in how these children viewed these events forty years later.

Grouping Gerda, Thomas, and Bernd as a cluster, I assumed that the scope of the problems with which they had struggled might be very different from those of the children of other perpetrators, since they had been more directly exposed to their parents' commitment to Hitler and his ideology. But my assumption was not substantiated. I was astonished at how little of all this emerged during our conversations. All three were young adults (fifteen to twenty-three) when the war ended, and all three have clear and vivid memories of the Reich. Bernd remembers how Berchtesgaden became a kind of fortress—

the farmers were driven out and the children forced to carry ID cards; he also recalls Himmler's visits and his father's decision to send him to an SS boarding school. Thomas tells how he paraded down the staircase of his uncle's palace in Prague. Gerda, the oldest of the interviewees, recalls riding to Nazi meetings with her father as a small child and Hitler's visit to her father's house.

Alongside these details are descriptions of middle-class family life: the warmth in Thomas's home, Bernd's many siblings, Gerda's sorrow over her parents' divorce. Even disagreements between parents and minor problems of child-rearing seem familiar and ordinary. Very little is mentioned about the larger drama going on outside these homes, and nothing of the criminality of the regime.

Over the past forty years, the vocabulary of these individuals has been purged of those idioms and euphemisms that once enshrined the beliefs of the Third Reich. Yet an odd sentence here and there, a slip of the tongue, hints at the prevalence of some of those attitudes. When Bernd describes his reaction to the Nazi regime's antagonism toward the Catholic church, he says that the confrontation with the Jews was over and finished, "taken care of more or less." In recalling how soldiers conversed about the camps and the shootings, Gerda refers to a Russian village as "liberated" by the Germans. Yet perhaps it is more astonishing that such moments are so rare, and that so little remains of these catch-phrases of the Nazi era.

All three experienced very real practical problems when the war ended: Gerda assumed a pseudonym in order to be able to go on with her professional career. Bernd, using a false name, hid in the Tyrol with a farmer's family until he joined the church and found refuge in more than one sense. While the Russians held his mother in prison in Berlin because of her Heydrich connection, Thomas and his younger siblings were taken in by a family he describes as an emotional "deep freeze." All of them confronted drastic changes in the political reality for which their parents had not prepared them and from which they could not protect them.

That Gerda's and Bernd's fathers were deeply committed to the Nazi government and involved in its operations is beyond question. Still, it is Gerda who emphasizes "how little they knew" and how distant they were from their children. When I ask her to elaborate, she surprises me with an account of the "wonder bomb" her father had believed in as late as the winter of 1944–45, and how deeply disillusioned he became when he found out it did not exist. Bernd's description of the end of the "Thousand-year Reich" evokes the turmoil of those final days: first, the military collapse, then the collapse of belief and the epidemic of suicides. His words still convey the weight of these events in the mind of a fifteen-year-old admirer of the Führer. Only Thomas is able to describe this period in his life with a touch of irony: at the outset, he shouts "Heil Hitler!" like the rest but a few months later can enjoy a play satirizing the Nazi regime.

Bernd admits that his father must have known about the full scale of the extermination process but does not excuse him, because, as he says, "responsibility presupposes freedom," but Gerda can acknowledge her father's awareness only indirectly. She herself found out about the atrocities during her flight from Berlin, when she heard soldiers on the road talking about villages they had burned in the east. At that point, her father was no longer around, and it is doubtful that she would have tried to confront him with questions. Thomas refers to a few incidents in which his uncle, a key figure in organizing and carrying out the extermination process, would release Jews in whom his mother or father had expressed a personal interest.

None of the three can recall any direct experience of the extermination process. Perhaps, as children of decisionmakers who lived at a distance from the scenes of the atrocities, they had little firsthand opportunity. The closest one can get is Bernd's description of the inmates from Dachau who worked at his SS boarding school, although to him they looked "well fed." All three report that the extermination program was never openly discussed at home, and certainly not in front of the children. And why in fact should it have been mentioned? It was one of the Reich's top secrets, and one would expect that those involved would keep it from their wives, their close relatives, and their children. These children were no different from anyone else at the time who might have known a few bits and pieces but could make little sense of them. The scale of evil was beyond human comprehension.

Like Thomas, Bernd can recall his reaction when he first heard about the atrocities and it slowly dawned on him that his father was involved. But he tries to explain these events away by claiming that the extermination camps "were set up in connection with the overcrowding in the concentration camps, and that probably wasn't until the war started to go against the Germans." Listening to Gerda, I am astonished at how little she seems to have reflected on these events. Yet what I first attribute to indifference or insensitivity I come to appreciate as the response of a devoted daughter deeply troubled by the connection between her father and the extermination program. When she shows me her father's last testament, in which he attempts to clarify his views, she is trying to let me know that, in the end, he regretted his persecution of the Jews. More than any of the other interviewees,

Gerda teaches me a valuable lesson: one must evaluate a person within her own context and not in relation to some general or external norm. It is Gerda who gives me a real sense of the painful difficulties children of high-ranking Nazis have experienced in trying to achieve a life of their own.

Thomas has achieved this before I meet him. He describes in detail the nineteen years during which he did little but deal with his family's past and its relation to the Holocaust, with the question of whether he was "good" like his father or the "Devil incarnate" like his uncle. He says of himself at one point in our conversation, "Speaking this way is a kind of liberation for me, a way of breaking free a bit."

Bernd is open and sincere, and his words carry considerable weight, a fact I do not want to underemphasize, especially since he consented to discuss these difficult issues with a virtual stranger. Yet he presents a kind of "closed circle" when he speaks about his relationship with his father, Christianity, and the Holocaust. Like Thomas, he has invested a great deal of effort in constructing a balance he can live with, and he does not want to inquire further.

Gerda, who still faces a number of issues, seems to me to be the most willing to approach the subject anew. Is she on the way to opening her own "hidden suitcase"? Will she be able to integrate her disparate insights on her own? Since I am not her therapist, I am left with questions, yet I wonder if I have played a role in the process and if this says something about the loneliness of those like her: children of heroes who overnight became children of criminals.

In my mind, I picture Thomas, Gerda, and Bernd, so different from one another yet all trying to live their lives in a society that for forty years has avoided coming to terms with the past. They want their dilemma acknowledged; at the same time they also want it forgotten. Having been drawn by their parents' beliefs and choices into the vortex of a drama involving unspeakable deeds, all three now wish to live quietly.

The majority of the interviewees are children of *Täter*, or "doers," as the Germans identify them today. The fathers of Monika and Renate were commanders of Einsatzgruppen; those of Helmuth and Manfred were physicians involved in the euthanasia program. Peter's father was stationed at Auschwitz and Hilda's father served in various concentration camps. Fritz's father and Menachem's father were in the Gestapo; the former was executed and the latter was not brought to trial, but their specific involvement in the extermination process could not be clarified by their children or through independent research. Dieter's father claimed to have been in the Einsatzgruppen, but the historian who tried to verify his membership has serious doubts that the father ever took part in the atrocities he described to his son. Rudolf's father, who witnessed the shooting of his Jewish workers in Poland, was a railway employee.

Rudolf, Hilda, and Helmuth are old enough to remember family life during the Third Reich as well as several grimmer experiences. Helmuth was a dreamy child who quite by chance on a class hike stumbled upon a machine-gun emplacement near one of the watchtowers at Buchenwald. He also saw camp inmates working near the town who looked "gaunt and emaciated," and after an Allied bombing raid he witnessed injured inmates being driven through the streets. But he never asked his parents about these events or about the comment made by one of his father's colleagues that Buchenwald was an "infamous stain."

Helmuth's most troubling memory is that of overhearing a conversation between his parents when he was eleven about whether the whole family should commit suicide, as friends in Berlin had done, or only his father. As a result, he refused to eat at home for several years, even after his father had killed himself. He must have realized that something was not quite right when he heard his father tell his mother, "What we have done to them will now be done to us." His feeling of being victimized by his parents has become intermingled in his mind with that other, distant victimization connected with his father.

Helmuth describes in a matter-of-fact way his father's view of "burdensome individuals" whose lives are "not worth living," and refers to gassing as an aspect of the "mania about Aryan cleanliness." It is the difficult experiences within his family that are more immediate to him: he still broods about an incident in which his mother warned him to stay away from the fireplace to protect his new suit, not out of concern for his safety. Helmuth is haunted by fears that one cannot view as totally unrealistic, especially since his own son has committed suicide: "Am I a victimizer too?"

As her father's favorite child, Hilda stayed with him in the barracks at the concentration camps where he worked. One day she witnessed an inmate being beaten, tried to intervene, and ran away in panic. After that, she would not allow her father to continue the bedtime story he has told her every night. During the interview, she suddenly remembers her nickname at the time, "camp doll," but she does not connect it with the dolls given to her by the women who came to parties in the barracks or with the rag doll shown to her by the Gypsy girl who told her about the gassing of Gypsies and children.

The experiences of Helmuth and Hilda, and to some extent Dieter, reveal how external violence and victimization are linked in their memories with the emotional violence and isolation in their families. Hilda, who is blamed when her father is sent to the front after the incident in the woods, is unable to talk to her mother. Helmuth feels like an outsider in his family, where his father attacks him as "weak," his sister teases him about being afraid to eat, and his mother does not intervene. When his father finally reveals a more tender, emotional side, it is to say good-bye before he leaves his son forever.

The home environment Dieter describes is a kind of "madhouse": a father weak in the eyes of his wife and his own father who is violent toward his children and full of contradictions; a tyrannizing mother; an older sister sliding into mental illness. In this house, stories about the father's involvement in the killing of men, women, and children in Russia do not seem to surprise or disturb the child. Dieter prefers to accept his father's terrible deeds rather than to see him as an insignificant nothing.

Rudolf heard about Nazi atrocities directly from his father when the latter returned home from Poland, physically and mentally broken. As an enthusiastic member of the Hitler Youth, Rudolf did not really believe him and suspected his father of running away from the front out of disloyalty and fear. Only years later can he understand and accept the truth of his father's experience. His story shows once again that even if knowledge about the extermination process was available early on, the proregime belief system made it seem, in one interviewee's words, like "pure BBC propaganda."

Peter, Monika, Renate, Menachem, and Fritz were all born during the war years and remember little if anything from that time. Manfred and Dieter were born after the war. As they make clear in the interviews, their fathers never mentioned a word about their wartime activities at home. In fact, because Peter's father was tried and acquitted after the war and former inmates visited their home, Peter assumed that his father helped rescue them. The interviews of this father and son reveal interesting differences. The expressions the father uses to describe Auschwitz—"gassing capacity," "work load," and so on—are missing from the son's conversation. Where the father sees Mengele as an "enthusiastic idealist" and an "intellect," the son describes him as a person who only obeyed orders. Beyond this, although the father tells his son about his refusal to participate in the selections, he does not tell him about the young physician who took his place in the selection process and later committed suicide, or about his schoolmate Leo Oppenheim. For me, this is a vivid example of how, after the war, parents tried to prove to their children how normal and emotionally intact they were. The sense of normalcy is supported by the facts (the father was acquitted), but in the interviews, the ghosts creep out. Auschwitz was not "normal," and the best the son can do is to shift attention from his father's experiences through generalizations about the all-pervasiveness of evil—it has happened before and it will happen again—although he acknowledges that he has never really thought about the matter or discussed it with his father.

I visualize this situation not as a unilateral case of parental silence, but as an interaction, a "double wall" phenomenon: the parents have erected a wall around their feelings about the atrocities they have witnessed or carried out, and their children have reacted by building their own protective wall. If those on one side try to find an opening, they encounter the wall on the other side. The children who have made an effort to confront the truth see themselves as the only members of their families willing to do so. What the interviews also reveal quite clearly are the larger, societal dimensions of the postwar silence about the Nazi years. Most of the interviewees report that the schools only reinforced their parents' reticence: history stopped at Bismarck.

Throughout our conversations, the interviewees bring in the German people as a kind of "Greek chorus" in the background. Peter describes those he meets at local bars who would be willing to "do it again" to Turkish immigrants in Germany. Monika reports the reaction of her students' parents on the one hand, who ask her to acknowledge that "we Germans have suffered too," and of her intellectual friends on the other, who are unable to understand how she can go on talking to her mother. Even her therapist is unwilling to deal with the Nazi period and views Monika's preoccupation with it as symptomatic of her problem. Fritz shows me some of the hate mail he has received attacking him for his public statements about the Nazi past. Manfred says that in compiling biographies for a scholarly study he could find little or no information about his subjects lives between 1933 and 1945. Menachem describes his parents' friends as "living entirely in the past," that is, in the Nazi era.

It may well be that all of these descriptions are biased, that they have been mentioned by my interviewees to emphasize how difficult it is to deal with the past in contemporary German society. Still, since they are so congruent, they seem to confirm that my interviewees' dilemma as children of perpetrators remains an unmentionable issue. Today, when there is heated disagreement in Germany about what belongs in the collective memory, it would seem that the children of perpetrators are unhappy reminders of the burden of the past rather than a source of truth. German society prefers a more convenient history, more comforting illusions. It is not surprising that the interviewees express a common experience of solitude and isolation. Victimizers' children are expected to deal with their situation by themselves.

Children who have tried to penetrate their parents' silence have first had to be aware that there were gaps or distortions in their parents' accounts; then they have had to identify the motives behind these versions of the past, confront them, and find a way to work through to the untold story. Most of the interviews reflect their failure. By accusing her father, Renate distanced herself from him; only now, years after his death, does she feel that she might have been able to help him to acknowledge his guilt. In contrast, through her sensitivity and persistence, Monika, the only one who reports any success, has brought her mother to the point where she can admit that she loved a man "who had incurred guilt."

In this atmosphere of collective silence, what sense did the children make of their parents' involvement in the Third Reich? Over quite a few years, none at all. Indeed, for several, the emotional and physical distancing was beneficial. Peter claims that "you can't repress what you don't know" but leaves home early and chooses a profession in direct opposition to his parents' aspirations for him. Menachem also "leaves home"—by converting to Judaism, emigrating to Israel, and becoming a rabbi. He claims that his is an intellectual decision unrelated to his father or to the war, but such "breaking away," while it can provide a shelter against the past, cannot resolve conflicting emotions. Perhaps this is why Thomas says of him, "He hasn't started at all to deal with what has occupied my mind for the last nineteen years."

The interviews all suggest a degree of ambivalence about the fathers' role in their children's lives. The father was not around during the child's formative years; he was "on duty," "away at war," or later, in prison. Some fathers were executed or committed suicide. Manfred gives the most extreme description of his father's absence: "He was a nonperson for me." Monika did not know her father but, encouraged by her mother, she clung to an idealized version of him that was later shattered. When Fritz discusses his father he always speaks angrily about "that man," and one can feel a need for love that was not—and probably could not be—fulfilled. Those fathers who did return, such as Renate's or Rudolf's, sought to reestablish their presence in the family. These parental figures, whether absent or present, were important to their children, however negatively. Psychologists have traditionally tended to stress the importance of mother-child relationships and to deemphasize the role of the father. The interviews seem to show otherwise. In the typical German family of the 1930s, the mother was subordinate to her husband's authority. The family was a microcosm of society. Nazi ideology was male-oriented, and the historic role of the male warrior was highly visible and greatly valued. For Thomas and Manfred, however, the influence of their mothers remained decisive and ultimately proved to be a saving grace. Thomas's mother rejected the Nazi regime epitomized by her brother-in-law; this, along with her warmth and affection, helped her son face the family past. Manfred's mother prepared her son for the difficult acknowledgment they both had to make; through her storytelling over the years, her sharing of the past, she gradually enabled him to accept the truth about his father.

For several interviewees, the interview process itself became an opportunity for exploring and integrating the past. Manfred read Gitta Sereny's book about Treblinka, met his mother's Jewish friend from Tel Aviv, and began to question the fact that he had not been troubled with nightmares over the years. Peter asked himself what he would have done if he had been in his father's place at Auschwitz. Renate was finally able to open the "suitcase in the attic" and read the written evidence of her father's activities during the war. But many interviewees seem to find it difficult to work through that past and start anew. They struggle and fail to establish stable relationships and families of their own. Thomas, Manfred, Fritz and Maya, and Gerda address this issue openly. Perhaps this is a characteristic difference between children of victims and children of victimizers: the former were charged with the task of biological survival; the latter seem afraid that they will hand on a "bad seed."

As I reflect on my encounters in Germany, two images recur: the dark side of the mind and the quest for hope. The dark side of the mind is like the dark or far side of the moon. Like the more clinical terms, denial and repression, this image expresses the existence of knowledge or awareness that has been shifted away from consciousness. The bright and dark sides of the moon are two inseparable parts of one whole, yet one side is visible while the other remains in darkness. Unlike the moon, however, the mind can rotate, although it is unclear where the "axes of rotation" are and what activates them. In the case of my interviewees, their emotional isolation within the family and society, the victimization to which they were sometimes exposed, their own fear of some inherent "bad seed" of evil or abnormality, their conflicting feelings toward their fathers—all of these, like a heavy weight, held them in the past and interfered with their attempts to disentangle themselves and move forward into the future. The "quest for hope" is a "working through" process that involves a gradual movement away from the euphemisms and distortions of the parents, which project a false reality, and toward an acknowledgment of what happened and what meaning those events have, especially for those who suffered.

I think of Debora, a Holocaust survivor, who came to me as a patient in her midforties. At the time, she was trying to discover when her father, a noted lawyer, had been killed in Auschwitz. He and her mother had divorced shortly before the war broke out. As a young girl, Debora had thus "lost" her father twice: through divorce and then through the Holocaust.

Over the months we met together she had a recurring dream. In her dream, she is four years old. Wearing a white dress, she sits in the living room near a window, listening to her father play the piano. Suddenly the Germans enter the room and take her father away, leaving her all alone. During the first stage of therapy, Debora attributed the dream to her sadness. She had missed her father all those years and hoped he would return, a hope she had never given up. She was very depressed at the time and suffered from terrible guilt. The dream seemed self-explanatory.

About a year later, when she was feeling better, Debora had the dream again. This time, however, she experienced events from the perspective of her father, who plays the piano while his loving daughter sits nearby. I could see a connection between this version of the dream and Debora's feelings of assertiveness and lessening guilt.

Toward the end of her therapy, Debora reported the dream a third time, and this time, she was one of the German soldiers. According to her own interpretation, at last she could experience how angry she was with her father for separating from her mother and leaving her, and admit that she wanted to "kill" him. At this stage, she felt that she understood the dream, and it did not recur. What impressed me most about this unusual experience was how much more hopeful Debora had become. Although she will never be free of her past, by acknowledging that she felt "like the Germans" she was able to let go of her anger and her overpowering guilt and begin to imagine a future.

My interviewees have approached the "dark side of the mind" in different ways. Peter lives very much in the present tense, wary of the "meat eaters" who could make "it" happen again. For Gerda, the desperate need to hold on to the image of her father as a good man ("er war so ein Mensch") has imprisoned her in a past that controls her future. Fritz's self-definition through opposition to his father locked him in negativity and isolation until his wife, Maya, offered a way out. Hilda brings to mind her memories of her father and the camps and then retreats into silence again. Manfred has been able to go on with his life because his mother exorcised his father's presence. Thomas wears his identity like a banner. Menachem and Bernd have embraced the religious traditions their fathers scorned, while Renate has become a social activist and lawyer, as if to counter her father's Fascist ideas. Monika, unlike many of the others who choose not to see too closely, is trying to learn as much as she can about who her father was in order to understand.

As I mentioned earlier, before I went to Germany, Tova asked me to find out if the children of victimizers "wish to kill in their dreams as I wish to die in mine." When I returned, I told her that I had not found the answer, but I believed that in their dreams they also wished to die. Their parents, zealously committed to Hitler's ideology, did not prepare them for defeat. When the Third Reich collapsed, the parents were afraid and disillusioned. They became preoccupied in the years after the war with defending themselves, unable to lead their children out of the past.

I undertook this research with an idea: to locate and interview children of the Nazi generation in Germany. I could not be sure anyone would consent to talk with me—a Jew, an Israeli, a psychologist—with the burden of the past between us. Nor could I predict how I myself would react, whether my fear and anger would dominate, whether I would retreat into intellectualization. Yet I was gratified to discover not only that such encounters could take place, but that they could provide a setting for very different individuals to talk together, to learn and unlearn. These interviews record our conversations and our interaction—questioning, probing, commenting. For me, these journeys toward hope have become signposts for my own.

In July 1988, I join my German hosts at the university in Wuppertal to organize a conference centered on my research. During the planning, I decide to invite my interviewees along with my professional colleagues. I write each of them a letter in which I try to explain myself and wait impatiently for their replies. They arrive one by one. Both Manfred and Dieter are newly married and are unable to come. Helmuth writes that he "consulted his father and decided he was not a perpetrator after all." When I phone him to assure him that this was not one of the criteria for the invitation, he says he is not the "groupy" type and prefers to work on these problems on his own. Hilda sends an annoyed postcard and asks to be "omitted from my mailing list," since she does not want anyone to recognize her name. Peter does not answer my letter, and I am unable to get in touch with him. Thomas is busy performing, and Menachem is in Israel and would not come to Germany solely for this purpose.

I am about to conclude that my idea has been a failure when a few other letters arrive: Fritz and Maya will come, as will Monika and Rudolf and several others whose interviews I have not included here. I also get hesitant but positive answers from Renate, Bernd, and Gerda, although each needs some additional persuasion before deciding to participate: Renate reminds me of how far away she lives, Bernd and Gerda worry about the possibility of sensational journalists. In the end, they all come.

A couple of days before the conference I decide to show a videotape and choose Rudolf's, because it is so moving and so atypical. When I phone him to let him know, he asks if his wife can attend the conference with him. "Of course," I say, "and I think you are a very brave man." He hesitates for a second and replies, "No secrets anymore. I have carried my father's letter for too many years all by myself."

To allow the interviewees to remain anonymous, we dispense with the usual name tags. But the child of a Dutch collaborator introduces himself and suggests we go around the room. There is a moment of silence, and I am about to suggest that we not continue, when the person next to him says his name and adds, "And I am an interview-partner of Dan Bar-On." But it is not easy for everyone. After watching the videotape we take a short break, and I see Gerda leave the room crying. Only after the conference can she meet with a small group to read her father's testament.

Then, in a separate room, my interviewees gather together for the first time. With them are a few of the children of Dutch collaborators who organized themselves as a self-help group in 1981. There is tension in the air but also an eagerness to find out about each other. A few ask Bernd what he knew about the Holocaust and are amazed to find out that he had known as little as they did, and maybe even less. At one point, Renate tells Rudolf that she envies him. "Your father felt guilt and was not a perpetrator himself. You can be proud of him. I can't feel that way about my father."

They are all very gentle with each other, trying to sort out who knew their father and who did not, when they found out about their father's involvement in the Holocaust, how they reacted, who had children. They must outline their differences before they can begin to look for similarities. There are unexpected outbursts of anger and guilt.

The gathering sparks a spontaneous group process that continues throughout the conference—during dinner, over lunch breaks, in the corridor. Maya and Fritz talk to members of the Dutch group, and with Rudolf, Renate, Monika, and a few others, they decide to try to establish a group of German children of *Täter*. They ask a few of the Dutch group to come to the first meeting to advise, and they also ask me. I am happy that they have taken the initiative and agree, intrigued by the fact that this movement has developed out of my interviews, but I am not sure to what extent I will be able or willing to be a part of it. It has become their own endeavor.

After the conference, I take my seventeen-year-old daughter, who has attended with me, to Heidelberg to see the house where her grandfather grew up. On the train I read the letter Fritz has handed to me just before I left in which he has recorded his personal impressions of the gathering in Wuppertal.

> To write things down in proper order. To express feelings. And to do this as a man, a German, the son of a lawyer involved in terrible deeds, and as one who is married to a Jewish woman . . . The conference itself is a bit chaotic too, though there is a good reason for that: nobody expected that almost everyone invited would attend. Now they are all here, and the room is too small.
>
> The vice-chancellor welcomes us, yet uncomfortably, stressing that he has nothing to do with the fields involved. But that is exactly the main point: it isn't a meeting of specialists.
>
> I sit watching people. Over there, to the left of the window, they are probably from Holland. I hear the familiar sounds that remind me of the happy childhood days I spent with Dutch relatives. But what is that I hear? The child of a collaborator? Maybe I am not so alone after all . . .
>
> The pretty woman sitting in front of me, is she Jewish? And that older woman, very alert and involved, way up front—she is probably Jewish too. So I classify people—and it turns out that I am not mistaken—yet I *know* this is nonsense. (There was a time when such classifications were lethal.) Something else: these people are going to ask questions, without pity, questions that are going to be a bit biased (which is no surprise), I am certain about that. And what about myself? I am still unable to see people *simply* as human beings. It is hard to forget the "legacy" of what I read, what I heard after the war . . .
>
> We children of perpetrators form into a separate discussion group. A son of one of the big Nazis is talking (oh, *that* name I think when he introduces himself, but all right, after all, *they* had

children too). His salvation was an intense Christian faith—his version of the antidote that all of us have. Christianity! What good did it do against the barbarity? I keep my objections to myself.

A woman my age is speaking now, and soon it is clear: we are going to try to set up a self-help group like that of the Dutch where we can tell the stories of our lives. She has her own program too: work on behalf of the defenseless in this society. Almost all of us are teachers, attorneys, social workers, and so on.

Many people are visibly upset. Tears are already beginning to flow. Suddenly my wife exclaims, "Look, accept your feelings, whether Christian or not, it's OK! What is happening here— that, after all, is what makes living in this country possible for someone like me."

I feel a sense of shame. Once again, it is a Jew who takes the initiative here, who gives us encouragement. Slowly we feel a sense of mutual affection.

Should I join in? After all, I have arranged things so well for myself: a clear attitude toward my father, arguments now and then with old Nazis—and with younger ones. And repeated encouragement from my wife. But then there are the migraines, the asthma, the fear of too many feelings. And sometimes, cynically, I give in.

During the course of the conference, I learn a bit more about the delayed effects of all this on us, the generation after. The one thing that remains is what the Dutch group has shown us: we are the only thing that counts. Politics and religion should be kept out of it (most of these problems have been worked through by now anyhow).

But then the others show their claws: to depoliticize is to relativize history. I appeal to the group to avoid mixing levels in the discussion. But how hard it is: we are all reacting to the expressions that irritate us . . .

I have little desire now to listen to the lectures, which are factual, informative. I note words that are consoling, disturbing, demanding. Yet for me, my personal problems are what continue to matter.

Then things get heavy: there are two interviews with those who were involved in the war (at last!). Warsaw. Horrible facts. And those who remember are tormented by their memories. So long ago, and yet so actual, so near! A few of us listening begin to cry. I have to leave the room, can't bear it any longer. What was it my mother wrote in a letter I came across? "The attempt to avoid letting unavoidable harshness exceed its customary limits."

The older I get, the more sensitive I become. New experiences with death, with brutality, the horror sensed deep within one's own self, and the ability to translate information into palpable images, must, I think, all join to produce this effect.

Other people have the same experience. Maybe they too are thinking of those who shaped and made the past. And perhaps also about what is still possible, even today.

A comforting point: the third generation is likewise asking questions about this, as we learn from another lecture.

Once again, it is a Jewish woman who pulls us away from these terrors. She gives us courage, telling us—and herself—that we must not let ourselves get lost in these horrors, that we have to draw the line and derive strength from the simple fact that not everyone is running away from the problem. There are some who have the courage to confront it.

Glossary

Einsatzgruppen Special action mobile killing units under the SD (Security Service) of the SS. Organized to clear Nazi-occupied territories in Poland and the USSR of Jews, Gypsies, the intelligentsia, and other designated groups.

Einsatzkommando A detachment of an Einsatzgruppe.

Euthanasia Program The Nazi plan to rid Germany systematically of "burdens to society," beginning with handicapped and retarded children and later expanding to include mentally ill and handicapped adults, most often by gassing.

Gestapo Geheime Staatspolizei; Secret State police. Founded during the Weimar Republic to keep watch over political extremists, including the Nazis, the Gestapo came under the control of the SS in 1937 when Heinrich Himmler was appointed chief of the German police. Thereafter, Gestapo officials held both civil service and SS ranks.

Kristallnacht November 9, 1938, "The Night of Broken Glass," a nationwide Nazi pogrom against the Jews.

NSDAP Nationalsozialistische Deutsche Arbeiterpartei; National Socialist German Workers' Party, Nazi Party.

Racial Hygiene The idea, which gained popularity in the biomedical community in the late nineteenth century and was vehemently promulgated by Alfred Ploetz and others in the Society for Racial Hygiene (Gesellschaft für Rassenhygiene), that the human race could be improved and racial degeneration countered through careful eugenic husbandry.

SA Sturmabteilungen; Stormtroopers, Brownshirts. One of many miscellaneous paramilitary groups of nationalistic ex-soldiers to emerge after the German defeat in 1918, the SA served as the paramilitary arm of the Nazi movement, aiding Hitler's rise to power through strong-arm tactics and street violence. Purged of its leadership, including its founder Ernst Röhm, during the "Night of the Long Knives," June 30, 1934.

SD Sicherheitsdienst; Security Service, headed by Reinhard Heydrich. The SD was originally the Nazi Party's own foreign—and domestic—intelligence unit. Its primary purpose was to spy on political opponents, but Heydrich also accumulated vast files on fellow Nazis. During World War II, the SD increasingly became Germany's primary espionage organization.

SS Schutzstaffel. Created by Hitler in 1925, the SS was originally part of the SA. A very small formation, its members served as bodyguards for Hitler and other high-ranking Nazi leaders. After the Röhm affair in July 1934, the SS became independent of the SA, and under its ambitious leaders Himmler and Heydrich evolved into an elite "state within the state" totally loyal to the Führer. With its black uniforms and jackboots, and the skull and crossbones insignia of its Death's Head Units, it became the major vehicle for domestic intimidation and terror, and for carrying out Nazi policies, including running the death machinery of the Final Solution.

Totenkopf-Verbände and **Verfügungstruppe** Death's Head Units and Special Duty Troops. The two divisions of the SS that were primarily responsible for running the concentration and extermination camps.

Waffen SS Armed SS. The elite military unit of the SS. Incorporated into the Wehrmacht in 1939.

Wehrmacht The German Armed Forces.